Critical Essays on William Styron

Critical Essays on William Styron

Arthur D. Casciato
and
James L. W. West III

G. K. Hall & Co.   •   Boston, Massachusetts

Library of Congress Cataloging in Publication Data
Main entry under title:

Critical essays on William Styron.

    (Critical essays on American literature)
    Includes index.
    1. Styron, William, 1925–   — Criticism and interpre-
tation—Addresses, essays, lectures. I. Casciato,
Arthur D. II. West, James L. W. III. Series.
PS3569.T9Z63   813'.54   81-24002
ISBN 0-8161-8261-2   AACR2

This publication is printed on permanent/durable acid-free paper
MANUFACTURED IN THE UNITED STATES OF AMERICA

CRITICAL ESSAYS ON AMERICAN LITERATURE

This series seeks to publish the most important reprinted criticism on writers and topics in American literature along with, in various volumes, original essays, interviews, bibliographies, letters, manuscript sections, and other materials brought to public attention for the first time. This volume on William Styron by Arthur D. Casciato and James L. W. West III is the most comprehensive collection of criticism available on America's most controversial living writer. It contains thirty-nine essays on Styron's works from *Lie Down in Darkness* to the recent *Sophie's Choice*, along with a special section on Styron in France that features an original essay by Valarie M. Arms. Among the reviews and reprinted articles are selections by Howard Mumford Jones, Malcolm Cowley, Roger Asselineau, Arthur Mizener, Louis D. Rubin, Jr., Larzer Ziff, John Gardner, and Melvin J. Friedman. We are confident that this volume will make a permanent and significant contribution to American literary study.

JAMES NAGEL, GENERAL EDITOR

Northeastern University

CONTENTS

PREFATORY NOTE

In compiling this volume we have followed certain guidelines. We have included only reviews and articles that have not been republished in other collections on Styron, and we have excluded interviews for lack of space. Because we have been particularly keen to emphasize Styron's standing in France, we have had two of the better French essays translated for this volume. We have also included two articles by American scholars on Styron's reputation among the French. For each of Styron's five novels, we have also included a brief item by Styron himself. These Styron items relate, in each case, to the composition, publication, or reception of the particular book.

The reviews reprinted here for each novel are not all necessarily favorable, nor do they necessarily represent a cross-section of the novel's reception (though that is sometimes the end result). And no attempt has been made to reprint all of the important documents in the controversy over *The Confessions of Nat Turner*. We do present a good sampling of opinion, but readers who wish to pursue the *Nat Turner* matter in depth should consult two casebooks: *William Styron's The Confessions of Nat Turner: A Critical Handbook*, ed. Melvin J. Friedman and Irving Malin (Belmont: Wadsworth, 1970), and *The Nat Turner Rebellion: The Historical Event and the Modern Controversy* (New York: Harper & Row, 1971).

This collection is meant to be a basic resource for scholars and students, making available some of the more useful work published on William Styron over the last thirty years.

A.D.C.
J.L.W.W. III

INTRODUCTION

William Styron in Mid-Career

James L. W. West III*

William Clark Styron, Jr., was born June 11, 1925, in Newport News, Virginia, the first and only child of William Clark Styron and Pauline Margaret Abraham. The boy's ancestry on both sides was Scotch, Scotch-Irish, Welsh, Swiss, and English. On his father's side, young William was descended from "Stiorings" who came to Virginia as early as 1650. His paternal grandfather, Alpheus Whitehurst Styron, served as a courier on Confederate General Hoke's staff during the Civil War and later became a pioneer steamboat operator along the eastern seaboard. It is a family tradition that this grandfather "possessed much native writing ability," was a "ready raconteur," and had "a vivid imagination." William's paternal grandmother, Marianna Clark, grew up on her father's plantation in lower Beaufort County, North Carolina. The Clarks, "a proud stiff-necked people," settled in North Carolina during the late seventeenth century and became well-to-do planters and slave-holders. William's maternal grandfather was Enoch Hamilton Abraham, a successful coal and coke operator in Western Pennsylvania and an associate of Henry Clay Frick. William's father, a graduate of North Carolina A & M College (now North Carolina State University), was an engineer at the Newport News shipbuilding yards for most of his adult life. William's mother, a Northerner from Uniontown, Pennsylvania, studied piano and voice in Vienna and taught public school music before meeting her husband-to-be at the Newport News YWCA during World War I.[1]

William was an unusual child. He showed such a keen desire to learn spelling and reading that a neighbor, Sally Cox Hayes, herself a schoolteacher, taught him to read well before he entered the first grade. He was an excellent speller, mastering such words as "formaldehyde" during his first year in school.[2] An undated but early analysis of his handwriting showed him to be "bright, even witty at times, able to mimic others, and embellish a story by exaggeration, in order to make it more interesting."[3]

Shortly after William's birth, his mother developed a malignancy

*Reprinted in part from The Mississippi Quarterly, 34 (Winter 1980–81), 3–14, by permission of the journal.

from which she never recovered. She was an invalid for most of her son's childhood and died shortly after his fourteenth birthday. Perhaps troubled by his mother's death, William became unhappy and disobedient and so in 1940 was sent by his father to Christchurch, an Episcopal boys' school on the Rappahannock River near Urbanna, Virginia. Christchurch was small and intimate, more like a loosely knit family than a formal institution of learning. Years later Styron remembered it as the only school he ever attended which "commanded something more than mere respect—which is to say, my true and abiding affection."[4]

After two years at Christchurch, young Styron entered Davidson College in June 1942. He was a member of Phi Delta Theta social fraternity there and wrote reports for the school newspaper and poems for the literary magazine.[5] He was unhappy at Davidson, though, finding its atmosphere repressive and sanctimonious. In the spring of 1943, a year and a half after Pearl Harbor and shortly before his eighteenth birthday, Styron enlisted in the Marine Corps. At the end of that academic year, he joined the Navy's V-12 program and was transferred from Davidson to Duke University.

At Duke, Styron enrolled in Professor William Blackburn's creative writing course. Blackburn, a gifted teacher and scholar, praised the young man's literary efforts and encouraged him to become an author. Styron was an indifferent achiever in his other subjects—his grades were only a little above average—but under Blackburn's guidance he became passionately interested in literature, especially in the Elizabethans and in modern American writers such as Thomas Wolfe and John Dos Passos. With Blackburn's encouragement, Styron tried his hand at writing short stories, and seven of these early fictional efforts were published in Duke's literary magazine, *The Archive*.[6] Blackburn was a major influence on young Styron during this period:

> Reading aloud from Spenser's *Epithalamion* with its ravishing praise, or the sonorous meditation on death of Sir Thomas Browne, his voice would become so infused with feeling that we would sit transfixed, and not a breath could be heard in the room. It would be too facile a description to call him a spellbinder, though he had in him much of the actor *manqué*; this very rare ability to make his students *feel*, to fall in love with a poem or poet, came from his own real depth of feeling and, perhaps, from his own unrequited love, for I am sure he was an unfulfilled writer or poet too. Whatever—from what mysterious wellspring there derived Blackburn's powerful and uncanny gift to mediate between a work of art and the young people who stood ready to receive it—he was unquestionably a glorious teacher.[7]

In late 1944 Styron left Duke and went to Marine training camp at Parris Island. He chafed under military discipline there, but in May 1945 he moved on to officer-candidate school and in due time emerged with a commission. At least one experience at Parris Island was of permanent importance to him: he was incarcerated in a venereal disease ward with a case of trench mouth which was incorrectly diagnosed as syphilis. The episode gave Styron the basis for his play *In The Clap Shack*, written over twenty years later. As a Marine officer, Styron also served for a time as a guard at the Naval Disciplinary Barracks on Hart's Island in New York harbor. From this experience came material for a novella that he began in 1953 but was unable to finish.

Styron was discharged from military service late in 1945 without having seen combat. He spent a short period in Newport News with his father and step-mother Elizabeth and then in March 1946 returned to Duke and began finishing requirements for his bachelor's degree. During the summer of 1946 he worked his way to Trieste and back on a cattle boat and also attended Bread Loaf Writers' Conference at Middlebury. In February of his senior year, Styron narrowly missed being named a Rhodes Scholar; he made a strong personal impression on the selection committee, but his mediocre academic record counted too heavily against him. In any case, he had already decided against additional formal education, preferring instead to go to New York City and make his way as a writer.[8]

In the late spring of 1947, after graduating from Duke, Styron took a job in New York as an associate editor in the trade book division of McGraw-Hill publishers. His tasks included writing blurbs and reading unsolicited manuscripts in the "slush pile." It was Styron's plan to write fiction during his free hours, but the work at McGraw-Hill proved so enervating that he found literary composition difficult. He did enroll, however, in a creative writing class under editor Hiram Haydn at the New School for Social Research. Styron had been guided to Haydn by Professor Blackburn, and under Haydn's tutelage the young author continued to learn his craft. Haydn was much impressed by what Styron wrote and urged him to begin a novel.[9]

Meanwhile, the job at McGraw-Hill became more and more unbearable and Styron's performance of his tasks more and more perfunctory. In October 1947, at the end of six months there, he was released by Edward C. Aswell—who, incidentally, had been Thomas Wolfe's last editor.[10] Styron was actually relieved to lose the job. He wrote to his father, "I'm very glad that you see eye to eye with me about my present attitude concerning my attempts at writing, and about the loss of my job. I realize that I've finally come to grips with myself, and that the job was in reality merely a delaying action. Writing for me is the hardest thing in the world, but also a thing which, once completed, is the most satisfying. . . . I am no prodigy but, Fate willing, I think I can produce art."[11]

Styron's father agreed to support his son while he wrote a novel, and in the fall of 1947 Styron began serious work on the manuscript that would become *Lie Down in Darkness*. For a time he lived in Durham with former schoolmates from Duke and then moved back North to

Brooklyn in the spring of 1949. He worked on the novel for a lengthy stretch at Valley Cottage, a village near Nyack, New York, at the home of Sigrid de Lima, also a young author, and her mother, who was publicity director at the New School. The eventual published novel was dedicated to Sigrid.[12]

Styron had difficulty beginning the novel—twice he had to make fresh starts—but after he got under way, he progressed steadily. His pace quickened at Valley Cottage, where he stayed until May 1950. He then returned to New York City and continued his work, still supported by his father and encouraged by Haydn. Early in 1951, Styron was recalled into the Marine Corps for the Korean conflict, but Haydn managed to have the induction postponed until Styron could complete *Lie Down in Darkness*. Styron finished with a burst: he wrote the final section of the manuscript—Peyton Loftis' interior monologue—in less than three weeks, during which time he lost fifteen pounds. The novel was complete by early April; Styron and Haydn went over it carefully, and with Styron's consent Haydn made some editorial changes. The book was scheduled for fall publication by Bobbs-Merrill, the firm for which Haydn worked. Bobbs-Merrill, however, insisted on expurgation of some sexually explicit passages in Peyton's monologue; and Styron, a first novelist with no leverage, gave in and allowed most of the "offensive" lines to be cut or toned down.[13]

Styron re-entered the Marines that summer, and for him "the experience of putting on that uniform again and facing anew the ritualistic death dance, had an effect which can only be described as traumatic."[14] Fortunately, his second stint in the Marines was brief. A congenital cataract in his right eye prevented him from firing a rifle accurately, and he was given a medical discharge in the late summer of 1951. Before leaving the Marines, however, he underwent two nightmarish experiences at Camp Lejeune that eventually would reappear in his novella *The Long March*. The first episode was grisly: eight young training-camp recruits were blown to bits by a stray mortar shell; the second was brutal: Styron's unit was sent on a 35-mile forced march which left them mentally and physically shattered.

Styron was discharged from the Marines shortly before publication of *Lie Down in Darkness* on September 10, 1951. Nearly all of the reviews were excellent, and Styron's career was off to a favorable beginning.[15] Backed by strong advertising from Bobbs-Merrill, *Lie Down in Darkness* sold well, particularly for a first novel. Less than a month after publication, it was into its fourth trade printing and had sold some 28,000 copies.[16] Subsequent marketing in paperback by Viking, Signet, and Penguin has kept *Lie Down in Darkness* a steady seller down to the present day.

Styron won the Prix de Rome of the American Academy of Arts and Letters in 1952 for *Lie Down in Darkness*. The award, given each year to a promising young artist, carried with it a year's stay in Rome.[17] Styron sailed to Europe in the spring of 1952; he toured England and Denmark and lived in Paris before going to Italy. The idea for another novel was germinating in his mind, and in the late spring he wrote to his father asking for books and information about Nat Turner, the leader of an 1831 slave insurrection in southeastern Virginia.[18] For a short time Styron contemplated writing a novel about Nat Turner's Rebellion, but postponed his idea in favor of a stronger vision: "the persistent image of eight boys killed by a random mortar shell and of a long and brutal march."[19] In June and July of 1952, while living in Paris, Styron wrote a novella about a forced march in a Marine Corps training camp. The working title was "Like Prisoners Waking."[20] Almost eleven years later, Styron recalled that everything went "just *right* during the composition," that form and substance seemed almost magically to "fuse into a single harmonious whole."[21] Under the title "Long March," the novella was published in February 1953 in the first issue of *discovery*, a periodical in paperback book format. A separate Modern Library paperback edition of the book, retitled *The Long March*, appeared in October 1956.

While living in Paris in 1952, Styron became friendly with a group of young writers—among them George Plimpton, Peter Matthiessen, Donald Hall, Harold Humes, and Thomas Guinzburg—and he helped them launch *The Paris Review*. Styron's "Letter to an Editor" in the first issue is an early statement of his artistic principles. He says in part that literary magazines should "emphasize creative work—fiction and poetry—not to the exclusion of criticism, but with the aim in mind of merely removing criticism from the dominating place it holds in most literary magazines and putting it pretty much where it belongs, i.e., somewhere near the back of the book."[22] Styron's association with *The Paris Review* has continued; he has published there throughout his career and maintains an active interest in the journal's progress.

Styron left Paris and arrived in Rome early in October 1952. He lived at the American Academy there and traveled throughout Italy. In Rome he renewed his acquaintance with Rose Burgunder, a member of a wealthy and socially prominent Baltimore Jewish family and a promising poetess herself. (Styron had met Rose briefly during the winter of 1951 in a seminar at Johns Hopkins.) William Styron and Rose Burgunder were married on May 4, 1953, in Rome; they spent that summer and fall in Ravello, where Styron worked on a novella based on his experiences as a prison guard on Hart's Island. By October he was 7000 words into the story but was unable to complete it, and the novella was aborted.[23]

In October 1954, the Styrons settled in Roxbury, Connecticut, in a white frame house which has been their permanent home ever since. By then Styron had begun his third novel, *Set This House on Fire*, but his work went slowly. (Throughout his career Styron has been a painstaking, deliberate writer who finds the act of composition difficult and painful.

He follows a certain regimen, always composing in pencil on long yellow legal pads, and he rarely revises after initial composition.[24]) *Set This House on Fire* was completed late in 1959 and was scheduled for publication in the spring of 1960. Styron's publisher was now Random House; he had moved to that firm with Haydn. Contrary to his usual practice, Styron made heavy cuts in both the typescript and the galleys of *Set This House on Fire* in order to remove gratuitous commentary by his narrator.[25] The novel was published on May 4, 1960, Styron's seventh wedding anniversary.

Set This House on Fire was expected to consolidate for Styron the praise that had greeted his earlier writings. The book, however, is long, complex, and challenging, and is quite unlike either *Lie Down in Darkness* or *The Long March*. Perhaps as a result, the American reception was mixed. Some critics saw the novel as a major achievement, but others characterized it as maudlin and boring. Many of the reviewers were more puzzled than negative: *Set This House on Fire* proved too difficult a book to be dealt with in a 500-word newspaper notice.

The French reaction to *Set This House on Fire* was quite different, however. Maurice-Edgar Coindreau, an important critic and translator who was Faulkner's first literary advocate in France, read the novel and recognized its true worth. He persuaded his French publisher, Gallimard, to acquire rights to the book, and he executed the translation himself. When the novel was published in France in February 1962, it received excellent reviews and an enthusiastic popular reception. Styron's literary stock in France, and indeed in all of Europe, has been high ever since. Like Poe and Faulkner, Styron was more quickly recognized as a major writer in France than he was in his own country.

After publication of *Set This House on Fire*, Styron became a more active, visible, and politically involved writer. During the 1960s and early 1970s, he fought against capital punishment, supported Eugene McCarthy, sought equal rights for blacks, protested infringements on academic freedom, and spoke out against political persecution of writers in both Russia and Spain. On numerous occasions, he came out publicly against America's involvement in Viet Nam. Through his personal efforts two victims of the American legal system—a mentally incompetent black man and a wrongly convicted young white boy—were aided.[26] Styron also began appearing in print more frequently as a reviewer and essayist, usually in *The New York Review of Books, Harper's, The New York Times Book Review,* or *Esquire.*

During the 60s, Styron also began writing a novel about Nat Turner, the historical figure who had intrigued him for so many years. In composing the novel, Styron set himself the task of entering into the mind of the mysterious black man who had led the only significant rebellion in the history of black slavery. The creation of the book was a six-year process, during which Styron studied the few historical documents available to him and visited Southampton County, where the rebellion had occurred in 1831. The story of his search for traces of Nat's revolt is told in the essay "This Quiet Dust," first published in the April 1965 issue of *Harper's*.

Completed in early 1967, *The Confessions of Nat Turner* was published by Random House on October 9 of that year. The United States was at that time in the midst of serious racial conflict; hostility between Negroes and whites was strong, and race riots were a constant threat. Styron's book was in some ways aided and in other ways victimized by this racial situation. Initial reviews by the established press were highly favorable: several influential critics even suggested that *Nat Turner* should be viewed as a white intellectual's answer to current racial conflicts. Sales were excellent. *Nat Turner* went through six large trade printings in less than a year, and thousands of additional copies were distributed through Book-of-the-Month Club and Literary Guild. The novel also sold widely as a Signet paperback and as a Modern Library hardback. *Nat Turner* was Styron's first big commercial success.

But all was not favorable: other reactions to the book were negative and even hostile. Black militants, then striving for racial identity, were angered that a Southern-born white man should have attempted to enter into the consciousness of a Negro. They leveled two charges at Styron— that he had made Nat into a weak "Uncle Tom" character and that he had been historically inaccurate in his portrayal of Nat and the rebellion. Negro opposition culminated in the publication of *William Styron's Nat Turner: Ten Black Writers Respond*, a collection of polemical essays attacking Styron and his novel. *Nat Turner* became the center of a strident and sometimes bitter controversy. Styron answered his critics by pointing out that he was a novelist, not an historiographer, and that he was bound only by the limits of his own imagination. Styron was at least partly vindicated in 1968 when *Nat Turner* was awarded the Pulitzer Prize for Fiction. In 1970 the novel also won the Howells Medal of the American Academy, given every five years to the most distinguished work of fiction published by an American writer during the preceding five-year period. In his acceptance speech for the Howells Medal, Styron insisted "that a novel can possess a significance apart from its subject matter and that the story of a nineteenth-century black slave may try to say at least as much about longing, loneliness, personal betrayal, madness, and the quest for God as it does about Negroes or the institution of slavery."[27]

The controversy over *The Confessions of Nat Turner* subsided, and Styron went to work on a variety of new projects. He wrote the play *In The Clap Shack*, which was produced by the Yale Repertory Theatre in December 1972 and published by Random House in 1973. He also collaborated with John Phillips on a screenplay titled "Dead!", which appeared in the December 1973 issue of *Esquire*. Styron continued to publish reviews and essays, but his public and political activities decreased. His major creative energies during the early 70s were channeled into a novel called "The Way of the Warrior." This book, still in progress, treats the period in Styron's life immediately following publication of *Lie Down in Darkness*. The hero of the story is quasi-autobiographical; he is a young writer who, after publishing his first novel, is recalled to active service for the Korean War. In training camp he meets a charismatic officer named Marriott, the central figure of the narrative.[28] Somewhere past the middle of the projected plot, however, Styron bogged down and became temporarily unsure of his direction; and shortly thereafter he was struck by a demanding vision which shouldered aside "The Way of the Warrior." This new idea grew into a manuscript called "Sophie's Choice: A Memory." Styron worked over this narrative for six years, during which time the manuscript—and its theme—grew from relatively modest projections to major length and significance. The book was completed late in 1978 and was formally published by Random House, under the shortened title *Sophie's Choice*, on June 11, 1979—Styron's fifty-fourth birthday. The Madison Avenue critics were mixed in their notices (perhaps an inevitability for an important writer today), but other reviewers in American newspapers and journals were almost uniformly laudatory in their comments. Sales have been excellent and overseas publishers have been eager to issue the novel. The exception is South Africa: to Styron's credit, *Sophie's Choice* has been banned there for its profanity and for its attitude toward Negroes.

Styron is presently at work on several reviews and essays, and he plans to publish a collection of shorter writings within the next year or two. He also means to return to "The Way of the Warrior," which will become his sixth novel. Unlike many of his contemporaries, Styron has remained loyal to the traditional novel as a literary form. At mid-career he remains innovative and productive.

Notes

1. The information and quotations in this paragraph are taken from pp. 1–3 of "The Genesis of William Styron," an unpublished eight-page typescript written by W. C. Styron, Sr. In 1951, while collecting promotional data for *Lie Down in Darkness*, Bobbs-Merrill asked the elder Styron for a sketch of his son's life. Mr. Styron, an amateur genealogist, responded with the lengthy "Genesis," most of which was of no use to his son's first publisher. The document is of course quite valuable now; it records much information about Styron's ancestors and gives several anecdotes from his childhood. Copies of "Genesis" are at the Lilly Library among the Bobbs-Merrill Archives and at Duke University Library among the Styron Papers, Manuscript Department.

2. "Genesis," p. 4.

3. This handwriting analysis is pasted into the first of three large scrapbooks of memorabilia and clippings at Duke University Library. These scrapbooks were prepared over a period of years by Styron's father and were donated by him to Duke in February 1969.

4. Styron, *Christchurch* (Davidson, N.C.: Briarpatch Press, 1977), p. 3.

5. See James L. W. West III, *William Styron: A Descriptive Bibliography* (Boston: G. K. Hall, 1977), entries E 3–7.

6. Ibid., entries E 8–19.

7. Styron, Untitled sketch of Blackburn in *Duke Encounters* (Durham: Duke Univ. Office of Publs., 1977), p. 79. See also "William Blackburn and His Pupils: A Conversation," *The Mississippi Quarterly*, 31 (Fall 1978), 605–614.

8. See Styron's "Almost a Rhodes Scholar: A Personal Reminiscence," *South Atlantic Bulletin*, 45 (May 1980), 1–6.

9. Haydn's recollections of the youthful Styron are recorded in his volume of memoirs *Words & Faces* (New York: Harcourt Brace Jovanovich, 1974).

10. Styron has painted a fictional portrait of Aswell as "The Weasel" in Chapter 1 of *Sophie's Choice*. The holograph MS of that novel, presently on deposit at Duke, reveals that Styron originally called the character "Carl Asbury."

11. Styron to his father, 28 Oct. 1947. W. C. Styron, Sr., saved his son's letters home and donated them to Duke University Library, where they are now housed. This quotation is reproduced with William Styron's kind permission.

12. Sigrid de Lima has published five novels: *Captain's Beach* (1950), *The Swift Cloud* (1952), *Carnival by the Sea* (1954), *Praise a Fine Day* (1959), and *Oriane* (1968).

13. See Arthur D. Casciato, "His Editor's Hand: Hiram Haydn's Changes in Styron's *Lie Down in Darkness*," *Studies in Bibliography*, 33 (1980), 263–276. Internal Bobbs-Merrill house memos, recently discovered at the Lilly Library, show that the impetus for the censoring came from the publisher. This article is reprinted on pp. 36–46 of this collection.

14. Styron, "Afterword to *The Long March*," *The Mississippi Quarterly*, 28 (Spring 1975), 188, reprinted on pp. 69–71 of this collection.

15. For annotated citations to the reviews of Styron's novels, see Jackson Bryer and Mary Beth Hatem, *William Styron: A Reference Guide* (Boston: G. K. Hall, 1978), and Philip W. Leon, *William Styron: An Annotated Bibliography of Criticism* (Westport, Conn.: Greenwood Press, 1978).

16. Lois Stewart of Bobbs-Merrill to James L. W. West III, 5 March 1975. Promotional materials and lists of recipients of review copies of *Lie Down in Darkness* are among the Bobbs-Merrill files at the Lilly.

17. The jury for the Prix de Rome that year included Malcolm Cowley, John Hersey, Van Wyck Brooks, Allen Tate, and W. H. Auden.

18. A portion of this letter, dated 1 May 1952, is published in Arthur D. Casciato and James L. W. West III, "William Styron and *The Southampton Insurrection*," *American Literature*, 52 (Jan. 1981), 564–577, reprinted on pp. 213–25 of this collection.

19. "Afterword," p. 188.

20. The setting-copy TS of this novella, together with some editorial correspondence about it, is at the University of Florida Library. These materials were donated to that library by Vance Bourjaily, co-editor of the first volume of *discovery*.

21. "Afterword," p. 187.

22. Styron, "Letter to an Editor," *The Paris Review*, 1 (Spring 1953), 11.

23. The unfinished TS of this novella is housed in the Manuscripts Division, Library of Congress. Manuscripts, typescripts, and proofs for Styron's first four novels are also among the Styron papers there.

24. For details about Styron's writing habits, see "A Bibliographer's Interview with William Styron," *Costerus*, n. s. 4 (1975), 13–29.

25. Ibid., pp. 19–22.

26. See Styron, "The Death-in-Life of Benjamin Reid," *Esquire*, 57 (Feb. 1962); "The Aftermath of Benjamin Reid," *Esquire*, 58 (Nov. 1962); and Styron's introduction to Joan Barthel, *A Death in Canaan* (New York: E. P. Dutton, 1976).

27. "Acceptance by Mr. Styron," *Proceedings of the American Academy of Arts and*

Letters and the National Institute of Arts and Letters, 2d ser., no. 21 (1971), publ. #269, p. 31, reprinted on pp. 226–27 of this collection.

28. Portions of "The Way of the Warrior" have been published; see "Marriott, the Marine," *Esquire*, 76 (Sept. 1971), and "The Suicide Run," *American Poetry Review*, 3 (May/June 1974), 20–22.

LIE DOWN IN DARKNESS

A Rich, Moving Novel Introduces a
Young Writer of Great Talent

Howard Mumford Jones*

"Lie Down in Darkness" illustrates the hold which certain conventions now have upon the American novel at the same time that it shows how these formulae, properly mastered, can contain a rich, full and moving story. For, despite its echoes of familiar authors, "Lie Down in Darkness" is satisfying work. It is planned with mature intelligence, it is written in a style everywhere competent and sometimes superb, and its slow and powerful stream is fed by insights into human beings beyond the capacity of many better-known novelists.

To get the conventions out of the way first, one notes that the title comes from Sir Thomas Browne ("it cannot be long before we lie down in darkness and have our light in ashes"), and that the theme is the familiar theme of the doom of a Southern family, this time in Virginia. The weakling husband is a dipsomaniac, the wife one of those narrow moralists whose intermittent matrimonial charity is a function of suppression. She is jealous of her beautiful daughter and dotes on the idiot sister. We have, in one sense, seen these daughters before—Maudie the crippled mental imbecile, and Peyton, beautiful and corrupted, whose father fixation recalls that of Temple Drake in "Sanctuary." There is a mistress, inevitably named Dolly and inevitably a little overblown. The conclusion turns on a stream-of-consciousness section leading to Peyton's suicide, reminiscent of "The Sound and the Fury" and more remotely of the Molly Bloom section of "Ulysses." And the style from time to time is like the rhetoric of Tom Wolfe.

I have deliberately listed these echoings because they place the book in its special category of horror, beauty and doom. But they should not be overestimated. When they are listed, almost everything is said (with one or two exceptions) that can be said against the shock of recognition of genuine talent. Mr. Styron has fertility of invention, he knows how to manage a long novel, and in the economy of his tale he proves himself a craftsman of the first water.

The story opens upon the return of Peyton's body to "Port Warwick"

*Reprinted from *New York Herald Tribune Book Review*, 9 Sept. 1951, p. 3, by permission of the author.

(in Virginia). After her marriage to a New York Jew she committed suicide. Her corpse was barely rescued from the Potter's field. The funeral ritual at Port Warwick, from the arrival of the gritty train to the final disposition of the body in the cemetery, drags its slow length along with consummate art until it grows almost unbearable. This is the hinge upon which the body of the novel is made to swing. The coffin is received into a hearse perpetually developing engine trouble, and the hearse is followed by a limousine containing an undertaker (a beautiful job of characterization), the father, his mistress and a Negro servant. At each stoppage of the ghastly little procession time becomes immobilized, and the author moves into the past slowly to reveal another complexity in the life of the Loftis family. By this subtle management of chronological time the whole married life of Milton and Helen Loftis unfolds in fits and starts of meaning, becoming the more credible because of the seeming irregularities of revelation. But the irregularities are only apparent; each is cunningly planned to fit into the total scheme of the book. The sense of doom, implicit in the Kafkalike difficulty of getting the body to the mortuary chapel, is imperceptibly transferred to the whole fable, so that in the end the reader accepts accumulated disasters as inevitable.

Mr. Styron has had the courage to be a moralist. He has a thesis. Like "Vanity Fair" his novel pictures a set of people living without God in the world. But where is God to be found? The wife clings to her Episcopalianism, to her so proper, so comforting, so sterile, but when as her agony increases she turns to the Rev. Carey Carr, all that she finds is what the reader finds: the breeding and the bewilderment of a gentleman. While the white family disintegrates, the counter-theme starts among the Negroes, who follow a "Daddy Faith" into a series of revivalist meetings which have at least a deep elemental satisfaction. The last one sees of Helen Loftis, her daughters dead and her husband a sot, is, ironically enough, of her being supported by Carey while she moans: "Nothing! Nothing! Nothing! Nothing!" whereas the last one sees of the Negroes is the triumphant affirmation of a mass baptism. Somewhere between these extremes Christianity must operate.

Mr. Styron has not everywhere avoided a merely literary touch. Milton Loftis appears so monotonously drinking or drunk, the literary formula grows tedious. I, for one, am not persuaded by Peyton Loftis, who dies of the last chapter rather than of necessity. Somehow I find the wanderer-in-Greenwich-Village motif for suicide a little hard to take. Her concluding scenes lack the observed reality of the railroad station at Point Warwick and of a score of other episodes in the book. But these are matters of taste which can be disputed. It is more important to see how, for Mr. Styron, the visible world exisits, not as myth but as actuality. It has people in it, and if you cut them, they bleed. What they do and what they fail to do has meaning in proportion to its morality; and though no system of morality can be explicitly drawn from these pages, Mr. Styron believes there is a moral law. Few recent writers have had the courage of this affirmation, and few have had the capacity to mingle beauty, wisdom and narrative art as he has done.

The Faulkner Pattern

Malcolm Cowley*

Lie Down in Darkness is a novel built around a private funeral. Young Peyton Loftis, daughter of a Virginia family connected with the Byrds, has gone to New York, married a Jewish artist, left him for other men and then committed suicide; now her body is back in Newport News. Only two cars follow the hearse. In the first are her desperately grieving father, her father's silly mistress and an old Negro servant; in the second are her half-crazy mother and the Episcopalian rector. The trip to the cemetery, on an intolerably hot late-August afternoon, is delayed by several accidents, and meanwhile the characters take turns remembering all the events that led to Peyton's death. Peyton remembers, too, by novelistic license; and the most impressive passage in a long, confused and often powerful book is her stream of consciousness during the six hours before she took off her clothes and jumped from the window of a loft building in Harlem.

The structure of the novel seems daring at first, then teasingly familiar; soon one remembers that *As I Lay Dying* was also a novel about a funeral, with the story told in a series of interior monologues by different members of the family, including the woman who had died. With this clue one examines the novel more closely and finds that it is as full of reminiscences as if it had dealt with Yoknapatawpha County instead of tidewater Virginia. Many of the new writers have been learning their craft from William Faulkner; that is among the leading tendencies of the day; but I can't think of any other novel that applies the lessons so faithfully or, for that matter, with so much natural authority and talent.

Take for example Styron's approach to the story. Instead of starting with a first event and making other events follow it in temporal order until we reach the final tragedy, as if at the end of a journey, he starts with an already tragic situation and keeps moving around it in narrowing circles; the story ends when we have grasped the situation in all its inner causes and consequences. That is still a new approach to the novel, but it was newer in 1929, when Faulkner published *The Sound and the Fury*;

*Reprinted from *New Republic*, 8 Oct. 1951, pp. 19–20, by permission of the author.

there his method was so completely circular that we couldn't understand the first section of the book until we had read the fourth and last.

Not only has Styron followed the method but he has also remembered most of the characters in Faulkner's novel. *The Sound and the Fury* had for its subject the decline of a Southern family. The father, Jason Compson III, was a scholar, a gentleman and a drunken lawyer; the mother was selfish and hysterical; the daughter, Candace, felt herself to be doomed and accepted a career of high-class prostitution. There were three sons: the oldest, Quentin, committed suicide in the North after his sister's wedding; the second, Jason IV, became a mean-spirited businessman; and the youngest, Benjy, was an idiot. At the end of the book the family was mourned only by an old religious Negro servant, who said of them, "I seed de first en de last."

It wouldn't be fair to say that Styron copied this family. I would guess that his characters were partly created, partly observed, like most characters in fiction, and that the germ of the story was some event that touched him closely. It is interesting to note, however, that most of the characters end by following the Compson pattern. The father, Milton Loftis, is a witty and drunken lawyer; the mother is selfish and hysterical; one of the daughters is an idiot; and their epitaph is spoken by an old religious Negro servant. There is no one who corresponds to Jason IV, but Peyton Loftis, the heroine, combines the promiscuity of Candace Compson with Quentin's will to suicide. She is, however, a convincing figure in herself and she tries to speak for others of her age. "They thought they had had it," Peyton says. "Those people back in the Lost Generation. Daddy, I guess. Anybody who thought about anything at all. They thought they were lost. They were crazy. They weren't lost. What they were doing was losing us."

It is a general rule that novels which stay close to their literary models have no great value of their own, but *Lie Down in Darkness* is an exception; in this case the example of Faulkner seems to have had a liberating effect on Styron's imagination. One might even say that his book is best and most personal when it is most Faulknerian. Peyton's wanderings on the day of her suicide are much like those of Quentin Compson on his last day and some of the symbols are the same: for example, Quentin carries an old-fashioned watch and broods about it, while Peyton carries an alarm clock. Yet Styron gets inside her character, makes her more understandable and pitiable than Quentin, and it seems to me that this one passage, at least, is better than its model.

Dissolution of a Family

Harvey Breit*

Since it was said at once that I had affection for Mann's novel, let me say at once that I have little affection and considerable admiration for William Styron's *Lie Down in Darkness*. And lest this be regarded as a contradictory remark, I remind the reader that Forster was careful to qualify his "test" with the word "final." Let me also add that for the 25-year-old Thomas Mann's *Buddenbrooks* I had more admiration than affection.

Lie Down in Darkness is an appallingly and terrifyingly effective (and sometimes even moving) novel. The author opens his story with a funeral. Milton Loftis, a prominent citizen of Port Warwick, Virginia, is waiting at the railroad station, with hearse, black limousine, and mistress, for the dead body of his beautiful daughter. As he waits, as he a little later almost succumbs to his need to escape the ordeal, as he still later rides to the cemetery in the mortuary car, the terrible, black, black story is unfolded in fragments. Put together, the fragments articulately and eloquently tell a story of the total dissolution of a family: Milton Loftis, his wife Helen, his two daughters, Peyton and Maudie (crippled, innocent, imbecilic, and dead years before her sister's insane leap from a toilet window onto a Harlem street).

The trouble in this one house has a number of excellent contributive factors. I think it would be fair to say that chief among them are the drinking and altogether self-indulgent habits of Milton, who loves Peyton and neglects Maudie, as against the ascetic and egocentric "style" of Helen, who protects Maudie and hates Peyton. One is the sin of sloth and the other the sin of pride. In the Loftis household it makes for a frightful warfare. But it is Peyton who is at the center of the novel and she is harder to understand. I would guess that what Styron has demonstrated is a simplified working out of Mendel's law: Peyton appears to have inherited the sin of each parent. It is the least convincing element of the book.

If there is a key word in the novel, it appears to me to be "need": people "need" each other, Milton needs Peyton, Peyton needs her hus-

*Reprinted from *Atlantic Monthly*, Oct. 1951, pp. 78–80. Copyright 1951, by The Atlantic Monthly Company, Boston, Mass. Reprinted with permission.

band, Helen needs Maudie. I don't mean that Styron isn't aware of this. At one point, Peyton's husband says he doesn't want her to need him, he wants her to love him. The point for me is an ironic one: I felt no "need"—no logical necessity really—for the story to evolve in the way that it does, for the relentless, perhaps willful, dirgelike monotone, not only unrelieved but given an additional turn of the screw in its last drawn-out section dealing with Peyton. It starts out a bleak and black book and it ends as one; there is no catalyst here. That is why I can have no affection for it. I am profoundly aware, though, that in wanting to cite its perhaps inevitable defects, I have placed my criticism in an improper focus.

For example, the book is not bleakly written. On the contrary, it is richly and even (in the best sense) poetically written. If Peyton is improperly motivated, she is nevertheless a fascinating creature and her beauty, her fatal attraction, is visible and tactile and altogether sensory. If the parts seem to succeed each other with no apparent logic or dialectic, each part is brilliantly made and lovingly accomplished. If the long, terminal inner-soliloquy appears immature, there is so much else that is overwhelmingly adult. If, finally, there exists a fugitive sense that the author has gone to Joyce for his structure and to Faulkner for his rhetoric, it is only fugitive and consequently intelligent and probably assimilated. Not least among its virtues, the novel is deeply absorbing. It is a basically mature, substantial, and enviable achievement, powerful enough to stay with you after you have shut it out.

A Grasp of Moral Realities

Robert Gorham Davis*

"Only that story deserves to be called moral," says the narrator at the end of Goethe's *Procurator*, "which shows us that man possesses within himself the force to act even contrary to his inclinations through a conviction of something better."

The great interest of William Styron's *Lie Down in Darkness*—apart from the marvelous talent which it constantly and variously displays—is a moral one. His principal characters, members of a fairly prominent, fairly respectable, fairly well-to-do family in a Virginia sea-coast city, do not themselves, it is true, meet Goethe's test. They are as weak and neurotic as any of the damned or doomed in recent naturalistic fiction. At the decisive, irredeemable moments, when everything depends on their not doing so, they take too many drinks, go to bed with the wrong person, yield to habitual and destructive impulses of self-righteousness, jealousy, vengefulness and deceit.

From the outside—or even from the inside in limited Dreiserian perspective—their behavior may seem determined. Indeed, Milton Loftis, the father, occasionally excuses his corrupting treatment of his wife, his mistress and his daughters, by references to determinism, to man's moral helplessness. But William Styron, who was only twenty-five when he finished *Lie Down in Darkness*, has an uncanny ability to move into the minds and feelings of people like the middle-aged Loftis parents and their friends, to reproduce their inner experiences with utterly convincing completeness. In this fullness of consciousness the important moments present themselves as moments of inescapable choice, and if past behavior has helped to determine the choice now, it has also taught more and more emphatically the consequences of such a choice. The characters cannot hide from themselves the fact that what happens is what they themselves have really willed. Milton and Helen Loftis have flashes of clear insight into what they are doing so terribly to each other, to themselves and to their daughter Peyton, and they have impulses to save themselves which they finally deliberately block or evade.

*Reprinted from *American Scholar*, 21 (Winter 1951), 114, 116, by permission of the author.

William Styron has dazzling gifts with language, and great observational powers in describing moods, incidents, landscapes and conversations. But it is the moral tension of his best scenes that gives such dramatic interest to a story which in outline is so familiarly depressing (it is all told in flashbacks on the day of the daughter Peyton's funeral) and to characters which are not, on the whole, very likable or amusing. Their depth and humanity derive from the constant sense of moral election implicit in the situation, and it is with real anguish that we experience their failure. Styron tells the story with such an imaginative grasp of moral realities that we can sympathize profoundly and yet judge quite objectively. To know all is not to pardon all; quite the contrary. This applies quite as much to Helen Loftis, shielding herself behind the church and her love for her defective daughter Maudie, as it does to Milton Loftis, living on his wife's money and overtly incestuous in his affection for his daughter Peyton.

It is only in his treatment of the younger generation, his own generation, that the author lets his intuitive sense of individual responsibility be replaced by the myth of a doomed generation, a myth taken directly from the novelists from whom he has learned his art. Maudie and Peyton Loftis are quite incapable, the first physically, the second spiritually, of determining their own fates. They are simply the symbolic consequences of their parents' failings. The explicit assumption is that both in a family and in a society a weak or lost generation can be followed only by one weaker and even more desperately lost, although this is implicitly denied by the creative strength and the Goethean conviction of something better in Styron's own work.

Peyton's career, though it is done brilliantly as far as details are concerned, is simply a greased slide down through drunkenness and nymphomania to a suicide leap and shipment to Potter's Field. Peyton combines the fates of Quentin and Caddy Compson in Faulkner's *The Sound and the Fury*. (Faulkner says of Caddy, "Doomed and knew it, accepted the doom without either seeking or fleeing it.") Styron takes over from Faulkner not only his lost lovely heroine, but also some specific symbolism, such as that of the clock, and the idea of ending the novel at a Negro revival meeting. The Negroes in the novel are all originals, however, wonderfully known and respected, and Milton and Helen Loftis, Milton's mistress Dolly, and the servant La Ruth are in the best tradition of the novel of character of the nineteenth century, a tradition which *Lie Down in Darkness* shows to be far from exhausted. Styron is remarkably mature already in his novelist's art and in his understanding of human nature. A conceptual maturity consistent with his vision of life and freed from some of the philosophic clichés of recent literary convention is bound to follow.

Private Emotions
Privately Felt

Elizabeth Janeway*

Whatever disappointment 1951 presented in the work of older novelists, it gave us some fine first novels. J. D. Salinger's *The Catcher in the Rye* is the best, a really extraordinary accomplishment, mature and expert as few first novels manage to be, speaking with its own voice, its strength controlled. Set beside it, William Styron's *Lie Down in Darkness* is seen at once to be less satisfactory. It has been called derivative, another book about a decadent and corrupt Southern family. This is nonsense. The members of Styron's Loftis family are hardly conscious enough to be decadent, and they suffer too much to be corrupt—these words imply a kind of evil complacence which is entirely absent from the moral atmosphere of the book. Neither are they particularly Southern in the literary sense.

Is the book derivative? I don't think so. It is true that it is a more usual type of novel for a *first* novel than *The Catcher in the Rye*, because it is undisciplined, and Salinger's writing is not undisciplined. But it is wider in range, it attempts more, and a great deal of what it attempts it brings off. Also it does not suffer from Salinger's one fault, which is, it seems to me, a kind of elfin sentimentality-in-reverse. *Lie Down in Darkness* is not in the least sentimental. Moreover, though the jacket blurb leads one to expect a certain amount of younger-generation self-pity, whatever of this weakness Styron may have started with has been burned off, to leave behind that much more useful emotion (for a writer, at any rate)—bitterness.

The action of the book is supposed to take place during a journey behind a hearse, from railroad depot to cemetery. The journey is made by Milton Loftis, an alcoholic lawyer of Port Warwick, Virginia. The body in the hearse is that of his daughter Peyton, a suicide. Loftis is accompanied by his mistress, Dolly Bonner, and an old Negro servant, Ella Swan. Helen Loftis, his wife who refused to go with him, makes her own pilgrimage to the graveyard. Her companions are her minister, an uncertain soul named Carey Carr, and the ghost of another dead daughter,

*Reprinted with permission from *New Leader*, 21 Jan. 1952, p. 25. Copyright American Labor Conference on International Affairs, Inc.

Maudie, who was a feeble-minded cripple. (Does this gruesome catalogue of the family seem to lend weight to the charge of "corruptness"? It should not. One is persuaded, reading, that such things really do happen to people.) All about the hearse and the mourners (Mourners? No, the stunned—only Ella Swan mourns) foams another pilgrimage of white-robed Negroes on their way to—not a revival meeting, certainly, but rather a celebration of a new religion whose God is a satisfying tangible personage called Daddy Faith.

I say the action is supposed to take place during this journey. Actually the book is a dizzying composite of flashbacks and flashbacks within flashbacks. If Styron intended the span of the journey to the cemetery to impose a kind of form upon his story, he at once proceeded to ignore his own intention. Indeed, the device has been used to permit a much looser structure than a straight narrative would have provided. It is never entirely clear *why* we learn what we do learn about the disastrous past life of the Loftis family *when* we do. The book has about as much continuity as a river in spate. Under the bridge on which we lean pours a torrent of the past, bearing with it a debris of incidents, as the river carries a hen-house, a ladder, a door, a mattress, a farmwagon upside-down. Here is Loftis as a man, as a boy, kissing Dolly, marrying Helen, drunk when Maudie is dying. Here is Helen mad, Helen sane; Peyton drunk, Peyton in love, Peyton marrying. It is a great compliment to Styron's conviction and power that these incidents are heartrending and immediate, for one does not build to the next. But the massive flood of emotion charges them with intensity. Story and characters alike are muddy and ill-defined. They both communicate themselves to the reader, nonetheless, by their sheer impact.

And at the end, Styron does more than this. My river metaphor fails. In the long passage leading to Peyton's death, Styron builds a tower right up to the sky—tragic, noble, beautiful—from whose highest, most exquisite turret Peyton flings herself down like one of the flightless birds which have haunted her for so long.

In those birds, in the role that crippled Maudie plays, in the Negro servants and their new religion (about which Styron writes very seriously, saying: What religion is not fantastic and delusive? Do we not need the strength of fantasia and delusion?) as well as in the more obvious symbology of the journey to the grave, there is achieved effortlessly something that most writers find extremely difficult and too many ignore. This is, to plumb private emotion *as it is felt privately* in obscure half-articulate symbols and to communicate the weight of this emotion to the reader. This has nothing to do with story-telling. It is a search for meaning. Unless more writers dedicate themselves to it, the stories we tell will wear even thinner than they already have.

Paradise Lost: Styron's
Lie Down in Darkness

Jonathan Baumbach*

> Son, you don't have to be a campfollower of reaction but always
> remember where you came from. The ground is bloody and full of guilt
> where you were born and you must tread a long, narrow path toward
> your destiny.

This mythic, almost absurd voice of Milton Loftis's father, comes as
an echo from Tiresias, chanting in oracular rhetoric the ritual theme of
Lie Down in Darkness (1951)—sin and guilt, guilt and death. These are
the trinitarian fruits of the fall. Port Warwick, Virginia, the soil of
William Styron's first novel, is a decayed and decaying paradise, haunted
by illusions of a glorious past. With the progressive deterioration of its
romantic ideals, the aristocracy of Styron's South falls from innocence
into decay, from decay into guilt, and finally from guilt into redemption
through death. This theme, though recurrent in southern fiction, has
been inherited intact, along with some characters and episodes, from
William Faulkner's *The Sound and the Fury*. Nor is that Styron's only
literary debt. The style of *Lie Down in Darkness*, studded with jewels of
rhetoric, indicates Styron's acquaintance with the writing of at least
Faulkner, Warren, Fitzgerald, Wolfe, and Joyce. However, given its
weaknesses, its often unassimilated indebtedness, its self-insistent verbal
virtuosity, its final failure to achieve focus, *Lie Down in Darkness* remains the most ostentatiously talented first novel of the period. The
prodigious brilliance of its performance resides in the richness and grace
of the language and the intricate, almost impossible complexity of the
structure.

The plot structure of *Lie Down in Darkness* has all the aspects of a
puzzle—a methodic search through a maze of mirrors for a truth hidden
in its symbolic reflection. But as a puzzle it is never intentionally obscure.
We are given at the outset the first clue: the fact of Peyton Loftis' suicide,
a symbol of the final disintegration of the Loftis family. The novel on its
narrative level, then, becomes an investigation of the events leading up to
Peyton's death, in effect an intensive exploration of a southern family's

*Reprinted from *The Landscape of Nightmare: Studies in the Contemporary American Novel*
(New York: New York Univ. Press, 1965), pp. 123–33, by permission of the author.

almost effortless self-destruction. On its symbolic level, *Lie Down in Darkness* is a tragedy of decaying values, a study of a paradise fallen into chaos, the end result of a romantic conception of morality. This is a morality corroded with paradoxes: purity and original sin, chivalry and slavery, innocence and decadence. The social order of the southern slavocracy is long dead, but the dream of glory persists—an idiot ghost haunting its descendants.

The entire forward progression of the novel takes place in less than three hours, a stunning self-imposed limitation. The time present of the novel is the burial of Peyton, a ritualistic symbol of the completion of the life cycle—a going back at last to the starting point of existence. It is no accident that the final scene in *Lie Down in Darkness* is a baptism, a symbol of the renewal of life. The technical problem of exposition that Styron has set himself is Ibsenic:[1] he must move backward and forward in time simultaneously; he must delay revelation of the past so that each discovery further illuminates our understanding of the present, the final discovery, the lifting of the veil, illuminating all. To effect his intention, Styron employs five narrators (six including the author) who reconstruct the significant events of the past that are connected with the final tragedy. Each of the narrators is equipped with the faculty of complete recall and, in some cases, a God-like intuition, which might be considered a kind of cheating on Styron's part. However, the stylized use of internal monologue is a schematic device employed with reasonable consistency throughout.

Milton Loftis, who is the fixed center of a destructive three-cornered relationship, standing uneasily between his daughter Peyton, and his wife Helen, is the first mind through which the narrative (past and present) is filtered. It is a mind dulled by alcohol, guilt, and indulgence. Milton seeks in the storehouse of remembered experience to discover where he failed Peyton, what particular moment, what action (if he could but undo it!) triggered Peyton's destruction. At first he finds no answer, but he feels that somewhere in his weakness, in his sins, in the sins of his tradition, he is responsible. Unable to live with the knowledge of his guilt, Milton succors himself in the narcosis of drink, looking not for expiation but only painlessness.

Milton, as seen through the eyes of Dolly Bonner who loves him but who is not loved in return, whose body is used by him as another anesthetic against the pain of memory, is a man whose charm of personality would make him most likely to succeed in his chosen field, law or politics. But Milton has already sold this possibility of personal achievement along with his manhood to Helen, for the price of comfort. His failure to realize his latent potentialities is not tragic but pathetic. Pampered by self-delusion, the habit of his traditional past, he is a romantic without romance. He must live in the idealized image of himself even though the picture never comes into focus for him. His obsessive, drunken search for his beautiful daughter Peyton, at a football game, while Maudie, his crippled, idiot daughter lies dying in a hospital nearby symbolizes the fruitlessness of his activity, the nightmare of his failure. Styron makes this graphic for us by having the inebriated Milton carry in his arms a Confederate flag, "a trophy without honor." Milton is good but lost, well meaning but irresponsible—a remnant of a tradition that did not require responsibility.

Milton's romantic yearning, unrewarded in Helen, grows into his incestuous attachment for Peyton, a love which becomes obsessive and is, in part, the cause of her destruction and his disintegration. Unable to consummate his attraction to his daughter, Milton drifts into an extended affair with the vulgar but sexual Dolly Bonner, which, Styron suggests, is a kind of vicarious incest. "Poor blind Milton," says Peyton in a moment of ironic revelation, and this is, in implication, his epitaph. But at Peyton's wedding reception, the nightmarish climax of the novel, Milton does achieve his moment of realization.

> Across the room he sees Peyton break away from the young lieutenant, her arm crooked at the elbow in a curious disjointed way. . . . He wishes to go to her side, to talk to her alone, and explain. He wants only to be able to say: forgive me, forgive all of us. Forgive your mother too. She saw, but she just couldn't understand. It's my fault. Forgive me for loving you so.
>
> But at this moment, when he suddenly sees Helen, white with fury, throw a coat over her shoulders and go out onto the porch with Carey Carr, he knows that explanations are years too late. If he himself could love too much only Helen could love so little.[2]

In a moment of pure unillusioned sight, Milton becomes aware of the irremediable nature of their three-personed tragedy. His discovery, however, only intensifies his helplessness, and so he drinks to forget; soon all that remains of his vision is a blurred sense of discomfort, a vague prescience of undefined and undefinable danger. Nevertheless, this has been Milton's first admission of his excessive love for Peyton, which has, in part, created Helen's obsessive jealousy of her daughter—her devout, self-righteous hate. Helen, Milton, and Peyton are, in effect, like Sartre's trinity in No Exit, one another's inescapable Hell. Under the catalytic influence of the wedding, the thinly disguised pattern of their lives manifests itself: Milton drunkenly mauls Peyton; Helen accuses Peyton of being a slut, of using her sexuality to exhort gratuities from her father; Peyton digs her nails into her mother's face. What happens is an intensification of what has been implicit all along; the patina of respectability is torn away, revealing the horror.

Further complicating the process of unraveling the puzzle is the use of narrations within narrations, flashbacks within flashbacks, creating a view of a view of a view—an extended perspective of perception. Styron's technique of indirect narration is most effective when he uses Carey Carr,

an acquiescent Episcopal minister, as reporter of the behavior, feelings, and thoughts of Helen Loftis. Carey is Helen's confidant, psychiatrist, father, and spiritual lover all in one. He is a man of love who searches hopefully, but always in vain, for the manifestation of God's goodness in man. A frustrated poet, Carey constructs or rather creates Helen's thoughts and feelings out of the incoherent material of her confidences. His interpretation of her motives is rather overly indulgent at the beginning of their relationship. But he discovers at Peyton's wedding, during which a series of explosive revelations are detonated (a kind of dramatic chain reaction), the ineradicable blackness of Helen's soul. Helen is psychotic, and there is no salvation for her except the escape provided by her madness. She represents for Carey his first confrontation with evil. In a moment of insane revelation, Helen tells him, "Your God is a silly old ass—and my God—my God is the Devil!" The minister, limited by his gentleness of spirit, is unable to cope with the malignancy of Helen's god.

Helen, even in Carey's gracious interpretation of her behavior, is the least sympathetic of the three central characters. Perhaps, because she is an amalgam of two corrupt traditions, the southern and the military, her corruption has been compounded. There is some reference to an unresolved sexual attachment to her martinet father, which might account for her emotional and sexual frigidity. Her fondest memory is of her father in his officer's plumage sitting masterfully atop a silver gelding. The memory image suggests Helen's secret wish to replace her father astride the emasculated horse; in effect, she aspires to dominate and, at least symbolically, emasculate her husband. Helen's justification of her unforgivingness is her pride, the echo of which is reiterated amid the empty ruins of her life. Finally, her pride becomes a masochistic self-indulgence, a persistent picking at a sore.

Using the morally responsible Carey as narrator of Helen's most offensive behavior, Styron stacks the deck against her. She is a victim as well as a murderer, but she becomes so totally despicable by the end of the novel that we are unable to feel pity for her suffering. Helen is incapable of love except a perverted self-love extended to her lame, simple daughter Maudie, the physical personification of Helen's crippled spirit. Helen, like Truman Capote's nether-world inhabitants, can love only "the broken image of herself."

Published when Styron was twenty-six, *Lie Down in Darkness* has some of the zealous faults of young writing. It is at times overwritten; rhetoric occasionally pours forth like unimpeded flood waters, and the structure seems to crumble at the end, perhaps unable to bear the pressure of the style. But these are flaws in an otherwise remarkable book. If Styron's metaphorical language is used indiscriminately at times, it is rarely less than equal to the highest demands of his story. For example, Peyton's fall from grace with Dickie, the first in a long line of compulsive affairs, is evoked by Styron as the Fall, the precipitative moment of her destruction, which is in symbol all our destructions. Her going to bed with Dickie, "whose mind was a sheet of paper upon which no thoughtful word had been written" (p. 342), does not have the romantic justification of passion or tenderness; it is a gratuitous submission. In a sense, this is her first suicide—a moral death that is an endless retribution for her endless guilt. Ivan Karamazov says, "If God is dead, everything is permissible." When Peyton discovers that God, her father, is for all intents and purposes dead, she sins compulsively, committing herself to the implications of a chaotic universe.

Peyton's act of sexual surrender is, in its universal implications, the death of innocence. In the resonance of Styron's prose this becomes a revelation:

> The act of love had exhausted them but they slept restlessly, dreaming loveless dreams. The sun rose, began to descend, and afternoon brought a flood of light to the room. The radio, playing faintly from the living room, sent through their dreams a murmurous flow of intrusions: the war, a preacher said, was general throughout the world and at the smoky edge of sleep between wakefulness and dreams, their minds captured words like Christ and anti-Christ only to lose them and to forget, and to stir and dream again.
>
> Sleeping, he took her in his arms; she drew away. A dog barked across the wintry fields. There was dance music and later, Mozart, a song of measureless innocence that echoed among lost ruined temples of peace and brought to their dreams an impossible vision: of a love that outlasted time and dwelt even in the night, beyond reach of death and all the immemorial descending dusks. Then evening came. Arms and legs asprawl, they stirred and turned. Twilight fell over their bodies. They were painted with fire, like those fallen children who live and breathe and soundlessly scream, and whose souls blaze forever. [p. 237]

Peyton is a fallen innocent lost in a world of irreconcilable opposites ("Christ and anti-Christ") which are reconciled for her on the level of ultimate meaninglessness. Her Hell, in which she symbolically burns, is a boundless vale of impossible hopes and irrevocable losses.

In their separate ways Helen, Milton, and Peyton all attempt indulgently to escape the consciousness of guilt; Helen through insanity, Milton through drink and adultery, and Peyton (successfully) through death. Life for Peyton is a football game in which her body takes part and is broken, while her spirit sits like a spectator on the sidelines weeping tears of pity. Where Milton is an idealist without ideals, Peyton is, correspondingly, an innocent without innocence. Loved too much by her father and hated by her mother, beautiful and spoiled, obsessed with death ("how short my time is"), she is a mass of neurotic contradictions. Peyton is aware of her masochistic drives, but she is unable to resist the least of her compulsions. She is without conscious will, and, by divorcing the intent from the act, retains the dream of her innocence. On the borderline of psychosis before her death, Peyton is still able to rationalize her motives:

> Oh, I would say, you've never understood me, Harry, that not out of vengeance have I accomplished all my sins but because something has always been close to dying in my soul, and I've sinned only in order to lie down in darkness and find, somewhere in the net of dreams, a new father, a new home. [p. 385]

Peyton regresses at the end to infantilism. Because she cannot find a paternalism on earth to replace the one she has lost, she must go beneath the earth to find "a new father, a new home." Frustrated and lost, she drowns in self-pitying tears as she inexorably lives out the last reel of her phantasmagoric life. She thinks, while climbing a staircase to the height from which she will jump to her death: "I thought that only guilt could deliver me into this ultimate paradox: that all must go down before ascending upward; only we most egregious sinners, to shed our sin in self-destruction, must go upward before the last descent" (p. 385).

Peyton's suicide has all the ritual aspects of a purification. She strips off her clothes (the vestments of her corrupt life) before she jumps, returning to nature in the state of innocence in which she came. Ironically, it is through "falling" that Peyton achieves her redemption. Styron's point is that only through hell—the ultimate Fall—can one finally come to heaven.

Despite the intensity and brilliance of Styron's handling of Peyton's stream-of-consciousness during the moments preceding and leading up to her death, the structure of the novel seems to collapse at this crucial point. Taking place in New York, outside the main setting of the book, Peyton's interior monologue has an alien sound, as if she were another character in another book. Even if the episode in New York can be justified in terms of structure, as necessary for the completion of the puzzle—the final filling-in of all retrospective exposition—it is still inordinately long and dissipates itself as well as the cumulative impact of the novel. Coming as it does after the wedding scene in which her death becomes inevitable, Peyton's state of mind at the moment of suicide seems irrelevant and anticlimactic. Styron tells his story peripherally, in ever-narrowing circles, working toward an ideal, if impossible, center. In attempting to produce that infinite point (that final illuminating) delineating what the novel has already successfully implied, Styron disappoints our expectations. Peyton, by virtue of her complex reality as character, remains finally a mystery.

Symbolism abounds in the over-fertile soil of Styron's novel. Styron evokes the classic myths through transplanting, in a sense, the tragic tradition of the house of Atreus to the marshlands of Port Warwick. I think a fair case can be made for Peyton's being a distant relation of Electra (also Orestes). The flightless birds which follow Peyton to her death are a sort of psychotic manifestation of the furies. Peyton's behavior can be interpreted as a somewhat perverse sublimation of the Electra drive (avenging her father's death by killing her mother in herself). Though the mythic allusions give the novel a further resonance, on occasion symbols seem employed, as in a Tennessee Williams play, merely to create a sort of poetry of atmosphere. One analogy that makes the reader uneasy throughout is that the dropping of the atom bomb on Hiroshima is the national correlative of the central action of the novel. "Don't you realize that the great American commonwealth just snuffed out one hundred thousand innocent lives this week," Harry tells the disoriented Peyton, who a few minutes later jumps to her death. The moral disintegration of the South is a symbol of the disintegration of all of us, and consequently Peyton's suicide is an exemplary act of conscience. The parallel is not wholly invalid, but by overinsisting on it—the bomb is referred to significantly at least a half a dozen times in the novel—Styron makes it seem if not arbitrary, only abstractly relevant.

The ferry ride that separates Port Warwick from the mainland is employed symbolically to suggest the classic voyage across the river Styx into Hades. The fallen paradise of Port Warwick is, like Hades, peopled by the shades of those who once lived:

> The ferry slip is not far from the railroad station, in fact adjoins it, in an atmosphere of coal dust, seedy cafes, run-down, neon-lit drug stores where sailors buy condoms and Sanitubes and occasionally ice-cream cones. The salt-air is strong here. The wind rustles the weeds in vacant lots. Along the railroad track the Negro cabins are lit with the yellow glow of oil lamps, and in the moonlight a black figure appears to pull down the washing. [p. 315]

Port Warwick is a marshland, a quicksand of decay. The landscape acts as a kind of mirror of the spiritual condition of its inhabitants.

> Death was in the air . . . but wasn't Autumn the season of death and all Virginia, a land of dying? In the woods strange, somehow rather marvelous fires were burning across the gray day, the road still shining with last night's rain, gray smoke drifted, bringing to his nostrils the odor of burned wood and leaves. [p. 188]

Virginia is a land of dying, Styron says. But it is a place for degenerative dying. Release, Peyton's fall to death, can only happen outside the narcotic atmosphere of Port Warwick. While Peyton has ended her suffering, Milton and Helen remain, still drowning in the morass of their self-indulgence and self-pity. They are dying too, but slowly, without awareness, engulfed in the sweet-smelling anesthetic of decay.

Harry, Peyton's husband (and father substitute), is used as a symbol of creativeness in contrast to the indolence and self-destruction of Peyton's tradition. Unfortunately, he is unconvincing as a human being and consequently makes a factitious and ineffective symbol. It is ironic that Styron's

conceptual representative of life—the New Yorker-Artist-Jew—has less
real life as character than his various rotting-on-the-vine southerners.
However, the artist as sympathetic character has traditionally been an
unaccommodating conception for the writer, who tends to intrude
himself, the most sympathetic artist he knows. Mainly, Harry's talk is
bad. His literary love making to Peyton ("My blessed Beatrice"[3]) sounds
like undergraduate self-consciousness. This is in striking contrast to the
maturity and control of so much of the writing.

Like Faulkner, Styron also has his symbolic idiot, Maudie. The death
of Maudie's innocence, narrated by Helen in a moment of rare understanding, is one of the tragic echoes of the novel. Maudie, crippled and
simple-minded, represents another aspect of the southern tradition—its
fragile innocence. She retains her innocence until she comes in contact
with one of nature's own spirits, Benny[4] (half-Indian, half-Negro), who
performs feats of magic to entertain her. He awakens in her the tender
wonder of love and she comes each day to meet him, experiencing
unalloyed happiness for the first time in her life. But her idyl must finally
end; innocence and pure love are merely transient. The death of Maudie's
heart comes when she realizes that Benny will leave her, that love does
not go on forever. The death of her body follows soon after. What Benny
offered her was, after all, only sleight of hand. The symbol of Maudie's
disillusionment extends into the following scene in the dramatic sequence
of the novel—Peyton's fall from grace with Dickie. They are, essentially,
parallel scenes.

The symbol of the southern Negro in *Lie Down in Darkness* as a child
in a child's world, who can find salvation through simple faith, has its
antecedents in Faulkner's novels. While the southern gentility disintegrates, the descendants of the slave class endure. Ella in *Lie Down in
Darkness* and her prototype Dilsey in Faulkner's *The Sound and the Fury*
rear the family and try to hold it together, while the family compulsively
destroys itself. The source of the Negro's strength is his unquestioning
faith in God, as opposed to the gentry's religion, which has formalized
God out of existence. For all his benevolence and intelligence, Carey Carr
is a less effective man of God than the absurd Negro evangelist Daddy
Faith. There are comparable scenes of religious ecstasy at the end of both
(Faulkner's and Styron's) novels. Coming after the burial of Peyton, the
Daddy Faith baptismal ceremony achieves a special resonance as a
symbol of the redemption of Peyton's life and of the possible salvation of
our own.

One of the problems of the novel is the paradox of Peyton's moral
responsibility set against the amoral backdrop of Port Warwick. Is she
completely a victim, the end product of a cursed and decaying southern
tradition, or does she have the possibility of survival? Peyton says in protest against the irresponsibility of her parents' generation: " 'They
thought they were lost. They were crazy. They weren't lost. What they

were doing was losing us' " (p. 235). However, through Carey, his moral raisonneur, Styron holds her responsible—at least in part responsible. Carey says of Peyton, " 'Other children have risen above worse difficulties.' " It is this immutable absolute of judgment, the last standing pillar in a chaotic, disintegrating society, that gives the novel its final importance.

Though it may fail ultimately, *Lie Down in Darkness* is a brilliant first novel. Yet our brilliant first novels have been followed more often than not by a drying up, by a substitution of will for creation, by second and third novels that fail to go beyond the promise of the first. It would be pleasant to report that this does not apply at all to Styron, but to a limited extent it does. His second book, *The Long March* (1952), a novelette, though more controlled and concentrated than the first, is considerably less ambitious; for all Styron's insistences, the noble defeat of its hero Mannix never quite achieves tragic dimension. When Styron's second full-length novel, *Set This House on Fire* (1960), finally appeared, an anticlimax to his waning reputation, it was inevitably a disappointment. In the accounting house of our popular criticism, measured against its ambitions, *Set This House on Fire* is a failure. Yet it is in many ways an advance over the first novel and it is remarkably better than the general verdict of its curiously unsympathetic press.

" 'What's the matter with this world?' " a nameless hillbilly singer chants dolefully at a propitious moment in *Set This House on Fire*. The singer, one of Styron's prophetic voices from other rooms, answers his own question: " 'Your soul's on sinking sand, the end is drawing near: That's what's the matter with this world. . . .' "

If anyone still wondered at this point why it had taken the author of *Lie Down in Darkness* eight years to complete his second full-length novel, these lines which inform its experience provide the explanation. Further indicative of Styron's attitude is that all of his sympathetic characters are alcoholics or reformed alcoholics, as if he were unable to conceive of a sensitive human being who could withstand the nightmare of existence without the anesthetic of drink.

Set This House on Fire attempts the improbable: the alchemical transformation of impotent rage into tragic experience. Styron's rage is the hell-fire heat of the idealist faced by an unredeemably corrupt world, for which he as fallen man feels obsessively and hopelessly guilty. To understand the quality of Styron's anger, one has only to set his protest along side that of the so-called angry young men (Messrs. Braine, Wain, Amis, and Osborne), who seem in comparison nothing so much as choir boys wearing tight shoes. Contemporary man for Styron is an infinitely corruptible Adam, repeatedly violating the terms of his existence, falling farther and farther out of Paradise. Each Adam experiences in the house of his body the torments of a private Hell, the solitary confinement of damnation. The novel contains a series of nightmare visions of Doomsday, at once a prophecy of impending atomic holocaust and an externaliz-ing of a raging interior guilt. But Doomsday does not so much threaten from without as from within, as Cass Kinsolving, the most central of Styron's three central characters, discovers to his horror and perhaps, final salvation. Cass is, in Styron's over-insistent conception of him, a neo-Dostoevskian hero who goes from the death of sin through the purgation of guilt and suffering to the potential resurrection of redemption. It is an exemplary spiritual voyage which Styron suggests makes possible, through the symbolic resurrection of Luciano de Lieto ("like the Phoenix risen from the ashes of his own affliction"), the salvation of all of us damned souls. The novel fails, like the later novels of D. H. Lawrence, because Styron permits his didactic purpose, when it is at odds with his impulses as a novelist, to govern and shape his book. As a result there is often an ir-reconcilable disparity between the experience resident in the novel and Styron's insistent explication of the experience.

Once we have faced up to the novel's weaknesses—its overexplicit-ness, its undramatized sermonizing (Styron unabashedly commenting on contemporary civilization through the masks of his sympathetic characters), and its unconvincing "hopeful" ending—we must also, though perhaps with greater difficulty, face up to the fact that *Set This House on Fire* is an original and serious novel which survives, if not wholly transcends, its flaws. Styron's world is a Dantean inferno; he takes us on a descent through levels of disillusioning experiences, some horrify-ing, some grotesquely comic, in which everything, even what seems most pure, turns out on closer view to be unreclaimably corrupt. Ultimately, the novel is a symbolic pilgrimage into Hell in search of, of all things, the sight of God.

As in *Lie Down in Darkness*, the plot structure is informed by a mystery whose unraveling, we are led to believe, will reveal some essen-tial truth of existence. In both novels, the final discovery is anticlimactic. At the outset of *Set This House on Fire*, we are presented with Peter Leverett, a nondescript Nick Carraway, as first-person narrator and ap-parently central character. Peter seeks, as the way to his own salvation, the meaning of a nightmare experience in Sambuco, Italy, in which his unholy friend Mason Flagg apparently raped and murdered an Italian servant girl and then killed himself. With the aid of Cass Kinsolving, Mason's antagonist, Peter attempts to reconstruct what actually took place. Along the way, however, the concern of the novel shifts from Peter's quest to Mason as the incarnation of evil (he is, of course, less evil than we had suspected) and then to Cass as a drunken sufferer for an unregenerate world. Cass's chain of self-revelations, through which the mystery is finally uncovered, becomes more significant than the mystery itself. When we actually lift the veil, the secret it has to yield has ceased to be important. Though Cass achieves a kind of redemption through Mason's death, Styron avoids overstating the obvious allegorical parallels.

As Mason is not quite Mephisto, and Peter not quite the rock on which the new church is built, Cass is not quite Christ, though these parallels are suggested.

Cass's sleeping nightmares are hardly less real than his waking ones. They are in one way or another recurrent evocations of destruction, sometimes personal, sometimes universal, in which he as southern white, haunted by the guilt of his tradition, is alternately tortured and saved by strangely familiar Negro effigies. Styron's liquid, rhetorical prose, which at times seems to flow on unbidden, is at its best in rendering the nightmare of Cass's hallucinatory visions:

> The sea was placid, held in momentary abeyance, but the sun had grown hotter still, hung in the sky fiery, huge and, like some dead weight, oppressively heavy and near. The bugger is exploding, Cass thought as he edged back into a shadowed place, it's going to shrivel up like a bunch of gnats in a flame. [p. 483]

There are other, more brilliant passages, but this one suggests both the power of Styron's writing and the central vision of the novel. The swelling sun is a projection of Cass's exploding guilt, but no less a real spectre of contemporary (hydrogen bomb) reality. Despite the philosophical justification for the hopeful ending, this scene and its echoes, and the various parables of corruption and doom that mythically underlie the basic experience of the novel, make the resurrection in the epilogue seem gratuitously appended. The vision of the undying, half-crushed dog offers, I suspect, a more accurate clue to the meaning of Styron's work. Cass witnesses a doctor trying in vain to put the incurably maimed dog out of its misery by beating it on the head with a stick. Although Cass leaves, the vision remains of "the dog's head, mutilated, bleeding, still mouthing its silent, stunned agony to the heavens." The suffering creature, refusing to relinquish its last painful breath to the hand of impotent and brutal mercy, is Styron's metaphor for existence.

Set This House on Fire, a bitter satire on the self-deceit and degeneration of contemporary civilization, a nightmare vision of Doomsday, an allegory of the corruption, death, and redemption of man, does not add up to a complete experience. Although it has its shattering moments, Styron's second novel does not achieve anything like the tragic catharsis of *Crime and Punishment*, which has similar concerns. That its failure can be measured against Dostoevsky's achievement, however, indicates somewhat the quality of its ambitions and the level of its imperfect accomplishment. Like *Lie Down in Darkness*, *Set This House on Fire*, in its romantic search for truth, a search that in its final implications is perhaps fruitless, in the almost Biblical chronicling of the Fall and Redemption of man, stands without need for apology in the great tradition of the American novel.

Notes

1. Notably Ibsen's mastery of retrospective exposition influenced the narrative technique of James's later novels.

2. Styron, *Lie Down in Darkness* (Indianapolis: Bobbs-Merrill, 1951), p. 291. All quotations are from this edition.

3. There is some suggestion that Harry as artist is a kind of symbolic Dante, and his trip to Port Warwick to marry Peyton a descent into purgatory, which may be an excuse, but a poor excuse nevertheless, for his calling Peyton "Beatrice."

4. Faulkner's idiot Benjy was christened Maury and later had his named changed. The names Maudie and Benny suggest the extent that Styron had Faulkner in mind when he wrote *Lie Down in Darkness*.

His Editor's Hand: Hiram Haydn's Changes in *Lie Down in Darkness*

Arthur D. Casciato*

A study of the relationship between a writer and his editor can be revealing. Knowledge of the career of Maxwell Perkins, for instance, contributes significantly to our understanding of Wolfe, Fitzgerald, and Hemingway—all three of whom were Perkins' authors. The same is true (though in a less positive sense) of Faulkner and his first editor at Random House, Saxe Commins. Yet this bond between an author and his editor is at best fragile, if only because of the author's sensitive ego. Often an author minimizes his editor's contributions to his work, rationalizing that it is after all his genius that supplies the necessary grist for the editor's mill. Gerald Brace Warner, a novelist himself, has written frankly about this delicate alliance:

> Any writer is lucky to have a hard-headed editor whom he trusts, but even so, and even after repeated experience, most writers are reluctant to admit their faults. After the long hard work, after the intense devotion of mind and imagination, what is done must clearly be done well, and any suggestions for change simply represent the opinion of an outsider with different values and concepts. Writers take pride in being stubborn in their own defense. They assume that men of talent, like themselves, are misunderstood by all who are not writers, by editors and publishers and agents and those who have to do with the commerce of writing. Writers have delusions of their own importance.[1]

William Styron seems not to suffer from such delusions. He has always acknowledged the important role that his Bobbs-Merrill editor Hiram Haydn played in the composition of *Lie Down in Darkness*, the novel which rushed Styron suddenly to prominence on the American literary scene in 1951. Haydn's influence on *Lie Down in Darkness* predates Styron's conception of the novel. In 1947, with only William Blackburn's creative writing classes at Duke University under his belt, Styron enrolled in Haydn's fiction-writing seminar at the New School for Social Research in New York City. Impressed by his new pupil's short-story efforts, Haydn challenged Styron "to cut out the nonsense and start

*Reprinted from *Studies in Bibliography*, 33 (1980), 263–73, by permission of the journal.

a novel."[2] Styron immediately conceived a story about "a girl who gets in a lot of trouble."[3] When Styron had written only twenty pages, Haydn took out an option on *Lie Down in Darkness* for Crown Publishers, then his employers. But after about thirty more pages, Styron's writing bogged down completely. The young Virginian returned to the South and spent an unproductive year among his familiar haunts at Duke University. Haydn sensed that Styron was foundering and urged him to return to New York. Styron did so, and after a short stay in New York City he took up residence in Nyack, New York, with the family of another novelist named Sigrid de Lima. Later Styron moved to West 88th Street in Manhattan, and approximately a year and eight months after his return he finished *Lie Down in Darkness*. During this period he frequently visited the Haydn home, receiving the encouragement due a "*de facto* member of the family."[4] More importantly, Haydn interceded when the Marine Reserve board recalled Styron to active service before he had finished the concluding section of *Lie Down in Darkness*. As a result of Haydn's efforts, Styron received a three-month deferment and finished his novel. Meanwhile Haydn changed publishing houses; Styron and *Lie Down in Darkness* followed him to his new position as editor-in-chief at Bobbs-Merrill.[5]

Haydn contributed more to *Lie Down in Darkness* than advice, support, and intercession with the military. Many of his suggested emendations and deletions were incorporated into the published version of the novel. Again Styron has indicated candidly, if not quite accurately, the presence of Haydn's hand in *Lie Down in Darkness*:

> And when finally [*Lie Down in Darkness*] was done, I remember how I found truly remarkable [Haydn's] ability then to exercise the editorial prerogative and point out where *he* thought things had gone a little haywire. There were never any major things at all in the book, as I recollect, that he changed; but certainly there were a myriad of little tiny points where he had this marvelous ability . . . to detect you at your weakest little moment where your phrase was not felicitous, or accurate, and you thought you could get by with what you put down . . . . He was not altering the nature of the book, or even much of the prose, but was catching me out in accuracies and grammatical errors, and an occasional badly chosen word. And I think this is beautiful when an editor can do this. It can only improve the book, without compromising the author's intent.[6]

Certainly Styron is correct in stating that many of Haydn's changes involved "little tiny points." But close scrutiny of the holograph manuscript, the "working" typescript, and the "editorial" typescript of *Lie Down in Darkness*—all now housed at the Manuscripts Division of the Library of Congress—reveals that many of Haydn's emendations constitute more than mere editorial tinkering. The two typescripts, "working" and "editorial," reveal a unique compositional process.

Styron remembers sending the novel to Haydn in four or five in-
stallments. Haydn, recognizing Styron's native ability and not wishing to
dampen his enthusiasm, refrained from suggesting any changes during
the initial composition of *Lie Down in Darkness*. A working typescript
was prepared from the complete holograph manuscript, and Styron made
changes and cuts throughout this typescript. A second typescript was then
prepared from the emended one, and this clean "editorial" typescript was
given to Haydn who marked his own suggested deletions and emendations
on it. Finally, Styron approved each of Haydn's suggestions individually
by incorporating them *back* into the first typescript. The end product is
two typescripts which have almost identical texts. A third typescript was
apparently prepared from Styron's twice revised "working" one and was
sent to Bobbs-Merrill to serve as printer's copy. Though this typescript
and the proofs for *Lie Down in Darkness* do not survive, a collation of the
"working" typescript and the published novel shows that the usual
changes in punctuation, spelling, and other accidental features, as well as
some small revisions for style, were made before publication.

Haydn made several kinds of minor emendations: deletion of italics,
word changes, trifles of phrasing, and grammatical niceties. His deletion
of italics throughout the editorial typescript, in fact, is rather significant.
Styron himself has spoken often of having to rewrite the initial third of *Lie
Down in Darkness* in order to rid the novel of Faulkner's influence.[7] Obviously, the use of italics to highlight a character's thoughts is pure
Faulkner. Haydn's deletion of italics, then, is a good example of his helping Styron to exorcise the "Faulknerian ghosts" from *Lie Down in
Darkness*. Haydn suggests twenty-eight of these cuts in the first third of
the "editorial" typescript; and Styron incorporates each of these suggestions in the published novel.

Sometimes Haydn's minor changes emphasize an effect. In the first
chapter, for example, a middle-aged Helen Loftis dreams of her family's
visit to her brother Eddie's farm in the Pennsylvania mountains. At the
age of twenty-four she is already neurotically attached to her crippled
first-born daughter Maudie. Both the editorial and working typescript
versions of this section originally read: "The baby, waking from strange
darkness into unfathomable light, began to cry but became quieter, after
a while, in her mother's arms."[8] In the editorial typescript Haydn reduces
this passage simply and more directly to "Helen crushed the child into her
arms." This change more powerfully suggests the cloying and destructive
nature of Helen's love, and Styron wisely adopts Haydn's emendation in
the published novel.[9]

At other times Haydn merely adds new phrases or sentences without
deleting the novelist's original wording. One such example occurs in the
second chapter where Loftis invites Pookie and Dolly Bonner to his home
for late Sunday afternoon drinks. In this scene Loftis wants to indulge his
own lustful but as yet unrealized itch for Dolly. His initial overture to her

is a cruel ridiculing of her husband. The editorial and working typescripts originally read this way:

> "The hell with that," Loftis repeated to Dolly. "Somehow, somewhere, you got stuck."
> With what seemed infinite tenderness she gazed at him. She was discontented, she had had too much whiskey, and she was vulnerable to about any emotion, especially that of lust. "You're beautiful," Dolly whispered. "You're wonderful."

Immediately following Loftis' remarks, Haydn adds: "They sat there for a few minutes in silence. Then Dolly stirred" (p. 61). By slowing down the movement of this passage for several beats and by freezing these two would-be adulterers in silence, Haydn dramatically underscores the importance of Dolly's reaction. When Dolly responds favorably, Loftis is sure of her receptiveness to an affair.

Still, these are only minor alterations in the text. At other times Haydn's emendations are more clearly significant. He supplies what Styron calls "accuracies" to an intricate plot structure, sometimes pointing out certain narrative and rhetorical inconsistencies. Haydn also suggests numerous deletions and emendations in Peyton's interior monologue in an effort to temper that section's sexual explicitness. Most important among these are the cuts and changes muting the incestuous relationship between Peyton and her father.

Haydn's editorial ability is clearly illustrated in the letter that Loftis receives from Peyton shortly after her death. In this letter she tells him about the terrifyingly abstracted thoughts that plague her. In both the working and the editorial typescripts, the passage in its unrevised state reads:

> They've first started lately it seems, I've had these moments before, but never for so long—and they're absolutely terrible. The trouble is that they don't—these thoughts—seem to have any distinctness or real point of reference. It's more like some sort of black, terrible aura like the beginning of a disease, the way you feel when you're catching the flu.

In the editorial typescript Haydn emends the single word "aura" to "mistiness"—but the emendation is significant. Haydn apparently remembered from his reading of the complete holograph manuscript that Peyton often complains of a sense of drowning in her interior monologue; "mistiness," with its dreary, oppressive connotation of wetness, is much more appropriate than "aura," a word which carries lighter, almost ethereal connotations. Styron defers to Haydn's judgment here and changes "aura" to "mistiness" for the published novel (p. 38). Similarly in the second chapter, Helen, furious with her husband for inviting the vulgar Bonners for drinks, rebukes him about his desire for Dolly. The editorial typescript originally read:

> "Don't hand me that sort of thing," she retorted. "You know exactly what I mean." She ran her hand feverishly over her brow—a theatrical gesture, he thought—raising her eyes skyward. *She's neurotic,* he thought with an oddly pleasant feeling of solicitude. *There is really something wrong with her.*

Here, besides deleting the italics, Haydn changed "neurotic" to "queer." By substituting the suggestive "queer" for the exact, almost clinical "neurotic," Haydn understates Helen's problems appropriately. At this point in *Lie Down in Darkness* we have had only glimpses of Helen's destructive personality; we have yet to witness her total depravity at Peyton's wedding. Therefore, Haydn's word choice keeps Styron from tipping his hand too early; the reader only becomes curious about this "queerness" of Helen's. Furthermore, the use of the psychologist's term "neurotic" is inconsistent with Loftis' character. A Tidewater Virginia lawyer who thinks of himself as a Southern gentleman is more likely to ameliorate his wife's aberrant behavior by labeling it with a quaint word like "queer." Once again Styron heeds his editor's advice; "queer" appears in the published version of the book (p. 59).

Another example occurs in the chronology of *Lie Down in Darkness*. In both the holograph manuscript and the working typescript, Styron begins the desolate journey of Llewellyn Casper's hearse and limousine on "a weekday morning in August in the nineteen forties." In the editorial typescript, however, Haydn specifies the date as "1945." Styron's editor again remembered from his reading of the manuscript that Peyton kills herself on the day of the bombing of Hiroshima—6 August 1945. No matter how one views this bit of gratuitous symbolism, the ambiguous dating of the novel at the beginning is inconsistent with its exact dating at the conclusion. Haydn recognized the disparity, and Styron changed the date to "1945" (p. 11).

Haydn again supplies both narrative and rhetorical consistency in the letter from Peyton to Loftis. Although it appears early in the novel, this letter accurately represents Peyton's pre-suicide mental state. In the working-typescript version of the letter Peyton complains to Loftis about the poignant disorientation which is characteristic of her breakdown:

> Thinking of you helps some, thinking of home—but I don't know, nothing seems to really help for long. I feel adrift, as if I were floating out in dark space somewhere without anything to pull me back to earth again. You'd think that feeling would be nice—floating like that—but it isn't. It's terrible.

In the editorial typescript Haydn emends both occurrences of "floating" to "drowning"—Peyton's most frequently repeated word later in the interior monologue which precedes her suicide at the end of the novel. In the published novel Peyton therefore writes to her father of "drowning" and a connection is established between letter and monologue.

Haydn makes one other seemingly minor change that demonstrates his keen eye for consistency. Early in the same letter, Peyton tells her father about the noisy taproom that she lives above: "There's a bar downstairs (I remember you haven't seen this apartment since I moved up from the village) full of the loudest Irishmen imaginable." Haydn realizes that "Irishmen" is inconsistent. Peyton's lover Anthony Cecchino is Italian; her landlady Mrs. Marsicano is Italian; and she meets another Italian, Mickey Pavone, in the same bar that she describes to her father. Peyton must be living in an Italian neighborhood, so Haydn changes "Irishmen" to "Italians" in the editorial typescript.[10]

Haydn's most important emendations are his sexual cuts in Peyton's interior monologue. In 1951 when *Lie Down in Darkness* was published, America was still in many ways a repressive society, especially in the presentation of sexual matters. Haydn's changes reflect these inhibited attitudes: the editor repeatedly tones down the explicit nature of the sexual passages that fill Peyton's rambling monologue.

Haydn first censors the passages in which Tony Cecchino, the milkman lover, forces Peyton to make love during her menstrual period. The editorial typescript of this passage reads:

> He came near me, erect, stiff and with veins on it like blue ink leaked out from a pen. Then it dropped some, looking silly and pink; the pain went away, receding in short little gasps, I wondered if I was bleeding yet.

Haydn excises the accurate though explicit metaphor "with veins on it like blue ink leaked out from a pen" from the typescript. And Haydn (or perhaps Bobbs-Merrill) apparently reduced the entire passage still further in proof so that the published novel only reads "He came near me. I wondered if I was bleeding yet" (p. 337). Later in the editorial typescript, after Cecchino and Peyton finish their lovemaking, she says "When Tony came out, he had blood all over his belly and I was weeping." Haydn cuts "he had blood all over his belly and" from the line. Once again this sentence appears to have been edited further in proof: "When Tony came out" is changed to "When it was over." The whole sentence, now entirely tamed, appears in the published novel as "When it was over, I was weeping" (p. 339). Finally Haydn emends the passage describing Peyton as she prepares to leave to visit her estranged husband, Harry Miller. The editorial typescript reads:

> I remember I was bleeding and I went into the bathroom and stuffed myself up. Quilted, absorbent, it was my last one; and I left hanging out the convenient thread. I scrubbed my face and brushed my lovely hair, for I must be pretty for Harry: like the tampax, "you are always out of things, darling . . . ."

Haydn reduces "Quilted, absorbent, it was my last one; and I left hanging out the convenient thread" to "It was my last one." The entire passage appears in the published version of *Lie Down in Darkness* as:

> I remember I was bleeding and I went into the bathroom and fixed myself. It was my last one. I scrubbed my face and brushed my lovely hair, for I must be pretty for Harry: he would have scolded me for forgetting. "You are always out of things, darling . . . ." (p. 343)

In proof, Haydn or Bobbs-Merrill must have substituted "fixed myself" for "stuffed myself up" and deleted "like the tampax."

Several of Haydn's emendations in Peyton's tragic soliloquy concern the Hungarian abortionist who comes to her aid. Peyton's promiscuity has already been established for us through her affairs with the mystery-writer Earl Sanders and with Cecchino. Haydn apparently felt that an additional sordid interlude with an oily and lascivious abortionist would be unnecessary and unattractive. He therefore deletes from the text all mention of a sexual encounter between Peyton and her doctor. The initial allusion to the Hungarian abortionist in the editorial typescript suggested Peyton's desire for him:

> He was a Hungarian, and when I squirmed because the tube made me feel hot he said, "Does it teeckle? Dot's allride, only pwobing," and he probed some more and I got so hot I could hardly stand it, wanting him, powdered Hungarian face and flicking moustache and insolent thoroughbred flesh."

Haydn substitutes "looking at the" for "wanting him," muting Peyton's sexual arousal. The second reference to the nameless abortionist alludes even more explicitly to some sort of sexual encounter:

> Out loud I said, "Protect—" but didn't finish, remembering the guilt, for the second time, which I had not even told Harry: the doctor, only probing, with his finger in me and not the instrument, at all, the chloroformed straining Hungarian flesh.

Haydn changes the passage drastically, deleting "with his finger in me and not" and substituting "merciless inside twitching" for "chloroformed straining Hungarian flesh." The passage in the published novel speaks only of Peyton's guilt over the abortion and not of any sexual guilt:

> Out loud I said, "Protect—" but didn't finish, remembering the guilt, for the second time, which I had not told even Harry: the doctor, probing, the instrument, the merciless inside twitching. (p. 376)

In her interior monologue Peyton's disorientation centers on the various men in her life—Milton Loftis, Dickie Cartwright, Harry Miller, Earl Sanders, and Anthony Cecchino. We observe her frenzied mind jumping from memory to memory of her lovers, distorting each affair into a jumble of sexual allusions. Haydn edits these passages carefully. For example, in the editorial typescript, Haydn censors the passage in which Peyton compares the sexual organs of three of her lovers:

> Harry's was just right, not big and gross like Tony's, and he said I could
> make it hard with the merest switch of my tail. Once he asked me who
> took my maidenhead and I said a bicycle seat named Dickie Boy.

By deleting "not big and gross like Tony's, and he said I could make it
hard with the merest switch of my tail," Haydn makes this passage far less
explicit. Shortly thereafter, Haydn steps in again as Peyton compares her
sexual relations with Tony and Harry:

> [Tony] had hair on his shoulders like wires; he was always taking it out to
> show me how big and he pressed my head down there once but I
> screamed. Harry and I did it because we loved each other. . . .

Here Haydn cuts the line "he was always taking it out to show me how big
and he pressed my head down there once but I screamed." He also edits
the passage in which "Dickie Boy" Cartwright, Earl Sanders, and the
strange, flightless birds appear together in Peyton's tortured mind:

> I wanted so for Dickie Boy to get it up but only when we were drunk and
> we were always drunk; but he couldn't get it up and I'd play with him un-
> til it hurt him. Then the birds would come around, I'd want it so badly I
> could have died, anything—Dickie Boy, anybody . . . or when I lay
> down in Darien with Earl Sanders once we were standing up, in the
> shower stall, and then the wings and feathers all crowded through the
> yellow translucent curtain: so I slumped down against him in the pelting
> spray and I bit him where he wanted me to, and I thought oh Harry, I
> thought *oh my flesh!*

The editor's deletion of "and I bit him where he wanted me to" is simply
the cutting of some 1950s sensationalism. But Haydn's excising of the first
two sentences in this passage is more significant. In these lines Styron
seems to indicate that Peyton's "bird" hallucinations are the result of sexual frustration, in this case caused by Dickie Cartwright's impotence. Actually, throughout the published novel, these "birds" are symbols of
Peyton's futile search for love. Haydn's motives here would seem to be artistic as well as censorious.

    The most important of Haydn's sexual emendations concern the in-
cestuous relationship between Peyton and her father. Their incestuous
urges, though sublimated and never actualized, are implied throughout
the novel—the playful fondling between father and daughter, Peyton's
sugary nickname ("Bunny") for Loftis, her father's jealousy of her beaus,
and his boyish excitement when Peyton returns home and his correspond-
ing depression when she leaves. All these are tinged with feelings apart
from mere paternal love. The incestuous action of the novel culminates
with Loftis' sexual anxiety at Peyton's disastrous wedding, climaxed by his
openly affectionate kiss that permanently shatters whatever familial ties
still bind the Loftises together.

But several times in the editorial typescript of Peyton's interior monologue, Styron does more than imply subconscious feelings of incest: he indicates that Peyton and Milton may have made abortive attempts at sex. The first instance occurs when Peyton describes a summer night in Lynchburg, Virginia, with "Bunny."

> But there were chimes in my soul, I was drowning in the summer night and I knew God was not a prayer automaton, but pitched half-way between Bunny and Albert Berger: love is a duality, one part dislike, one part soft-soap, so said Albert Berger, but oh how I have loved him: once in Lynchburg Bunny got me drunk off beer, and then we drove up into the hills and parked in the moonlight; he put his arm around me. I didn't care but the chill up my back—better than Dickie Boy—and then we both got embarrassed at the same time and didn't say anything for five minutes.

This passage reveals urges that are certainly more than subconscious; Peyton and Loftis are embarrassingly aware of their mutual desire, if only for an instant. Wishing to mute a subject that would undoubtedly scandalize many 1950s readers, Haydn strikes the entire passage from the editorial typescript, substituting in its place the innocent line "But I remembered grass, and gulls" (p. 363).

An even more explicit example occurs later in Peyton's interior monologue when she pleads with her husband Harry to return to her. The editorial typescript reads:

> Then I would say: oh my Harry, my lost sweet Harry, I have not fornicated in the darkness because I wanted to but because I was punishing myself for punishing you: yet something far past dreaming or memory, and darker than either, impels me, and you do not know, for once I awoke, half-sleeping, and you were still inside me and I ran my hand down your back and murmured, Bunny dear.

Again Haydn realizes that this is far too explicit for Styron's audience. He changes "for once I awoke, half-sleeping, and you were still inside me and I ran my hand down your back and murmured, Bunny dear" to a more moderate "for once I awoke, half-sleeping, and pulled away. 'No Bunny,' I said" (p. 377). Haydn's emendation here may also have an artistic motive. Until this point the incest has been one-sided. Loftis alone subconsciously wants his daughter, but Peyton, though aware of her father's desire, never reciprocates. Haydn therefore makes this passage consistent with the rest of the novel by removing Peyton's physical longing for Loftis from the text.

Haydn's sexual emendations, then, range in importance from his significant muting of the incestuous relationship between Peyton and Milton to his rather prudish substitution of "other things" for "brassiere and pants" at the conclusion of Peyton's soliloquy (p. 385). Ironically, Haydn was accused by David Laurance Chambers, president of Bobbs-Merrill, of "sexual obsession" because he championed *Lie Down in*

Darkness (Haydn, p. 49). One might logically assume that Haydn's suggested changes were the result of censoring by Bobbs-Merrill or pressure from Chambers. Styron, however, feels otherwise:

> I think Haydn was merely following the accepted pattern when he wanted me not to be too explicit. I don't think Bobbs-Merrill or Chambers exerted any *direct* pressure on Haydn, though he may have been vaguely intimidated by the firm, since it was the most wretchedly reactionary and stuffy publishing house in the business. It was only because of Haydn's great faith in the book that those Neanderthal mid-Westerners backed down and the book was published as successfully as it was. In short, I think Haydn's suggested cuts were due less to the shadow of Bobbs-Merrill and Chambers than to his own feelings which were honest though unadventurous.[11]

Whatever the case, Haydn's "unadventurous" changes did not alter the basic sexuality of the novel. *Lie Down in Darkness* remains a frank and sexually candid work. But future editors of the novel would do well to consider restoring many of Haydn's sexual cuts. Few of today's readers would be shocked by the explicitness of the sexual language deleted from *Lie Down in Darkness*.

Much of *Lie Down in Darkness* is the end product of a unique cooperation between novelist and editor. Styron himself was intimidated neither by Bobbs-Merrill nor by Haydn. In fact, many of Haydn's suggestions were rejected by the novelist, and none of them, sexual or otherwise, was incorporated into the novel without Styron's full approval ("A Bibliographer's Interview," p. 24). Instead of chastising Styron, as Bernard De Voto did Wolfe for his collaboration with Perkins on *Of Time and the River*,[12] we should applaud the then young novelist's good sense and maturity in relying from time to time on his editor's experience and judgment. *Lie Down in Darkness* is a stronger, more consistent novel because of Styron's wise acceptance of Haydn's help.

Notes

1. Gerald Brace Warner, *The Stuff of Fiction* (1969), pp. 141–142.

2. Jack Griffin, Jerry Homsy, and Gene Stelzig, "A Conversation with William Styron," *The Handle* (undergraduate magazine of the Univ. of Pennsylvania), 2 (Spring 1965), 17.

3. John K. Hutchens, "William Styron," *New York Herald Tribune Book Review*, 9 Sept. 1951, p. 2.

4. Hiram Haydn, *Words & Faces* (1974), p. 279.

5. Interestingly, Styron again followed Haydn to his next publishing firm, Random House, which today remains Styron's publisher. But in 1960, Styron declined to accompany Haydn to Atheneum, the firm of which Haydn was a founder. Of Styron's defection Haydn writes, with what appears to be a bit of pique, that the novelist "was tired of having people think and say that he owed everything to me; he wanted to stand on his own feet." See Haydn, p. 281.

6. James L. W. West III, "A Bibliographer's Interview with William Styron," *Costerus*, N.S. 4 (1975), 23–24.

7. See, for example, E. P. H. [Eloise Perry Hazard], "The Author," *Saturday Review of Literature*, 34 (15 Sept. 1951), 12; and Hutchens, p. 2.

8. Quoted from the "working" typescript of *Lie Down in Darkness* at the Manuscript Division of the Library of Congress. This and subsequent quotations from the typescript are published here with Mr. Styron's kind permission.

9. *Lie Down in Darkness* (1951), p. 30. All future quotations from the novel are cited parenthetically.

10. Haydn's one remaining emendation to Peyton's letter is also important. At the end of the paragraph describing her fear of "floating," Haydn adds the line "then when I see the birds it seems [something crossed out]." This addition enhances the passage in two ways: first, Haydn's phrase "[something crossed out]" enables Styron to reap the full benefit of his epistolary technique. These crossed-out words are tantalizing to both Milton and the reader. Second, Haydn introduces the crucial image of the "birds" into the novel for the first time. Peyton speaks often of these wingless and hairless creatures in her interior monologue. The typescript sheet bearing Haydn's emendation is facsimiled in "A Bibliographer's Interview," p. 25.

11. Styron to Casciato, 8 July 1978. Quoted here with Mr. Styron's permission.

12. Bernard DeVoto, "Genius Is Not Enough," *Saturday Review of Literature*, 25 April 1936, pp. 3–4, 14–15.

The Prevalence of Wonders

William Styron*

[*Editorial Note*: The following short essay is an early statement by Styron of his artistic principles. It was prepared in 1953, by invitation, for a symposium in *The Nation*, and is republished here for the first time since that initial appearance.]

Rome

I hardly think that anyone in so short a space can do much justice to what he believes, and perhaps least of all should this be attempted by any writer, whose works, finally, should be sufficient expression of his credo. Lots of writers find themselves hopelessly baffled when it comes to dealing with ideas, and even though I suspect that this is a grave and lazy weakness, I none the less count myself among the group and, in a symposium of this sort, flounder about in a vague wonderland of notes and inconclusive jottings. But I was asked to write a "frank and honest statement of your feelings about your art, your country, and the world," so I will proceed, as frankly and as honestly as I can.

About my art: I know little of the mechanics of criticism and have been able to read only a very few critics, but I respect those people — critics and readers — who feel that the art of writing is valuable, since, like music or sailing or drinking beer, it is a pleasure, and since, at its best, it does something new to the heart. I for one would rather listen to music or go sailing, or drink beer while doing both, than talk about literature, but I am not averse to talking about it at all, just as lawyers talk about law and surgeons about surgery. And I take it quite seriously. I have no conscious illusions of myself as teacher or preacher; I do know that when I feel that I have been writing my best I am aware of having gathered together some of the actualities of myself and my experience, projected these whole and breathing on the page, and thereby have enjoyed some peculiar poetic fulfilment. This is self-indulgence; but I trust that it sometimes approaches art, a word which I'm not ashamed to use from time to time, and I trust that it might also please some reader, that person who, in my most avid self-indulgence, I am not so ingenuous as ever really to forget.

*Reprinted from *Nation,* 2 May 1953, pp. 370–71, by permission of the author.

So I might say that I am not interested in writing propaganda, but only in that sort of personal propaganda engendered by afternoons of vicious solitude and the weird, joyful yearning which it pleases oneself to think, just for a couple of seconds, that Bach must have felt. If out of all this, placed as vividly as I can place them in their moment in time, there are people who emerge worthy of a few moments of someone's recollection, I am satisfied. Good people and bad people—bad enough to justify the truth at every signpost in one's most awful nightmares, good enough to satisfy every editor on *Time* magazine, and so much the worse.

I would like to say something in regard to my feelings about America. I have lived in France and Italy for something over a year now—not a long time but long enough for me to feel well ahead in my postgraduate education. I have been here under a large handicap, though a handicap which, as I will try to demonstrate, might have its redeeming qualities. This handicap may be explained simply by the fact that I am one of those people who are unable to enjoy a painting, a piece of sculpture, a work of architecture, or, for that matter, practically any visually artistic representation. To suffer such a lack while in Italy is somewhat like being let loose, while suffering from ulcers, in one of those wonderful, large West Side delicatessens; yet, as Clive Bell, to whom I have run for refuge as apologist, so sympathetically points out in his essay called "The Aesthetic Hypothesis," there *are* people congenitally incapable of such an experience, just as there are people born without the sense of smell, and no more to be blamed than their equally sensitive friends who can visualize in the aerial, clear abstractions of a Vivaldi concerto, only horses galloping, nymphs and shepherds, or the first girl they ever kissed. So, deprived as I am in a place so rich in wonders as Rome of the means to assimilate those wonders, I have been thrown a bit on my own devices, so that my viewpoint, as an American living abroad, has probably often been closer to Burbank and his Baedeker among the ruins of Venice than any number of generations of comfortably adjusted artists. Many people can feel the true rapture at the façade of Chartres, and these are no doubt a step further toward an affection for France and its people than the aesthetically more limited who, attuned to the night clubs of Montparnasse or *escargots* primarily, are outraged, stricken, and resentful when it dawns upon them that the French consider them jackasses. Not all art lovers, of course, are nice people. But a warm and tolerant feeling of brotherhood for man is, I believe, often measured by the extent of one's love for man's monuments and man's artifacts, and not a few American tourists, like myself, don't know a Piero from a peanut.

I think this blindness of mine, though, has had its worthy effects, for if it has helped to keep me from understanding the more beautiful things about Europe it has also conspired with a sort of innate and provincial aloofness in my nature to make me much more conscious of my *modern* environment, and self-consciously aware of my emotions as an American within that environment. And thus at last, after more than a year, I think that I am as "adjusted" as I ever will be, having succumbed neither to the blandishments of exile nor to any illusions of a faultless America. There cannot be much dogma about nations when one lives in One World, eighteen hours from home, and for me now things are pretty well balanced.

The "U. S. Go Home" signs no longer offend me, since I have learned that they are the work of the Communists and don't mean *me* but the American army encamped nearby. I have even come to the point where I can sympathize with the signs and ask myself: "Suppose New York were full of Swedish soldiers all mouthing orders for beer in an alien, thick, jaw-breaking tongue. Would I not want to scrawl 'Swedes go home!' on every available wall?" I have learned, too, that anti-Americanism is many different things: unjustified among the spoiled and snobbish Italian upper class, with whom it's currently the vogue, and among whom was the famous actress heard at a party recently to utter the most slanderous anti-American remarks, and enplane the next day, via TWA, for New York; justified when a Parisian reads about McCarthy in *Figaro*, or when our most widely read weekly editorializes upon France and compares it to a whore; non-existent, finally, among most Italians, whose happiest tradition has been an inability to be anti-anything and each of whom has a cousin in Brooklyn.

What I suppose I've really learned is the elderly truism that all of us can learn something from each other. That whereas our radios are better, no car from Detroit can match a fleet, shiny Alfa Romeo; that our planes work, crack up less often, and are generally on time, but that the dreadful snarl on Madison Avenue might be alleviated by a study of the marvelous Paris bus system; that, on the other hand, a bottle of Châteauneuf du Pape is ambrosia, indeed, but that there's still nothing like a Coca-Cola on a hot summer day, as every Frenchman knows but won't admit; that the man from Chicago gobbling hamburgers on the Champs Elysées is undoubtedly a fool, but there is something wonderful to be said about his brother, the July tourist with his straw hat and his lurid tie and his camera, and his almost pathetic eagerness to find, in a strange land, some kind of dazzling and miraculous enlightenment: sometimes his manners are bad but he's making the effort at least, and one finds few French tourists outside of France; that our mass production is the world's finest: "Oh," says the American, "your Italian sports cars are great, but in the states everyone can own a car." "But Signore," is the reply, "here not everyone *wants* a car"; that our Park Avenue head-feelers are the very best: "But Signore, here we do not *need* psychoanalysis." It's simply a matter of balance.

One must end a credo on the word "endure," but I think we will do just that—Americans and Italians and Frenchmen, in spite of all those who threaten us momentary harm. Humans have become involved too much in life, and the wonders are too thick about us, to be daunted by a handful of madmen who always, somehow, fall. The hope of heaven has flowered so long among us that I just can't envision that hope blighted in our time, or any other, for that matter; perhaps the miseries of our century will be recalled only as the work of a race of strange and troublous children, by the wise old men in the aeons which come after us. Meanwhile, the writers keep on writing, and I should like to think that what we write will be worth remembering.

THE LONG MARCH

Following *The Long March*

Roger Asselineau[*]

Published between *Lie Down in Darkness* (1951) and *Set This House on Fire* (1960), *The Long March* (1953) has not received, as of now, the attention it deserves. It has been neglected because of its brevity. The profuseness of the novels which preceded and followed it has been preferred to its somewhat austere simplicity. Yet this long short story, with its fine and very pure lines, whose art is more that of drawing than painting, is worthy of consideration.

At first glance *The Long March* is a satire in which career militarists are dealt with quite severely. Colonel Templeton is shown to be both a poseur and a sadist. If he shows any concern for the well-being of his subordinates, he does so because of duty and not through any humane feeling: "He had too long been conditioned by the system to perform with grace a human act."[1] The hero of the work, Reserve Captain Mannix, therefore does not hate the man himself, but *"the Colonel,"* the Marine Infantry Colonel who has been hardened and dehumanized by his profession. The military *esprit*, as Colonel Templeton says in French, is, according to Styron, the very negation of *l'esprit*, the mind. The Army stupefies. For Mannix, it is but "a group of morons, morons who had been made irresponsibly and dangerously clever" (p. 43). Considered on any level, be it at the Colonel's or at the roupes', military life is similarly "degrading" (p. 54). It condemns the officers to an artificial, unreal and shallow existence on their bases, and imposes an inhuman segregation on drafted soldiers who normally should live with their wives and children. Thus *The Long March* is, among other things, the protest of an American civilian against the presence within a democratic society of a professional army whose nature is essentially anti-democratic. Seen in that perspective, the book can be placed in a rather long tradition which goes back to Whitman and Melville. And on occasion this protest is scathing. For example Captain Mannix goes so far as to compare to "an SS man" a drill sergeant particularly convinced of the importance of his mission: "He's

[*]Reprinted from *William Styron, Configuration Critique*, no. 11 (Paris: Minard, 1967), pp. 73–83. Translated from the French by W. Pierre Jacoebee. Reprinted by permission of the author.

gonna come down here and cut your balls off. You Jewish?" (p. 47). He adds later, "I'll bet [he]'d sell [his] soul to be able to drop a bomb on somebody" (p. 48).² This violent anti-militarism can be explained by circumstances. *The Long March* is set in the Korean War era when reservists, veterans who had been back in civilian life for several years, saw themselves being snatched suddenly and unexpectedly by the military machine because of a "frigging international incident" (p. 54), as Captain Mannix says in his language, which is more a soldier's than a pedant's. This intrusion of history into the private lives of individuals for the second time in one generation could indeed have appeared intolerable, especially to Americans for whom such an invasion was a new and therefore more scandalous phenomenon.

In any case, by abnormally magnifying the facts, a crisis of that order illustrates in a particularly vivid way the relationship between the individual and the society to which he belongs: individual rights are abolished and, in the name of national security (public safety), the demands of the community become exorbitant, barely tolerable. Man is then tempted to revolt, as can be seen in *The Long March* where Captain Mannix is in a constant state of anger. But this revolt remains virtual, it never bursts out. Like the hurricane lamp which lightens the officers' tent at the beginning of the narrative, its fire burns with rage but only gives light. Any revolt is vain and doomed to failure: "Born into a generation of conformists, even Mannix . . . was aware that his gestures were not symbolic, but individual, therefore hopeless, maybe even absurd, and that he was trapped like all of them in a predicament which one personal insurrection could, if anything, only make worse" (pp. 55–56). Mannix is in fact compared to a "tormented beast in the cul-de-sac" (p. 62). As for his friend Lieutenant Culver, in spite of his anger, "he stumbled on behind the Colonel, like a ewe who follows the slaughterhouse ram, dumb and undoubting, too panicked by the general chaos to hate its leader, or care" (p. 85). The training they have undergone has conditioned them like Pavlov's dogs. Whenever they hear an order, they obey, whatever they may think of it. They are no longer free men, but soldiers in the Marine Corps (pp. 102–3).

The satirical tone of many a passage is thus neutralized by the understanding of the futile nature of revolt. Moreover, Styron is too conscious of the complexity of human problems to make of *The Long March* a mere debunking of the military. He cannot bring himself to condemn Colonel Templeton entirely. He shows him to be "a man who might be fatuous and a ham of sorts, but was not himself evil or unjust—a man who would like to overhear some sergeant say, 'He keeps a tight outfit, but he's straight' " (p. 30). At the end of the narrative, Lieutenant Culver does not know what to think: "The Colonel had had his march and his victory, and Culver could not say still why he was unable to hate him" (p. 117). He could not because here Styron is one with all his characters, career officers included, and consequently he cannot judge them. He has said so himself. "I sometimes feel that the characters I've created are not much more than sort of projected facets of myself."[3] This complete sympathy, in the etymological sense of the word, gives him the same aptitude Keats praised in Shakespeare and called *negative capability*. Keats defined it as the capacity "of being in uncertainties, mysteries, doubts, without any irritable reaching after fact and reason."[4] It is not by chance that we find Shakespeare mentioned here. He appears with Marlowe among the great writers of the past to whom Styron has publicly admitted his debt, and in *The Long March* tragic elements always mix with satire. As in any tragedy, moreover, there are dead bodies. They occupy the proscenium at the very moment the curtain rises. They are the corpses of young soldiers, mangled during an exercise by badly set mortar shells. One may ask what they are doing there: they have no reason for being, no part to play in the action. They are the essential accessories of tragedy. They are there to create a certain atmosphere, to give this narrative a tragic dimension, and Styron does not allow us to forget them. He reminds us of their existence several times, harmonically as it were (pp. 93, 115, 116), so as to convince us of this tragic truth: that living and acting are synonymous with suffering. In one sense, then, *The Long March* is a tragedy in short story form, in which two protagonists, Captain Mannix and Colonel Templeton, confront each other. Once, at least, the reader has the impression of watching a Greek tragedy: "In the morbid, comfortless light [the two protagonists] were like classical Greek masks, made of chrome or tin, reflecting an almost theatrical disharmony" (p. 29). Neither is it accidental that the narrative is divided into five acts or parts. In the present case, the first act is more a prologue in which the corpses of the young soldiers are shown. The long march, the order for which has just been confirmed, is announced in the second act, an act of introduction. During the third act we see the beginning of the march. The stress between the reserve captain and the career colonel rises very rapidly. At the end of the act, the captain rather vulgarly refuses to act upon the advice given to him by the colonel—to abandon the march formation and get into a truck. The crisis becomes imminent. It breaks out, as it should, in the fourth act; he is put on house arrest and will be court-martialed. The fifth act, like the prologue, is very short. It is in fact an epilogue. Apparently defeated, Captain Mannix comes out of the conflict greater and victorious. As Faulkner says of his black characters in the Compson Appendix to *The Sound and the Fury*, Mannix has "endured."[5] He has dragged his swollen leg for hours, but he has reached the goal he had set for himself; he has been able to accomplish of his own free will what they intended to force upon him. He acted as a free man, not as a slave. But when questioned by a Negro woman, who resembles Faulkner's Dilsey a great deal, he concludes, "Deed it does [hurt]."

The Long March gives us a tragic vision of life. It shows both the greatness and the misery of man. The greatness because it centers on Mannix who, "Atlas-like," bears "the burden of his great weariness" (p. 81) and takes the blows without flinching, thus defying the powers who thought him to be at their mercy. Also the misery, because Styron relentlessly reminds us of the precariousness of human life suspended between being and non-being, like Captain Mannix when two drunks hold him by the ankles above the emptiness from the tenth-floor hotel window. Everything happens as if we were "adrift at sea in a dazzling, windowless box, ignorant of direction or of any points of the globe, and with no way of telling" (p. 34). Man is doomed to loneliness in the vastness of the universe. Human life is an unending long march in the night and the "never-endingness of war" (p. 118) like "a movie film pieced together by an idiot" (p. 92).

In spite of the epilogue's calmness, fear and horror occupy a considerable if not dominant place in the tragic narrative. Moreover, startled cries are heard on several occasions: screams of the wounded in the initial killing, the scream of Mannix, suspended in the air, who shouts at the top of his lungs not realizing that the clamor which deafens him comes out of his own mouth. One could almost say that *The Long March* itself is one long artfully modulated scream of horror.

It is not simply that, however. One could also say that it is a metaphysical detective novel. The bodies are there, still warm, in the first pages of the book. Who is guilty? How can one close in upon the evil forces at work in the world? Where is evil? Is it the military? The government? Those of whom Mannix complains when he moans, "Won't they ever let us alone?" (p. 63). But in fact evil is everywhere, in Mannix who submits despite his revolt, in Templeton who leads the operations. Everyone carries it inside. Everyone is guilty in the end. Everyone, thus no one. Hence the calmness of the conclusion.

But of course making a tragedy, a terrified scream, or a detective novel of *The Long March* is but a game. This narrative is simply a short story, a very free and very simple short story. Not a skillfully constructed, then cleverly unraveled one. Its subject is one of those rare moments, one of those intensely experienced inner adventures, the usual material for one of Sherwood Anderson's short stories. Styron explained himself on this subject in an interview given to the *Paris Review*. With him, writing is not a gratuitous exercise of the imagination, but an art in which he is completely engaged. It allows him either to relive the past, thus exorcising his ghosts, as when he tells of Captain Mannix's terrible adventure on the tenth floor of the hotel,[6] or to experience indirectly, by proxy, adventures which could have happened to him, if this or that part of himself had had the opportunity to manifest itself freely, which is another form of exorcism. Through his work, then, he both lives what he has been and what he could have been. Said he, "When I'm writing I find it's the only time that

I feel completely self-possessed." He frees himself by doing so. Indeed, he adds, "It's fine therapy for people who are perpetually scared of nameless threats as I am most of the time" (WW, p. 272). In this manner he cures his own neuroses (he himself uses the word—WW, p. 282). In other words, he purges himself of his passions; from that perspective also, his esthetic is akin to that of tragedy.

But however close his concept of the short story may be to Sherwood Anderson's, the movement Styron gives his narrative is the very reverse of the movement in Anderson's short stories. Indeed Sherwood Anderson, at least apparently, seeks to illustrate, by means of the "exceptional moments" he evokes, the passing from innocence to experience. Styron on the other hand attempts to recapture original innocence beyond experience. He has the nostalgia of childhood. This tendency is clearly visible in *The Long March* where the vision of the two graceful little girls reappears insistently, like a leitmotiv: "He recalled himself at a time which already seemed dark ages ago . . . to an earlier, untroubled day at the end of childhood. There, like trembling flowers against the sunny grass . . . two lovely little girls played tennis, called to him voicelessly, as in a dream, and waved their arms" (p. 10). "Across the rim of his memory two little girls playing on the sunny grass waved to him" (p. 59). "He only felt that all of his life he had yearned for something that was as fleeting and as incommunicable, in its beauty, as . . . those lovely little girls with their ever joyful, ever sprightly dance on some far and fantastic lawn" (pp. 116–17). Moreover, what does the very name "Mannix" suggest? It is of course a real Jewish name. But is it not composed of "man" and "nix"? "Man" and "no." In one sense, Mannix is a no-man. Despite his age, upon which Styron is repeatedly insistent, Mannix has remained a child and behaves like one. He is also the man (or the child) who says no: no to experience, no to adult life with its ugliness and turpitude. And at the end of the painful pilgrimage represented by this unending long march, as he unfastens his bathtowel, he finds himself as naked as a new-born child. His revolt has cleansed him of the impurities of experience. He has recaptured his first innocence like Peyton who, in *Lie Down in Darkness*, throws herself naked from the window in order to kill herself and purify herself forever from the blemishes life has left upon her.

Such is, in the final analysis, the meaning of this short story. It is, then, definitely, a "fable" in the sense Faulkner gives to the word, but the moral remains discreet and the narrative remains the overriding concern. For this small work is of an extreme concrete density, despite its brevity. The characters in particular are intensely alive. They take precedence over the plot which, in this case, is almost nonexistent. Such is Styron's method generally. When he writes, he allows his characters to develop freely and strives to give them three dimensions, as he explained in his interview with the *Paris Review*. There, going back to E. M. Forster, he makes the distinction between "round" characters and "flat" ones. It is true that in *The Long March*, one could reproach him for having been able to give only two dimensions to Commander Lawrence and Colonel Templeton. Always seen from outside, and with less than perfect empathy, they remain "flat" and never gain the intensity of Mannix.

This short story has also a remarkable temporal density. As Styron has noted, "The business of the progression of time seems to me one of the most difficult problems a novelist has to cope with" (WW, p. 275). Styron's mastery, therefore, is also recognisable in that respect. Even though *The Long March*, with its preparations and after effects, lasts scarcely twenty-four hours, we have the impression that Mannix's entire life has been told. This is achieved through a series of very adroitly introduced, and at times barely sketched, "flashbacks." Without breaking the continuity of the narrative, we are taken back to Mannix's Brooklyn radio store, his action in the Pacific, his return to San Francisco after the war, and the beginning of his second training period in South Carolina. With the appearance of the two graceful little girls gamboling on the grass, whose memory has always remained deep within him, we are even brought to his earliest childhood. *The Long March* itself is thus surrounded by a series of concentric circles which widen it to infinity. As for the march itself, it takes place in time as well as in space, thanks to the changes in light and temperature between nightfall and dawn of the following day, all carefully noted by Styron. Thus we progress little by little through a moving duration as well as through continuously changing landscapes and terrains whose very nature changes by the hour under the feet of the soldiers. At times the ground is spongy, sometimes sandy, at other times hard.

In all this, Styron shows great mastery and consummate art. The ranges of his voice, in particular, are uncommonly varied. He passes easily from the most vulgar military slang to the most polished and articulate language, and this within a few lines, as in the following:

> One boy's eyes lay gently closed, and his long dark lashes were washed in tears, as though he had cried himself to sleep. . . . Around his curly head grasshoppers darted among the weeds. Below, beneath the slumbering eyes, his face had been blasted out of sight. . . . The Captain was sobbing helplessly. . . . "Won't they ever let us alone, the sons of bitches," he murmured. [p. 63]

Styron also knows how to play *leitmotiv*: the leitmotiv of the hurricane lamp, the leitmotiv of the two little girls, the leitmotiv of the melody by Haydn which reappears now and then in counterpoint.

The smallest details are calculated with the greatest care. Colonel Templeton, for instance, who through affectation loves to use French words from time to time, ignorantly says "comprend?" where we would expect "compris?" Styron's perfect knowledge of French (and Italian) which he demonstrated in *Set This House on Fire*, does not leave us any doubt that what we have here is the willful search for an effect.

Like Flaubert, whom he admires and whose influence he acknowledges, Styron is a stylist. He writes very slowly, not on a typewriter but by hand. This permits him to correct himself and to collect his thoughts along the way. He has said, "I seem to have some neurotic need to perfect each paragraph—each sentence, even—as I go along" (WW, p. 271). And he added, "I used to spend a lot of time worrying over word order, trying to create beautiful passages. I still believe in the value of a handsome style. . . . But I'm not interested any more in turning out something shimmering and impressionistic. . . . I guess I just get more and more interested in people" (WW, p. 276).

This confession is important. It confirms what, in truth, just the reading of *The Long March* could have confirmed: that Styron does not believe in style *per se* but that, in this short story at least, he subordinates his stylistic effects to his intention of preserving a past experience in transparent amber. Therefore, inversely to what happens in his novels, where time waves criss-cross and blurs the outlines, he has in this case courageously simplified and stylized. In this instance Flaubert is his master much more than Faulkner or Joyce, whose complexity he appreciates but whose excessive confusion he criticizes (WW, p. 275). His ideal is what he calls "total communicability" (WW, p. 274).

In short, one can say that he has succeeded in *The Long March*, and that in this instance he may be closer to European writers than to his own countrymen. His care to compose tense and complex narrative in a perfectly clear style and in a simple and harmonious order makes him, at least in the case of *The Long March*, a writer who is more French than American.

Notes

1. William Styron, *The Long March* (New York: Random House, 1956), p. 89. Subsequent references are to this edition and are indicated in parentheses immediately after the quotation.

2. Styron's anti-militarism is also apparent in his review of General MacArthur's memoirs. See *New York Review of Books*, 8 October 1964, pp. 3–5.

3. *Writers at Work*, ed. Malcolm Cowley (New York: Viking Press, 1958), p. 276. Hereafter cited parenthetically as WW.

4. John Keats, *Complete Poems and Selected Letters*, ed. Clarence DeWitt Thorpe (New York: Odyssey Press, 1935), p. 528.

5. One finds in Faulkner the same tragic vision of life. Styron has recognized his indebtedness to him; see *Writers at Work*, p. 274. One even finds in *The Long March* some of Faulkner's favorite words, such as "fury" and "outrage," reappearing constantly.

6. Styron has told us that he himself lived through that adventure.

The Long March: The Expansive Hero in a Closed World

August Nigro*

Although it received favorable reviews, William Styron's *The Long March* has not received the critical examination it deserves and apparently needs. In the only two studies devoted to the novella, Eugene McNamara and Peter Hays present two somewhat contrasting interpretations, both of which are incomplete. McNamara's thesis is that *The Long March* reveals Styron's belief that, in an age of conformity and absurdity, the individual protest is hopeless and doomed. For McNamara, the Marine Corps is symbolic of a "monastic order, united in love, symbolized by the ritual which must be entered into unquestionedly, with complete obedience." Because the hero Mannix remains obdurate and rebellious, like the "recalcitrant Old Adam" and like Satan, he not only remains fallen, but he also damns himself.[1] Hays agrees with McNamara as far as he goes, but feels he does not go far enough. By extending McNamara's method of drawing analogy between Mannix and mythic rebels, Hays discovers analogies in the novella between Mannix and such rebels as Prometheus and Christ. Such analogues, Hays concludes, put Mannix's rebellion in a more favorable light; for Mannix becomes part of an heroic tradition characterizing the endurance of the indomitable will in spite of pain and suffering.[2] Hays' article is helpful in that it questions McNamara's conclusion about the sympathy and position of Styron; however, Hays himself fails to go far enough in his interpretation of the mythic significance of *The Long March.*

A close examination of the novella reveals that Styron has written a fable in which a few concrete images and symbols tell at least three related tales: the story of a forced march in a Marine camp, which demonstrates Styron's belief "that military life corrupts and we would be a lot better off without it;"[3] the story of the American experience in which the individual's dream of a free and peaceful Utopia is betrayed by the suppression and bondage of a closed, tightly-organized society; and finally the story of the degeneration of the hero in western civilization, from a figure who personifies the aspirations of the common man and the values of society to a grotesque anti-hero who makes a futile, but

*Reprinted from *Critique*, 9 (Winter 1967), 103–12, by permission of the author.

necessary, attempt to assert his personal freedom and identity in the face
of a society which is consistently demanding that he sacrifice both.

The Marine Corps, rather than symbolizing a "monastic order united
in love," represents a social condition in which the individual is suppressed, almost enslaved, into an order which necessitates insincerity, insensitivity and subservience. The Corps uses "boy scout passwords" as
"part of the secret language of a group of morons . . . who had been
made irresponsibly and dangerously clever."[4] All members of the group
are expected to "essay some kind of answer" when questioned about
anything. Even the long march is undertaken with the provision of dog-
pound trucks to pick up recruits who are expected to make a little gesture
and subsequently "crap out." Not only does the Corps nurture sham and
imposture, it is equally adept at desensitizing the individual. Such dehumanization is apparent in Colonel Templeton, personification of what
the Corps stands for. Templeton is one "to whom the greatest embarrassment would be a show of emotion" and one who "had too long been conditioned by the system to perform with grace a human act." With his
pearl-handled .38 revolver and swagger stick, "Old Rocky" is the neuter
commander—the marine and not the man.

And it is against the marine, not the man, that Mannix and to a lesser
extent, Culver, rebel. Early in the book, before the march commences,
the fury and suffering reflected in Mannix's face are described as those of
a "shackled slave" and later, after the march is well under way, the men
are referred to as "zombies" and "robots" and their tired, worn expressions "like faces of men in bondage who had jettisoned all hope, and were
close to defeat" (95). Mannix's rebellion against this enforced bondage is
of course ironic: on the one hand, it is an assertion of his will and pride,
and regardless of his failure to bring in his company and of his impending
court martial, the reader feels and sympathizes with the humanity of his
suffering and the dignity of his protest. However, Mannix's endurance
and rebellion as a shackled slave are incongruously and grotesquely juxtaposed to his demonic fury as a driving master of his own men. His
rebellion in reverse, his "rocklike" resistance of "Old Rocky," ricochets
on his men and he becomes to them what Templeton is to himself; he
becomes the force against which he rebels: the enslaver.

Thus, Styron demonstrates that the Corps—all military life—corrupts. On the one hand, the Corps instills and augments the very pride
that moves Mannix to rebellion, and yet it also provides the bondage and
humiliation which force Mannix to rebel and become that against which
he rebels. The corruption and destruction of the individual dramatized in
the ordeal of Mannix are complemented by and reinforced by the lamb-
like submission of Culver, who stumbles "behind the Colonel, like a ewe
who follows the slaughterhouse ram, dumb and undoubting, too panicked
by the general chaos to hate its leader, or care" (85).

When the central action and main characters are viewed with more perspective and the richly suggestive images and symbols considered in their full significance, Styron's indictment of military life becomes a more general indictment of American life. The "fishy struggles" under the sea become not only the conditions of marine life, but also the general conditions that underlie the social world. The Corps and the long march become representative of a larger world, Mannix representative of a cultural hero and the encounter between the hero and the world a conflict, which once more dramatizes the discrepancy between the American Dream and the American Nightmare.

This discrepancy between dream and nightmare is apparent from the beginning of the novella. The six years of freedom and tranquility, associated with childhood innocence in Culver's reveries, become so remote in the new world of the Corps that they become almost nonexistent:

> He felt suddenly unreal and disoriented, as if through some curious second sight or seventh sense his surroundings had shifted, ever so imperceptibly, into another dimension of space and time . . . as if they were adrift at sea in a dazzling, windowless box, ignorant of direction or of any points of the globe, and with no way of telling. What he had had for the last years—wife and child and home—seemed to have existed in the infinite past or, dreamlike again, never at all . . . All time and space seemed for a moment to be enclosed within the tent, itself unmoored and unhelmed upon a dark and compassless ocean. [34–35]

The preceding passage not only describes effectively how the terrible experience of Culver renders his innocent past nonexistent, but also presents a rich and suggestive metaphor of the world of *The Long March*. In the first place, it visualizes two conditions of the world in which Culver, and of course Mannix, find themselves. It is a world of containment, a world like a windowless box, but also a world which is itself a minute atom upon a compassless ocean. Such a metaphor brings to mind a similar fictional world—the ship of state used by Melville in *Billy Budd* to render the social order in microcosm. Moreover, the association extends the symbolic importance of the Corps and the march, for both become, like Melville's ship and voyage, analogous to the American experience.

This analogy between the fictional worlds of Melville and Styron is complemented by a similarity between the symbols of authority in both novellas. Templeton is to the Corps what Captain Vere is to the *Indomitable*: both represent the corruption of the individual human being by the institution. Vere is one who is "always acquitting himself as an officer mindful of the welfare of his men, but never tolerating an infraction of discipline; thoroughly versed in the science of his profession, and intrepid to the verge of temerity."[5] Moreover, he is stoical in his ability to control his emotion with his reason and will and perfect in his fidelity to the maritime law, a devotion which necessitates his sacrificing the life of Billy Budd and negating the basic human tendency towards mercy.

"Old Rocky," like Vere, has developed an impersonal detachment in his devotion to the Corps; for him the "greatest embarrassment would be a show of emotion." He too is well versed in the science of his profession, fair and adamant in his attitude toward his men, and equally intolerant of disobedience. But whereas Vere's stoic stance is explained in terms of his philosophical adherence to truth, Templeton's is explained metaphorically in terms of a religious pilgrimage. With all his emotions emanating from a "priestlike, religious fervor, throbbing inwardly with the cadence of parades and booted footfalls" (30), Templeton is the priest leading his men to "some humorless salvation" (88).

This extension of the metaphor of Templeton as priest and the "westward" march as a pilgrimage to some salvation suggests that the maritime ordeal described literally in *The Long March* is once again the American adventure in which an ideally conceived Christian democracy, devoted to the principle of individual freedom, has to abandon that principle in peacetime as well as in war. Even this aspect is somewhat illuminated by comparison to *Billy Budd*, in which Melville describes the efforts of the ship's clergyman to minister to the doomed hero in the following words:

> Bluntly put, a chaplain is the minister of the Prince of Peace serving in the host of the god of War—Mars. As such he is as incongruous as a musket would be on the altar at Christmas. Why then is he there? Because he indirectly subserves the purpose of the religion of the meek to that which practically is the abrogation of everything but force. [198]

Is not this the very nature of Templeton's office and the Corps in *The Long March?* Here is the advocate of a "grandiose doctrine," the leader of a westward march to some humorless salvation, the priest who has been too long conditioned by the system to perform a human act, becoming the "creator of such a wild and lunatic punishment" as the march (101). Thus, the "black triangular wet spot plastered" at the back of the Colonel's dungarees, symbolic of his service to the Prince of Peace, contrasts violently with the pearl-handled revolver, emblematic of his service to the god of war.

Into the contained world of Templeton comes the expansive Mannix: a "big, relaxed mass," "huge," "enormous," "formidable," "Towering," "passionate," "sullen, mountainous," "Atlas-like,"—"a great soft scarred bear of a man." This last description of the expansive hero is only part of a consistent analogy drawn between Mannix and the bear—an analogy which calls to mind one of the most important literary expressions of the discrepancy between the American Dream and Nightmare—Faulkner's "The Bear." Examination of this analogy sheds some light on the meaning of the encounter between the expansive hero and the contained world.

Like Old Ben in Faulkner's novella, Mannix is described as a

"Tormented beast in a cul-de-sac," with the "baffled fury of some great bear cornered, bloody and torn by a foe whose tactics were no braver than his own, but simply more cunning" (97). To Culver, Mannix is an "Old great soft scarred bear of a man" (107), who is depicted in the final scene "clawing at the wall for support" (119). The analogy is explicit and effective: like Old Ben, Mannix represents that which is primitivistically and innately free, noble and grand in America, and he is confined, baffled and destroyed by an army of American Christian soldiers preaching a "grandiose doctrine" and practising rapine and bondage contrary to that doctrine. The Faulknerian element of the analogy is even more evident in the following passage in which the containment of the bear-like Mannix is juxtaposed with the archetypal symbol of American bondage, the Negro:

> Tormented beast in the cul-de-sac, baffled fury, grief at the edge of defeat—his eyes made Culver suddenly aware of what they were about to see, and he turned dizzily away and watched the wreck of a Negro cabin float past through the swirling dust; shell-shattered doors and sagging walls, blasting facade—a target across which for one split second in the fantastic noon there seemed to crawl the ghosts of the bereaved and the departed, mourning wraiths come back to reclaim from the ruins some hot scent of honeysuckle, smell of cooking, murmurous noise of bees. [62]

When Mannix's size and sensitivity are seen in more human terms, the analogy is one with another noble savage, Adam. Mannix is the innocent too sensitive and honest for his own good; he is a "huge hairy baby soothed by the wash of elemental tides, ready to receive anything, all, into that great void in his soul which bitterness and rebellion had briefly left vacant . . ." (58–59). Thus, Mannix is not the unfallen Adam, like Billy Budd, but rather the fallen Adam, like Ahab, who Melville writes, feels "so very, very old . . . deadly faint, bowed and humped, as though [he] were Adam staggering beneath the piled centuries since Paradise." Mannix too has suffered and his suffering has "left a persistent, unwhipped, scornful look in his eyes, almost like a stain, or rather a wound, which spells out its own warning and cautions the unwary to handle this tortured parcel of flesh with care" (49).

Thus, extending the analogy of the Melville and Styron fictional worlds, one finds an Ahab-like hero who encounters the contained world of the Corps; and like Ahab, Mannix becomes the tyrannical enslaver of his own men. The tragic irony is explicit: the Adamic hero—sensitive, enormous, primitive, childlike—outraged by his exile from innocence and peace, tormented by the betrayal of youth around him and by his own suffering, rebels against the world that enforces bondage and nurtures insincerity and insensitivity. His rebellion is noble in that he attempts to assert the self and the natural and ideally conceived right of freedom; however, the pride and will that move him to rebellion are also the tragic flaws that blind him to his own tyranny. Thus, Mannix's defeat is ironically a self-inflicted one; and the subsequent insubordination and impending court martial are more anti-climactic, external wounds which only compound his destruction. Styron's description of Mannix's finishing the march completes the picture of the grotesque victim:

> Mannix's perpetual tread on his toe alone gave to his gait a ponderous, bobbing motion which resembled that of a man wretchedly spastic and paralyzed. It lent to his face . . . an aspect of deep, almost prayerfully passionate concentration—eyes thrown skyward and lips fluttering feverishly in pain—so that if one did not know he was in agony one might think that he was a communicant in rapture, offering up breaths of hot desire to heavens . . . it was the painted, suffering face of a clown, and the heaving gait was a grotesque and indecent parody of a hopeless cripple, with shoulders gyrating like a seesaw and with flapping, stricken arms. [113–114]

This portrayal of Mannix introduces a third analogy which reinforces the dramatic presentation of the discrepancy between the American Dream and the American Nightmare: Mannix as Christ. Mannix, who is constantly invoking Christ, who is himself in his passion pierced by a nail, whose wound is described as "fat milky purple," who in a moment of agony clutches the wall, naked except for a towel around his waist, and who is identified during the march as "Christ on a crutch," does in fact become a grotesque caricature of Christ. The incongruity of Mannix as a hero is furthered when the transformation of Mannix is contrasted to the transfiguration of Melville's hero in *Billy Budd*, at whose tranquil death "the fleece of the lamb of God seen in mystical vision" hovers over the *Indomitable*.

For Melville, the hero in his death is transfigured into the resurrected Christ; for Styron, the hero's defeat suggests a beaten, whipped and spasmodic Christ. In Melville, the Christ-like resurrection of the hero contrasts with the perversion of Christian values in the microcosmic world, illustrated in the sterile service of the priest aboard a man-of-war. In Styron, the contrast becomes more violent and incongruous, as the torment of the Christ-like Mannix drastically intensifies the perverse office of the priest-like Templeton. In Melville, the individual rises above a society that seeks to destroy him; in Styron, he is crushed by that society. This is the real significance of the religious imagery throughout *The Long March:* to point out the continued crucifixion of the individual in a Christian, democratic America, and not as McNamara would have it, to demonstrate the necessity of an organizational society.

The analogies of Mannix to Old Ben, Adam and Christ are only a few examples of Styron's more general application of what T. S. Eliot calls the "mythical method." According to Eliot, James Joyce's method in *Ulysses*, of "manipulating a continuous parallel between contemporaneity and antiquity," is a way of "controlling, of ordering, of giving shape and a significance to the immense panorama of futility and anarchy which is contemporary history."[6] Styron employs the same mythical method not only to bring order to the futility of contemporary life, but also to sharpen that sense of futility. Through simile, analogy and allusion, Styron identifies Mannix with a series of heroes from the literature and myth of western civilization, all of whom rebel against social and traditional authority. This identification works paradoxically: on the one hand, it transfers to Mannix an heroic tradition and heroic characteristics; but on the other hand, it sharpens the absurdity of his defeat by juxtaposing it to the grandeur of their defeats.

The first analogy is suggested in the early episode in which Mannix and Templeton are likened to Greek tragic heroes. In the tent and in what approximates a war council, Mannix, the sensitive, brooding, massive Captain, protests against the actions of his superior Colonel. The setting and the general development of verbal conflict between the warriors and the allusion to the "classical Greek masks," which their countenances suggest, convene in a drama quite comparable to the Achilles-Agamemnon conflict that opens the *Iliad*. The identification here between Mannix and Achilles is reinforced later in the march when Mannix is crippled by the wound in his heel—a wound that parallels the internal as well as the external flaw of the Greek hero. For the vulnerable heel of the Greek hero is really the physical correlative to his more significant internal flaw—his passionate *hubris*. So it is with Mannix, for the skin that is peeled away from his heel is symbolic of his heightened sensitivity, which makes him prone to rebel. Shortly after Culver notices the "sharp pinpoint of torture" on Mannix's heel, he makes this observation about the vague, unpredictable and brooding Marine: "It puzzled Culver; the explosion seemed to have stripped off layers of skin from the Captain, leaving only raw nerves exposed" (66). Thus, Mannix, like Achilles, becomes increasingly sensitive to a subordination enforced by a military superior.

Another Greek mythic figure with whom Mannix is more directly identified is Atlas: "It was as if his own fury, his own obsession now, held up, Atlas-like, the burden of his great weariness" (80–81). This comparison and the tableau in which Mannix's countenance is compared to a tragic Greek mask suggest another analogy pointed out by Hays—a similarity between Mannix and the titan-brother of Atlas, Prometheus, a Greek who rebels against divine omnipotence on behalf of suffering humanity. Still another rebel with whom Mannix is likened is Satan. Mannix's despite for "Heaven's Gate," the pleasure-dome for officers only, is figuratively as well as literally a hatred for Heaven's Gate; and Mannix's confinement to it and resentment of it echoes in essence Satan's scorn for heavenly existence: "Both Mannix and Culver hated the place," which "seemed to offer up, like a cornucopia, the fruits of boredom, of footlessness and dissolution . . . they were bound to the pleasures of the place by necessity—for there was no place to go for a hundred miles, even if they had wanted to go—and therefore out of futility" (54).

Finally, Styron draws an analogy between Mannix and Moses. In the following passage an allusion to Exodus clearly points out that Mannix's quest is one to liberate his people from bondage: "Dust billowed up and preceded them, like Egypt's pillar of cloud, filling the air with its dry oppressive menace" (99). But the analogy is ironically extended and just as Mannix becomes an enslaver, so his voice takes on the "sound of a satrap of Pharaoh, a galley master. It had the forbidding quality of a strand of barbed wire or a lash of thorns . . ." (77).

This evocation of traditional heroes works contrapuntally and the reader feels the heroic dimensions of Mannix's act, but also the sharp incongruity between their grand defeats and Mannix's ignoble defeat—between Achilles' powerful lament and vengeance for the death of Patroklus, Atlas' staggering labor beneath the pillars of heaven, Prometheus' ordeal on the rock of ages, Satan's titanic fall from heaven to hell, Adam's temptation and fortunate fall, Moses' struggle in the exodus from Egypt, Christ's passion and resurrection, Ahab's magnificent failure to destroy the white whale—between all these and Mannix's paralyzed, spastic, bobbing entrance into camp. One feels with Culver that the absurdity of Mannix's defeat is compounded by the fact that his stance is "not symbolic, but individual, therefore hopeless" (55–56); nevertheless, this does not alter the basic integrity and nobility of that stance. That Mannix's rebellion is not representative of the accommodation to bondage made by the other marines is a further indictment of the meek, will-less masses who give up their freedom without even a whimper.

This protest against bondage is the main theme that emerges from Styron's fable; it is given form and vitality by the ironic and dramatic presentation of the discrepancy between the American dream of innocence and the experience of evil, between the dream of an ideal Christian, democratic America and the nightmare of an organized America which violates Christian and democratic principles. This discrepancy is sharpened by the encounter of a primitive, expansive hero with a closed, contained society; and this American experience in turn is reinforced by and translated into more universal significance through allusion to the rebel tradition in the literature and mythology of western civilization.

Notes

1. "William Styron's *Long March:* Absurdity and Authority," *Western Humanities Review*, 15 (Summer 1955), 20.

2. "The Nature of Rebellion in *The Long March*," Critique, 8 (Winter 1965–66), 72.

3. William Styron, "If You Write for Television . . .", *New Republic*, 146 (April 1959), 16.

4. William Styron, *The Long March* (New York, 1956), p. 43. Hereafter all references to the novella will be to this edition and will be cited in the text.

5. Herman Melville, "Billy Budd," *An Anthology of Famous American Short Stories* (New York, 1953), p. 154. Hereafter referred to in the text.

6. "*Ulysses*, Order and Myth," *The Dial* (November 1923), reprinted in *James Joyce: Two Decades of Criticism*, ed. Seon Givens (New York, 1941), p. 204.

Afterword to *The Long March*

William Styron*

[*Editorial Note*: Styron's second novel *The Long March* is one of the best-known and most frequently republished works of American fiction from the fifties. *The Long March* appeared initially in December 1952 as a contribution to the first issue of *discovery*, a periodical edited by John W. Aldridge and Vance Bourjaily and published by Pocket Books. Since that first appearance, *The Long March* has been reissued separately in five English-language editions—three in America and two in England.

The Long March has also been widely translated. Editions of the novel have appeared in France, Germany, Italy, Portugal, Brazil, Romania, Poland, Czechoslovakia, The Netherlands, Mexico, Russia, Denmark, Sweden, and Norway. The 1963 Norwegian translation, published in Oslo by J. W. Cappelens Forlag, is of particular interest. Cappelens issued *Den lange marsjen* in its series "Verdens Unge" ("Young Authors of the World"), a series which included writings by such authors as Jack Kerouac, Marie-Claire Blais, Bernard Malamud, J. D. Salinger, Yevgeny Yevtushenko, and André Schwarz-Bart. To this Norwegian edition of *The Long March* Styron contributed an "Etterord," which he composed in English, but which was translated into Norwegian by Karna Dannevig and printed at the conclusion of the Cappelens text.

Styron's Afterword is an important document. It establishes the autobiographical basis of *The Long March* and reveals significant information about the circumstances out of which the novel grew. Styron's description in the Afterword of his state of mind while composing *The Long March* helps to explain the nervous, compelling quality that many readers sense as they progress through the book. Though Styron has been interviewed frequently throughout his career, he has never commented at length on the composition or meaning of *The Long March*. And he has published almost no written comments about the novel. For these reasons, Styron's Afterword deserves attention from critics and students of his work.

The English text published here is taken from Styron's original holograph manuscript of the Afterword. That manuscript is among the Styron papers in the Manuscripts Division of the Library of Congress.

*Reprinted from *Mississippi Quarterly*, 28 (Spring 1975), 185–89, by permission of the author and journal.

Seven minor emendations have been made in the manuscript text; these have been approved by Mr. Styron.—J. L. W. W. III]

AFTERWORD

I am happy that *The Long March* is the first of my books to be published in Norway since, although not nearly so long nor so ambitious as my other works, it achieved within its own scope, I think, a unity and a sense of artistic inevitability which still, ten years after the writing, I rather wistfully admire. Lest I appear immodest, I would hasten to add that I do not consider *The Long March* even remotely perfect, yet certainly every novelist must have within the body of his writing a work of which he recalls everything having gone just *right* during the composition: through some stroke of luck, form and substance fuse into a single harmonious whole and it all goes down on paper with miraculous ease. For me this was true of *The Long March*, and since otherwise the process of writing has remained exceedingly painful, I cherish the memory of this brief work, often wondering why for a large part of the time I cannot recapture the sense of compulsion and necessity that dominated its creation.

Possibly much of the urgency of the book is due to factors which are extremely personal. As the reader may eventually begin to suspect, the story is autobiographical. To be sure, all writing is to some degree autobiographical, but *The Long March* is intensely and specifically so. I do not mean that the central figures are not more or less imaginary—they are; but the mortar explosion and the forced march which are central to the entire narrative were actual incidents in which I was involved, just as I was bound up, for a time, in the same desolating atmosphere of a military base in the midst of a fiercely hot American summer. If the story has a sense of truth and verisimilitude it is because at the time of the writing all of these things—the terrible explosion, the heat of summer and the anguish of the march itself—still persisted in my mind with the reality of some unshakable nightmare.

Perhaps it was an even larger nightmare I was trying to create in this book, and which lends to the work whatever symbolic power it has the fortune to possess. Because for myself (as I do believe for most thoughtful people, not only Americans but the community of peaceable men everywhere) the very idea of another war—this one in remote and strange Korea, and only five years after the most cataclysmic conflict ever to engulf mankind—possessed a kind of murky, surrealistic, half-lunatic unreality that we are mercifully spared while awake, but which we do occasionally confront in a horrible dream. Especially for those like myself—who had shed their uniforms only five years before in the blissful notion that the unspeakable orgy of war was now only a memory and safely behind—the experience of putting on that uniform again and facing anew the ritualistic death dance, had an effect which can only be described as traumatic. World War II was dreadful enough, but at least the issues involved were amenable to reasonable definition. To be suddenly plunged again into war, into a war furthermore where the issues were fuzzy and ambiguous, if not fraudulent, a war that could not possibly be "won," a senseless conflict so unpopular that even the most sanguinary politician or war-lover shrank from inciting people to a patriotic zeal, a war without slogans or ballads or heroes—to have to endure this kind of war seemed, to most of us involved in it at the time, more than we could bear. War was no longer simply a temporary madness into which human beings happily lapsed from time to time. War had at last become *the* human condition.

It was this feeling I believe I was trying to recapture when some time later, in the summer of 1952, I found myself in Paris still unable to shake off the sense of having just recently awakened from a nightmare. My own ordeal and the ordeal of most of my Marine Corps friends (including one or two who died in Korea), was over—yet the persistent image of eight boys killed by a random mortar shell and of a long and brutal march lingered in my mind. Senseless mass slaughter and a seemingly endless march, the participants of which were faceless zeroes, were all that in retrospect appeared to me significant about this war without heroes, this war which lacked so utterly a sense of human identity, and which in so sinister a fashion presaged the faceless, soulless, pushbutton wars of the future. All right, I would write about this faceless, soulless march. Yet, all my intentions to the contrary, I began to understand, as I wrote, that even in the midst of an ultimate process of dehumanization the human spirit cannot be utterly denied or downed: against all odds, faces emerge from the faceless aggregate of ciphers, and in the middle of the march I was creating I found Captain Mannix slogging and sweating away, tortured, beaten, but indomitable. A hero in spite of himself or me, he endures, and in the midst of inhumanity retains all that which makes it worthwhile to be human. I myself cannot be sure, but possibly it is the hopeful implications derived from this mystery—this kind of indefatigable man—which are all an artist can pretend to suggest, however imperfectly, in his struggle to comprehend the agony of our violent, suicidal century.

Roxbury, Connecticut, March 1963.

SET THIS HOUSE ON FIRE

Some People of Our Time

Arthur Mizener*

Since the publication of William Styron's "Lie Down in Darkness" in 1951, there has been some suspense over whether he might not become an important novelist. There is real power in "Lie Down in Darkness," despite a certain factitious solemnity about The Meaning of It All. It has intelligence, technical skill and a readiness to tackle tough situations—which are so well worked up that you expect them to be resolved significantly, despite their tendency to end in the easy out, as does Peyton Loftis' story. Peyton's psychosis is not a problem to be dealt with by an ultimately responsible heroine; it is the irresistible determinant of her character and action. As such it makes the climax of "Lie Down in Darkness" romantic melodrama rather than tragedy.

"Set This House on Fire" is the story of narrator Peter Leverett's deciding between two men, Mason Flagg, the charming, wild son of a rich Northern movie mogul turned Virginia gentleman, and Cass Kinsolving, a Carolina farm boy who is potentially a talented artist. Their lives are joined when they finally come together in a small southern Italian town called Sambuco, in a palace where Cass lives in squalor on the lower floor and Mason in expensive elegance upstairs. A movie company, filled with grotesque characters, is on location in the town. Driven by some metaphysical guilt, Cass has become a sodden drunk and falls under the power of Mason Flagg, who has a half-sinister, half-pathetic need to dominate people, to assert his personality with innocent malevolence.

Cass is about to be saved by the naïve love of Francesca (a peasant girl who happily poses for him in the nude in remote glades) when Mason rapes her. She scarcely has time to tell Cass about it before she dies, in mysterious circumstances. The death rouses Cass to avenge his loss. The effort (in a fashion which will not be revealed here) brings about his regeneration. All this is lively stuff. There is a great deal more than there is room to describe—essays on the mystic vision and on segregation, a lambasting of Eisenhower, descriptions of beat joints and sex orgies.

Mr. Styron certainly means this long book to answer the question

*Reprinted from *New York Times Book Review*, 5 June 1960, pp. 5, 26, by permission of the author.

raised by "Lie Down in Darkness," to fulfill his publisher's promise that "in the most ambitious and profound way [he] has written a major novel about contemporary America." Nobody who had not meant to do something like that would have flourished the eloquent and extravagant epigraph out of Donne's Sermons from which the title comes. And all the immediately impressive talent of "Lie Down in Darkness" is here. The story of "Set This House on Fire" is revealed to us by an extraordinary and skillfully arranged series of narratives. The sense of the striking scene and of how to deploy events to make the most of it, the fine ear for dialogue, the sharp observation of cities and scenery and interiors—all these things give the novel an admirably interesting surface life.

The gentle voice of Peter Leverett will say with a Fitzgerald feeling (perhaps an all-too-Fitzgerald feeling) of the Flaggs' expensively preserved Virginia plantation house, "the renovated castle in the morning mists loomed with a drowsy parvenu splendor amid its garlands of extinguished lanterns." Cass Kinsolving's Carolina farm-boy's voice will say, "she was quite a bimbo, that Rosemarie. A real foursquare, fluid-drive . . . machine"—and you know you are in expert hands. The same effect is produced by the novel's brilliantly illuminated scenes, like the one in Mason's palatial living room when a quietly sensitive movie director suddenly picks up a drunken Bogart-type by his shirtfront and confounds him with a few impressive words. Or the one in which, in the middle of the night, a self-confessed Fascist policeman steps out of a corner of Cass' grubby bedroom and begins to talk gently about "the humanist philosophers."

The trouble is that all of this sharply observed and represented material is solemnly hopped up, emotionally and metaphysically. Every character is presented as a special case of profound significance. The girls are all beautiful, perhaps a little mad and terribly sad—like Celia, who loves Mason Flagg in some inexplicable, self-tortured way, or like Cass' Francesca, the peasant girl as idyllic pastoral nymph. All the men are tragic in the best modern way, as is Mason Flagg, the rich boy who is desperately trying to convince himself of how "religious the orgiastic principle is," or Cass Kinsolving, driven by a romantic sense of guilt like some Carolina Manfred.

The whole novel reminds you just a little of George Eliot's wry observation that "some gentlemen have made an amazing figure in literature by general discontent with the universe as a trap of dullness into which their great souls have fallen by mistake." Despite the skill and sophistication with which Mr. Styron presents these characters, despite the fashionable metaphysical trimmings he provides them with, they remain the stock figures of romantic melodrama. This melodramatic quality is also evident in the book's long, explanatory meditations on Being and Nothing, The Denial of Life, and a host of other very big topics, most of which Mr. Styron tosses around with the ease of a man who has heard them all discussed by the best expatriate minds.

As this straining after tragic significance becomes gradually evident, so does a commonplace quality that underlies much of the surface brilliance of the writing. You begin to notice, too, how much standard "sensitivity" there is in the book: Werther-like young Americans brooding over Roman sunsets from their flats on the Gianicolo or observing with disgust the gas-station and neon degeneration of the American scene. This sensitivity is, of course, accompanied by plenty of shock stuff like the account of Mason's library of pornography, or a priest's reporting of the gruesome particulars of spouting blood when a man dies of miliary tuberculosis (Mr. Styron's favorite disease).

In its mild Victorian way, "The Oxford Companion to English Literature" describes perhaps the most famous of the "Gothic" novels, Matthew Gregory Lewis' "The Monk" (1796), as a "mixture of the supernatural, the horrible, and the indecent," and adds that "it has power, contains some notable [writing], and attained a considerable vogue." "Set This House on Fire" and "The Monk" are remarkably similar, in narrative structure, in subject-matter (in "The Monk's" climactic scene, Friar Ambrosio rapes and then murders the impossibly beautiful and innocent Antonia), in the sensational manipulation of metaphysical speculation.

It all no doubt makes for good, if not exactly clean, fun if you do not take it too seriously. But this is not what Mr. Styron once seemed to promise and apparently means this book to do.

Styron's Appointment in Sambuco

Abraham Rothberg*

Of the American writers who emerged after World War II, three stood head and shoulders above their contemporaries in talent, Norman Mailer, Ralph Ellison and William Styron, and they wrote three of the most promising contemporary novels: *The Naked and The Dead, The Invisible Man* and *Lie Down in Darkness*. Now, almost a decade after the last, William Styron has written a new book, *Set This House on Fire*, which further fulfills the promise of his talent.

Peter Leverett, the character who tells the story, says that the book is about "a murder and a rape which ended, too, in death, along with a series of other incidents not so violent, yet grim and distressing." But the novel is far more than that. "A man cannot live without a focus," Cass Kinsolving says, and this book is the search for a focus of three men—Cass Kinsolving, Mason Flagg and Peter Leverett—as they seek it in themselves, in others, in sex, in drink, in violence, in art; it is a story in which these three who might be three aspects of a single man, or three American "brothers Karamazov," move (to paraphrase Styron) through dooms of love, through griefs of joy, in the lonely search for meaning, for virtue and for identity, as they struggle not only with their own anarchies but with the political, economic and spiritual anarchies of our time.

The three expatriate Americans meet in a small Italian town, Sambuco, where Mason Flagg, a rich, upper-class Yankee, is supposed to be writing a play but is instead moving swiftly through his vices to his death; where Cass Kinsolving, a lower-class, almost white-trash Southern Methodist, is supposed to be painting and is instead drinking himself to death, and through love—for an Italian girl, Francesca—and compassion—for her father, Michele, who is dying of poverty and tuberculosis—through violence and error, comes to his true self; where Peter Leverett, good middle-class Virginia gentleman, a lawyer who has been working in Europe for an American "aid agency," has come to vacation with his boyhood friend and schoolmate, Mason Flagg, witnesses a tragedy, but fails to understand it or his own role in it.

Writers of novels attempt to impose pattern and meaning *on* life, or

*Reprinted from *New Leader*, 4–11 July 1960, pp. 24–27, by permission of the author.

to put it another way, though probably conveying the same thing, they attempt to perceive pattern and meaning *in* life, and then to communicate it, endow it with passion and artistic vitality. William Styron sees and communicates a contemporary life shot through with corruption, guilt, sin, remorse and envy, and he uses those magnificent old words (and concepts) in a passionate discernment and dissection of betrayals of self and betrayals of others, of individual and collective betrayal. Most important, he is able—neither pompously nor apologetically—to speak openly of evil (that term we have almost "understood" and "tolerated" and "explained" out of existence) and he has Cass say it clearly:

". . . this business about evil—what it is, where it is, whether it's a reality, or just a figment of the mind. Whether it's a sickness like cancer, something that can be cut out and destroyed, with maybe some head doctor acting as the surgeon, or whether it's something you can't cure at all, but have to stomp on like you would a flea carrying bubonic plague, getting rid of the disease and the carrier all at once."

There are the personal evils of Mason Flagg (is the name symbolic of America?), a fusion of Beverly Hills and Bohemia, who is a sadist and a faddist, an exhibitionist and a pornographer, a rapist, an incipient homosexual, an intellectual dilettante—altogether a psychopath who destroys wife, mistresses and friends; of Cass Kinsolving (is the name symbolic kin-solving?), an artist and an alcoholic, a man of dignity, courage and intelligence, and also a man debased, a trained seal, a drunken cowardly fool, an impossible father and husband who, even in his deepest degradation, struggles for a virtue and probity he wishes for but cannot apprehend.

There are the collective evils of politics, economics and religion. Styron sees man's miserable condition and exemplifies it both in the misery of the Southern Italian peasant and the Southern American Negro, and has Michele—Francesca's dying father—cry out against God in the accents of Job: "He is evil, is He not, to put us down in this place where we work and slave for fifty years, making ninety thousand lire a year, which is not even enough to buy *pasta*. Ninety thousand lire! Then all the time He sends the tax collector from Rome. Then after draining us dry—of everything—at last He throws us away, as if we had cost Him nothing, and for a joke He punishes us with this pain. He loves only the rich men in Rome. He is evil, I tell you! I shit on Him! I shit on Him because I do not believe!"

And Styron devotes the same scalding scorn to fat, prosperous Americans, "a bunch of smug contented hogs rooting at the trough. Ciphers without mind or soul or heart." As the "Lost Generation" of the '20s fled prosperous Babbitty America, so many of the generation of the '50s also seemed to be fleeing the materialism, machine and new prosperity to Europe (and some—like the "Beat Generation"—are in internal emigration from them), but if it is in Europe that they "find" themselves, it is to the United States that they return with their "changed selves." All three of Styron's characters do—though one in a coffin—and all three have that strange ambivalence expatriates have for America: a hatred of the people, the culture (or lack of it) and the products (or the plethora of them); and a moving, nostalgic love of the natural landscape.

Set This House on Fire is rich in description of American scenes, brilliant description, and swarms particularly with "southern weather, southern voices, southern scenes." Styron has genuine feeling for scenery everywhere—Paris, Rome, Sambuco, Tramonti, New York—but he is at best in his own Virginia countryside.

But the book's value is in its human scenes, moving and beautifully rendered: Cass in Paris finding the final edge of joy, then terror, in drunkenness; Cass' seduction of Vernelle Satterfield, the juvenile Jehovah's Witness; Mason taking Peter to a "gang shag"; Michele denouncing God; the Italian women, like beasts of burden, bearing their loads of fagots; the dog, half-crushed in the street, with the audience watching it die; Cass wildly drunk in the PX; the incredibly touching interchange in jail between Luigi, the Facist policeman, and Cass, when Luigi refuses to permit Cass the indulgence of guilt, self-destruction and martyrdom in a magnificent act of Christian charity. These are but a few; there are a myriad such.

There is also the power of the language, a complicated, sinuous and sometimes even tortuous prose style filled with expletive and coarseness, subtlety and delicacy, libertinism and puritanism, simplicity and complexity, a whirling gyre of language which deals with art and literature, landscape and character, ringing the discreet changes necessary and appropriate for each, and moving easily from humor to seriousness, from humble to grand, from irony to candor. As with the scenes, to take just a few random well-turned examples does Styron no justice, but it is worth doing nonetheless: "I saw him doing the mambo on countless Grace Line cruises to Brazil, with women forever taller than himself"; "In each Jew resides a frustrated mother"; "He would of sympathized with cancer if he thought it was à la mode"; ". . . you may sentimentalize sex by confusing it with love, and still be read, but if you equate sex with unpleasurableness, you may expect your audience to be obscure, whether your bias is puritan or pornographic."

And, the discerning reader will now ask, did not even Homer nod? I would like to reply with Hemingway's pithiness that one pitcher should not tell any batters about another pitcher's curves, but that would be presumption on my part in more ways than one. The answer is, of course, yes; Styron's book has shortcomings, flaws, even serious faults, and if the book is not a masterpiece, quite, but only a magnificent attempt at one, it *is* magnificent and it *is* an attempt. Here one is in the presence of a great talent setting itself a great artistic task, and in its smallest sparks struck one can see more light and more illuminated than in the perfectly modulated beams of lesser talents who focus on lesser tasks.

With those two other splendid postwar American talents—Mailer and Ellison—Styron shares the strange difficulties that Jews, Negroes and Southerners who write in our country have in common, perhaps because they are all "oppressed minorities," or "defeated," or perhaps because those groups more than others were nurtured on the Bible (although I doubt that): those four horsemen of the literary apocalypse: self-pity, sentimentality, rhetoric and melodrama. Styron, as are the other two, is prey to all four.

Perhaps most grievous is the form Styron has chosen to tell his tale, half involuted detective story with information deliberately withheld about a murder, half Greek tragedy with inevitable doom descending like a mushroom cloud and rising up out of character, a stink in the nostrils and a miasma under the sky. This inadvisable combination led Styron into using one major unnecessary character, Peter Leverett, the narrator, who is unsuccessfully and uninterestingly projected, and perhaps 200 pages of unnecessary material which, if cut, would have given a swiftness of pace and tension which, as is, often slacken. The story told straightaway, without flashback and digression and Leverett interpolation, by Cass Kinsolving, whose story it truly is, would have made a firmer, finer book.

There are other weaknesses too: Styron cannot create a real woman character. His women—Poppy, Cass' elfin wife, the succession of Mason's pneumatic mistresses, the primitive perfection of Francesca—are failures and sentimental fantasies; and hence his man-woman relations are always slightly unreal, melodramatic and oversimplified, lacking the passionate contradictoriness of his man-man relations. Nowhere with men and women does Styron reach the heights of artistic characterization as he does with the relationships between men: between Cass and Michele, Cass and Mason, Cass and Luigi, Cass and Lonnie, and even between Cass and Peter—which is perhaps the least successful of all.

There is a flaw in the dialogue. His people, speaking to each other in normal discourse, are more stilted than when his characters pour out (in what is really monologue) their stories. There is even the small flaw of an inappropriate title to the novel, from a beautiful and appropriate epigraph chosen from a John Donne sermon, a title which sounds like a book about arson.

All too often, Styron is overwhelmed by things, by words, in that old Whitmanesque tradition (and not one confined only to him and to American writing) in which instead of artistic selection, there is enumerating, inventorying, cataloging. Too many incidents, too many characters, too many descriptions, too many incidents, too many emotions, and too many words, words until the ones that count, that are meaningful, are lost. Styron's torrent of talent has still to be disciplined by levees of fictional control to run swifter, deeper and truer in course.

But these are genuinely motes in the literary eye. This is a magnificent book, whose pages—at least for me—echo with Melville and Faulkner and Fitzgerald (literature makes stranger bedfellows than politics, and if that be *double entendre,* make the most of it!). I do not say this merely to record Styron's indebtedness—for if he has borrowed, what he has borrowed he has made his own and imprinted it with his own singular signature (that essential token of the genuine talent)—but to place him in the mainstream of American letters.

If it is also, in those terms, a bitter book, "disenchanted," it remains a book intimately concerned with understanding and evaluating the individual and social consequences of human experience. If Styron, denying Alexander Pope's "Essay on Man," presumes to scan God— ". . . God was not even a lie, but worse," Cass says, "that He was weaker even than the evil He created and allowed to reside in the soul of man, that God Himself was doomed. . . ."—he does not avoid studying mankind, and he does not presume. In fact, Styron goes back to that essential knowledge so frequently forgotten, ignored or deliberately set aside, Socrates' "Know Thyself," and distills from Cass' anguish the shards of human and personal wisdom that are life's most precious and painful possessions and achievements.

"The only true experience," Cass says, ". . . is the one where a man learns to love himself. And his country!" "The single good is respect for the force of life," Luigi, the Fascist (and most Christian) policeman, says, ". . . the primary moral sin is self-destruction."

Finally, out of the awareness that everywhere, in persons as in politics, in Italy as in the United States, there is power and corruption, nepotism and graft, stupidity and blindness Styron can ring his faith (and Cass') out of Cass' (and his own) despair in a Job-like affirmation: "man's own faith, vain perhaps, but nonetheless faith in his hardwon decency & perfectability & his own compassionate concern with his mortal, agonizing plight on a half burnt out cinder he didn't ask to be set down on in the first place."

A Second Novel

Harvey Breit*

In 1951 William Styron published his first novel, *Lie Down in Darkness*. It made a durable mark; failing to stimulate the mind, it nevertheless haunted, as though the dark shadow of a large hand hovered over the heart, affecting one with a sense of calamity and doom (and gloom). Immature in some ways (the novelist was still in his twenties), the book insinuated, encircled, herded the attuned reader into an emotional experience that shattered tranquil days long after the last pages were a faint memory. It somehow hung on, in spite of ratiocinative dismissals. Power, the capacity to construct powerful equivalents in fiction of what was his idea of the world, was then Mr. Styron's striking gift, his most remarkable virtue.

Now nine years later Mr. Styron's second full length novel comes to us—but what a nine years it has been! What an unholy, inactive lot we were during that time. Bitter, cynical, indifferent, supine, momentous events proceeded without us, the world advanced in spite of us, life ebbed and flowed in vast movements while we loafed on beaches and in television rooms. How sad for most of us, who rode out our nation's unconnection, remaining unconnected, solitary, alien, complacent. Yet for a "happy few" this evil time was transformed into an auspicious time in which to mature. How can this come about? Some human law has to be operative: the complacent chorus breeding the anxious solo, the organization tentacles missing the corners where individuals were at work on their own idiosyncratic tasks; "And on a heath beneath winking stars a fox with merciless bright eyes scraped in the earth, listened, scraped up the earth, listened, scraped and scraped."

For me, who may be only a poor minority, *Set This House on Fire* is an immeasurable gain in maturity over the author's fine first novel, though I would not know how to calculate those nine years of growing up. Because of the rapidity and intensity of the upheavals in the world; because of their instantaneous relevance to each inhabitant of each continent; and, more important, because the evil of our own isolation and

*Reprinted from *Partisan Review*, 27 (Summer 1960), 561–63, by permission of the journal. Copyright © 1960, Partisan Review, Inc.

dislocation and inaction permitted the individual for the first time in this period (before there had been mass depression, collective politics and total war) to conduct an uninterrupted dialogue with himself, call it ninety years. To finish off the conceit, then, the new novel appears to me to be ninety years more mature (in the sense that one is supposed to be learning all the time), more knowing, more directed and controlled, than Mr. Styron's first book.

Not that the novel is a complete success. There are flaws, though perhaps it would be more accurate to call them mistakes of the will. The entire beginning is just such a mistake, opening with a monologue by the narrator of the story, which then turns into a dialogue between the narrator and the protagonist of the novel, a painter called Cass. Together they reconstruct the events that led to rape and murder in the Italian village of Sambuco, with its cliffs and sea, its villas and peasant hovels. The emphasis is false; the novel itself proves the significance of the narrator to be invalid. What he contributes to the fulfillment of the puzzle (the pattern, the design) is unnecessary. And because his function is artificial, willed as it were in terms of structure, he contributes a tone that is too high-pitched, recalling too easily the macabre tones of the Gothic-shudder school of story-telling. How the novel itself, as it slips into gear, rids itself of this superfluity, is one of its major delights, a triumph of art over craft, of the organic over the willful. To be fair to Mr. Styron, the events that succeed the opening pages are of moment and their intensity is unflagging, so that in retrospect one may justify the initial tone and conceivably find a correspondence between atmosphere and act, though I do not think so. The bulk and heart of the novel is so swift, so sure, so true that it needs no aggrandizements, no outside jacking-up, no preparatory bolstering. Two men talking, exploring, finding something out—it goes beyond story-telling, no matter how profound the story; it somehow seems less frivolous, less an idle act. I must halt at the frontiers of the psychology of art. No matter; mistake or no mistake, the novel grows, expands and literally runs, carrying its burden of beauty and corruption with singular ease.

With the exception of Malcolm Lowry's Mexico in *Under the Volcano*, I know of no modern novel that unfolds and conveys a sense of place as this one. Not only a sense of it, but a physical knowledge of it, so that road, street, cliff, square, palazzo and hut are all around us, visible, smellable and tactile. The characters are astonishingly good, all of them, major and minor, mural and miniature; each comes to individual life, distinct and clear and unexaggerated. Mr. Styron's language, in the beginning a little self-conscious, patently sheds its Faulknerian heritage, grows into an efficient (though still formal) machine, exact and solid. His themes, multifarious and hidden, entwine and grow one into the other, so that issues and people are inseparable, and consequently "non-paraphrasable." The question of evil is uppermost, but just who is evil is not as obvious as appears; and the questions of guilt and sin and responsibility are also intrinsic to this book.

I have seen other reviews of *Set This House on Fire*, less affirmative or enthusiastic than this estimate. In the long run, critical judgments will not affect the significance and durability of the novel which, in spite of defects or weaknesses, I consider a first-rate work. Come to think of it, at its heart, it has a good deal of Lowry's *Under the Volcano*. The painter of Styron has much in common with the Consul of Lowry: the excess, the alcohol, the relationship to landscape, the illusory line between reality and dream, the delusions and visions and nightmares. Only the bitter hopelessness in Lowry, steadfast and eternal, is replaced by a bittersweet, possibly tougher, tentative hopefulness. I am not hinting at even an influence; I am suggesting a similar concern, a diving deep into place and people and discovering at the depth a world of tragedy and violence. At the heart of Mr. Styron's story I found myself being pulled into too deep water; in Lowry's story I drowned, as, of course, one drowns in Dostoevsky's novels. I mean only that one gives over completely. Mr. Styron, in his new novel, is close to that tyrannical power.

William Styron and the
Age of the Slob

Charles A. Fenton*

> It's the age of the slob. If we don't watch out they're going to drag us under, you know.
>> William Styron, *Set This House on Fire*
>> (1960)

One of the heartening episodes of the post-World War II American literary scene was the establishment of the *Paris Review* in 1952 by a group of young Americans living momentarily in Europe. For the literary historian the episode was almost divinely delivered. It confirmed or extended a number of recurrent literary facts of life, including the instinct for expatriation, the coterie factor in literature, and the reappearance of the little magazine after two decades of stately literary quarterlies. It was also a refreshing declaration of the refusal of a new generation of creative writers to submit to what one could, and a few did, querulously object to in 1952 as an Age of Literary Criticism.

Unlike so many of the little magazines of the 1920's, however, the *Paris Review* has been durable and eclectic, a consequence perhaps of the measured stability of this postwar, non-beat literary generation, or perhaps no more than a tribute to the new trough of foundation benevolence. It has been a comforting as well as an exciting magazine, a vehicle for new talent and a showplace for older artists who have been superbly displayed through the *Review's* series of interviews on technique. Even more comforting than the magazine itself, however, is the career of one of its founders, William Styron, who subsequently became himself the subject of an excellent interview and the sponsor of a collection of short stories from the magazine.[1]

As a novelist Styron represents, it seems to me, a denial of the hardy bromide which declares that there are no successors, either potential or actual, to Hemingway and Fitzgerald and Faulkner. His most recent novel, *Set This House on Fire*, is also going to constitute, I think, a fresh refutation of the ancient critical whine that most American literary careers end in midflight or drag on to a discredited end. Styron's *Set This*

*Reprinted from *South Atlantic Quarterly*, 59 (Autumn 1960), 469–76, by permission of the journal.

86

House on Fire is a meaningful piece of fiction. It grants us in 1960 the same exhilarating confirmation of a major talent which *A Farewell to Arms* must have represented in 1929 and *The 42nd Parallel* in 1930 and *Tender Is the Night* in 1934.

Before the publication of *Set This House on Fire* in June of this year, in other words, one could have argued, with that earnest search for creative decay which often passes for lofty critical adjudication—one could have argued that Styron's *Lie Down in Darkness* (1951), though it won him a Fellowship to the American Academy in Rome, was an extended exercise in derivative Gothicism, and that *The Long March* (1952), though it had a remarkable publishing and critical history, was so technically accomplished as to be very nearly the work of a cynical journeyman. Now, however, one can properly identify those two books as appropriate stages of development. *Set This House on Fire*, the clearly sweated labor of five years, gives Styron a solid body of work. It also undeniably establishes him and Norman Mailer, I would say, as primary writers in the generation which is only just now, after artificial delays and rebukes, taking its begrudged place as the contemporary literary generation.

Younger than Mailer—he was born in Newport News, Virginia, the son of a native of North Carolina, in 1925—Styron has been the beneficiary of the excellent collegiate courses in writing which so often identify the mature work of his generation. He had a year at Davidson, after preparing for college at Christchurch School, and then he transferred to Duke in 1943 as a member of the Marine Corps unit. His first short stories, written during his seventeenth and eighteenth years, were published in Duke's *Archive;* two of them were later reprinted by his principal teacher, William Blackburn, in the latter's notable *One and Twenty: Duke Narrative and Verse, 1924-1945.*

Even before the publication of *Set This House on Fire* Styron had received some remarkably generous and acute praise. Philip Toynbee told an English audience some time ago that Styron was the only living American writer who could be decently compared with Faulkner. *Lie Down in Darkness* was applauded by critics as professionally far apart as Alfred Kazin, Howard Mumford Jones, John Aldridge, and Maxwell Geismar. It's impossible to imagine that *Set This House on Fire* isn't going to extend his reputation.

There are a number of sources of the power of *Set This House on Fire.* The conventional requirements of conventionally successful fiction—provocative characters, suspenseful narrative, stylistic vigor, authentic and ample dialogue—are all abundantly present. The sense of structure and scene which in *The Long March* was virtually deafening is here fleshed out by a technique of flashback which permits Styron the expert use of at least three layers of time. Belonging as he does to a generation schooled in Lubbock and Forster and Joseph Conrad, Styron is equally deft in his handling of point of view. His narrator—"My name is Peter

Leverett. I am white, Protestant, Anglo-Saxon, Virginia-bred, just past thirty, in good health, tolerable enough looking though possessing no romantic glint or cast, given to orderly habits, more than commonly inquisitive"—Styron's narrator, as you can see, is a model of Jamesian central intelligence, refined by such successors as Hemingway's Jake Barnes and Fitzgerald's Carraway. The older convention of a narrator with a literary sensibility, on the other hand, is given a further diminishment by Styron. His Peter Leverett is a failed composer turned lawyer, so that, like James Jones' Pvt. Prewitt, Leverett's acuteness is authentic and persuasive, but, again like Prewitt, he is also sufficiently ordinary so that his attitudes and responses are in no way special.

But each publishing season, these days, casts up innumerable novels with smoothly-functioning machinery and sleek, knowledgeable, disengaged but readily wounded narrators. If *Set This House on Fire* were no more than proficient it would be cause for pleasure rather than rejoicing. What separates it from the machine-tooled facility of so many of our seminar-trained novelists, it seems to me, is the magnitude of its theme and the massiveness of its landscape. Styron himself, as the dedicatory epigraph reminds us—"L'ambizione del mio compito non mi impedì di fare molti sbagli"—is diffident about the fulfilment of his undertaking. It is indeed a large enterprise, for Styron's theme is nothing less than the stagnation and regeneration of the spirit.

This is hardly a fresh topic; it is one which major literary artists have manfully wrestled with throughout the century. More often than not, however, the novelists have controlled the theme by orderly simplicity and manageable symbol and myth, as in *The Old Man and the Sea*, or they have shirked its magnitude by creating a confident, careless bulk, as in the later Malraux, or they have lazied themselves into pretentiousness, as Faulkner did in *A Fable*. It has been tempting for writers to define the stagnation through the hysterical melodramas of Tennessee Williams, or the neat cameos which Malcolm Cowley has correctly identified, under the label "A Tidy Room in Bedlam," as a distinct genre.

Styron, however, has undertaken an enormous narrative spread, a twenty-year time span, several major characters and a number of minor ones, all of this firmly controlled by the techniques which during the past decade have been largely restricted by his contemporaries to tight narratives and nuances of relationship. The result is what we seek from a major literary artist: an adult affirmation without mawkishness and possessed of stylistic force and technical elegance. This is also, to repeat, a novel of our times—the great political events of the past twenty years are not concealed or dismissed, and Styron clearly regards history as meaningful rather than embarrassing—and the measure of its success is nowhere more apparent than in the thematic validity of its situation.

The principal action of the novel occurs during a brief period in an Italian town, Sambuco, where an American film company is shooting a hasty and bogus extravaganza. The most important cultural fact in the lives of millions of twentieth-century human beings—the movies—and a cultural fact which is peculiarly identified with the United States, is thus a central fact in Styron's statement. "Flicker creeps," as the novel's hero, Cass Kinsolving, refers to the stars and their creatures, are therefore present as a kind of depraved chorus for the grotesque tragedies which occupy the focus of Styron's narrative.

> The greatest art form ever devised by man [says Cripps, the literate and defeated movie director] and what do we get? A void . . . *cosa da nulla* . . . nothing . . . We are not even barbarians. We are mountebanks.

This presence of a band of corrupt and opulent Americans in Italy, against a background of a devastated, exhausted Europe, permits Styron to add another document to the extensive body of literary alienation from America.

> Some day, [a sensitive Italian points out to Kinsolving] the Russians will have the refrigerators and the bathrooms that you Americans have. But though it is repressed at the moment, the Russians have a fund of spirituality which you Americans have never developed. They will be educated people with refrigerators and bathrooms, and the educated people will triumph.

It is with spirituality, in fact, that Styron is particularly concerned. The monstrous quotation from Donne—"what torment is not a marriage bed to this damnation, to be secluded eternally, eternally, eternally from the sight of God"—alerts us, but it is Styron who gives contemporary body to the seventeenth-century sermon. Styron's narrator is aware of and responsive to the need for spirituality, but he has long since made his compromise and adjustment. He is a receptive audience for Cripps. "Let me give you some advice," Cripps tells Leverett gently. "Form regular habits, don't try too hard for anything, forget about—well, honesty, or effort, or it'll all get you like it's got me."

Leverett, to be sure, has recognized a kind of spirituality in his own Virginia father, who "had managed to work out a shaky compromise between his honest piety, on the one hand, and his enlarged human views, on the other, and the resulting tension had helped to make him the only true liberal I think I have ever known." The elder Leverett, however, is in his own way as desperate at the end of his life of liberalism as Cripps is at midpoint. "These are miserable times," the father tells his thirty-year-old son. "They are miserable times. Empty times. Mediocre times. You can almost sniff the rot in the air. And what is more they are going to get worse."

All these various stages of incomplete or withered or nonexistent spirituality—the flicker creeps, the Italians, Mason Flagg's women,

Leverett, the latter's father—are a prelude to and a substantiation for the two major carriers of moral exhaustion. The situations of Mason Flagg and Cass Kinsolving are joined in Sambuco. Their relationship is ugly and mean and destructive, the sterile Flagg bent on the humiliation of Kinsolving and his talent. I am not at all certain, to be sure, that Flagg may not be Styron's single creative failure in *Set This House on Fire*, or at least the most difficult to accept fully. Flagg is rich, reckless, wholly fraudulent, so nearly evil and so transparently a representation of contemporary America that he is always in danger of becoming a caricature. The personal charm which he is alleged to possess was never fully believable to me, and if this is a responsible diagnosis it is certainly a weakness in the novel. Flagg's function, on the other hand, is powerfully clear and direct. When Cripps asks Leverett how long he has known Flagg, Leverett replies that he has known him practically all his life. Then, of course, Leverett realizes that this is far from true.

> "Well, not really all my life," I added. "I was at prep school with him near my home in Virginia. Then for a while after the war I saw him in New York. But there's something about Mason that makes you feel you've known him forever, even when you don't see much of him."

In the characterization of Cass Kinsolving, however, drunk, gifted, desperate, courageous, blasphemous, there is no flaw whatsoever. If this is a major novel, as I think it surely is, Cass is as surely a major creation. His torment is vivid, his regeneration is plausible. Styron's capacity for the deeply operative symbolic episode is nowhere more effective than in the superb, extended encounter with the fundamentalist nymphet, Vernelle Satterfield, who tells Cass prophetically after a bedroom misadventure, "Why you *pore silly*. Look down there! Look what you done! Why the divine spirit just flowed right on out of you."

There are a number of such episodes—some brief, like the extraordinary vignette of the Italian cows so undernourished that the laboratory tests denied to their yield the normal properties of milk, or Leverett's near-drowning during boyhood, some of them elaborate and recurrent like the bootlegged American drugs—and there are passages to remind us that if *Set This House on Fire* is the American novel which most completely delivers the 1950's to us, it is also very much a fine novel about World War II.

> Someone said the Second World War was fought just like the War Between the States—between the Potomac and the Gulf of Mexico—and my God it's true. Think of all us millions of men and boys prowling the streets of a thousand dusty southern towns, and the boredom, and the beer joints, and the bus stations, and the bootleg whiskey and the endless, endless search for girls. And the rain and those dead, black skies of winter and the M.P.'s. How few of us escaped it! It's a mood that lingers in the heart of a whole generation. And behind it all, shadowing all of it, is the

memory of the time when all the lovely girls had vanished from the land.
The time when only the whores were abroad. . . .

As one reads and ponders *Set This House on Fire*, it becomes increasingly plain, in fact, that what Styron has undertaken, and what he has in large part achieved, is nothing less than a rendition of national mood dramatized in terms of powerful characters of fiction. It is this, I think, which sets his novel above the ample shelves of those other serious-minded novels of the 1950's, so competent, so assured, so modest. What one senses as he finishes *Set This House on Fire* is an encounter with a greatly gifted writer—but there are many of great gifts—who has laboriously picked up the pieces of his gifts and his training and his torment and swept them into effective unity. There is no hedge in *Set This House on Fire*. Styron took his chances with this novel; it could have been a catastrophe, but happily it was not. Styron has undertaken the major effort which American critics have blandly urged on so many other skilful craftsmen in the past few years—O'Hara, Steinbeck, Marquand, Wescott—and which so seldom has been realized.

It is all here, all the ingredients of the American literary achievement and experiment of the past forty-five years, congealed into this single massive statement which will take its place with the other massive literary statements of our time. It is heartening and electrifying, a signal that the renaissance has been consolidated, that there is more to our national literature as the 1960's commence than the amusing but rather nasty beat parodies of Diana Trilling or the trivial niceties of yet another imitative critical essay. One is reminded too of the calm confidence with which Styron himself rebuked the detractors of his literary generation, back in 1953.

"There are signs," said Styron, seven years ago, "that this generation can and will produce literature equal to that of any in the past." In verification he cited, in 1953, Jones's Private Prewitt and Mailer's Sergeant Croft. Certainly his own Cass Kinsolving now belongs in the same company. There is even the bizarre fact that Styron's publishers bought a very learned journal's entire back cover with which to advertise, this last summer, *Set This House on Fire*. It appears that Styron belongs by right as well as by purchase in both American literature and *American Literature*. All that's needed now is for the Modern Language Association to pin him as an Honorary Fellow, along with such present Fellows as T. S. Eliot and St. John Perse. That would be a seedy finish for a writer who once said, cogently—and who now disproves his own cogent statement—that "the literary magazines seem today on the verge of doing away with literature, not with any philistine bludgeon but by smothering it under the weight of learned chatter."

You'd better read *Set This House on Fire* now, before Styron gets enshrined and explicated, before they tell us that Cass Kinsolving is really a

Christ-figure and that Sambuco is actually a lost Garden of Eden under a hydrogen sky. It's nothing of the kind. It's a story of men's eternal combat, in each generation, with their own hypocrisy and meanness. "Son," the elder Leverett tells his boy, "life is a search for justice." Then, noting that his father was "betraying not a flicker of self-consciousness at the immeasurable phrase," young Leverett considers his parent and states as well as it can be stated Styron's timeless theme of what he calls spirituality. "I know now," Leverett reflects, "that he never found justice, but perhaps that matters less than that he moved through dooms of love, through griefs of joy, in his lonely seeking."

Note

1. Peter Matthiessen and George Plimpton, "The Art of Fiction V: William Styron," *The Paris Review*, 2 (Spring 1954), 42–57; republ. in *Writers at Work: The Paris Review Interviews*, ed. Malcolm Cowley (New York: Viking, 1958), pp. 268–82. *Best Short Stories from The Paris Review*, intro. by Styron (New York: Dutton, 1959), pp. 9–16.

An Artist in Bonds

Louis D. Rubin, Jr.*

Ten years ago William Styron published *Lie Down In Darkness*, a first novel that caused many persons to consider him the most promising of all the post-World War II writers of fiction. After that he brought out only one long story, and speculation about what he might eventually do has been widespread. He was known to be "at work" on a second novel; several times it was even announced for publication. Norman Mailer, for one, grew tired of waiting, and in that cantankerous book entitled *Advertisements For Myself* accused Mr. Styron of being a consummate literary politician who had parlayed a single novel into a reputation that many an author of a dozen books might envy. Meanwhile the 1950s went by, and no novel.

Well, at last the new Styron novel has appeared—a big book, 200,000 words long, complete with an epigraph from John Donne's sermons. The newspaper and magazine reviews have been mostly unfavorable. Arthur Mizener, in the Sunday book section of the *New York Times*, found it melodramatic, overblown, turgid. *Time* Magazine pronounced it self-pitying and un-American. Though at this writing the returns are not yet complete, it is clear that the new Styron novel has earned its author comparatively few journalistic laurels, and that for the time being Herman Wouk and Mackinlay Kantor are still safe.

What the Sunday book supplements and the newsmagazines think about literature is, in the long run, not very important, of course, and I suspect that by the time Mr. Styron gets around to publishing a third novel, the present hostilities will have blown over. But in a way I am rather glad that things have worked out in this fashion. For I have never felt that Mr. Styron's first novel received decent critical attention in the serious literary periodicals that ultimately mean most for an author's reputation. Hailed in the press, *Lie Down In Darkness* was all but ignored by the quarterly reviews, when it was the quarterly reviews, not the Sunday book supplements, that *should* have recognized its worth. For William Styron was not and is not a "middlebrow" novelist; his work is in no way flashy and meretricious, but quite original. So that now, perhaps,

*Reprinted from *Sewanee Review*, 69 (Winter 1961), 174-79, by permission of the author.

the bad press he is getting in the dailies and weeklies will serve to emphasize this fact.

I had better admit my bias openly and at the start: to my mind Mr. Styron is the most impressive writer of fiction of his generation. *Lie Down In Darkness* was a remarkable novel, and *Set This House On Fire* is an even better novel. Indeed, so far as I am concerned it is like nothing else that has been written in the past decade, and deserves the respectful attention of anyone seriously interested in fiction—this despite a grievous structural flaw which in the hands of a less gifted author might have sufficed to spoil it entirely.

There are three main characters in *Set This House On Fire*: Mason Flagg, a would-be playwright, Cass Kinsolving, a painter, and Peter Leverett, a lawyer. Flagg is a wealthy, clever, bedevilled young man, who is always "going to write" a play but never does. Handsome, conversant in the arts, a brilliant talker, he spends his days and nights in quest of some ultimate sensation, usually sexual. Sex, he keeps insisting, is the only frontier left to modern man. Essentially he is a fraud, a poseur, in some ways reminiscent of the character Starwick in Thomas Wolfe's *Of Time And The River*.

Cass Kinsolving is a painter who cannot paint. A Southern boy, he is wedded to a sweet and not very intelligent woman named Poppy, and they have several children. A considerable portion of his time is spent in getting and remaining drunk.

Peter Leverett, through whom much of the story is related, is a boyhood friend of Mason Flagg's, who goes to visit Flagg in the Italian coastal town of Sambucco, where the major events of the novel take place. Peter is from Port Warwick, Virginia, the scene of Mr. Styron's first book. The novel begins when Peter travels to Charleston, South Carolina, where a now-regenerate Cass Kinsolving is living and painting, and together they piece out the details of what happened in Sambucco, where a young peasant girl had been raped and Mason Flagg killed.

We see Mason Flagg, in other words, through the eyes of two persons—Peter Leverett, who knew him as a youth and as a young man, and Cass Kinsolving, who knew him in Sambucco just before his death. It is here that the chief structural flaw of the novel resides, as we shall see. For if this novel were primarily a study of Mason Flagg, what made him into the harried and driven man he was, what drove him to his death, then the structural scheme that Mr. Styron chose to give his story might have sufficed.

But important though the character of Mason Flagg is in this novel, it is not in Flagg that the chief meaning of the story is to be found. Rather, the central figure is the painter Cass Kinsolving.

For most of the novel, Cass is a man in bondage. In Paris, before he goes to Sambucco, he lives in an alcoholic daze, tortured by his inability to paint, spending his time drinking, wandering about, pitying himself, doing everything but confronting his talent. At length he moves down to Italy, where he comes under the sway of Mason Flagg. In return for food and drink money, he allows himself to be dominated by Flagg. At one point Flagg even forces him, in exchange for his largesse, to paint a pornographic picture for his collection. Cass also becomes enamoured of an Italian peasant girl, and steals medicines in a hopeless attempt to save the life of her father, an old man in the late stages of tuberculosis.

Peter Leverett, about to leave Rome for the United States, drives over to Sambucco to visit Mason Flagg, arriving in time to witness the cataclysmic events that end the novel. The peasant girl is raped by Mason Flagg, then brutally murdered. Flagg is found dead at the foot of a cliff. The solution to these crimes is discovered by a philosophical young Italian policeman, who allows the culprits to go unpunished by the law.

The meaning of these events exists, as I have said, not in Mason Flagg's life but in Cass Kinsolving's. When Peter Leverett and Cass meet several years later to analyze what happened at Sambucco, Cass is a well man again, doing the painting he could not do in Europe, earning a living, caring for his wife and family. And though this novel is a murder mystery, the principal question it undertakes to answer is why Cass was in bondage for so long, unable to paint the pictures he wanted to paint, to receive and return the love of his wife and children.

In the events that come to a climax at Sambucco, I think, we do find out why. It was because Cass was unwilling to accept the responsibility of his own talent, unwilling to face up to the fact that it alone could accomplish its own perfection. He wanted to find a form for his art outside of himself, when it was he alone who could give his art, and therefore his life, its reason for being. He would not put up with his creative limitations and work his way out of them.

This was the hold that Mason Flagg had on him. For Mason could provide wealth, afford the glamour and excitement of "Life," "Experience"— or so Cass tried to pretend. Throughout the novel Cass attempted to deny the responsibility of his talent, attempted to substitute external experience for the dedication to artistic creativity that for him could be the only true account. He sought escape into "Life," in alcohol, in false moments of Wordsworthian "ecstasy" that gave him the illusion of beauty, in Mason Flagg's largesse and phony dilettantism, in an insubstantial, idyllic romance with the peasant girl, in a quixotic and hopeless attempt to doctor the old man back to health. All these activities were ways of avoiding his only refuge and mission—the remorseless requirements of learning how to discover and paint the pictures he wanted to paint.

The attainment of this realization, through grief and pain, constitutes the development of this novel, and though it requires 500 pages and 200,000 words, as a story it is dramatically and artistically convincing. When at last we put this novel down, we have witnessed the resolution of a tremendous conflict within a man.

Why, however, is Cass so constituted that it takes him so long to find out what at last he learns? We accept the reality of his bondage to "Life"—but how, we may ask, did it come to be? The answer is there but—and this, I think, is the major structural defect of *Set This House On Fire*—it does not lie in the experience of Cass Kinsolving at all. Instead, it is found in the characterization of Peter Leverett.

For it was Peter, not Cass, who grew up with Mason Flagg, who was exposed through him to the delusion of artistic self-fulfillment through "experience," instead of by artistic creativity itself, who was progressively tempted by Mason Flagg's advocacy of false gods. The spiritual duel between Mason Flagg and Cass Kinsolving that constitutes the dramatic struggle of *Set This House On Fire* was begun long before Cass went to Sambucco and encountered Mason Flagg. It commenced in Virginia, when Mason and Peter were young.

Mason's last, despairing attempt to "own" Cass Kinsolving by raping Cass's girl friend was the culmination of a long battle. Why did Flagg try to dominate first Peter Leverett and then Cass Kinsolving? Because he knew that they alone, of all those who comprised his acquaintanceship, could judge him as a writer. Tempted though they both were, they alone did not confuse what Mason did with the true artistic responsibility. He could bribe others, but he could not bribe them. They would not be owned.

But what is Cass Kinsolving's relationship to Peter Leverett? In this novel ostensibly they are both friends of Mason Flagg, and that is all. Dramatically, psychologically, however, they are more than that. *They are one and the same person.* We meet Cass Kinsolving in mid-passage, a painter who cannot paint, a created, believable character. It is Peter Leverett's past history, not Cass's, that explains why Cass cannot paint. Peter Leverett, in other words, *becomes Cass Kinsolving.*

Now from a strictly logical point of view, that ought certainly to compromise Mr. Styron's novel. How can the experience of one character serve to create the characterization of another and entirely different man? But the point I want to emphasize is that nevertheless we *do* believe in Cass Kinsolving. As a character, he is convincing, and the events that give this story its conflict and its resolution happen to him, not to Peter Leverett. So perceptive and imaginative is the characterization of Cass that the explanation of how he got that way, though interesting, is not finally of primary importance. Though logically we know that the early experience happened not to Cass but to Peter Leverett, dramatically and psychologically the development of the characterization is so secure that as readers we do what in terms of plot logic we should not do: we give Cass Peter Leverett's experience.

Building upon it, Cass emerges as a tremendous characterization, a figure that almost anyone who has ever attempted to paint or write or otherwise create artistic work can recognize. Cass Kinsolving is a familiar and crucial figure of our time, the artist seeking reality, confusing it with "Life," struggling to locate it in his work. One recalls Allen Tate's remark about Hart Crane, that "he is betrayed, not by a defect of his own nature, but by the external world; he asks of nature, perfection—requiring only of himself, intensity." And what Mr. Styron makes his fictional artist learn is what Mr. Tate pointed out that Crane did not learn: the obligation "to define the limits of his personality and to objectify its moral implications in an appropriate symbolism." The Cass Kinsolving whom Peter Leverett visits in Charleston several years after the events of Sambucco has accepted that obligation, though he never speaks of such things at all. Wrongly structured or not, the characterization is there.

Mr. Styron might have done it better, and perhaps some day he will, but even so he has given us a novel of great perception, with moving and believable characters. Even the partial failure of *Set This House On Fire* is more instructive than ten "successful" novels. It shows us that *Lie Down In Darkness* was no fluke—that those who saw in William Styron a major talent were not mistaken.

Cass Kinsolving: Kierkegaardian
Man of Despair

Lewis Lawson*

During the short history of William Styron's *Set This House on Fire*,[1] several critics have hinted at its existential element. Soon after its publication Robert Gorham Davis wrote that it was "more or less existentialist,"[2] and David L. Stevenson placed it "in an existential world."[3] John Howard Lawson wrote a little later that its "existentialist frame of reference is more pervasive than the psychological element in *Lie Down in Darkness*; . . ."[4] Even more recently, Ihab Hassan has said that it "reminds us that existential fiction has become as indigenous to America as it is to Europe."[5] Yet, for all the widespread agreement upon an existential element in the novel, no one has fully examined the importance of that element.

But only when Cass Kinsolving, the protagonist, is viewed as a Kierkegaardian man of despair does his life take on enough significance to justify its very full presentation. For although he seems unaware of it, Kinsolving's descriptions of his thoughts and actions during his exile in Europe are couched in Kierkegaardian terms. The introduction of the theme of despair into the novel is Kinsolving's exploration of his spiritual life in Paris. At that time, after having driven his family from him, he encounters a tart he knows, who tells him *"Cass, tu es malade!"* And though he had denied his sickness then, Kinsolving, back in the United States several years later, admits the truth of the girl's observation, when he tells Peter Leverett:

> And the thing was, you see, I *was* sick. . . . What I was really sick from was from despair and self-loathing and greed and selfish and spits. I was sick with a paralysis of the soul, and with self, and with flabbiness. . . . I was very nearly sick unto death, and I guess my sickness, if you really want to know, was the sickness of deprivation, and the deprivation was my own doing, because though I didn't know it then I had deprived myself of all belief in the good in myself. The good which is very close to God. (STHOF, 269–270)

*Reprinted from *Wisconsin Studies in Contemporary Literature*, 3 (Fall 1962), 54-66, by permission of the author.

Though Cass has apparently never read Kierkegaard, Styron surely has: "despair," "self-loathing," "selfishness," "self," "sick unto death"—all suggest that Styron is positing Kinsolving as a character who travels through the stages of despair until he reaches the faith that saves him from madness. Styron relies mainly, of course, upon Kierkegaard's *The Sickness Unto Death*.[6]

The sickness unto death is, says Kierkegaard, despair (TSUD, 7). This sickness can be regarded in two ways: (1) "Despair regarded in such a way that one does not reflect whether it is conscious or not so that one reflects only upon the factors of the synthesis" (TSUD,7); (2) "Despair viewed under the aspect of Consciousness" (TSUD, 8). There are two forms of "Despair viewed under the aspect of Consciousness": (a) "Despair which is Unconscious that it is Despair," and (b) "Despair which is Conscious of being Despair" (TSUD, 8). Of "Despair which is Conscious of being Despair," there are two forms: (1) "In despair at not willing to be oneself," and (2) "The despair of willing desparingly to be oneself" (TSUD, 8). Each form of despair viewed under the aspect of consciousness can be seen in succession in Kinsolving as he searches Europe for spiritual peace.

The most vivid action in *Set This House on Fire* is the conflict between Mason Flagg and Cass Kinsolving, which is eventually resolved through the murder of Flagg by Kinsolving. But the motive force for the novel does not result from this conflict; Cass intrigues the reader not because he wars against Flagg, but because he wars against himself. And he knows that the source of his difficulties was not Flagg. As he emphatically tells Leverett some years after Flagg's murder, "It didn't *start* with Mason, I'm telling you, . . . It started in me, early, way back. . . . But it really started in Paris the year before, when I was sick and these here nightmares began to come upon me. It began *then*, . . . " (STHOF, 249)

And in his loquacious, half-erudite, half-illiterate speech, Cass begins to characterize his condition in Paris. He had been drunk, sexually unfaithful, unable to paint. "You know, you can't work without faith, and, boy, I was as faithless as an alleycat," he says (STHOF, 250). He is interpreting, however, an event which had occurred years before; had he known then that his salvation lay in faith, he might have avoided the inhuman punishment that he later gave himself. But only after he has murdered Flagg and has been given his freedom by Luigi Migliori, the philosophical Italian policeman, does Cass gain faith, the only Kierkegaardian antidote to despair (TSUD, 216). The element of retrospection also invalidates another comment about his Paris condition that Cass later makes: "Boy, Kinsolving pitted against Kinsolving, . . . " (STHOF, 250) This statement implies that Cass knew at the time that his condition resulted from his self being in conflict with itself; his comments immediately afterward show that he had not known the cause of his condition.

For as he admits, he had "had no such notions or insights there in Paris" (STHOF, 254). That he is aware as he talks to Leverett of what his trouble was in Paris is clear, though, by the redundancy of his references to his self for a few pages (STHOF, 254–255). But at the time, Cass had not known the cause of his condition. He had been so tied up in himself that he could not analyze himself.

On that day in Paris, having driven his family from him, Cass drunkenly wanders around the apartment, his steps carrying him to a window overlooking the city. He tells Leverett later,

> Well, I stood there for a long while. . . . And then finally, in a sort of doze, and with all my hatred and poison lost for the moment, or forgotten, I looked up. And I'll swear at the moment as I looked up it was as if I were gazing into the kingdom of heaven. I don't quite know how to describe it—this *bone-breaking* moment of loveliness. . . . Ah my God, how can I describe it! It wasn't just the *scene*, you see—it was the sense, the bleeding *essence* of the thing. It was as if I had been given for an instant the capacity to understand not just beauty itself by its outward signs, but the other—the *elseness* in beauty, this continuity of beauty in the scheme of all life which triumphs even to the point of taking in sordidness and shabbiness and ugliness, which goes on and on and on, and of which this was only a moment, I guess, divinely crystalized. . . . What was it, really? I just don't know—the weakness, the light-headedness, the booze, the vertigo. Yet it was there, and for the first time—the first moment of reality I think I had ever known. And the strange thing was that it was in the midst of this, in the midst of a time when I was most wrapped up in self and squalor and meanness, I had a presentiment of selflessness: . . . It was no longer a street that I was watching; the street was inside my very flesh and bones, you see, and for a moment I was released from my own self, embracing all that was within the street and partaking of all that happened there in time gone by, and now, and time to come. And it filled me with the craziest sort of joy . . . (STHOF, 256–257)

According to the forms of despair that Kierkegaard views under the aspect of consciousness, Cass is starting to move from unconscious despair to despair conscious of its existence. His vision marks him as a Kierkegaardian *immediate* man:

> The *immediate* man . . . is merely soulishly determined, his self or he himself is something included along with 'the other' in the compass of the temporal and the worldly, and it has only an illusory appearance of possessing in it something eternal. Thus the self coheres immediately with 'the other, . . .'
>
> Now then there *happens*, befalls (falls upon) this immediate self something which brings it to despair; in no other way can this come about, since the self has no reflection in itself, that which brings it to despair is

merely passive. That wherein immediacy has its being, or (supposing that after all it has a little bit of reflection in itself) that part thereof to which it especially clings, a man is deprived of by 'a stroke of fate,' in short, he becomes, as he calls it, unfortunate, that is, the immediacy in him receives such a shock that it cannot recover itself—he despairs. Or . . . this despair of immediacy occurs through what the immediate man calls an all-too-great fortune; . . . (TSUD, 80–81)

Uneducated though he is, Kinsolving discusses his experience by using Kierkegaardian images: e.g., Cass's "elseness" is Kierkegaard's "the other." When Cass discusses the vision, he suggests that liquor was responsible. The truth, though, was that he had gazed into "the kingdom of heaven," that he had established a God-relationship, and "the God-relationship infinitizes; but this may so carry a man away that it becomes an inebriation, . . . " (TSUD, 48) Or again, Kinsolving says that the vision was the result of vertigo, using a Kierkegaardian analogy to despair (TSUD, 19, 22). While he is still in unconscious despair, the vision has "happened" that propels him into conscious despair.

After Cass has his vision, he passes out. Later he tells Leverett, "I can't say how long this moment of *rapture*—I guess, that's what it was—I don't know how long it lasted, maybe not more than half a minute, . . . Then a strange thing happened. . . . I fainted, blacked out" (STHOF, 258). His sense of immediacy has been shattered by a vision of eternity, and his self reacts as Kierkegaard predicts: " . . . this is the only way immediacy knows how to fight, the one thing it knows how to do: to despair and swoon—and yet it knows what despair is less than anything else. It despairs and swoons, and thereupon it lies quite still as if it were dead, . . . " (TSUD,82)

There occurs then in Cass's recital the curious story of his youthful seduction of Vernelle Satterfield, which Styron slyly calls a "diversion" (STHOF, 259). Midway in it, though, Styron has Cass attach significance to the story:

> Maybe I seem to be getting away from the point. But you see, it was this girl and this moment in time which were so important to me that day in Paris, and I'll tell you about it. But I've often thought that it was not the girl so much—maybe because, whatever it was, it wasn't love—who was important to me, but the moment, the mood, the sad nostalgic glamour— call it what you will: the crystallization of a moment in time past which encompasses and explains and justifies time itself. (STHOF, 261–262)

The seduction takes on importance when Cass says that the mood surrounding Vernelle began to pervade his mind in Paris after his swoon; the mood came over him with a "heart-stopping and heart-rending immediacy" (STHOF, 266), until, as Cass says, "the joy was on me, the joy and the calm. It was a real euphoria" (STHOF, 267). Kierkegaard knows that happiness—and its peril:

Even that which, humanly speaking, is the most beautiful and lovable thing of all, a feminine youthfulness which is sheer peace and harmony and joy— even that is despair. For this indeed is happiness, but happiness is not a characteristic of the spirit, and in the remote depths, in the most inward parts, in the hidden recesses of happiness, there dwells also the anxious dread which is despair; it would be only too glad to be allowed to remain therein, for the dearest and most attractive dwelling-place of despair is in the very heart of immediate happiness. All immediacy, in spite of its illusory peace and tranquillity, is dread, and hence, quite consistently, it is dread of nothing; one cannot make immediacy so anxious by the most horrifying description of the most dreadful something, as by a crafty apparently casual half word about an unknown peril which is thrown out with the surely calculated aim of reflection; yea, one can put immediacy most in dread by slyly imputing to it knowledge of the matter referred to. For immediacy doubtless does not know; but never does reflection catch its prey so surely as when it makes its snare of nothing, and never is reflection so thoroughly itself as when it is . . . nothing. There is need of an eminent reflection, or rather of a great faith, to support a reflection based upon nothing, i.e. an infinite reflection. So even the most beautiful youthfulness which is sheer peace and harmony and joy, is nevertheless despair, is happiness. (TSUD, 37–38)

In the years since his Paris vision, Cass has learned well the dialectical, happiness-depair quality of immediacy. The mood induced by his memory of Vernelle he had thought then to be "a real euphoria," but then he adds, "And, God, how stupid I was not to realize that the whole thing was a fraud!" (STHOF, 267)

In the state of immediacy, of false happiness that is really despair, of "joy, serenity, the calm" (STHOF, 267) Cass leaves the apartment for the Luxembourg Gardens, thinking he will be able to paint for the first time in months. At this time the passage previously quoted occurs, in which Cass is told, "*Cass, tu es malade!*" In such a state of false happiness, Cass resents what he considers an intrusion into his personal life: "No Montparnasse tart—especially one who had confronted me as if she were my own guilt made incarnate—was going to spoil my balmy day, see? So I suppose I said something rude, . . ." (STHOF, 269). Kierkegaard knows, also, the angry reaction to a suggestion that immediacy is false: "So when a man is supposed to be happy, he imagines that he is happy (whereas viewed in the light of the truth he is unhappy), and in this case he is generally very far from wishing to be torn from that illusion. On the contrary, he becomes furious, . . ." (TSUD, 66). But, no matter how hard Cass tries, he cannot recapture immediacy; by the time he reaches the Gardens, he later says, ". . . I was feeling *bad*. . . . And to top it all, worse than this was the anxiety I'd begun to feel—this dread, this fear that something bad was about to happen" (STHOF, 270). This is the Kierkegaardian "dread of nothing"; Cass only knows that "something bad was about to happen." Unable to stand his anxiety, Cass runs for home in a panic, there to throw himself on the bed, trying to protect himself by "lying dead." He sleeps, but a dream terrifies him into wakefulness.

In the dream Cass is being taken to the North Carolina state prison by his uncle, and he says later of his dream feelings,

> . . . I can remember the feeling of despair I had, because for the life of me I couldn't figure out what my crime was, or anything about it, other than that I had done something unspeakably wicked—surpassing rape or murder or kidnapping or treason, some nameless and enormous crime— and that I had been sentenced not to death or to life imprisonment but to this indefinite term which might be several hours or might be decades. Or centuries. (STHOF, 272–273)

Before his dream Cass was still in a state of despairing over the earthly. But his dream reveals that he is progressing into the next stage of despair: "Despair over the earthly or over something earthly is really despair also about the eternal and over oneself, in so far as it is despair, for this is the formula for all despair" (TSUD, 97). As the dream continues, Cass, so he tells Leverett, is led to the lethal chamber:

> . . . then I woke up beneath the blanket half-smothered and howling bloody murder with the vision in my brain of the dream's last Christ- awful horror: which was my uncle, my kindly good old bald-headed un- cle who'd reared me like a daddy, standing with a crucible of cyanide at the chamber door, grinning with the slack-lipped grin of Lucifer hisself and black as a crow in his round tight-fitting executioner's shroud. . . . (STHOF, 274)

At this point Styron is again relying upon Kierkegaard for imagery. The dream reveals Cass's unconscious awareness of his despair over the eter- nal, but it reveals also his conscience at work. He is guilty, of what he does not know, but he is being executed by his foster father, a God symbol. It is the method of execution that suggests a Kierkegaardian image: "A man seated in a glass case is not put to such embarrassment as is a man in his transparency before God. This is the factor of conscience" (TSUD, 203).

Cass is thoroughly conscious now of despair, but contrary to what might be expected, his recognition is the first step toward his regenera- tion. As Kierkegaard says, unconsciousness "may be the most dangerous form of despair. By unconsciousness the despairing man is in a way se- cured . . . against becoming aware—that is, he is securely in the power of despair" (TSUD, 69–70). Almost everyone suffers from one of two kinds of despair; if one is not unconscious of despair, then one must be conscious of it. This is Cass's new state. But consciousness of despair can take either of two forms: "despair at not willing to be itself; or . . . despair at willing to be itself" (TSUD, 74). With his recognition of despair, Cass wills not to be himself.

When he first awakens, he thinks of suicide: "Then for the first time

in my life, I guess, I honestly, passionately yearned to die— . . ."
(STHOF, 274) He does not kill himself, though, because of the dream:

> . . . I think I would have willingly done myself in in an instant if it hadn't
> been that the same dream which pushed me toward the edge also pulled
> me back in a sudden gasp of crazy, stark, riven torture: there wouldn't be
> any oblivion in death, I knew, but only some eternal penitentiary where
> I'd tramp endlessly up gray steel ladderways and by my brother-felons be
> taunted with my own unnameable crime and where at the end there
> would be waiting the crucible of cyanide and the stink of peach blossoms
> and the strangled gasp for life and then the delivery, not into merciful
> darkness, but into a hot room at night, with the blinds drawn down,
> where I would stand again, as now, in mortal fear and trembling. And so
> on in endless cycles, like a barbershop mirror reflecting the countless faces
> of my own guilt, straight into infinity. (STHOF, 274–275)

Cass's soul is at this point still within a Christian frame of reference:

> . . . humanly speaking, death is the last thing of all; and humanly speak-
> ing, there is hope only so long as there is life. But Christianly understood
> death is by no means the last thing of all, hence it is only a little event
> within that which is all, an eternal life; . . . (TSUD, 12)

Still, Cass plans to kill himself and his family when they return, so he lies in
wait for them. While waiting, he dreams again, this time of immediacy:

> And I saw some southern land with olive trees and orange blossoms, and
> girls with merry black eyes, and parasols, and the blue shining water. . . .
> there seemed to be a carnival or a fair: I heard the strumming music of a
> carrousel, which wound through it all like a single thread of rapture, and I
> heard a liquid babble of tongues and I saw white teeth flashing in laughter
> and, Lord love me, I could even smell it—this smell of perfume and pines
> and orange blossoms and girls, all mixed up in one sweet blissful fragrance
> of peace and repose and joy. (STHOF, 276)

Part of the dream comes from the memories of past happy experiences,
but the most important part is "one sweet blissful fragrance of peace and
repose and joy." Here Cass uses almost verbatim Kierkegaard's characterization of immediacy: "Even that which, humanly speaking, is the most
beautiful and lovable thing of all, a feminine youthfulness which is sheer
peace and harmony and joy—even that is despair" (TSUD, 37). Although
Cass has despaired, he still thinks he can substitute immediacy for faith,
the only answer to despair (TSUD, 77).

The next morning the delusion that he can regain immediacy forces
Cass to forget his plans for murder and suicide. Beset by his guilt, he
welcomes his family, embracing his wife and thinking, as he tells
Leverett, ". . . of the day before, and the long night, and even Vernelle
Satterfield and what she said about the divine spirit, which had indeed
flowed right on out of me, and which to save my very life I knew I had to

recapture" (STHOF, 278). The seduction of Vernelle has become symbolic: he had become so excited that he had been unable to perform the sexual act, and she had said, "Why, you *pore silly*. . . . Why the divine spirit just flowed right on out of you" (STHOF, 265). The flowing-out of the divine spirit, falling into despair, has its counterpart image in Kierkegaard: "Whence then comes despair? From the relation wherein the synthesis relates itself to itself, in that God who made man a relationship lets this go as it were out of His hand, . . ." (TSUD, 22).

After his dream of immediacy, Cass tries to force his consciousness of despair from his mind. Going to a doctor, he embarks upon a "regime which he was later to call his period of 'dull reasonableness' " (STHOF, 280). Kierkegaard knows, too, the attempts of the "immediate" man to regain immediacy, after having despair befall him:

> Meanwhile time passes. If outward help comes, then life returns to the despairer, he begins where he left off; he had no self, and a self he did not become, but he continues to live on with only the quality of immediacy. If outward help does not come, then in real life something else commonly occurs. (TSUD, 83)

Cass fears the recurrence of his despair, but it comes, the result of an unpleasant incident with an American tourist couple (forerunners of the McCabes in Rome, when he has another attack). The memory of "the blue southern waters, the carrousel, the laughing girls—vaulted into his consciousness, no longer just a promise and a hope, but a command, rather, and an exhortation" (STHOF, 282), and he knows that he must seek his vision of immediacy in the south.

The Kinsolvings leave Paris for the south, where Cass hopes to find his vision. En route, the children contract scarlet fever, and it seems a miracle that they survive. They do, though, and the family settles in Toulon to recuperate. Here Styron first presents the solution to Cass's despair. When Cass talks to his Catholic wife about his fear that the children would die, she says that she had known that they would get well. And Cass, so he writes in his journal, had said:

> How did she know. And she said—why I had FAITH, thats all silly. And then I blew my top—saying something on the order of Faith my ass, it was a man named Alexander Fleming who did it you idiot, and penicillin & 75,000 francs worth of medical care product not of faith in some disembodied gaseous vertebrate, and an hermaphrodite triply-damned incestuous one at that, but of mans own faith vain perhaps, but nonetheless faith in his hardwon decency & perfectability & his own compassionate concern with his mortal, agonizing plight on a half burnt out cinder that he didn't ask to be set down on in the first place. . . . Then she said again quite firmly & finally: I had faith. (STHOF, 294–295)

Poppy knows that "the believer possesses the eternally certain antidote to despair, viz. possibility; for with God all things are possible every instant. This is the sound health of faith . . ." (TSUD, 61) But Cass still rejects faith.

In conscious despair, his first impulse had been to commit suicide, in despair to will not to be himself. At Toulon he articulates for the first time his death-wish, mentioned earlier in the novel (STHOF, 55, 118, 195, 196, 238) but not earlier chronologically; he writes in his journal, "At least I understand the quality & quantity of what I do possess which is a mysterious self-hatred . . ." (STHOF, 293). He hates his weakness, as Kierkegaard predicts that a despairer should: "Just as a father disinherits a son, so the self is not willing to recognize itself after it has been so weak. In its despair it cannot forget this weakness, it hates itself in a way, . . ." (TSUD, 100).

In his state, Cass can find no peace, so the Kinsolvings move to Florence, then to Rome. Again Cass tries to "live on only with . . . immediacy" (TSUD, 83). "The world of taste and sight and sound—all the sweet sensations Nature granted to the most uncomplicated mortal—were his once more; the air dripped sunlight, his nostrils quivered to long-forgotten odors, he felt he might live to a ripe old age" (STHOF, 296). Cass is still the "immediate" man: "He now acquires some little understanding of life, he learns to imitate the other men, noting how they manage to live, and so he too lives after a sort" (TSUD, 83). The card game with the McCabes ends Cass's attempts to live the conventional life. At its cataclysmic conclusion, he rushes out into the life that he had abandoned in Paris.

Again filled with despair, Cass had drunkenly picked up a whore. Though he does not know the reason for his actions, Kierkegaard does: the despairer "will seek forgetfulness in sensuality, perhaps in debauchery, in desperation he wants to return to immediacy, . . ." (TSUD, 105). When he had become conscious, Cass found himself lying naked in a filthy hotel room.

> For long perplexing minutes he grappled with the question of how came he there, and when, and why; there was a terrifying instant when he could not recall his own name. . . . All identity had fled him and he lay there quietly breathing—. . . After a time, by the slowest of stages, he regained his bearings; memory and reality came slipping back, as did his name, which he spelled out slowly to himself—K-i-n-s— . . . (STHOF, 309)

He is still the "immediate" man, for "the immediate man does not recognize his self, he recognizes himself only by his dress, he recognizes . . . he recognizes that he has a self only by externals" (TSUD, 84).

Here again Cass has the vision of "whirling carrousels and orange blossoms and the black eyes of girls" (STHOF, 311) that symbolizes immediacy to him. And here too Cass moves into a further stage of despair. He had been in despair at not willing to be himself; still Christianly oriented, he had despairingly thought of suicide, but fearing no end of his despair in death, he had attempted to keep his self drugged by immediacy or inebriation. Now he wills despairingly to be himself; he is defiant about his condition. As he sprawls on the vermin-infested bed, he screams, "*Dio non esiste!*" and, again, "*Non c'è Dio!*" (STHOF, 311) These screams mark his entry into the new state of despair:

> In order to will in despair to be oneself there must be consciousness of the infinite self. This infinite self, however, is really only the abstractest form, the abstractest possibility of the self, and it is this self the man despairingly wills to be, detaching the self from every relation to the Power which posited it, or detaching it from the conception that there is such a Power in existence. (TSUD, 108–109)

The recurrent vision of immediacy lures Cass again. He flees south to Sambuco, where he finds the externalization of his vision; deciding to stay there, he returns with his family. His life becomes again a drunken nightmare of anxiety (STHOF, 341) and deathwishes (STHOF, 362). He continues to have the same conscience-stricken dream, only the Kierkegaardian "glass case" now becomes an airplane shower stall in which he is executed (STHOF, 368).

In his half-mad state, Cass meets three people who will change his life: Mason Flagg, Luigi Migliori, and Francesca Ricci. Francesca comes to symbolize the vision of happiness for him; he later tells Leverett, "No, I found some kind of *joy* in her, you see—not just pleasure—this joy I felt I'd been searching for all my life, and it was almost enough to preserve my sanity all by itself. *Joy*, you see—a kind of serenity and repose that I never really knew existed" (STHOF, 439–440). And through her, Cass meets the sick Michele, her father, who becomes Cass's chance to escape the torments of his despairing self.

The dream in which Cass had always been guilty of some enormous, nameless crime and had been executed for it had always contained Negroes. Once Cass tells Leverett of this dream: "Ever since I'd been in Europe about half of whatever nightmares I'd had—the ones I remembered, anyway—had been tied up with Negroes. Negroes in prison, Negroes being gassed, me being gassed, Negroes watching me *while* I was being gassed. Like that terrible dream in Paris" (STHOF, 369). Finally in Sambuco, Cass had thought of the repressed origin of his guilt; as a boy he had participated in an act of cruelty to a Negro sharecropper, so for years he had been plagued by a guilty self-hatred. At his meeting with Flagg, Cass had betrayed his guilt by saying, "The only true experience, by God . . . is the one where a man learns to love himself. And his country!" As he later says,

> And as I said these words, and turned around, why so help me God that nightmare I'd had came crashing back like a wave, and then those Negroes and that ruined cabin so long ago and all of that, which seemed

to be the symbol of the no-count bastard I'd been all my life, and I became absolutely twisted and wrenched with a feeling I'd never felt before— guilt and homesickness and remorse and pity all combined—and I felt the tears streaming idiotically down my cheeks. (STHOF, 398)

As he struggles to live in his nightmare, Cass is torn between two people. He sees in Francesca the vision of immediacy, and he receives from Flagg the liquor he uses to keep his self drowned. His going to Michele's hut is the incident that tears him from Flagg, for the smell prompts him to think, "It is niggers. The same thing, by God. It is the smell of a black sharecropper's cabin in Sussex County, Virginia. It is the bleeding stink of wretchedness" (STHOF, 416).

Cass immediately grasps at the opportunity to expiate his old guilt by helping the consumptive Michele. Since he has no money, his only method of securing drugs is to ask Flagg for them. Flagg agrees—but only if Cass will virtually become his slave. Cass does anything Flagg asks, for as Cass later says, ". . . the paradox is that this slavish contact with Mason that I had to preserve in order to save Michele freed me to come into that knowledge of selflessness I had thirsted for . . ." (STHOF, 443).

When Francesca is raped and killed, Cass kills Mason, the assumed rapist-murderer. Then he runs from the town, "running not from punishment but as if from the last shred and vestige of the self with which he had been born, . . ." (STHOF, 478). Thereafter he hides, until he decides to return home, there to kill his family and himself. On his way to town, he learns of Michele's death, and at that he faints.

As he later remembers, he awakened in the police station with but one idea, "And that was that I should be punished . . ." (STHOF, 490). He wills in his despair to be himself, but Luigi shows Cass the solution. To Cass's pleas for judgment, Luigi shouts, "You *sin* in your guilt!" (STHOF, 494), thereby applying the Kierkegaardian definition of sin: "Sin is this: before God, or with the conception of God, to be in despair at not willing to be oneself, or in despair at willing to be oneself" (TSUD, 123). Then Luigi says, "Consider the *good* in yourself!" (STHOF, 499).

When Luigi sets him free, Cass realizes that "the anxiety and the anguish—most of it, anyway—had passed" (STHOF, 499). Whether he is free of despair, he never says; evasively he says only "that as for being and nothingness, the one thing I did know was that to choose between them was simply to choose being, . . ." (STHOF, 500). Whatever the state of his soul, Cass Kinsolving is most appropriately named: throughout the novel he struggles desperately to solve the relationship between his God and himself.

Notes

1. William Styron, *Set This House on Fire* (New York: Random House, 1960). Hereafter, references in the text will be to STHOF.

2. Robert Gorham Davis, "Styron and the Students," *Critique*, 3 (Summer 1960), 44.

3. David L. Stevenson, "Styron and the Fiction of the Fifties," *Critique*, 3 (Summer 1960), 47.

4. John Howard Lawson, "Styron: Darkness and Fire in the Modern Novel," *Mainstream*, 13 (October 1960), 17.

5. Ihab Hassan, "The Character of Post-War Fiction in America," *English Journal*, 51 (January 1962), 7.

6. Sören Kierkegaard, *The Sickness Unto Death*, trans. Walter Lowrie (Princeton: Princeton Univ. Press, 1941). Hereafter, references in the text will be to TSUD.

Adjustment, Tragic Humanism and Italy: Styron's
Set This House on Fire

Anthony Winner*

"How shall I ever again endure the restraint and bondage of Boston?" asked W. W. Story, the American sculptor, writing home from Italy in 1848. In Boston, he said, "there is no such thing as flesh and blood. . . . the sky itself is cold and distant. The heart grows into stone."[1] Story was a professional expatriate and hence a special case, but his opinions were shared by many other Americans who, coming to Italy in search of Tradition and the picturesque, became fascinated by the country's sensual warmth. In the nineteenth century, when amateur anthropology or psychology did not compete with simple tourism, the prevalent image of Italy was that suggested by Van Wyck Brooks' title, "the dream of Arcadia." Longfellow may be taken as typical of general opinion when he refers to Italy as "the land of sun, and the land of song. . . . the land of dreams and visions of delight."[2] This sunny image, however, was often modified by a titillating consciousness of the darker possibilities of an exotic Italy. And, for a selected few, the gothic expectations fostered by Washington Irving out of Walpole and Mrs. Radcliffe seemed to conform to a reality far more ambiguous than that associated with ghost tales or Byronic poses. For those sensitive to the less smiling aspects of life, Italy inspired nightmares as well as visions of delight. Describing Rome in a letter of 1900, William James employs a vocabulary that would be equally appropriate to an imaginative evocation of the mysteries of the unconscious:

> The things the eyes most gloat on, the inconceivably corrupted, besmeared and ulcerated surfaces, the black and cavernous glimpses of interiors, have no suggestions save of moral horror, and their tactile values, as Berenson would say, are pure gooseflesh. Nevertheless, the sight of them delights.[3]

William James' description comforms to a gothic tradition which uses Italy to provide settings for dark dramas of evil and guilt. Speaking of this symbolic Italy, Leslie Fiedler notes that "it is Italy, the Mediterra-

*Reprinted in abridged form from Studi Americani, 7 (1961), 311–61, by permission of the author.

nean South with its overtones of papistry and lust, that is the true ghost"
haunting the protagonists of gothic fables. "Through a dream landscape,
usually called by the name of some actual Italian place, a girl flees in terror and alone amid crumbling castles, antique dungeons, and ghosts who
are never really ghosts."[4] This plot is varied by Hawthorne, touched on by
Henry James and most recently revived by William Styron in *Set This
House on Fire,* a novel we shall presently discuss at some length. Despite
its often absurdly theatrical devices, the gothic romance seems to provide
an apt set of symbols for those who would plumb what Hawthorne, in
The Marble Faun, terms "those dark caverns into which men must de-
scend if they would know anything beneath the surface and illusive
pleasures of existence." Gothicism's thematic bias is well described by
Leslie Fiedler:

> Implicit in the gothic novel from the beginning is a final way of
> redeeming it that is precisely opposite in its implications to the device of
> the explained supernatural, a way of proving not that its terror is less true
> than it seems but more true. There *is* a place in men's lives where pictures
> do in fact bleed, ghosts gibber and shriek, maidens run forever through
> mysterious landscapes from nameless foes; that place is, of course, the
> world of dreams and of the repressed guilts and fears that motivate them.
> This world the dogmatic optimism and shallow psychology of the Age of
> Reason had denied; and yet this world it is the final, perhaps the essential
> purpose of the gothic romance to assert. Between the lapsing of orthodox
> doctrines of original sin and the emergence of modern scientific theories of
> the unconscious, Europe possessed no dignified, recognized vocabulary
> for expressing certain dark truths about the human soul.[5]

Gothicism is also an intimate and perhaps inevitable corollary to the
dream of sun-drenched, sensual and luxuriant Italy. For the very promise
of flesh and blood, the license vouchsafed man's animal nature, contains a
threat of anarchy. To cater to the exigencies of primal forces is always to
court engulfment. Hence Italy becomes an extreme symbol combining not
only the dangers of the primitive but also the hazards which world-weary
European experience holds in store for American innocence. For those,
such as Henry James, who are concerned with this latter theme, the attractions of European culture are generally vitiated by the presence of
corruption and sin. As in the case of the dark crime of the de Bellegarde-s,
in *The American,* there is always a skeleton in the European closet. But
whereas England and France may offer terrible examples of accommodation with evil, Italy is frequently considered to be in and of itself mortally
dangerous. The country itself seems to exude poison vapors, like that
which struck down Daisy Miller. There is always the chance that in thaw-
ing out "restraint and bondage" primal forces may be unleashed and the
reign of terror which constitutes the gothic nightmare may become reality. To the decadence of European experience is added the threat of pre-
social evil. Luxuriance and exotic beauty may mask moral horror, as in

Hawthorne's "Rappaccini's Daughter," where Italy becomes a poisonous garden, a kind of anti-Eden.

The usefulness of Italy as a stage for foreign actors lies precisely in the balancing of gothic and what we may call Arcadian aspects. Italy's Arcadian qualities derive from the permissiveness of what Hawthorne termed "the particular mode of life, and its freedom from the enthralments of Society."[6] While partaking of the revivification of the senses which so appealed to W. W. Story, most Americans sought freedom from social rigidity rather than from moral restraints. If the charm of Italy was, as Stendhal said, akin to that of being in love, the love affair was in general platonic and the love-object that "accumulation of history and culture" on which James placed such a premium in his study of Hawthorne. Innocent tourism, artistic training, the pleasures of nature: these were the order of the day. Though many regretted Italy's "wicked misery" and attacked the tyranny of Austria or the Church, such negative reactions usually gave way before the country's exoticism, simplicity and human warmth.[7] Yet the innocent freedom of Arcadia was a pure delight only for those who could believe that man was by nature good and that there were no snakes in Eden. For those, such as Hawthorne or James, who conceived of original sin as an ineluctable part of the human condition, the state of nature fundamental to Arcadia threatened to encourage those dark forces which law and society had striven to restrain. As Daisy Miller found out to her cost, natural innocence *per se* is no protection against the gothic. Donatello, in *The Marble Faun*, is another case in point. In his story the sunny, picturesque and innocently amoral Arcadian Italy must confront the darkness, guilt and moral horror of the gothic Italy. Donatello's fall from innocence is a re-enactment of the drama of original sin. And it is notable that, from Hawthorne to William Styron, the Italian background has inspired a consideration of the dilemmas of innocence and evil.

Hawthorne and James were essentially concerned with the metaphysics of evil. Mr. Fiedler notwithstanding, one cannot properly equate their vision of man's imperfections with the forces psychology has subsumed within the concept of the Id. Numbers of modern writers have, however, made this equation. The idea of Italy as representative of the sensually impulsive South, geographical analogue to man's torrid libido, has come to re-inforce many assumptions already implicit in the gothic. In Thomas Mann's "Death in Venice," for example, Italy becomes the effective setting for the fulfilment of Aschenbach's vision of an over-ripe primeval wilderness, symbol of the festering impulses he has tried to repress. This vision makes Aschenbach "throb with terror, yet with a longing inexplicable" and draws him South to Venice, disease and death.

The current dream of Italy adds the insights of psychology to the generalized promise of sensual refreshment under a Southern sun. Though the dangers of the primitive inevitably lurk, like Mann's crouching tiger, in the background, the prevalent emphasis is on the therapeutic virtues of a "siren land." The basic attitude emerges clearly from D. H. Lawrence's explanation of why the Italians so delight in D'Annunzio's poetry:

> It was the language which did it. It was the Italian passion for rhetoric, for the speech which appeals to the senses and makes no demand on the mind. When an Englishman listens to a speech he wants at least to imagine that he understands thoroughly and impersonally what is meant. But an Italian only cares about the emotion. It is the movement, the physical effect of the language upon the blood which gives him supreme satisfaction. . . . He is like a child, hearing and feeling without understanding. It is the sensuous gratification he asks for.[8]

Unfortunately, Italy was not as unresponsive to D'Annunzio's message as Lawrence, writing in 1913, suggests. But we are concerned with an image whose necessities deal highhandedly with fact. The elements fundamental to Lawrence's description—emotionalism, sensualism, intense personalism and a closeness to childhood—recur insistently in the works which determine the modern American conception of Italy. One need only think of Ernest Hemingway's A Farewell to Arms. More recently, the kind of fascination Italy now exerts on American writers has been well stated by Eleanor Clark in Rome and a Villa. As in the nineteenth century, Italy is viewed as a land of dreams; however, Longfellow's innocent visions of delight have given way before psychoanalytic sophistication. Roman spaces seem to "open out or close up before you suddenly as in dreams, and a tormenting dreamlike sexual gaiety seems to rise you cannot tell how from the streets."[9]

> You walk close to your dreams. Sometimes it seems that these pulsing crowds, with their daily and yearly rhythms established so long ago none of it has to be decided any more, with their elbows and knees and souls and buttocks touching and rubbing and everybody most pleased and agreeable when it is like that, in a bus for instance, will in another minute all be naked, or will have fishtails or horses' behinds like the characters of the fountains. For the Anglo-Saxon mind, ruled by conscience and the romantic, rigid in its privacies, everything here is shocking—an endless revelation and immersion; this is the vocabulary of our sleep; and the key image is always water.[10]

Like Lawrence, Miss Clark slips a proselytizing note into her observations. It would be a good thing if the Anglo-Saxon conscience were shocked. We are in need of a therapeutic immersion; our arthritic rigidities should submit to "the gallant assault of Rome": an assault which is "total and terrible." This point of view is contingent on a belief that immersion in the unconscious is essentially salutary: that the primitive is a source of creativity and strength rather than a heart of darkness. Serious American writers, almost compulsively attuned to "the horrors of the

half-known life," tend to be less sanguine. Yet from the "beats" to the protagonists of Saul Bellow's *Henderson the Rain King* or William Styron's
Set This House on Fire, experience of, and rapprochement with, the
forces of the primitive are considered imperative. The significance of the
image projected by Lawrence and Miss Clark lies in the suggestion that
Italy is a country in particular and intimate relation with man's elemental
nature: an idea which, replacing the attractions of Tradition, now forms
the vital basis of Italy's appeal.

That Italy is closer to the essential and the natural than other countries, that Italians deal with life *ad hominem* undercutting the abstract
and the formal by insistent recourse to the personal, that in Italy man is
his own creature and not society's: these and other generalities constitute
a time-honored myth. Hawthorne, in the preface to *The Marble Faun,* explains that he has chosen Italy as his scene because it affords "a sort of
poetic or fairy precinct, where actualities would not be so terribly insisted
upon as they are, and must needs be, in America." In Italy, as Miss Clark
says, "you walk close to your dreams." In a world of poetry or dreams
characters are freed from irrelevant "actualities" and from "the enthralments of Society" and can act out their profoundest desires or dilemmas. For those disaffected with an America increasingly definable in
terms of such phrases as "the organization man," "the hidden persuaders"
and the "lonely crowd," Italy provides a special precinct within which
man seems safe from repressive or depersonalizing influences.

Attempting to explain the American thirst for ruins and shadows,
Ruskin observed in a letter written in 1856:

> After the scraped cleanliness and business and fussiness of America,
> mildew and mould may be meat and drink to you, and languor the best
> sort of life, and weeds a bewitchment. . . . the very sense that nobody
> about you is taking account of anything, but that all is going on into an
> unspelt, unsummed, undistinguished heap of helplessness must be a relief
> to you, coming out of that atmosphere of calculation.[11]

Ruskin's analysis is pertinent to the contrast between an unnaturally
over-structured America and an Italy in which nature has gone to seed
from lack of control. More importantly, however, the emphasis on helplessness and muddle serves to introduce a crucial extension of Italy's usabil-
ity. Americans interested in living in or "using" Italy, rather than in tour-
ing or transacting business, tend to accept the cliché of chauvinistic
regionalism which states that in the current period of industrialization and
modernization northern Italy has become indifferently European. According to this point of view, only the South remains truly Italian. Above
Florence, Americanization, with its gadgets and efficiency and depersonalization, is destroying what, in the eyes of foreigners at least, have
seemed to be Italy's prime virtues. The Italy sought out by those in flight
from institutional conformity must remain humanly picturesque, un-

sullied by progress. It must not be cleaned up, must remain true to the image Ruskin evokes. Inevitably, such an Italy will include not only mildew and mould, but poverty, sickness and human misery. Behind the picturesque and the human there exists the underdeveloped and the brutalized.

Italy's rewards are thus bound up in the spectacle of what Hawthorne termed its "wicked misery." Mark Twain was merely reflecting the split consciousness of other "innocents abroad" when he defined Italy as "that vast museum of magnificence and misery." A characteristic modern attitude is expressed by the protagonist of Irwin Shaw's *Two Weeks in Another Town*. During a visit to Rome, the hero is approached by a "ragged, bent woman with a dirty child in her arms" who demands alms and runs after him crying " 'Americano, Americano,' holding out her other hand, clawlike and filthy." Though he gives her a hundred lire, she stares:

> after him, ungrateful, unappeased, and he had the feeling that the hundred lire he had given her did not make up for the warmth of the meal he had just eaten, for the pretty girl by his side, for the luxury of the hotel rooms he was approaching.
> "It is to remind us," [his companion says]. . . . "Remind us of how close we are to Africa here in Italy. . . . and how we pay for it."[12]

The guilty conscience created by the spectacle of poverty and underdevelopment is, for Mr. Shaw's hero, merely a passing mood. For others, however, the matter is more serious.

The human misery which is woven into the very texture of life in parts of Italy recalls the theme of persecution so dear to the gothic world view. Beyond the superficial tourist's guilt felt by the protagonist of *Two Weeks in Another Town* there can also be a profound sense of implication in the tragic discrepancies of the human condition. An attitude which activates the American's sense of guilt and calls into play his complex and haunted sense of mission.

Discussing the particular suitability of the gothic form for the portrayal and working-out of guilt, Leslie Fiedler notes that:

> In the United States, certain special guilts awaited projection in the gothic form. A dream of innocence had sent Europeans across the ocean to build a society immune to the compounded evil of the past. . . . But the slaughter of the Indians, who would not yield their lands to the carriers of utopia, and the abominations of the slave trade, in which the black man, rum, and money were inextricably entwined in a knot of guilt, provided new evidence that evil did not remain with the world that had been left behind.[13]

In the nineteenth century, a handful of socially conscious Americans found it easy to equate the tragic condition of the Negro with that of the Italian degraded and oppressed by foreign powers of the Church. Visiting a goldsmith's shop in Rome, Harriet Beecher Stowe was presented with the sculpted head of an Egyptian slave. "Madam," one of the owners said, "we know what you have been to the poor slave. We ourselves are but poor slaves still in Italy. You feel for us."[14] In the mid-nineteenth century as now the spectacle of poverty and tyranny could awaken that tendency towards officious and even diabolic reformism imputed to Americans by numbers of writers from Hawthorne to Graham Greene. Yet, in this century at least, the putative equation between the Italian situation and the American can evoke a less equivocal response. Since Italy's problems are not in point of fact America's, except insofar as all men are implicated in human misery, involvement in these problems can be relatively objective; relieved of the virulent guilts which arise from complicity in America's dark past, concern with Italy's dilemmas can prove a cathartic experience. Moreover, while the ramifications of America's moral condition have become impossibly complex, Italy's "wicked misery" presents a seemingly more manageable challenge. As a literary image if not as a human fact, Italy offers the disaffected American an opportunity to come to terms with his own country and situation. Administering a wonder drug to an ill and poverty-stricken peasant in the Tramonti, the protagonist of *Set This House on Fire* must humor the dying man by indulging his belief in America as a kind of Eldorado. The hero feels "sudden pain and longing himself, and annoyance at the demeaning nostalgia and . . . wondering at the feeling, [realizes] simply that whatever else he might say against his native land, there would not be this particular gross wrong and insult to mortal flesh."[15]

Set This House on Fire employs a southern Italian town as its setting, but the particular episode just referred to could just as well take place in Africa, India or any other "underdeveloped" area. Indeed, one might legitimately object that many of the aspects we have discussed are not necessarily peculiar to the current image of Italy. Africa provides a more traditional metaphor for the darkness of the unconscious than does Italy. Sensualism and unrationalized emotionalism are at least equally the hallmark of the "mysterious" East or of Pacific isles. Italy must vie with Germany or even the American South as a gothic setting. Nor is Italy unique in providing a synthesis of the foregoing qualities. What makes the image of Italy unique and compelling is the combination of these qualities with the "accumulation of history and custom," that increment of tradition which was for Henry James and others the very heart of "the denser, richer, warmer European spectacle." Especially for those who now react against the over-valuation of rationalism, against the myopic vision of man's potentialities and fate by the eighteenth century dream of progress, Italy's balancing of darkness and light seems profoundly pertinent. In fact, the point of view implicit in the modern ideal of Italy appears closely related to the message which John Strachey, in a recent article, discovers in the work of Koestler, Pasternak and other contemporary anti-rationalists:

Unless we give far greater weight to the subjective side of man, unless we recognize the power of Pasternak's *troika* of values [Christianity, love and art], we shall achieve only disasters. The creativeness of personal relations, of aesthetics or of religious experience, is what matters today, wherever at any rate the economic problem is on the way to solution.[16]

Particularly for those Americans who, rebelling against depersonalization and a purely mechanistic ideology of progress, seek a setting for subjectivism that will not at the same time involve a total capitulation to the primitive, Italy comes to represent a promised land. What is being sought is less a descent into the maelstrom of the unconscious than an accommodation of the darkness with the light. The African heart of darkness, the irresponsible sensualism of tropic daydreams, the paralysingly brutal misery of many areas of the world: each might offset American innocence and untangle the contortions created by American life. But such extremes would go beyond the intention of therapy; such shock treatment might maim instead of heal. Italy's social dilemmas are solvable; its gothic potential is balanced by that myth of the triumphantly unified ego, "the Renaissance man"; its sensualism is seen in the light of "the creativeness of personal relations." And if these statements seem too good to be accurate, we must remember that literal accuracy is not the province of dreams. The American dream of Italy merely projects upon a foreign background images of fear and hope which serve to suggest the dreamer's private necessities.

II.

In its hugeness of theme and scope, William Styron's *Set This House on Fire* is a most characteristically American novel. The title is taken from a passage in which John Donne speaks of God's efforts to win back the errant soul. All other methods of persuasion having failed, the body which houses the soul is set on fire as a symbolic foretaste of the utter desolation of damnation. To reject God's love is to invite eternal seclusion from this love, an eternally, unconsummated firing of desire. Mr. Styron's novel treats not only the themes of faith, love and evil, but also such matters as the problem of guilt, the role and education of the artist and the difficulties involved in achieving a viable identity as an American. Unfortunately, this grandness of intention is often compromised by tenuous structural devices and the presence of unsuccessful passages and scenes. Yet the level of achievement is in general high. The serious attempt both to examine and to resolve the crucial dilemmas already noted in this essay is conducted with a subtlety and awareness of complexity which are the evidence of mature and certain talent.

Set in a town named Sambuco, romantically isolated among the cliffs overlooking Amalfi, *Set This House on Fire* unfolds against a desolate and mysterious nighttime landscape. Most of the peripheral characters are drawn from film-land's *dolce vita*—a world which, as Nathaniel West realized, provides a wonderfully appropriate atmosphere for modern gothicism. Mr. Styron is almost hyper-conscious of the gothic tradition. The film being shot at Sambuco is a modern-dress version of the Beatrice Cenci story: a tragic tale of patricide and incest which figures importantly in both *Pierre* and *The Marble Faun*. While eschewing supernatural devices, the action is none the less devoted to the most extreme and melodramatic situations. The tone is set at the very beginning of the novel when the narrator, Peter Leverett, declares that the "awesome and shocking" events he is to describe include "a murder and a rape which ended, too, in death, along with a series of other incidents not so violent yet grim and distressing" (p. 4). The gothic role of hero-villain is divided between two characters: Cass Kinsolving, a self-destroying, guilt-ridden artist seeking to free himself into "the condition of love," and Mason Flagg, a wealthy American in search of sensation and dominance. In a similar fashion the "persecuted maiden" and the "living symbol of eternal motherhood," occasionally presented as one figure in gothic romances, are here separated. The former role is assigned to the beautiful Francesca, who is pursued, raped and finally murdered. The latter function falls to Cass's wife, Poppy, whose somewhat simple-minded refusal of all intellectual or rational complexity is highly appropriate to a stereotype of the female principle.

The novel's central action is compressed into one nightmarish day and night. Just before returning to the States after several years in Italy, Peter Leverett receives an invitation from Mason Flagg, whom he had known at school in Virginia, to spend a week in Sambuco. En route from Rome, Leverett runs down a cyclist; though in no way responsible for the accident, he must bear the hysterical insults of the young man's mother, who blames all Italy's woes on the Americans. Burdened with a dazed sense of guilt and totally exhausted, he arrives in Sambuco. The town is over-run by members of the film unit; Mason, who has rented the ancient and picturesque Palazzo d'Affitto, is acting as amateur impresario and host. After a troubled sleep, Leverett joins the guests at the Palazzo. The party, incongruous enough in its mélange of grotesque personalities, is made even stranger by a background of mysterious sights and sounds. A girl runs screaming down the corridors; Mason enters in angry pursuit, his face scratched and bloody; from the floor below a phonograph blastingly alternates a hillbilly revival song and Mozart's *Don Giovanni*. Cass Kinsolving, who, it turns out, lives in the Palazzo and owns the phonograph, enters, drunkenly ranting speeches from *Oedipus at Colonus*. Holding out the promise of a bottle of whiskey, Mason lures Cass into performing a series of obscene and humiliating imitations. Sickened by the spectacle, Leverett intervenes and, somewhat later, is persuaded by Cass to hike to a neighboring valley in order to help attend a dying peasant. Returning to the Palazzo, he falls into an exhausted sleep which is troubled by nightmare fantasies woven around mysterious cries and screams. When he awakens late the next day, he learns that these screams had been part of a reality more terrible than his dreams. The girl has been raped and murdered presumably by Mason, who has committed suicide.

This chain of events forms the subject of a series of encounters between Leverett and Cass which take place a few years later and in which the two men attempt to discover the significance of the gothic tragedy and their own roles in it. Their desire, of course, is to achieve catharsis. The first step in this direction, however, makes it evident that they must begin by trying to reach some conclusion about Mason, whose ambiguous friendship with Leverett and attempt to possess Cass' soul are crucial to the tragedy's meaning. Is Mason evil or merely vile? The name Mason Flagg suggests that its bearer may be particularly representative of his country. Is America then evil or vile? Partial answers to these questions are contained in two flashbacks dealing with Leverett's friendship with Mason in the years before the Sambuco episode. In the first of these, Leverett recalls Mason as he had known him when they were both at boarding school. Son of a multimillionaire investor and a doting, ego-centric mother, Mason appears superficially to have all the advantages: money, dynamic personal charm, intelligence. Yet he seems from the beginning a weird mixture of Claggart, Gatsby and Dmitri Karamozov. Mason's morals are more or less a product of the world inhabited by his shallow, self-indulgent and hysterically self-pitying mother, whose assumptions about life resemble those of the *dolce vita*. What Mason is to become, however, results from an attempt to reconcile this kind of degeneracy with the image of his father: an almost mythic figure, a modern robber baron who combines a pioneer's rectitude with a "sheer, annihilating authority," an "almost regal" power of will (p. 91). When Mason is expelled from school for having seduced a feeble-minded young girl, his father rejects him as a "contemptible *swine*" (p. 92). His mother, on the other hand, is fast won over by his charm. Whether Mason is a contemptible swine or a monster of evil is a question which must be set aside for later discussion. The point of this presentation of Mason's background is seemingly to suggest that his later triumphs are a successful attempt to imitate his father's kinetically masculine authority without any right to such authority. Mason's mother provides the model for his assertions of will and hence the world in which he will choose to live is one in which moral discrimination and integrity have been undermined by moral dissipation. Mason will live a dynamically false lie in a society of weaker lies; he will achieve his goals by an exploitation of the corruption and guilt in others.

The action in the second flashback occurs years later when Leverett encounters Mason in a Greenwich village bar. Mason is now an aspiring playwright. The play he is working on deals with his own experiences during World War II. As he tells it to Leverett, the story is a marvelous cloak and dagger affair taking place in Yugoslavia and including the love of a beautiful native girl, the death of a faithful comrade and a hair-raising last-minute escape. The life Mason leads seems almost as fabulous as his story. Living in an artist's studio, done up in such a way as to combine Beverly Hills and Bohemia, Mason has absorbed characteristics of both the Artist and the Beat. He has become a sort of walking encyclopedia of facts and theories, wearing "his really rather amazing erudition flashily and blatantly, like a man outfitted for a costume ball" (p. 147). As opposed to Leverett, who calls himself a "square," Mason is a fully engaged denizen of what he terms *"le nouveau libertinage."*

> Sex is the last frontier [he tells Leverett] . . . the only area left where men can find full expression of their individuality, full freedom. Where men can cast off the constrictions and conventions of society and regain their identity as humans. And I don't mean any dreary, dry little middle-class grope and spasm, either. I mean the total exploration of sex, as Sade envisioned it.

Following this cult, Mason explores the fringe world of drugs, orgies and occult erotica. With Carol, his lush mistress, he leads a night-time life of compulsive depravity; with Celia, his lovely wife, he becomes during the day a model of intelligent respectability and charm.

Leverett's reaction to Mason is one of fascination and disgust. He feels Mason to be "more imaginative, more intelligent than [himself], and at the same time more corrupt" (p. 136). During this period Mason pays the bills, supplies the girls and acts as stage manager for Leverett's life. The latter is awed and grateful but at the same time disturbed by the thought that it might be "possible to remain under Mason's aegis" for the rest of his days: "Because if I suspected that there was a lust for a kind of ownership in these big gestures of Mason's, I also realized with some shame that my willingness to be owned was stronger than I ever wanted to admit" (p. 149). Yet, if Mason's lust for ownership and extensive corruption disturb, the scale of his powers and activities is still extraordinary and impressive.

> The more I saw of Mason in this dual role of daytime squire and night-time nihilist . . . the more it became apparent to me that here was a truly distinctive young American—able in time of hideous surfeit, and Togetherness' lurid mist, to revolt from conventional values, to plunge into a chic vortex of sensation, dope, and fabricated sin, though all the while retaining a strong grip on his two million dollars. (p. 158)
>
> Rich, gloriously handsome, erudite, witty, gifted, a hero of the war, with a wife over whom the goddesses must grind their teeth in rage—what else could a man wish to be? Could the earth hold more youthful promise? Beside him . . . I felt pitifully small, and I gloomed over all that . . . forbade me to see all that I disapproved of in him as a superb Renaissance spilling-over, manly as a stud horse, instead of corruption. (p. 160)

The night before Leverett is to leave for Italy, Celia, Mason's wife, bursts into his apartment. Mason has attacked her and she is bruised and hysterical. From her Leverett learns that Mason's war record is a complete fabrication: a draft dodger, he was never in Yugoslavia and never wounded. Celia, however, is still hopelessly in love, and defends Mason's lie as "only a part of that breadth and vastness of his whole personality, part of his *vision* of life, which was so broad and encompassing that it just had to include exaggeration and stretchings of truth?" (p. 162). Celia, though lovely and charming, is only a superficially educated college girl; like Mason's other women, she regards him as a kind of matinee idol. She accepts his seeming deficiencies as part of a pattern too grand for her understanding. Innocent and vulnerable, she is a perfect subject for Mason's hypnotic mastery; indeed, as Leverett learns at this end of this, Mason has been systematically driving her insane by refusing to make love to her.

Celia's story and example are sordid enough illustrations of Mason's corrupt influence. Yet, in order to explain why, several years later, Leverett will accept Mason's invitation to Sambuco, they must be juxtaposed against a quite different idea of Mason's character. The morning after the episode with Celia, Mason appears on shipboard to wish Leverett farewell. Having stocked Leverett's cabin with a Midas horde of gifts, he proceeds to refer once again to his war experiences. Leverett, rebellious and enraged, calls him a liar. Seemingly stunned, Mason crumples before the charge, weakly pleading friendship:

> His shoulder still heaving as if with palsy, he took my hand, turning that simple gesture of farewell into the sorriest act of loneliness, of naked longing, I think I have ever known. . . . Before I could say another word . . . he was gone . . . leaving my hand clutched around a wad of French money. . . . Mortified, I tried to call out after him, but already he was lost from sight—except for one last brief glimpse I had of him at the top of a distant stairway: with his head bent down there seeking the steps he looked curiously clumsy and inept; not the old breezy magician but vulnerable, bumbling and for an instant wildly confused—future's darling, a man with one foot poised in the thinnest of air. (pp. 173–74)

Mason's last gift reminds Leverett of the story of the unpopular rich boy who spends his allowance buying other children's company; the gesture is "one of recompense and hire, and laden with the anguish of friendlessness" (p. 173). At the same time we remember that Mason's *nouveau libertinage* is a most gloomy cult: that at no point does he appear truly involved in his debauchery, remaining always somehow apart, serious and lonely. For Leverett, it is the mysterious contrast between pathetic insecurity and epitomized youthful promise that allows Mason to retain a measure of his original stature.

The first half of *Set This House on Fire* is devoted in large part to Leverett's bewildered description of the events at Sambuco and to the two flashbacks just discussed. Both because Leverett is incompletely realized as a character and because he partakes of the moral disorientation Mason personifies, his narrative is rarely convincing enough to permit a willing suspension of disbelief. However, in the second half of the novel, Leverett is set aside and Cass Kinsolving, the man whose house has been set on fire and the book's true protagonist, steps to the center of the stage. Seen in antagonism to Cass, Mason becomes for the first time a believably complex and meaningful character. As Cass relates the story of his life to Leverett, we come to realize that the Sambuco tragedy embodies for him the two extremes of the Italian myth. The pure and beautiful Francesca promises salvation in Arcadia; Mason, the evil genius whose power derives from the guilts and failures of others, threatens to corrupt Arcadia and to damn the searching soul to gothic darkness.

Cass's background is not presented with much fulness. A poor Southerner, he joined the army at an early age and suffered some form of shell-shock during the war. While recuperating, he meets a psychoanalyst who, though unable to help in any formal way, takes a liking to him and presses him to attempt a career as an artist. From this point onwards Cass develops into a complexly fragmented figure. Unable to believe in God, he none the less retains the manner of a Southern Baptist preacher; self-educated in bits and snatches, he uses what culture he has achieved (mostly, it would seem, Greek tragedy) to provide a correlative to his own dilemmas. These dilemmas are tremendous if obscure. Cass is afflicted with a lacerating sense of guilt which poisons his existence; convinced he is in some way evil, he tries to blind self-hatred with alcohol. But drunk or sober he must do battle: laying siege with despairing awkwardness to the repressed truths which somehow keep him from the freedom of self-knowledge and the uninhibited enjoyment of love and practice of art.

Through a process of self-analysis confusedly compounding Sophocles and Freud, Cass reconstructs the two seminal episodes of his early life. The first is a brief encounter with a young girl who manages to combine the vocabulary of Jehovah's Witnesses with an ingenuous yet somehow completely pure commitment to the wonders of the body and of love. From her, Cass learns of the redemption obtainable through love unmarred by guilt. The memory of their encounter becomes a vision of sensual honesty similar to that suggested by Lawrence. The second episode is equally decisive: a classically traumatic experience which Cass represses and which comes to light only near the end of the novel. At fifteen, spurred on despite his initial unwillingness by the vindictive rage of a salesman for whom he is working, Cass takes part in the brutal destruction of a Negro's home. Caught up in the salesman's orgasm of hatred, Cass becomes for a moment not a man but a beast. The vision of love born of the encounter with the girl leads Cass to marry Poppy, an earth-mother type, innocent of evil and complexity to the point of simple-mindedness, yet completely honest, good and devoted. The destruction of the Negro's home, combined in an unclear way with Cass' war record, produces an unfocused but overpowering sense of sin, a self-hatred which forces Cass to the verge of alcoholic suicide.

The two episodes Cass relates motivate and determine his actions during the period preceding his arrival in Sambuco. His story begins in Paris where, accompanied by Poppy and his brood of children, he has gone in hopes of finding an atmosphere exempt from the falsifications which undermine the honest practice of art in the United States. Even in Paris, however, he is driven to drink and, physically exhausted as well as emotionally depleted, he undergoes a peculiar type of nervous breakdown. He is seized by brief but remarkably intense visions whose effect is evoked by means of the vocabulary of mystical communion: rapture, perception of essence, of the "elseness" of beauty divorced from but including the self, achievement of passive selflessness before the in-dwelling of the Godhead:

> . . . when you try to describe a—a state like this. You end up like some shaggy tenth-century anchorite, hooting and hollering that he's been raped by a platoon of angels. . . . Well, anyway, maybe you can see how, if I got such a boot out of these spells, I didn't want to give up the very thing that caused them, even if the very thing that caused them was a self-destructive thing of booze and slow starvation and nervous exhaustion. Suicide, really. (pp. 257–58)

Though the vision of selflessness, of oneness with that natural goodness of grace which all men possess though few can realize, will have crucial implications in the novel, Cass rejects the state of rapture for what it is: "a sick drunken daydream, with no more logic or truth in it than the hallucination of some poor old mad starving hermit" (p. 270). The knowledge that the daydream is specious exacerbates Cass' sense of guilt and stimulates his urge to self-destruction, which now amounts almost to a lust for death. He conceives the idea of murdering his family and committing suicide, since "God was not even a lie, but worse, that He was weaker even than the evil He created" (pp. 275–76).

Before Cass can accomplish this massacre, however, he has a vision which seems to promise a far better life:

> And I saw some southern land with olive trees and orange blossoms, and girls with merry black eyes. . . . this smell of perfume and pines and orange blossoms and girls, all mixed up in one sweet blissful fragrance of peace and repose and joy. And over all of it, somehow, vague and indistinct but possessing the whole scene: a girl's sweet voice calling, some southern Lorelei calling me and beckoning me on. (pp. 276–77)

The dream, as Cass interprets it, is of some sort of salvation in Italy. The "southern Lorelei" promises a fulfilment of the hope of sensual wholeness born of the youthful episode Cass has already described. Drawn by this promise, Cass moves his family to the south of France, to Florence and finally to Rome, where he manages to re-establish a semblance of normal life. He removes "himself from the seductive world of the night and from erotic daydreams and sour semi-suicidal moods, brushing his teeth twice a day and polishing his shoes and cleansing his breath with Listerine" (p. 296).

> Yet this state in itself had its drastic shortcomings. . . . the closer he approached this condition of palmy beatitude—the whole man operating with all his God-given faculties wide-open—the closer, paradoxically, he saw himself coming to be a nice young fellow with a blurred grin, a kind of emotional eunuch in whom that necessary part of the self which saw the world with passion and recklessness, and which had to be flayed and exacerbated and even maddened to retain its vision had been cut away. . . . (pp. 296–97)

Convinced that life has become "flat, stupid, sterile" (p. 297), he lapses back into alcoholism at the first opportunity. Again the need to escape possesses him. Half-maddened, yelling revival hymns and gulping Grappa, he drives southward on his Vespa in search of his promised land. He runs out of gas near Sambuco, enters the town, and is arrested for making a drunken disturbance in the local hotel. At the Sambuco police station, Cass meets two of three characters who will preside over his fate: Francesca, a beautiful peasant girl, the Lorelei of his vision; and Luigi, a self-educated policeman who claims, paradoxically, to be both a fascist and a humanist. Taken by the beauty of the town and tantalized by the memory of the girl, Cass decides to settle down. He brings his family to Sambuco where, practically penniless, usually drunk, he passes the time until Mason's unexpected arrival.

Cass continually refers to his experiences in Europe as an awakening. From another point of view, his behavior suggests that of a man in the throes of a particularly tense and difficult course of psychoanalysis. Having refused the alien and mechanistic aid of a professional analyst, Cass is attempting alone the painful process of self-discovery and liberation. The interim period spent in Sambuco before Mason's appearance marks a crisis in this process. Alone, except for his loving but uncomprehending wife and for the occasional company of Luigi, who comprehends but cannot help, Cass manages to dredge up the repressed memory of the episode with the Negro. Since this memory is among the most essential causes of his self-castigating guilt, the fact that Cass can now contemplate it has crucial significance. As Cass explains to Leverett in the course of their long dialogue:

> No, there are no amends or atonement for a thing like that. But there is another thing, and though it won't bring back any busted stove or plaster bulldog . . . it's something, and it's strong. What I mean is, you live with it. You live with it even when you've put it out of your mind—or think you have—and maybe there's some penance or justice in that. (p. 379)

At this moment of recognition, and consequent intensification of trauma and self-hatred, Mason enters Sambuco in his cerise Cadillac: "this loose long lanky Mason, handsome as a Vitalis ad and looking about as American as it's possible to get" (p. 381). Mistaking Cass for an American sculptor with a vaguely similar name, Mason proceeds to flatter him and to praise his work with a great display of platitudinous erudition. Mason's tone, the general falsity of the situation and the man, taken with a vulgar remark he makes about Francesca who re-enters the novel at this point by coming to ask Cass for a job, rapidly create a nightmarish situation. For Cass, Mason seems the very image of all he had come to Europe to escape:

> . . . the man in all those car advertisements—you know, the young guy waving there—he looks so beautiful and educated and everything. . . . And he's *going* places. I mean electronics. Politics. What they call communications. Advertising. Saleshood. Outer space. God only knows. And he's as ignorant as an Albanian peasant. (p. 392)

Perceiving at once all that Leverett had been unable to see, or tried to explain or whitewash, Cass denounces Mason to his face. Mason reacts with the same pitiful air of deflation and misery which Leverett has already noted. Yet even before Cass takes in Mason's reaction, he is stopped in the midst of his diatribe by a realization of his own position:

> "The only true experience, by God," I said, "is the one where a man learns to love himself. And his country!" And as I said these words . . . that nightmare I'd had came crashing back like a wave, and then those Negroes and that ruined cabin so long ago and all of that, which seemed to be the symbol of the no-count bastard I'd been all my life, and I became absolutely twisted and wrenched with a feeling I'd never felt before— guilt and homesickness and remorse and pity all combined—and I felt the tears streaming idiotically down my cheeks. (pp. 397–98)

Cass' tears indicate that he achieved a state of contrition. Substituting religious for psychoanalytic terms (a legitimate exercise, since Mr. Styron seems to consider the two vocabularies complementary), we may say that Cass is ready to commence the positive task of regeneration and rectification of the will. This task is rendered almost impossible, however, by the fact that Cass can accept neither formal theology nor formal analysis; in particular, he is unable to formulate for himself any stage beyond that of contrition. Unable to hope for heaven, he places his faith on a tenuous vision, amounting to a quasi-mystical affirmation of adjustment's ideals, of a potential wholeness somehow available to every man. Cass' house has been set on fire in order to bring him to the realization that he has denied love (the guiltless, selfless condition of freedom) and to impel him to fight to repossess his right to love. Mason arrives at the moment of realization and it soon becomes clear that he is the antagonist Cass must overcome if the vision of wholeness through love is to be achieved. Self-recognition and contrition do not in themselves guarantee cure or salvation. Cass' recognition of what a "no-count bastard" he has been can lead him either to the positive penance of facing, trying to live with his guilt or to the negative penance of rejecting his self and passively inviting destruction. As we shall see, Mason will provide the means by which the latter alternative may be accomplished, while Luigi will insist on the difficult virtues of the former. Throughout the climacteric of the novel, which begins with Mason's entrance, Francesca will embody the vision of love and thus provide a counterbalance to Mason, who embodies the perversion of love.

Playing on Cass' evident weaknesses (his desire for self-abasement, his penury and craving for liquor), Mason gradually enslaves him. He inveigles Cass into painting a pornographic picture in return for food and drink. This perversion of his art along with his ever-increasing need to drink stimulates Cass' sense of guilt and forces him further into Mason's power. He sinks so low as to become a kind of obscene jester for Mason's guests, performing at his master's command humiliating charades in the course of which he abandons every vestige of human dignity. Feeling he has no right to exist, he gives himself over to Mason's diabolic tyranny asking as his only reward an uninterrupted supply of whiskey. Yet, during this terrible period, there remains one human sector in which Cass is able to retain a measure of self-respect. The only times he rebels against Mason's domination are when Mason, who has hired Francesca as a servant, makes lewd remarks or suggestions about the girl. With Francesca, Cass hopes to free himself into the condition of love. Together, they conspire to steal supplies from Mason. These they carry to Francesca's father, a mortally tubercular peasant who lives in the poverty-stricken Tramonti some distance from Sambuco. Co-ordinate with Cass' love for Francesca is his attempt to cure Michele, her father. By curing Michele, who inhabits a hut which exudes the same "stink of wretchedness" as "a black sharecropper's cabin," Cass hopes to expiate his participation in the destruction of the Negro's home (p. 416). Moreover, listening to Michele's daydreams of America—the pathetic promised land of the peasant imagination, Cass is able to revise his own conception of his homeland, realizing "that whatever else he might say against his native land, there would not be this particular gross wrong and insult to mortal flesh" (p. 418).

Yet, in order to aid Michele, Cass must debase himself even further before Mason, who alone can provide the necessary drugs. The final act of the Sambuco tragedy begins when Mason refuses Cass the miracle drug which might save Michele's life; or rather, Mason withholds the drug, making its delivery contingent on Cass's performance of the sickening charades which are the symbol of his degradation. For the drug, like the liquor or indeed even Francesca, are important to Mason only as means for establishing what comes to seem an ambiguously sexual domination over Cass. Something of the complexity of Mason's feeling can be seen in the look he gives Cass after having refused to hand over the drug: a glance "composed in part of such hatred, [yet] made up in at least equal part of something else not quite love but its loathsome resemblance" (p. 429). In this regard, Mason's rape of Francesca later in the evening contains a curious symbolism. As Cass attempts to explain to Leverett:

> [Mason] knew that for a while he had the pluperfect victim—a man he could own completely, and who lay back and slopped up his food and his drink, and who was so close to total corruption himself that he gloried in being owned. But he sensed, too, that his victim had changed now, had found something—some focus, some strength, some reality. . . . by raping [Francesca] he raped the two of us: that night I felt he had committed some filthy, unspeakable violation upon life itself. (pp. 443–44)

The fundamental components of the action Leverett arrives to witness are: Cass' alcoholic stupor during which he performs the ghastly rite demanded by Mason and from which he later recovers sufficiently to enlist Leverett's aid in stealing the drug and in hiking into the Tramonti to administer it to Michele; Mason's rape of Francesca; the murder of Francesca by a feeble-minded town beggar; Cass' assumption that Mason has murdered Francesca and his subsequent murder of Mason. After the murders, Luigi, the assistant to the local police sergeant, arranges the evidence to make it appear that Mason had killed Francesca and then taken his own life. Luigi's reasons for indulging in a deception which might well ruin his own career form the most direct statement of the novel's moral thesis. Cass wants to give himself up, to go to jail and thus to continue his guilt-inspired abdication of will. Cass finds the idea of liberty appalling: "Yearning for enclosure, for confinement, I was faced with nothing but the vista of freedom like a wide and empty plain" (p. 442). Luigi, however, insists that Cass go free:

> ". . . this existence itself [he says] is an imprisonment. . . . Once we were at least able to talk with our Jailer, but now even He has gone away, leaving us alone with the knowledge of insufferable loss. . . . to confine any but the mad dogs among us is to compound that knowledge of insufferable loss with a blackness like the blackness of eternal night. I have seen prisons, they are the closest thing to hell on earth. And you are not a mad dog. I suppose I lied to keep you from this kind of banishment. But I suspect that is not all. I know you and your hideous sense of guilt too well. . . . In jail you would wallow in your guilt. As I say, I did not wish to allow you that luxury" (p. 497).
>
> "Simply consider your guilt itself—your other guilt, the abominable guilt you have carried with you so long, this sinful guilt which has made you a drunkard, and caused you to wallow in your self-pity, and made you fail in your art. . . . Ask what it was. Ask yourself whether it is not better to go free now, if only so that you may be able to strike down this

other guilt of yours and learn to enjoy whatever there is left in life to enjoy. Because if by now, through what you have endured, you have not
learned *something*, then . . . fifty years in jail will teach you nothing."
He came close to me. . . . "For the love of God, Cass," he said. "Consider
the *good* in yourself! Consider hope! Consider joy!" (p. 499)

Abandoned by God, and tortured by the evils and guilts inherent in
his nature, man's condition is dark indeed. Yet Luigi states that there is
good as well as evil and that man must battle against the surrounding
darkness in order to reclaim this good. It is this knowledge that Cass finally accepts. The death of Francesca and the murder of Mason are symbolically if not realistically inevitable. For both characters are in this
sense externalizations of Cass' struggle and victory: Francesca, an impossible but necessary goal, Arcadia's embodiment; Mason, the tyrannous, gothic projection of Cass' guilt. As the novel ends, Cass, now living
quietly in the South with his wife and children and earning a small income from painting and political cartooning, sums up his experience:

> "Now I suppose I should tell you that through some sort of suffering I
> had reached grace, and how at the moment I knew it, but this would not
> be true, because at that moment [of return to wife and country] I didn't
> really know what I had reached or found. I wish I could tell you that I
> had found some belief, some rock, and that here on this rock anything
> might prevail—that here madness might become reason, and grief joy,
> and no yes. And even death itself death no longer, but a resurrection.
> "But to be truthful, you see, I can only tell you this: that as for being
> and nothingness, the one thing I did know was that to choose between
> them was simply to choose being, not for the sake of being, or even the
> love of being, much less the desire to be forever—but in the hope of being
> what I could be for a time. This would be an ecstasy. God knows, it
> would." (pp. 500–01)

Near the beginning of *Set This House on Fire* there is a brief but vital
episode in which Peter Leverett, on his way to see Cass and to begin the
series of exchanges which will form the bulk of the novel, stops off to visit
his hometown in Virginia. The town's charm, its intimate relation to the
land and sea, in short its "peculiar romance," have been destroyed by
"progress" (p. 10). Its personality has been lost amid a welter of super-
highways, super-markets, houses bristling with television antennas and
flashy, impersonal developments. What once seemed Eden has become an
anonymous suburb. Leverett feels lost, sundered from his roots; he suggests that "perhaps one of the reasons we Americans are so exceptionally
nervous and driven is that our past is effaced almost before it is made
present" (p. 18). For Leverett's father, however, the fate of the town is
symbolic of an even more profound blight; the specious constructions of
progress reflect a complacent evasion:

. . . what this great land of ours needs is something to happen to it. Something ferocious and tragic, like what happened to Jericho or the cities of the plain—something terrible I mean, son, so that when people have been through hellfire and the crucible, and have suffered agony enough and grief, they'll be men again, human beings, not a bunch of smug contented hogs rooting at the troughs. Ciphers without mind or soul or heart. . . . We've sold our birthright . . . and you know what we've sold out for? A bunch of chromium junk from Detroit put together with chewing gum and spit! (p. 15)

The demand for agony and grief recalls the functions Leslie Fiedler assigns to gothicism. America's values have been corrupted by unthinking conformity to the ideals of gimcrack progress. We are a nation of spoilt children. Paralysed in perpetual adolescence, we can experience neither the complex fulness of adult emotions nor the challenge of adult responsibilities. Yet we delude ourselves that ours is the best of all conditions: that inexperience signifies innocence, that the statistics of progress are as valuable as the ideas and feelings which constitute understanding. Given this situation, our only hope for maturity lies in the experience of those sobering truths about human nature which official culture has repressed. Only by facing the ambiguities and even terrors which are as profound an aspect of our inheritance as our material achievements can we become men again. The meretricious façade of modern America represents a denial of certain dark truths which none the less endure below the threshold of the national consciousness. Our roots and these truths are inextricably intertwined: to reject the latter is to abandon the former, to be lost and incomplete.

The interdependence on public and private maturity is one of the major theses of *Set This House on Fire*. The condition of love Cass seeks is a synthesis of self-love, love of a good woman and love of country. The reverse of this condition involves self-hate, loveless sexuality (or impotence or homosexuality) and rejection of country: antithetical reactions which are associated with or reinforced by the figure of Mason Flagg. Mason is, as Leverett claims, a most representative American, but what he represents is the distorted, corrupt America attacked by Leverett's father. Mason's *nouveau libertinage*, his philosophy of sex as individualism's last frontier, is a pretentious product of adolescent prurience, a symptom of unachieved "genital maturity." Mason's over-ripe and essentially pleasureless concern with the erotic along with his tendency to impotence (apparently he makes love only to women he can treat as whores or victims) convinces Cass that he is nothing but "a bleeding little prude" (p. 441). Though never fully clarified, the homosexual element implicit in Mason's attempt to "possess" Leverett and Cass is equally indicative of a failure to achieve normal fulfilment. In Mason's character the impulses of love are transmogrified into a lust for power, a tyrannous and sadistic delight in dominating others. Whatever the specific explanation of his sexual maladjustment, it seems clear that Mason represents a nightmare image, a pathological end-product of America's denial of love.

From another point of view, however, Mason's febrile concern with sex may be seen as the *reductio ad nauseam* of popular psychology's preoccupation with such concepts as "genital maturity." In this regard as in many others, Mason's life appears a grandiose realization of the ideals and daydreams of a morally disoriented culture. His charm is that of the Madison Avenue stereotype of the perfect young American. His erudition is founded on the quiz program ideal of intelligence: the walking almanac. His corruption realizes the wish-fulfilment fantasies nurtured by popular semipornography. Successful businessman and aspiring playwright, he has one foot in Wall Street and the other in Bohemia and yet avoids becoming either "square" or "queer." Fulfilling so perfectly the ideals established by American mass media, Mason becomes the representative hero of a nation of "smug contented hogs" (p. 15). Yet Mason is more than a mere embodiment of specious ideals; if he were only that he could never hope to triumph over Cass. The moral horror Mason inspires stems less from his intrinsic fraudulence (he is neither businessman nor war hero, his artistic career and sexual prowess are fictions) than from his attempt to command that authority and "almost regal" power of will which were his father's most impressive characteristics. Corrupted by the egoism, hedonism and petulant self-pity of his mother's world, Mason none the less desires to enact the role and command the respect American tradition assigns to the virile, dynamic pioneer or the empire-building businessman. Since the moral basis of the "sheer, annihilating authority" Mason wants to assert is purely negative, the empire he would create and rule must be corrupt: a new version of the cities of the plain. Given this prospective, the positive values symbolized by Francesca and espoused by Cass become subversive and must be eliminated if Mason's ideology is to triumph. Mason's ultimate victory is dependent on his ability to subdue those like Cass whose goodness has been compromised by guilts and fears and to win over those like Leverett whose moral integrity has been weakened by the vitiating ideals which blight American life.

As a tyrannical embodiment of a false America, Mason is wholly convincing. Unfortunately, however, Mr. Styron wishes us to view Mason not just as a personification of the corrupt and the specious but also as an essentially weak, pitiful man whose force derives from the manipulation of a nation's guilts and terrors. The discontinuity between these two viewpoints seriously affects our reaction to Cass' killing of Mason. If Mason embodies an absolute principle of corruption, then this act becomes a justifiable tyrannicide; if, on the other hand, Mason is merely the pathetic little rich boy of Leverett's image, contemptible but not evil if properly understood, then Cass must be taken as a murderer. This all-important ambiguity arises because Mr. Styron tends to define evil in terms of psychology while at the same time being unable to abandon the idea of evil as an absolute and inexplicable moral phenomenon. Psychologically, evil is defined in reference to the irrational guilts which corrode the personality and inhibit wholeness; morally, evil is postulated as man's inhumanity to man, the inexplicable desire to oppress others. Behind these two approaches to evil we find a tension between the assumptions of adjustment psychology and those of tragic humanism. This becomes particularly clear in Mason's case when we realize that we are being asked both to understand his problem (hence to view his maladjustment as the pathetic result of parental influences) *and* to judge him as evil by the absolute moral standards of tragic humanism.

Mr. Styron's effort to combine the goal of adjustment with the standards of tragic humanism appears to better effect in his portrait of Cass. Self-reliant, of the people, strong in native decency and latent creativity, Cass is potentially Mason's opposite: the personification of all that is good in America. That he is for a long while unable to fulfil this function, that he squanders his resources in dissipation and self-hate, is due to his youthful experience of the evil in his own nature. By repressing the memory of his participation in an act of racial oppression, Cass compounds moral with psychological evil. Mr. Styron accepts Leslie Fiedler's assertion that such oppression is the characteristic American version of original sin and that the guilt thus generated is fundamental to American gothicism. Insofar as Cass provides the center of consciousness in *Set This House on Fire*, it may be said that the entire gothic tragedy at Sambuco is a projection of his "dreams and of the repressed guilts and fears that motivate them."[17] Cass' working backward from his monstrous guilt to the crime which produced that guilt is intended as a model of the profitable interaction of tragic humanism's fearless exposure of dark truths and adjustment's goal of living with these truths. Until we come to terms with the crime in which we are all implicated we cannot hope to achieve wholeness: cut off by an obscure sense of guilt from self-respect, we must either destroy whatever potential goodness it is still in our power to achieve or allow ourselves to become human flotsam, slaves of any stronger will. Since oppression is absolutely evil, our complicity in it, whether active or passive, cannot be expiated. Following Dostoevsky and other great tragic humanists, Mr. Styron insists that no one must be allowed to relieve us of the burden of our crime. Yet the knowledge of our terrible complicity is also the price of our maturity. Living with this knowledge provides some sort of atonement, or at least permits the attainment of a tragic realism which not only makes easy sentimental acceptance impossible but also frees us to perform the duties owed to common humanity and self-respect.

It is at this point that *Set This House on Fire* deviates from Leslie Fiedler's conception of the American gothic. Mason, the persecuting principle of damnation, projects not just the moral horror lying below the threshold of consciousness but also the power of "all institutions which might inhibit that freedom."[18] Both the dark forces of the id and the tyrannical super-ego are postulated as evil: hence the novel's moral viewpoint cannot be defined either as radical (though it attacks the institutions Mason reflects) or as conservative (though it equates certain forces of the id with evil). Moreover, the minimal adjustment Cass achieves would perhaps be termed an evasion by Mr. Fiedler, since this *modus vivendi* suggests that acceptance of the assumptions of tragic humanism need not, indeed should not, involve engulfment in the "blackness of darkness." What Cass achieves is an awareness of the darkness of the human condition tempered by a belief that life is none the less to be lived in joy as much as in sorrow. After the deaths of Francesca and Mason, the extreme embodiments of his ideal love and his self-hate, Cass is somehow freed to return to wife and country. He teaches art to "Sunday amateurs" and has a small success as a political cartoonist (p. 505). As opposed, for example, to Hawthorne's Goodman Brown, whose perception that all men are tainted with evil turns him into "a stern, a sad, a darkly meditative, a distrustful, if not a desperate man," Cass is able to achieve a measure of adjustment and happiness.

That Cass is able to survive "hellfire and the crucible," to emerge as a man instead of a debilitated and shadowy shell, is due to William Styron's revision of the absolute commitment to gothic darkness demanded by Leslie Fiedler. This revision is closely and specifically connected with certain of the therapeutic aspects of the current American myth of Italy. Not only is Cass beckoned southward by an Arcadian vision, he is also saved from virtual suicide by Luigi's insistence on the lessons to be learned from an initiation into the gothic. For if Francesca represents the ideal of guiltlessness and wholeness in love expressed by D. H. Lawrence and Eleanor Clark, then Luigi speaks with the authority of that experience of evil so crucial to the Hawthorne of *The Marble Faun*. Since America has denied or perverted love and evaded or repressed the tragic realities of life, the American attempting to repossess a just perspective tends to romanticize both aspects of experience and to endow them with a preternatural vividness. At one point Luigi accuses Cass of being "a damnable romantic from the north" (p. 497). The judgment is accurate. Cass flings himself between the absolutes of innocence and experience, purity and guilt. Because America, in denying original sin and its ramifications, has obliterated the meaning of the past, Cass and other Americans must start from scratch: must confront the existence of evil and the vision of love as pristine facts. Cass is, of course, an exemplary rather than a typical case. An orphan, he seeks the father who will enable him to understand his ancestry; self-taught (a necessity in a culture which falsifies learning), he seeks a teacher who will help him to convert knowledge to wisdom. For though Cass' self-reliance and loneliness are both necessary and valuable, they are not finally sufficient: they provide no protection against the adolescent absolutism which reacts to the knowledge of evil by self-destructiveness and to the vision of love by a desire for the impossible. What Cass must learn from Luigi, America's European father and teacher, is an adjusted tragic humanism. Only through this philosophy can Cass survive to repossess his birthright and avoid defeat at Mason's hands. The ideal Francesca embodies and the possibility of exorcising guilt provided by Michele are vital aspects of the Italian background, but they are secondary to the lesson Luigi would teach. Luigi speaks for a revised conception of that "accumulation of history and culture" Americans once came to Europe to seek. The serious American now coming to Europe can no longer browse among aesthetic traditions and Arcadian landscapes, half-fascinated, half-repelled by the skeletons in the European closet. What Cass must discover is not so much Tradition as it is a way of dealing with the tragic facts and concomitant guilts with which European history has had to come to terms. Luigi's philosophy is not just a result of his experience of war (which teaches him we are all criminally guilty) nor of his discovery that we have been abandoned by God and are alone: rather, it is a product of the total knowledge of a race and of the realism enforced by this knowledge. Luigi reasserts the necessity of proportion in the face of man's gothic predicament. His advice to Cass comes as close as it is perhaps possible to come to a symbiosis of tragic knowledge and adjustment's ideal of love. His conviction that there is a "depth of joyousness" to counterbalance the depths of evil and of guilt may, of course, be said to constitute an evasion of the fullest implications of moral horror. Yet, by the same token, for those convinced of the fragility of our position in a God-less universe, any hope or faith may seem a futile subterfuge. One must at least believe with Cass that it is better to opt for life than to retreat into suicidal darkness and leave the stage to be occupied by such as Mason.

Notes

1. Quoted in Van Wyck Brooks, *The Dream of Arcadia: Artists in Italy, 1760–1915* (New York: Dutton, 1958), p. 100.

2. Quoted in Brooks, p. 68.

3. Quoted in Brooks, p. 168.

4. Leslie Fiedler, *Love and Death in the American Novel* (New York: Criterion Books, 1960), pp. 107–08.

5. Fiedler, p. 123.

6. Quoted in Randall Stewart, *Nathaniel Hawthorne* (New Haven: Yale University Press, 1948), p. 193.

7. These generalizations are drawn from Brooks.

8. D. H. Lawrence, *Twilight in Italy* (London: Heinemann, 1950), pp. 111–112.

9. Eleanor Clark, *Rome and a Villa* (New York: Doubleday, 1952), p. 17.

10. Clark, p. 34.

11. Quoted in Brooks, p. 125.

12. Irwin Shaw, *Two Weeks in Another Town* (New York: Random House, 1960), p. 70.

13. Fiedler, p. 127.

14. From a narrative by Mrs. Stowe's companion, Annie Fields, quoted in Brooks, p. 129.

15. William Styron, *Set This House on Fire* (New York: Random House, 1960), p. 418. All further citations refer to this edition and will be given in the text.

16. John Strachey, "The Strangled City(II)," *Encounter*, 15 (Dec. 1960), p. 37.

17. Fiedler, p. 123.

18. Fiedler, p. 111.

Oedipus Americanus

Michel Butor*

I. CONVERSATIONS IN CHARLESTON

The transcriptions, or summary, of fifteen days of conversations that take place in Charleston, South Carolina, between Peter Leverett and Cass Kinsolving, make up almost all of the novel; these fifteen days are decisive and mark a turn in the lives of the two men. But the dramatic aspects of the central subject matter around which these conversations revolve, and which are the events of a spring night at Sambuco, which is to say Ravello, may, at first, blur the main theme of the novel. However, when Peter Leverett decides to impose himself as a visitor upon Cass Kinsolving, he does so after experiencing quite a serious failure in love. He tries to put a good face on the matter, but he admits he is wounded: "The time spent in New Hampshire with my dazzling Annette was a total and sweeping catastrophe. . . . I went down to Virginia feeling mournful, grim, indescribably bereft" (pp. 9–10).

But after his stay in Charleston, he is in complete control of the situation. A letter from Cass, cited in an epilogue informs the reader about Peter's happy relationship: ". . . wanted to tell you how glad I am that N.Y. goes O.K. for you now. You didn't tell me her name but hope you will bring her down here some day" (pp. 505–6).

In the case of Cass Kinsolving, there is also a striking change for the better. In the letter he wrote to Peter in July, he stated: ". . . also teach a painting class though things go a bit slack both ways toward the end of Summer" (p. 8). In November, he not only informs us that now "the Sunday amateurs are keeping me busy & I'm up to my ears in work" (p. 505), but that his wife Poppy is expecting a baby in June. "Kinsey was distinctly wrong," he adds. "A man doesn't even get started until he moves in toward il mezzo del cammin" (p. 505). The Charleston conversations which have taken place in September coincide, then, with this new start.

All of this shows that these discussions, from a psychological view-

*Reprinted from the French edition of *Set This House on Fire* (*La proie des flammes* [Paris: Gallimard, 1962]), where the essay served as an introduction. Translated from the French by Ahmed Amriqua. Reprinted by permission of the author.

point, have been a perfect success. The two speakers are relieved from a burden which obsessed them both, Peter since his arrival in Sambuco, and Cass since his birth. Both of them have consequently found the answer to the question which they tried to clarify during their acquaintance. Cass, in his July letter, wonders "who M[ason] was, I mean really WAS & what was eating him & how he ended up the way he did" (pp. 8–9). As for Peter, if he imposes himself upon Cass by visiting him in Charleston, it is because "without knowing about Cass [he] could never learn about what happened in Sambuco—about Mason, and [Peter's] part in the matter" (p. 19). Therefore, Cass understands who the Mason he killed was; and this understanding justifies his action. Peter, on the other hand, not only learns what happened that night but also learns what part of the responsibility he had in those events. In other words, all that had begun at Sambuco finally ends during this meeting between Peter and Cass. The last appendix, the letter which Peter receives in December from Sister Marie-Joseph, places this ending, this closing of the events, on a symbolic level which largely goes beyond the psychology of the two individuals at stake. Indeed, Peter tells us that the tragedy began, for him, before his actual arrival in Sambuco. He comes from Rome, summoned by Mason; as he approaches Naples:

> All of a sudden exhaustion smote me like a fist. I came to a dead halt.
> For some reason I date the events at Sambuco—at least my participation in them—from this moment. Had I been able to sleep easily that night, I might very well have been spared my trouble of the next day. Without *that* misadventure, I most surely would have arrived at Sambuco as fresh as a buttercup: not haggard, shattered, and forlorn, my composure hopelessly unmoored, and cursed with a sort of skittish, haunted depletion of nerves from which I never quite recovered. [p. 26]

After reading the book, we understand the reason: he blames the accident which happened to him the next day, involving Luciano di Lieto and his scooter, on that fatigue and that painful night. From then on, di Lieto had swayed between life and death in a mysterious coma; during all that terrible night at Sambuco, and during the fortnight at Charleston, Peter wondered whether or not he was guilty of murder. His suspicion of Cass was rooted in his anxiety; he knew well enough that there had been some mistake and that he did not have anything in particular against di Lieto, though he could not assert his own innocence, because, furious as he was against another Italian, his "heart was full of murder," and he "was only dreaming of revenge" (p. 28). The head-nurse at the hospital finally informs him that "Luciano was in the profoundest slumber when, like the Phoenix risen from the ashes of his own affliction, he sprang up in bed complaining loudly of a violent hunger. Upon examination it was discovered that the pressure upon his brain had alleviated itself" (p. 506).

A "wondrous miracle," as this sister puts it, and the more so in that if we examine the dates, we see that this recovery must take place a very short time after the Charleston talks, thus obviously resulting from such talks, and expressing their success. We also see why Peter Leverett is unable to specify the link between these events: the reason is that it is not a question involving some determinism which is inherent in the anecdote as told, but rather a question of a poetic and illustrative rendering which slowly unfolds before our eyes the riches of an allegory.

The meeting of the two actors finally allows the tragedy and the performance which was staged at the Sambuco theatre (the presence of a whole film crew has completely changed the piazza into a set) to take their final shape and their meaningful power. At first, each one knows only half the tragedy, being cut off from its main sources by the thickness of a wall, by sleep, or by amnesia. Peter clearly remembers everything he has done and seen, but Cass, much more in the centre of the whirlpool, crossed the stage like a blind man, totally unaware of whole parts of his own behavior. He neither desires nor is able to remember; he is too frightened by what he feels is fluttering behind the veil of compassion. It is Peter's narrative which will gradually start, stir and awaken his own. He plays the part of the Chorus in a dialogue of *Oedipus at Colonus*.

> Chorus: Ill is it, stranger, to awake
> Pain that long since has ceased to ache,
> And yet I fain would hear—
>
> Oedipus: What thing?
>
> Chorus: Thy tale of cruel suffering
> For which no cure was found,
> The fate that held thee bound.
>
> Oedipus: O bid me not (as guest I claim
> This grace) expose my shame.

Cass's narrative is certainly not what he could have told himself, even, before Peter's intervention. It is, then, not the juxtaposition of the two memories, but the progressive assembly of another face of things. Of what things? What are they trying to resolve? They are not trying to find a solution to the Sambuco events as if they formed a police mystery: who did what exactly, where, when and how—but the why of everything, the reason behind these behaviors, which is the same as the reason underlying the basic interest which clings to these behaviors in the recollection of the two men and in every reader's mind. Let us examine once more the parentheses, the context in which the Sambuco performance appears to us. If Peter Leverett decides to force Cass Kinsolving's door despite the latter's silence, it is because, during a walk with his father in his childhood Virginia, he saw that what represented for him the centre, the omphalos, the very place of his roots, had disappeared under an Esso station: "My great-grandchildren's cleverest archeology will strive in vain to unlock that sun-swept marsh, that stream, those crawfish, that singing trolley car. Everything was gone. . . . my marsh had vanished, a puff into thin air, and nothing of it remained" (p. 18). This distressing vision, which has made of him a lost man, is only the specification, in his case, of an incomparably wider phenomenon, of which his father has just given, a moment earlier, a remarkable expression.

> 'Look out there, son.' He waved toward the sparkling water. 'That's where they came in, in the year 1619. Right out there. It was one of the saddest days in the history of man, and I mean black *or* white. We're still paying for that day, and we'll be paying for it from here right on out. And there'll be blood shed, and tears.' He mopped his brow. I turned my eyes eastward. A cloud passed across the day, then all was clear again, and for an instant I thought I could see those Dutch galleons, with their black bound cargo, lumbering up toward the muddy James. [pp. 14–15]

The preceding image finds a response in this one which, one might say, ends the Charleston talks (the following paragraphs are a commentary on them on an individual level). It is Cass who says:

> 'Then you know, something as I sat there—something about the dawn made me think of America . . . all of a sudden I realized that the anxiety and the anguish—most of it, anyway—had passed. And I kept thinking of the new sun coming up over the coast of Virginia and the Carolinas, and how it must have looked from those galleons, centuries ago, when after black night, dawn broke like a trumpet blast, and there it was, immense and green and glistening against the crashing seas. And suddenly I wanted more than anything in my life to go back there. And I knew I *would* go. . . .' [pp. 499–500]

We can see that what happens in Sambuco is no more than an allegory of the American condition, an invitation to transcend it. It is no surprise then that the author put this warning at the beginning of his book: "The ambition of my undertaking did not prevent me from making many mistakes."

II. THE SAMBUCO EVENTS

What did really happen in Sambuco? The official version is quite simple: a young American millionaire, Mason Flagg (let us point out the meaning of the word "flag" and the fact that the "masons" played a great part in the original making of the United States), raped a young Italian peasant girl, Francesca, with such brutality that she consequently died a few hours later. The murderer remorsefully kills himself by jumping off a belvedere.

Peter Leverett is more or less restricted to this interpretation of the story and keeps the reader confined to these facts until the end of his own narrative. However, we know that he has some doubts: first, he does not think that Mason had the courage to commit suicide; on the other hand, he is astonished at the atrocity of the rape. Cass points out to him:

> 'How though you could credit him [Mason] with an ordinary red-white-and-blue American-style rape you couldn't see him doing it in the all-out monstrous way he did it. Well, when you said that, it rang a bell. Because there in Sambuco, when it was all over, that was the way I felt too. . . . I couldn't see him doing that. What he did took something Mason didn't have. . . . Only I think now that, by God, I was wrong about all that.'
> [pp. 127–28]

Cass is playing on words here. He is trying to avoid a confession. We will learn, soon enough, that when he speaks of Mason's "doing that," he is not quite thinking about what Peter was saying, and that the inquiry never took place "when it was all over." But then, Cass will state that Mason did not commit suicide; it is Cass himself who killed him. That is when Peter's feeling of guilt starts taking shape because, had he suspected the thing, he could have prevented the murder. Now he thinks that Cass killed Mason in order to avenge the violence done to Francesca, and that he is sorry for his deed:

> 'I'm working on the assumption, of course, that you wish it hadn't happened, in spite of what Mason did. Right?'
> 'You're right,' he said, and the look of sorrow on his face was abruptly so total and painful that I turned my eyes away. 'Boy, you're sure right.'
> [p. 248]

However, here again, despite all sincerity, there is a misunderstanding which is willingly nurtured by Cass. Peter imagines that the murder could have been isolated from the rest of the events, whereas Cass would like to obliterate everything. Peter suspects, however, that he has not reached the final version of these events. " 'He ravished her, killed her. And for that you finished him off. All that's evident and plain. But what were these other things?' " (p. 248).

Cass, then, makes a crucial revelation: Mason did not kill Francesca. This fact seems to correspond to Peter's intuitions, but then the motive of the murder is not as clear anymore. The rape seems again an ordinary rape of the red-white-and-blue type. What is important is that Cass himself is worried by this possibility. If Mason were a monster, the reason for his murder would no longer be a problem. " 'But the guilt is not his [Mason's]! I been asking and asking and asking it from you, hoping you would show me he was *evil*. But no. He's still just scum. Don't you see? Nossir! The guilt is not his!' " (p. 249).

But even if the rape and murder of Francesca were separate, they remain, nonetheless, closely bound together. "I'll kill her," cried Mason to the terrified Peter, who did not know what had just happened; and if Saverio, the idiot, raped Francesca in turn, fatally wounding her because she resisted his attempts, it was only because, according to the carabiniere

Luigi's reassembling of the facts, which Cass finally relays and adopts, she had already been brutalized by Mason:

> For she had indeed encountered Saverio on the path sometime during the early morning. . . . She knew him well, and was not in the least afraid of him, but what Mason had done to her just that same evening clung to her flesh like some loathsome disease which she was fated to endure forever. So it was that when she met Saverio in the shadows and he put out his fingers harmlessly—perhaps no more than as a simple greeting—to stroke her, the intense male hand on her arm brought back, like horror made touchable, the touch and the feel and the actuality, and she found herself shrieking. She shrieked, and she scratched madly out at the flat lopsided face which now itself was stricken with panic. [p. 477]

We can see through these scratches that the very scene which had just taken place in Mason's room was re-enacted, as if automatically, in the woods. It is as if Saverio were a machine through which Mason, without suspecting it, fulfilled his wish. And Cass cannot, in his final interpretation, give up this link between the two rapes. "Now he is certain too that he convinced himself, despite all intuition that told him otherwise, that Mason *had* killed Francesca. . . . because that night, after a day spent somewhere in the hills . . . he had a witness" (pp. 477–78). It is because Peter told him about his return that he can finally be sure and make Mason responsible for Francesca's death. Luigi disclosed his discoveries to him only afterward. If Cass had not made this link, which seems to be contradicted by certain facts, but which remains indispensible, he would not have gone as far as murder:

> 'Had you told me even then, even in the midst of all my foaming, infuriate craze for revenge, that I would be capable of killing him—that indeed, within an hour, I *would* kill him—I would have said that you exaggerated my hatred and rage.' [p. 445]

In fact, when he learned of Francesca's rape by Mason, he did not think of it as an absolutely serious matter. He did not even insist on making Mason suffer; he only wanted to have a mark on himself, something to prove the scorn he felt for Mason, "even if it was only a hand bloodied with his blood, or a fist bruised and broken where I had driven it into that smooth, peerless, polished, vainglorious face" (p. 445). Until then, Mason was not a serious rival. Cass did not take any precautions against him because he considered him to be impotent: ". . . I just didn't think he was capable of it. I mean I had foolishly let my guard down. . . . I had just finally assumed that he couldn't get it up. I really had. That he just couldn't get it up, and that was that" (p. 441). Francesca's tale proved the contrary to him, but he still looked upon Mason's rape of her as a half-rape: "And when such a man don't produce any offspring—like Mason—you've got to be especially suspicious . . ." (p. 441).

Mason was sterile; everything he said was false; his actions themselves were lies; but when Cass learned that the business had gone too far, then everything changed and he finally understood that if Mason, as he felt, was quite unable to do much harm on his own, he was, however, strangely capable of corrupting indirectly, through the medium of other people, and that is where, in fact, lies the secret of Cass's own relations with him. As long as the link between Mason's and Saverio's rapes was not quite clear, Cass regretted the murder he committed. But after this link is well-established, the murder becomes a necessary deed through which Cass, as he well understands, must sacrifice part of himself. After telling Peter that he was sorry for the murder, Cass makes this astounding confession: " 'Who knows why he did it, but he *did* it, and at last I smashed his fucking skull in' " (p. 444), as if he had been awaiting for months this excuse to fulfill, at last, the deed for which he was fated.

He does not regret the deed so much as he does the horrible state preceding it.

As for Peter, he was not surprised in the least by the rape because, knowing Mason for a long time, he was very well aware that he was not physiologically impotent. But the occurrences which proved this fact to him have a singular character that closely links them to the Sambuco events. At seventeen, Mason was expelled from school for having been caught "playing leapfrog" with a thirteen-year-old girl. One feels that it was not at all an accident or a mistake, but that Mason planned the whole thing, knowingly risking his dismissal and the scene with his parents; he did all of this to advertise his virility. He was already talking a good deal about sex, but then, for the first time, he came up against what he called "the last frontier," which represented for him a barrier he could not overcome unless he had witnesses to watch him. Such was the scene specially staged for Peter in New York: ". . . when my knock went unanswered and, opening the door, I saw the two of them in the blazing light, Mason and Carole, naked as pullets and frenziedly abed, locked in that entangled embrace. . . . It seemed somehow so obviously staged . . ." (p. 145). Nothing, then, was possible without the presence of a spectator. If there was no one to shock, no loved person he could embarrass and affect in this manner, then nothing happened. Not only was the little girl from Saint Andrews school indifferent to him, but the outrage he could provoke in her home was insufficient; Mason did it because of the presence of his mother, "Wendy darling." In New York, the show was for Peter's benefit, and in Sambuco it was obviously not for Francesca's sake that he raped her, but in order to reach Cass through her:

'So that that night, if you discount the business about the earrings and his rage over Francesca's alleged thievery—which was just a cover-up for something deeper—and put aside for a moment this theory about his impotence—which must be only part of the story—then you come up with one answer: he was raping *me*.' [p. 443]

Since Mason's behavior remained meaningless without the participation of the audience for which it was intended (he was all lies and charm; women adored him, but he drove them mad), it was inevitable that sexuality presented such a problem for him, and that he could only find a solution for it in pornography. He had to succeed in changing his sexuality into something public; if it remained private, he remained impotent; he needed someone else's passion so that he could claim it and feed upon it. His greatest entertainment consisted in throwing sex parties as one would cocktail parties, but sex is precisely what was most lacking in this fabrication. That is the reason why the crucial place in his collection, the picture which he had Cass paint, strikes us by its simplicity. We could have expected some weird abomination suggested by *The Hundred and Twenty Days of Sodom*, but not at all; the picture showed as clearly as possible, the most simple and most natural sexual act. And that is what was most difficult for Mason. By owning this painting, he somehow stole the passion Cass felt for Francesca. His acquisition of it was the first step toward her rape. If Cass wanted so much to recover the painting on the day before the fatal night, it was because he vaguely sensed that its possession made Mason capable of the act he could not achieve otherwise. When he belatedly destroyed it, he was trying to destroy his own guilt in Francesca's misfortune.

Mason had tried to arrange with Cass one of those sex parties, or, as he called them, a "circus":

> . . . Mason, propositioning Cass at a fuzzy vulnerable moment with the idea of a circus, coyly divulged the information that this would engage the four of them—Mason, titanic broad-assed Rosemarie, himself and, implausibly, insanely, *Poppy*—in some co-operative bedroom rumpus; more tickled and bemused than horrified by the vision of his saintly little Irish consort sporting with Rosemarie, all naked as herring, he had laughed so uproariously that Mason gave up the venture straightaway, though sulking. [p. 414]

The circus on the night of the murders, and at which Mason displayed the hold he had on Cass before the crowd of actors, movie technicians and Peter, who had been especially invited for the occasion, was obviously a substitute for the "circus" he had not had with Cass, Poppy and Rosemarie. The rape Mason had just committed was incomplete in itself: it needed the presence of Cass. That is why Mason made him act out in public that scene which he could only partially perform. Earlier in the day he had warned him that he wanted to take his place:

> 'In the complete wreck you've become, dollbaby, I don't think you can fail to understand why I might be determined to get into her pants. Of what earthly use is a *lush* to her? After all, someone's got to give her a good workout—' [p. 429]

Incapable of passion itself, he stole that of others.

The only passion which held him and truly made up his whole existence was the mad envy inspired in him by the passion of others; what made him live was this insane desire to intercept it and display it to an audience:

> '. . . this *difficulty* I always suspected him of having, this failing which must be one of the most agonizing things that can afflict a man, this raging constant desire with no outlet, a starvation with no chance of fulfillment, which must fever and shake and torment a man until he can only find a release in violence.' [p. 442]

He was not attracted to Francesca. He was passionately attracted to the desire she aroused in Cass. It was this relationship which he wanted to appropriate in the eyes of others and this which he raped, because his intervention would inevitably corrupt everything. The murder which he could not commit by himself, but which he planned unknowingly triggering it, is the paradoxical proof of his impotence. He sentenced himself without appeal. He did not kill Francesca with his own hands, but he was the source of her death. He did not kill himself, but if he came all the way to Sambuco, it was because he was drawn there by his own death; if he adopted Cass, then pushed him to the limits, it was in order to groom himself a murderer. When Mason collapsed, when he was finally defeated, he blurted out tender words: " 'Dollbaby.' 'Dollbaby,' he whispered again, in a child's voice. . . . the pale dead face, which was so soft and boyish, and in death as in life so tormented . . ." (pp. 464–65). Cass could answer, like Oedipus to Creon:

> . . . and methinks my sire,
> Could he come back to live, would not dissent.

Thus, all of the investigation, all the successive aspects of the tragedy, all the details and surprise finally confirm the truth of the appearances.

III. OEDIPUS AT COLONUS

" 'Overpowering twagedy, my God. It's like the *Gweeks*, I tell you, but far worse!' " (p. 220), declares Windgasser, the hotel clerk, to Peter Leverett on the next day. He could not have put it any better. The novel is strewn with references to Greek tragedy, and particularly to *Oedipus at Colonus*. When Cass made his first appearance that evening, he jabbered one of the most famous choruses of this play and he would later assert that he was then as drunk on Sophocles as he was on whiskey; when Cass went to Mason's apartments in order to steal the miraculous drug and destroy his painting, Peter discovered in his studio a sketching pad on which he had copied, in a frenetic hand, Oedipus's love cry when he has just met his daughters again:

> *I hold to my Dear ones and now*
> *should I die I were not wholly*
> *wretched since ye have come to me*
> *Press close to me on either side*
> *Children cleave to your sire and*
> *respose from this late roaming so*
> *Forlorn so grievous!!!* [p. 203]

The last words which Peter heard him utter before leaving Sambuco are taken from the same quotation: "Bloody, with dazed and glassy eyes, he drew the children next to him in a smothering embrace. 'Press close to me on either side—' he began, then ceased" (p. 241). And when Mason came to see Cass for the first time, the latter used, in his description of Sambuco, another famous chorus from the second *Oedipus*, praising Attica.

The unfortunate king of Thebes is therefore a basic reference, and Cass identified himself with him more and more, as the night progressed. But we can already see that the interpretation which is given here is quite different from the one to which classical psychoanalysis has accustomed us. Here again, the gods ordained everything:

'. . . I can't help but believe that something *forced* me to go to Sambuco. These nightmares I had. . . . It was as if I had to go there—and that what happened there, to be fancy, was some sort of logical endproduct of what had been prefigured in these dreams.' [p. 248]

When Cass accepted the first bottle of whiskey that Mason gave him, he acknowledged his paternity. Mason becomes his suckling father, of course, but there was more than that: he discovered in Mason this legacy which was at the root of his own impotence, and that is the reason why his behavior in this scene is so closely related to the crucial experiences of his youth, particularly to the story of Lonnie who defined him as a Southerner:

'Mason,' he said slowly. 'Uncle Sugar. I got so that with Mason I was as helpless as Romulus, sucking on the fat tit of a wolf. . . . But never as long as I live will I forget standing down there in the courtyard, with that bottle like a big warm cow turd in my hand, and him hanging over the balustrade, so lean and so American, with the hungry look of a man who knew he could own you, if you'd only let him.' [p. 402]

Mason took him financially in charge; he would also have liked to take him in charge morally. He acknowledged him as a son. Mason was a sterile father who needed to use a real father as his tool; and naturally, he fully achieved this feeling of paternity at the moment of his death. When Peter saw Cass for the last time before his departure, he noticed in him a subtle, but decisive change:

I didn't know what there was about Cass that made him seem at my first glimpse of him another—a different—person. It was Cass—he was dressed the same . . . but it didn't quite look like Cass, an indefinable weird displacement of himself, rather, as if he were his own twin brother. [p. 237]

This new Cass was obviously the son engendered by Mason's rape of Francesca. We can see that the Oedipian incest has been achieved here in quite an unexpected manner, as if in reverse. As for the twin who disappeared, Cass evidently killed him by killing Mason, thus corroborating the decisive dream, the oracle which preceded their first encounter:

> . . . he [Cass] found himself taking off all his clothes. Then—wonder of wonders—he had withdrawn from himself. . . . he saw his other self, naked now, step into the shower. . . . Now naked and blue beneath the rush of gas, his other self grew rigid, skin shiny as a turquoise bead, and toppled soundless to the floor, all life extinct. [p. 368]

Whom did he kill, then, by killing this father and this twin? How is it that this murder became a blessing for his own country, America? He killed Mason's phrase, which occurs at the beginning of two chapters: "Art is dead." He killed what makes the root of this phrase, the historical oblivion in which Mason lived; he killed Laius's crime, the lie about the origins, resulting in the peculiarity that the young American had no real money, that he constantly fantasized his own life, without the possibility for this fantasy ever to become positive and take the shape of a literary work.

When we see Mason for the first time, we have the feeling that we have always known him, and that he is a member of the family; however, Cass says:

> All the time I spent with Mason, I felt I never knew him, never could put my hands on him. . . . a creature so strange, so *new*. . . . For him there was no history, or, if there was, it began on the day he was born. Before that there was nothing, and out of that nothing sprang this creature, committed to nothingness because of the nothingness that informed all time before and after the hour of his birth. [p. 446]

Cass Kinsolving's behavior, therefore, expresses an admonition to stand firmly on one's origins and to reformulate the whole of history. I wondered for a long time why the name Ravello had been changed to Sambuco. A lead toward one of the most essential cores of the book will perhaps be opened if we remember that this Italian word means "*elder tree.*"

This is a broken thread that must be tied up again; and Mason is that rupture, the dream of that flaw in all of us, whose birth naturally goes further back than the first arrival of Blacks in the Dutch galleons on the banks of the James River.

The Discarded Opening for
Set This House on Fire

William Styron*

Preserved among the William Styron papers at the Library of Congress is a discarded opening for his second novel, *Set This House on Fire*. Written in black pencil on long yellow legal sheets, this twelve-page holograph manuscript is important for several reasons. First, this false start is a significant step in Styron's creative process; it allows us to examine the imaginative seeds from which *Set This House on Fire* eventually flowered. Second, by comparing the discarded opening to its published equivalent, we are able to look over Styron's shoulder as he edits and recreates in order to achieve his fictional ends. Most importantly, a close scrutiny of this document supplies clues to Styron's original conception of the "square" narrator of the novel, Peter Leverett, a character who has always been a bone of contention among critics of the book.

Styron discarded the writing in this false start, but the subject matter and the method of development in it provide the basis of the opening for the published novel.[1] In the fragment Peter Leverett describes two ocean cruises. He remembers the first, which he took to Europe a few years after World War II, as "adventurous and grand." His expectations were clouded by a romantic fog; he anticipated ending up "in the cabin of some compliant and breathtaking girl," and he pictured himself as "flushed and palpitant and on the threshold of conquest."

Leverett's second voyage, however, is quite different. Peter remembers this cruise, on which he sailed from Naples to New York shortly after the violent events at Sambuco, as "a trip shorn of romance and of any illusions at all." Leverett scandalizes his cabin-mate, "an Evangelical Lutheran from out west," with his drinking, rudeness, and solitary debauchery. He also cuts his table companions and his waiter whenever one of them offers goodwill or fellowship. Peter returns home to America decidedly neurotic. Through the obvious contrast of these two cruises, Styron apparently meant to pique the reader's curiosity. What could have happened in Sambuco to transform an immature but harmless romantic into a jittery, almost hysterical candidate for analysis?

*Reprinted from *Mississippi Quarterly*, 34 (Winter 1980–81), 38–50, by permission of the journal and the author.

Although Styron abandons all talk of ocean voyages in the published opening of *Set This House on Fire*, the travel motif is still present. Styron begins his first chapter with an excerpt from a travel guide, Nigel's *Italy:* "The road is hewn nearly the whole way in the cliffs of the coast. An ever-varied panorama unfolds before our eyes, with continual views of an azure sea, imposing cliffs, and deep gorges."[2] The contrast between the two ocean voyages, which seems a bit contrived in the false start, is only skillfully implied in the opening of the novel. Styron sets the dead facts of Nigel's *Italy* ("We return to the sea and then make a retour round the grim ravine of Erchie, approaching the sea again at Cape Tomolo.") against the vivid, living, cataclysmic murders and the rapes in Sambuco.

In the false start one also finds Styron using melodies and lyrics of popular music to counterpoint his story. Leverett's initial romantic cruise has its own music: he remembers a three-piece band that seemed constantly to be playing "*C'est si bon*," that "imbecile, off-key tune uncoiling night and day from the ballroom." This carefree, lilting melody with its trivial love lyric is, of course, the perfect accompaniment for Peter's romantic illusions. "*C'est si bon*" is also part of the "enforced fun" of Peter's first ocean voyage. In similar fashion the published version of *Set This House on Fire* has its significant song, "What's the Matter with This World," which, like "*C'est si bon*" in the discarded opening, functions on at least two levels. First, the melody with its whining dulcimers and crying twelve-strings summons up for Peter and probably for Cass "southern weather, southern voices, southern scenes":

Country beer joints, pinewoods, dusty back roads and red earth and swamp water and sweet-fragrant summer dusks. (p. 121)

Peter describes the song as "so lovely and so horrible" because he associates it both with the innocent days of his youth in Port Warwick, Virginia, and with the American decadence—already far too pervasive in Sambuco—of the sterile and vicious dilettante Mason Flagg. But more importantly, the song's lyrics reflect Cass Kinsolving's self-destructive fascination with peering into the existential abyss:

This question we daily hear, no one seems to know . . .
What-a-at's the matter with this world . . .
Now this rumor we hear: another war we fear,
Revelations is being fulfilled . . .
Your soul's on sinking sand, the end is drawing near:
That's what's the matter with this world . . . (p. 121)

This apocalyptic vision will be shared, to a much lesser extent, by Leverett after he has witnessed the human depravity that occurs in Sambuco.

Although they disagree sharply about Styron's style and achievement in *Set This House on Fire*,[3] most critics feel that the novel's major flaw lies in Styron's conception of his self-proclaimed "square" narrator, Peter

Leverett. Donald Malcolm, for example, classifies Leverett as "a hopeless fathead" because of Peter's susceptibility to Mason Flagg's superficial and repulsive charm.[4] David L. Stevenson complains about the "un-novelized materials" in the narrative: Leverett's self-effacing thoughts about himself, his stunted affairs with women, and especially his didactic conversation with his father.[5] With characteristic truculence Robert Foster views Leverett as a gross, soulless caricature of Nick Carraway—a parasitic voyeur who "wants hotly to see everything, and what he can't see he craves to have described to him."[6] Abraham Rothberg sees Leverett as an uninteresting and unnecessary character whose deletion would quicken the pace and magnify the tension of a novel that is too long by two hundred pages.[7] Even Louis D. Rubin, Jr., an unabashed Styron admirer, finds the major defect of the novel to be the Leverett character.[8]

The discarded opening for *Set This House on Fire* is early proof of Styron's concern with Leverett. The false start, like the finished novel, is narrated by Leverett; but the narrator of the discarded opening is a different man from the narrator of the published novel. In the false start we already see what Styron would later call his narrator's propensity for "self-conscious reflections." Leverett is not content with divulging to the reader his intimate romantic fantasies about ocean cruises; he must also analyze them for us:

> Even so, the idea of a voyage had always had for me this high dazzle and enchantment, and it is no doubt an attribute of the young (or the stupid or the incurably optimistic) that they can face such an outing again and again with fine expectancy.

This false-start passage adds little to the characterization of the narrator. At the beginning of the fragment Leverett labeled himself as an "incurable optimist," and his preoccupation with the clichéd aspects of romance has already earmarked him as "average." Leverett is merely commenting gratuitously about himself, and his remarks constitute an excellent example of Stevenson's "un-novelized materials." In the eventual opening of the published novel Styron judiciously sidesteps the pitfall of Leverett's long-winded self-characterization; the narrator establishes himself as Everyman by simply admitting to the reader that he is "something of a square" (p. 5).

In the false start Leverett is equally loquacious as he talks about his post-Sambuco mental condition:

> And so during those first few months in New York I can recall only having been prey to sickening and degrading terrors; fearful of assaults from thugs and robbers; of fire and sudden falls and disease; of suicides plummeting down to crush me, like a bug upon the sidewalk; of taxi drivers and subway platforms and of all heights above six feet.

The list goes on, but the message is already clear: Leverett is neurotic. He even spells out his problem again: "As a neurotic first-class I must have been characteristic: paralyzed, evil-tempered, humorless, and abominably self-centered." In the novel Styron carefully avoids this extraneous summary and analysis, reducing all this nervous chatter to a simple admission by a more laconic Leverett that "the blood and the tumult and the shambles" of Sambuco had left him in "a really rather bad state" (p. 5). Just how bad is left, more satisfyingly, to the reader's imagination.

Styron chooses, in the novel, to temper his false-start characterization of Leverett. Instead of severely neurotic, Peter is merely "desperately stunned" by the carnage of Sambuco (p. 5). This alteration is more consistent with Styron's conception of his narrator. It is illogical to make Peter a neurotic: he lacks the artistic sensitivity of men prone to neuroses and psychoses.

Styron does not abandon his characterization of Leverett as a neurotic, however. He saves Peter's agitated sensibilities for a more suitable character—the blocked painter Cass Kinsolving (who is called "Ben" Kinsolving in the discarded opening). Leverett in the false start is in many ways similar to Kinsolving in the published novel. For instance, in the discarded opening Peter tells the reader that he returned to America "removed the width of a hair from lunacy." But in the novel it is Cass's hairbreadth escape from insanity that we witness.

Styron's purpose in drawing much of Cass's personality from the false-start characterization of Leverett is clear: by giving Peter and Cass similar though not identical characteristics, he means to create characters who are shadows of each other. In this way he can also merge together the first- and third-person points of view, a special aim of his in *Set This House on Fire*. In a May 1960 letter to *Publishers' Weekly* Styron wrote about this narrative experiment:

> I had never seen the welding of two points of view attempted in a work of fiction before: I had never seen a narrator who, beginning in the first person, could, convincingly, end up in the third person, the story so merging and mingling that one might accept without hesitation the fact that the narrator himself knew the uttermost nuances of another man's thought; and it was the fight to achieve this new dimension—involving over three and a half years of more tearing apart and putting back together than I care to think about—which gives to the book whatever power and tension it has.[9]

This discarded opening for *Set This House on Fire* is probably the initial step in Styron's long "tearing apart and putting back together" process. Here we see Styron flexing his creative muscles, deciding which characteristics to give Leverett and which to give Kinsolving. At first their personalities were too similar—perfect reflections where Styron was only aiming for slight echoes. Styron saw his error and began again, solving his problem by heightening certain characteristics in Kinsolving and tempering the same ones in Leverett.

A. D. C.

[THE DISCARDED OPENING]*

About some things I had been an incurable optimist. A voyage on an ocean liner, for instance, possessed for me an irresistible glamor. Perhaps this was because, a bachelor still, I had never been able to shed the illusion that all that enforced fun—the music, the games, the various hectic, pleasant tricks which are employed to fight boredom, much in the same way that fever is often artificially induced to cure certain diseases—that those imposed, light-hearted intimacies could only lead to my ending up, at one time or another, in the cabin of some compliant and breathtaking girl. It is a dream shared by bachelors and other lonely and frustrated persons but like all dreams it is as airy and as insubstantial as smoke. The girls are either not beautiful or, if so, are not willing or are accompanied by watchful husbands or are the ones who are shy and young and virginal and disposed to seasickness. Or, presuming some flirtation, once begun, contains the seeds of promise—plop! there you are in Plymouth or Havre, flushed and palpitant and on the threshold of conquest, but disembarking, bound for some other destination.

Even so, the idea of a voyage had always had for me this high dazzle and enchantment, and it is no doubt an attribute of the young (or the stupid or the incurably optimistic) that they can face such an outing again and again with fine expectancy, like sailors on liberty in Norfolk, avid for pleasure but haunted by the faint, nagging knowledge that this time, as usual, they will have to do without girls. Nor had I been so old or jaded that the first voyage I made did not still possess its own distinct identity—its own mood and meaning—and corresponded with a phase in my life which, as I looked back on it, seemed singularly adventurous and grand. It was as if that putting out to sea had been a sort of baptism washing me clean of the mistakes of the past, making an auspicious beginning, with the voyage itself an exciting preview in miniature of the world which would be opened up to me on the other shore.

And so whenever I remembered my first trip abroad—a few years after the war—I tried not to recall those items which reason told me made up, after all, the *real* essence of the voyage—my table-mates on that big French boat, for example, or Mrs. Fessenden. For even from the start, innocent as I was of world travel, I was aware that somehow Romance had not shipped aboard this trip—at least not in the person of my dinner companions, a glum British tractor salesman with a hyphenated name which I still cannot remember, and two young alumnae of the University of Florida whose names I've also forgotten, except that one of them seems to have been called Melba. They were like two fresh daffodils, those girls—ripe, erect, with flossy blonde hair—and they had the touching artlessness of grown Southern girls who have not been forced to study much, and they informed me early in casual tinkling tones that they were going abroad to visit their soldier husbands and certainly were not going to tolerate any impropriety, especially from all those Frenchmen. Inseparable, they clung to one another for the entire voyage, their soft brown eyes rolling wide with surmise and delighted alarm, like maidens during the sack of Atlanta. So, still drugged by their perfume, I would lurch my way alone to my cabin or, more often, to the bar, where a three-piece band constantly played *C'est si bon*. There now and then I talked to Mrs. Fessenden, a huge divorcée from Chicago who was transporting with her to Europe some secret and impressive grief, which she kept stoked with vast quantities of cognac. She wept often and showed me her jewels, calling me "Hon"; and one night late, while the clarinet piped high and shrill over the rushings of the wintry sea, she told me that I was the only one on earth who understood her, and she sort of whinnied, and drew me down close to her steaming and resplendent bosom.

No, it was certainly not these faces which lent to that voyage such an air of indescribable charm. It was something else—the music, perhaps, that imbecile, off-key tune uncoiling night and day from the ballroom; or the persistent clamor of the sea, which gave to my conscious hours such a feeling of quest and peril and adventure; or perhaps one other girl, whose name I never found out. She was French—that much I knew—a lovely-looking creature who, besides having the blackest eyes I had ever seen, was also somehow delectably sick, as if she had just recovered from or was about to succumb to some decently romantic illness, like tuberculosis. I never spoke to her but I followed her every move and gesture with hungry yearning. Her flushed, tormented beauty fascinated me, and when she brushed by me in a passageway I'd begin to sweat and feel my heart pounding stupidly. No doubt it was shyness (another name for vanity, after all) which prevented me from making some advance; in any case, our eyes met only once—at the harbor in Cherbourg—when from a distance, through a blizzard of confetti with *C'est si bon* still fluting madly from the ballroom, she glanced at me and gave me a sly and secret smile. It was a smile of invitation but also of farewell, for in a second she was gone and I never saw her again. Perhaps she had known my passion for her all along, and her smile had been a final token of sympathy; perhaps, more truthfully, it was just my imagination and she had not been smiling at me at all but only at the gray coast of France. Whatever, it took some of the curse off the Florida girls and the tractor salesman and Mrs. Fessenden, so that I was able to recall that moment as the glory of the voyage: standing alone on the windy deck with a new continent spread out base and vulnerable before me, and thinking of all the girls in Paris willing to smile upon me their sly and wistful smiles.

And it is in that way, I have no doubt, that most men regard themselves when they were younger: remote, mysterious, and fascinating—jaunty voyagers not yet debarked from the sea of illusions.

Why do I mention all this? Only by way of contrast, I suppose, to my

last—my final—voyage home from Europe a year or so ago—a trip shorn
of romance and of any illusions at all. Returning home from the wreck
and the confusion—from Sambuco, and all the ugly events that happened
there that summer—I was panicked, shattered, and left gazing inward
upon a conscience which for the first time in my life had begun to gaze
back at me. And for the first time in my life—with the chilling surprise
which must accompany the onslaught of some fatally incurable disease—I
had begun to know what it is to live constantly with fear. I was sick to
death of voyages, of adventure. I felt like the limpest of passengers—my
bright pennants furled, shaky and seasick like all the rest, and given to fits
of wild alarm.

On that voyage—it was from Naples—I shared my quarters with a
man of God—an Evangelical Lutheran from out west who exposed his
plump body daily to the late summer sun and rubbed himself with some
oil that filled the cabin with a fragrance of cinnamon. He was a nice man
but I was heartlessly rude, and made only muttered replies to his decent
gestures of fellowship. I don't suppose I spoke to him more than three or
four times during the entire trip. I felt utterly cowed by my sorrow and
bewilderment, and exhausted, and I lay on my bunk day after day gazing
upward toward nothing, while the ship plowed westward through calm
seas and burning sunlight past Africa, and into the wild ocean. It was an
American ship—a cocky overstatement of indigenous chrome, egalitarian,
cheerful, and grim—with the gift, such as the ships of no other nation
possess, of making one feel already on native soil. There were lots of Army
people aboard—the proconsuls of Munich and Frankfurt on leave with
their families: fat captains and skinny majors and women who herded
their offspring down corridors and passageways with incomprehensible
Texas cries. My waiter whistled as he brought me my hamburgers and
chicken pie, eager to establish some facetious *rapport*. He, too, I cut dead
without embarrassment, as with my table companions—three frail and
translucent old ladies—to whose quiet remarks about the wonders of
Venice and Rome I replied with mumbles of murderous scorn. I felt like a
bastard about it but I didn't care. I suppose I was a bit insane. I steered
clear of the bar, too, but bought whiskey by the bottle which I drank in
my cabin—to the concern of the Lutheran minister who would burst in on
my solitary debauch with paunch glistening, smelling of cinnamon, and
with a clamp-jawed air of censure. I slept until far past noon, numbing
myself with great long draughts of unconsciousness, and often I would
arouse myself only after the last glimmerings of sunset had begun to color
the remotest limits of the sea.

And so finally I came home again to America, removed the width of
a hair from lunacy, and not nearly so much alive as one quivering,
bottled-up scream. Nor do I mean to exaggerate. As I look back on it now,
it is a mystery how I got past the Immigration people—even equipped as I
was with a passport, but with hair unbarbered and flying, whiskers bris-

tling wildly, and with a watery glint of mania in my eyes. I can't remember having taken a bath. I must have stunk like an old shoe. Anyway, there is little I can recall about that debarkation day, save that somehow and in wicked delirium I got myself to a hotel near Times Square, where I slept for three days. It was not only a joyless homecoming, it was lacking in dignity, but I didn't care. Awaking finally one midnight to the raucous new clatter of America on the streets below, I felt like a man who on his knees has done night-long vigil, only to look up and see at the heart of the altar a pitiless and uncompromising sneer.

Fear. I had—almost overnight, it seemed—become the victim of the most ignoble, the meanest of emotions. And so during those first few months in New York I can recall only having been prey to sickening and degrading terrors; fearful of assaults from thugs and robbers; of fire and sudden falls and disease; of suicides plummeting down to crush me, like a bug upon the sidewalk; of taxi drivers and subway platforms and of all heights above six feet; of germs in restaurants, of madmen gone berserk upon the avenues, and of electrocution in the bath. Thoughts of blights like leukemia and sarcoma and Brights' disease drummed a steady litany in my mind, and I went to a physician named Rubinstein who tested me with syringes and blood pumps, and prescribed vitamins.

More than anything I longed for the faintest shadow of health, hungered greedily for a moment in which I could draw one tranquil breath. As a neurotic first-class I must have been characteristic: paralyzed, evil-tempered, humorless, and abominably self-centered. I tried to console myself with the easy thought that in my state I was a victim—and a part—of the temper of the times. Yet in my new job in an office above Fifth Avenue I still made no friends, sullenly each Friday collected my pay, and took my lunch alone in Schrafft's, surrounded by malodorous fumes of skin lotion and ladies from the suburbs deep in fretful colloquies. Horribly, I realized I had in my panic come to identify myself with these matrons; failing, a-flutter, and now womanish like them, I yearned moreover, in the sickly stew that my mind had become, to be crushed in tender solace against those stern and be-corseted forms. It was despicable.

Now in retrospect certain things have become clear to me about that period of my life—the most important among them being the fact that not once since leaving Europe had I given the slightest thought to the event (or rather series of events) which must have been the cause, or at least the trigger, for my unhappy condition. There had not been a time when my mind, even for an instant, had turned back to Sambuco, or had ever lingered upon that fantastic green-and-calcimine coast or upon the extraordinary events which took place there and which had caused in the end my headlong stampede for America. About the things which had happened to me in the recent past I had drawn a total blank, as if there were walled up in my brain vast zones of consciousness too bleak for recall.

Only recently—now that the letters I've received from Ben Kinsolving have managed to clear up much of the whole story—have I been able to face the memory of that summer with passable calm. And only *very* recently have I been able to picture in my mind Sambuco again—a quiet, lovely place which became after nine placid centuries the victim of all our meanness and discord.

Notes

1. At the end of the surviving draft of the discarded opening there is a cancelled passage which Styron did use in the published novel. This passage, which begins "Aloof upon its precipice," is Peter Leverett's opening evocation of Sambuco, the tiny Italian village where the tumultuous central action of the novel occurs (4.12–18 in the first edition of *Set This House on Fire*).

2. William Styron, *Set This House on Fire* (New York: Random House, 1960), p. 3. All future references are cited parenthetically within the text.

3. The critical reception of *Set This House on Fire* deserves extensive study. Many commentators (Styron among them) have characterized this reception as uncommonly harsh. Louis D. Rubin, Jr., in his book *The Faraway Country*, calls the reviews of *Set This House on Fire* "a torrent of critical abuse the like of which has seldom been seen in our time." In reality, however, the criticism of the novel can be assessed much more accurately as "uneven." For example, the reviewer for *Time* dismisses the novel as "a 507-pp. crying jag," while Abraham Rothberg, writing in the *New Leader*, calls *Set This House on Fire* "a great artistic task."

4. Donald Malcolm, "False Start, " *The New Yorker*, 4 June 1960, p. 154.

5. David L. Stevenson, "Styron and the Fiction of the Fifties," *Critique*, 3, No. 3 (Summer 1960), 52.

6. Robert Foster, "An Orgy of Commerce: William Styron's *Set This House on Fire*," *Critique*, 3, No. 3 (Summer 1960), 64.

7. Abraham Rothberg, "Styron's Appointment in Sambuco," *New Leader*, 43 (July 1960), 26.

8. Louis D. Rubin, Jr., "An Artist in Bonds," *Sewanee Review*, 69 (Winter 1961), 178.

9. "William Styron Writes PW About His New Novel," *Publishers' Weekly*, 177 (30 May 1960), 55.

THE CONFESSIONS OF
NAT TURNER

Styron's Nat Turner . . .

Shaun O'Connell*

Styron has run some risks with this novel. This is true despite its striking, contemporary relevance. Nat would have understood Stokely Carmichael's threat and gone him one better. When a honkie hits you, you indeed kill him, but first you *organize*, then you *plan* to kill them *all*. Still, this book is likely to raise some resentment. For Styron has presumed to *know* a Negro. A white ex-Southerner of the middle 20th century insists he knows enough to assume the guise of an early 19th-century black slave. Not only that but Styron admits—in an important essay, "This Quiet Dust" (*Harper's*, April, 1965) which explains his personal obsession with Nat—that "most Southern white people *cannot* know or touch black people," that the contemporary Negro "may feel that it is too late to be known, and that the desire to know him reeks of outrageous condescension." Yet, Styron insists on telling Nat's story in first-person narrative.

In a serious way he seems not to care *what* LeRoi Jones, say, might think of his presumption. This is something he had to do. In the desperately understated cliché, he is paying his dues, just as did Faulkner in *Intruder in the Dust* and Warren in *Who Speaks For the Negro?*. For, Styron says, "to come to *know* the Negro has become the moral imperative of every white Southerner." To argue that this is arrogant and futile is to resign oneself to fragmentation, alienation, violence. Styron chances a daring, imaginative leap into a tormented black psyche to better understand himself and his country. He has taken to heart Baldwin's wisdom— hatred destroys the hater; the American white man must "find a way of living with the Negro in order to be able to live with himself."

For Styron this personal, social problem "resolved itself into an artistic one." How could he best understand, embody, become Nat? He could be circled from the outside with historical documents, the actual *Confessions* and the only book on the subject, *The Southampton Insurrection* (1900) by W. S. Drewry. These scant notes could be amplified by close readings in the history of slavery. Though these works provide Styron with a framework of the actual, reference points which had to be touched, and an abundance of specifics from which to draw, he had,

*Reprinted from *Nation*, 16 Oct. 1967, pp. 373–74, by permission of the author and journal.

157

finally, to confront Nat's single, isolated self. Who was he? Why did only he, in the long history of American slavery, lead an uprising? Why, when about sixty whites were slaughtered, did he personally only kill one? She was 18, her name was Margaret Whitehead, a belle, and, as Nat actually confessed, "after repeated blows with a sword, I killed her by a blow on the head with a fence rail." Why did the thrust of Nat's rebellion flinch after this murder? Styron asks, "Did he discover his humanity here or did he lose it?" History can help but, finally, Styron had to depend upon his novelist's first-rate sense of self to create situation and character which would convince us that these questions can be answered.

Nat's humanity is both Styron's and, as he sees it, Nat's problem. He was "favored" as perhaps no Virginia slave had been before. Son of the cook, he ate well. A cute pickaninny, he was pampered by whites. Further, he had the "luck" to be owned by a man of unusually enlightened convictions, Samuel Turner—"Turner" is, of course, his name, not truly Nat's—who felt "that the more religiously and intellectually enlightened a Negro is made, the better for himself, his master, and the commonwealth." At first Nat responds gratefully to this benevolent despotism. He develops a sense of his own significance that a field hand could never know. He feels the joy of becoming; "I shiver in the glory of self." Spurred by his heightened sensitivity to the promises of life he mimes the whites, their talk, their style, studies his Bible, learns his carpentry and, he says, becomes "a pet, the darling, the little black jewel of Turner's Mill." He pushes so successfully against the barrier of his "niggerness" that Turner promises emancipation. But Turner is weak, caught in a depression caused by the exhaustion of tobacco lands, and goes back on his word. When Nat is sold, when it is clear that he will never be free, that he can never more *become* in that way, he

> experienced a kind of disbelief which verged close upon madness, then a sense of betrayal, then fury such as I had never known before, then finally, to my dismay, hatred so bitter that I grew dizzy and thought I might get sick on the floor.

Having been promised more—through the white man's "wanton and arrogant kindness"—and seeing that promise denied, Nat had to kill. The need to slaughter those who are most compassionate is, Nat says, "the central madness of nigger existence." Their philanthropy, however patronizing, creates a sense of self in Nat, but their refusal to accept that self as fully human creates in him the capacity to deny their human reality, to make their blood flow "in a foaming sacrament." He *will* grow, if not one way, then another. If he cannot become white then he will be black with an unimagined power of blackness:

> I knew that . . . the whole world of white flesh would someday founder and split apart upon my retribution, would perish by my design and at my hands.

Given the alternative by two-faced whites of being Sambo or Black Daemon he chooses the latter so that he can forever wipe out the sight of those white faces.

But it is Nat's curse and his nobility that he cannot wholly do to the white man what they have done to him. Even though he is betrayed by one master, whipped by another, even when he sees his mother raped by an Irish overseer, his best friend sold down the river, Nat cannot fully reduce the white man to a caricature, the Oppressor, whose lack of human characteristics justifies any retributive horror. Nor, despite the uprising, can he successfully suppress his own humanity. Nat's burden of intelligence creates in him an ambivalence. He can hold two opposed ideas in mind at the same time—hatred and understanding—and not quite go mad. Understanding is not forgiveness—he has sixty killed. But it diminishes his ferociousness—he might have killed 600. He is almost successful in stifling his apprehension of the humanness in his enemy but, with Margaret Whitehead, comes to a kind of love which, though it does not save her, keeps him from more murder and insures his own defeat and death.

Styron's Margaret is the Southern belle seen with compassion and understanding. She is a charming thing, full of little lyric bursts of froth, sentimental about the darkies' lot and squashed turtles, but a first-rate sensibility, trapped in taffeta, who can only talk to Nat—this odd, brilliant slave—whom she performs for, respects, patronizes, flirts with, she hardly knows what. For she is as blocked and profoundly isolated as he. Nat can articulate his isolation:

> I thirsted to plunge myself into the earth, into a tree, a deer, a bear, a bird, a boy, a stump, a stone, to shoot milky warm spurts of myself into the cold and lonely blue heart of the sky.

He reaches for shimmering visions of God and bloody revenge. But Margaret is as lonely and knows it less. She is disgusted by her brother—a smug preacher who likes to hunt runaway slaves—distressed by the nonsense she hears about Negro inferiority at her girls' seminary, yet caught in the only world she knows. She and Nat cannot come together in life, in love, so they seek each other in death, in murder:

> Then when I raised the rail above her head she gazed at me, as if past the imponderable vista of her anguish, with a grave and drowsy tenderness such as I had never known, spoke some words too soft to hear and, saying no more, closed her eyes upon all madness, illusion, dream and strife. So I brought the timber down and she was swiftly gone, and I hurled the hateful, shattered club far up into the weeds.

"Such as I had never known." Can there be a greater isolation? Never until then had either seen his own humanity reflected in another's eyes. For this the houses of their bodies are on fire; for this lack they lie down in darkness.

In this novel, as well as intensifying his complex, compelling vision, Styron extends his craft, modulates his style. The soaring, personal rhetoric of his other books is here held back to better delineate a range of characters. T. R. Gray, who set down the original *Confessions,* speaks in legalistic, Latinate rhetoric which luxuriates in revealing, polysyllabic distinctions, as when he defines Nat as *"an-i-mate* chattel." Hark, Nat's right-hand man, has an earthy, sharp rhetoric—"Nigger life ain't worth pig shit!" Jeremiah Cobb, who passes death sentence on Nat, speaks in a style which is at once boozy, grand, self-pitying and perceptive—"God, God, my poor Virginia, blighted domain." Nat is up tight, masked, cool, so his rhetoric is controlled, fluctuating between "nigger gabble," when that will serve his ends, and formal, perfect English. Thus Styron's flexible style helps him portray a variety of characters, a range of experiences—a dramatized paradigm of "the peculiar institution" in its several aspects—and amplify the thin original *Confessions* into a full, plausible statement of a man's groping understanding of the significance in his own life.

Nat is believable, the gap between color and times can be bridged, because he is first and last a man, not a Negro slave. That is, as an imaginative, sensitive man concerned with ways to live a meaningful life, Nat is not so far apart from Styron as at first it seems. Styron has been able to detect and describe the man beneath the murderer. We accept the man and are thus implicated in his deeds. For example: Nat sits alone in his cell, in a "web of chains," watching flies buzz "in haphazard elastic loopings" through huge motes of dust. He wonders if the motes hinder the flies' flight, but then decides that they can be no more obstruction than the "harmless, dazzling, pelting flurry" of October leaves to a man. He fancies an envy for the flies' brainless state, "unacquainted with misery or grief." But then he turns this idea around to see the flies as "God's supreme outcasts, buzzing eternally between heaven and oblivion in a pure agony of mindless twitching." He thinks, then, of the infrequency of suicide among slaves, how he had mistakenly interpreted this as evidence of their Christian forbearance, but now, sitting in chains, musing upon a fly:

> It seemed rather that my black shit-eating people were surely like flies, God's mindless outcasts, lacking even that will to destroy by their own hand their unending anguish . . .

Here Styron dramatizes Nat's marvelous associations in terms which any man, any time, could understand. Who has not mulled the significance of flies? Then he dramatizes an extraordinary sensibility, one able to yoke seeming dissimilarities in a striking synthesis. Which of us has construed the mote/leaf, fly/man connection? Thus we are swayed into provisional acceptance of the fly-slave analogy because we have already agreed with the logic of his previous metaphors. So it goes throughout the novel. Nat impinges. His humanness cannot be denied.

Comfort, however, should not be taken from Nat's humanity. Styron's novel should be as disturbing to white liberals as to black militants. For, given character and conditions, Nat had to do what he did. Seeing it all from his point of view forces us into the paradoxical situation of urging his revenge even though we know it will also mean general horror and his own destruction. We flinch from the horror—women scalped, a baby smashed against a wall—but Nat, despite Margaret, does not.

> *I would have done it all again. I would have destroyed them all. Yet I would have spared one. I would have spared her that showed me Him whose presence I had not fathomed or maybe never even known.*

God is love and love is Margaret and, as she cites from John, "he that dwelleth in love dwelleth in God, and God is him. . . ." But love does not conquer justified hatred, nor should it. God is also righteous wrath and, Styron demonstrates, Nat is in every way sympathetic and right when he leads in vengeance "a majestic black army of the Lord." Styron has written an apologia for no political position, but a stunningly beautiful embodiment of a noble man, in a rotten time and place, who tried his best to save himself and transform his world.

Rise and Slay!

John Thompson*

Once only in all the years of American Negro slavery did slaves organize a revolt. This was in 1831, in Southampton County, Virginia, a half-century after the Declaration of Independence, a third of a century before the Civil War. In the hundred years of false freedom following the Emancipation Proclamation, there was no important uprising by violence against the degradation imposed by America on its Negroes, until the summer of 1967. Then there occurred those bombings, burnings, and (to some uncertain extent) that gunfire directed against white Americans, acts said by some to have had the grand design of spreading so far as to force the recall of troops from Vietnam, and the disruption of American policy; but acts, anyway, upon which the governor of New Jersey conferred the title of "insurrection."

William Styron's new novel, *The Confessions of Nat Turner*, is based on that uprising in Virginia in 1831, which also was called in its time an "insurrection." Through the "confessions" of the leader of that insurrection, the book undertakes "to recreate a man and his era," and to answer for that episode of violence the questions that alarmed the whole South in 1831, as they now alarm white Americans in 1967. Why did the Negroes revolt? How widespread was the conspiracy? Why did Nat Turner fail? But most of all, it seems, the question still is, as it was for the South and as it must ominously be for us, why was the violence so limited? Why only one revolt? (Why only that fitful and even doubtful sniping in our cities, why only that ghetto looting when everywhere the white suburbs lie crammed with plunder, guarded by screen doors and poodles? Why did not the Negroes really seize Detroit or Newark? What will happen next?) Anyone who held slaves as Southerners held them, anyone who holds Negroes in degradation as white Americans hold them today, must realize that his head rests on a tender neck. Yet who dares justify the chop of the axe? And finally, what is the human condition which seems to nourish out of its essence an eternity of tyranny and murder?

*Reprinted from *Commentary*, Nov. 1967, pp. 81–85, by permission of the author.

These questions and many more related to them are argued, brooded over, dreamed of, and acted out in *The Confessions of Nat Turner*. (Why in Virginia, where slave conditions were relatively good? Why—as of the end of this summer—only in the North? What is a Negro?) One of the questions that will surely be asked about the book itself is whether or not the uncanny timeliness of its appearance, after the author's twenty years of study and five years of writing, is really a service or a disservice. The book aspires to be more than a tract, yet today, a book about a Negro who leads other Negroes to murder men, women, and children solely because they are white cannot avoid becoming the matter of editorials, sermons, panels, and shouting matches. It is hard to imagine, though, how anyone will be able to go beyond the author's determination and courage in facing the almost impossible question, that of the justification of murder. This is the book's central and very considerable intellectual distinction. Yet while it was absolutely necessary that the matter be held to without flinching, if the book was to amount to more than another bloody romance, this intellectual and moral problem could not be the author's major concern. "Perhaps," he says modestly in his brief foreword, "the reader will wish to draw a moral from this narrative, but it has been my own intention. . . ." It has been his intention, surely, to produce a work of art. And certainly he has succeeded beyond the reasonable hopes of almost any writer. *The Confessions of Nat Turner* is a superb novel. Later I will try to point out some of its achievements as art—worth doing, perhaps, especially because it has the particular excellence of being such a good story that no reader decently susceptible to stories will be likely to pause, his first time through, over the means of his enthrallment. Certain other questions about "timeliness," however, do affect the book as a novel quite aside from the kind of public notice timeliness may attract, and these must be considered later.

The novel is based on a pamphlet of twenty pages called "The Confessions of Nat Turner," published in 1832 following Turner's hanging. Styron says he has rarely departed from the few known facts about Turner and the uprising—and never from his understanding of the history of slavery in America. What he has added to that is an immense understanding of the human spirit and a fine novelist's ability to make us see—to force us to see, to shove our noses into it—to smell, taste, and feel these imaginary events, as if they were real, to live through them, according to the way we have been taught by novels to believe we are living when we accept, as so many of us still do, the language of novels as life. Finally there will remain a caution to be stated about that.

To relate in their order the chief events of Nat Turner's life is not at all to give an impression of the complex and rewarding structure of this book, which is like a treasure hunt where each clue is itself a treasure, but it may give us some bearings for comment. Turner was born at the very beginning of the 19th century, into good fortune for a slave. His mother was cook in a white kitchen, and as a house slave Nat was spared the total brutality of field labor.

Here it is irresistible to give a brief account of Nat's grandmother, whose misfortune allowed his mother, as an orphan, and thus himself as her son, the luck of the house such as it was. His grandmother had been brought over as a girl in a slave ship from the Guinea Coast, was impregnated by some black man on that ship, and she died, insane in her captivity, shortly after reaching the United States of America and bearing here her gift to its posterity. Her cedar headstone, standing for a time until the Negro graveyard is burned over for a yam patch, is one of the ironies of the book that so enters the soul, like iron, that there is incitement to murder in the pious arrogance of every letter of it.

"TIG"

AET. 13

BORN AN

HEATHEN

DIED BAP-

TISED IN CHRIST

A.D. 1782

R.I.P.

But Nat's luck, furthermore, was that when he passed to his second owner, Samuel Turner, he became the property of an eccentric gentleman who by chance perceived that Nat might be the subject for an experiment in educating Negroes, not an illegal proceeding in Virginia as it was elsewhere, but universally assumed to be about as impossible and useful as teaching cows to fly. Thus, Nat became the pet "darky" of the household, "the smart little tar baby," and learned to read. He acquired a passion for the Bible. Later, his owner had him instructed in the trade of carpentry and promised him the opportunity of earning his freedom—a further experiment to show that Negroes could be successful as freedmen, since a free Negro without a viable trade was worse off than a slave, even in Virginia. To Nat, then, Mr. Turner is a figure of biblical grandeur, a Moses or an Elijah: "My regard for him is very close to the feeling one should bear only toward the Divinity." But the land of Virginia goes barren; Mr. Turner, in despair and with self-loathing, deceitfully sells off his slaves. Nat is sold into Egypt—except again he is lucky; he does not go with so many of the others into the murderous plantations of Georgia or Alabama, but stays in Virginia where, however harsh his bondage, he is not lost beyond all bearings of hope. But he has to hate Mr. Turner. At last, after one thing and another, following one adventure after another with sottish whites, sadistic whites, sympathetic whites, indifferent whites, he begins to form his great plan. He has learned to identify all whites with the enemies of the children of Israel, even though, or indeed because, they sometimes pet him. Fully immersed in his project, he still recalls Miss Nell Turner who taught him as a child, and he remembers to breathe "a silent word of gratitude to this gentle and motherly lady, from whose lips I first heard those great lines from Isaiah: *Therefore will I number you to the sword, and ye shall bow down to the slaughter, because when I called ye did not answer."*

In those later years when he has turned thirty, Nat is again in a benevolent household, a skilled and trusted craftsman and a valuable property, "the smartest nigger in Southampton." He has become also a preacher of the Word to his people, and slowly gathers about him a small secret discipleship of slaves. He instructs them with stories of the captivity in Egypt, the triumph of Moses, and the wars of Joshua and David. Meanwhile, in the household of his benevolent master, Joseph Travis, Nat becomes ever more familiar with the other race. "Without knowing the white man at close hand . . . a Negro can only *pretend* to hate."

In still another household, where, rented out like a mule by his master, his talents as carpenter are highly prized, he is tantalized almost beyond endurance by the patronizing kindliness of Mrs. Whitehead and by the luscious, tender presence of her seventeen-year-old daughter, Margaret. In the Whitehead library he discovers a map of Virginia; and after a final, fast-induced vision, seeing in the heavens a black angel subdue a white angel, he completes his battle plan, based on that of Joshua. He will attack the farms, gathering recruits as he goes, seize the armory of the nearest town, and then retreat with his black army into the fastness of the Dismal Swamp, where, he believes, they can survive indefinitely, escaping in the end by sea to the North. By this time, his chosen few are prepared. When he tells them the time has come to reveal his purpose, they already know:

"Us gotta *kill* all dem white sonsabitches. Ain't dat what de Lawd done told you? Ain't dat right, Nat?"

The revolt begins well but soon fails. Joseph Travis and his family are slain, and the Whiteheads. Nat himself kills young Margaret. Altogether, sixty white people die. But only a fraction of the local Negroes join the rebels, many of the others aid the whites. After only two days the band is all dead or dispersed, and the whites undertake a riot of reprisal in which one-hundred and thirty innocent Negroes are cut down by mobs. Nat is captured, tried, and hanged. The first and last slave uprising in America has come to nothing.

As the few quotations I have given will have indicated, the story is told as if by Nat Turner himself. When the book opens, he is jailed, in leg irons and chains, awaiting trial and certain execution. After a few introductory pages from the deposition of the Southampton County court, the confessions begin, with a daring and totally assured flight of language into the heart and soul of Nat Turner.

Nat recounts the central dream or vision of his life. He imagines he is floating in some sort of small boat down an estuary toward the sea—which he has never seen—and toward a cape where stands a strange white marble building, a temple, sarcophagus, or monument, "endowed with a profound mystery." This vision—we may suppose it to be both death and birth, seen in this same symbolic white body—brings him always an "emotion of tranquil and abiding mystery." The book will close as it begins with this half-dream, half-vision. The passage has an extraordinary effect, no matter how we rationalize it with our modern interpretations of dreams. It creates at once sympathy, respect, and trust for our imaginary narrator. At the center of his soul is a dream of peace, beneath all the violence, hatred, and despair; and he conveys this to us in language of surpassing distinction. The dream itself may be beyond language, but it is language that brings it to us. And that the words are those of a Negro slave is made totally credible. The tone, so unfaltering and impeccable throughout the book, is slightly archaic, formal, and touched everywhere with the majesty of the King James Bible. Yet the author has claimed for himself a further daring, beyond his claims of this eloquence for a Negro slave. Nat Turner speaks not only as some genius of the 1830's might have spoken, but he insinuates himself across the years into our minds by his mastery—and strange as it may seem this too is totally successful—of the more exquisite strategies of 20th-century literary language. He says, and the reader believes Nat Turner is saying, "—as if by one single glimpse of this scene I might comprehend all the earth's ancient, oceanic, preposterous splendor." Here, *preposterous* is one of our modern sophistications. Or, he says, someone is "chewing upon the *gorgeous* syllables as if upon air. . . ." Or, "an ancient Elijah exploding in bearded triumph at the transfiguration of Christ." Or again, this time with the utter conviction of unrhetorical simplicity: "my tall, beautiful mother."

Very rarely does the style slip at all, perhaps it does not ever. I may misunderstand when I wish that Nat had not been made to echo the famous line of Marlowe in describing his first great vision, ". . . the blood ran in streams against the churning firmament." But all in all, the grand style is an achievement as necessary as the intellectual courage of the book, and the primary act of Styron's faith in his hero is this benediction of his finest language. It is a language somewhat of the kind that Styron—if we are to speak of the author now as we do in reviewing books, as enlisted in some competition for Parnassus—a language that Styron has used before but without quite the occasion for it. In *Set This House On Fire* he did seem to be chewing upon gorgeous syllables as if upon air. Here he has bitten off more than air, and the great words are authentic for Nat Turner. And those other obsessions of Styron's are necessary here, to speak again of the author, those obsessions with willful human debasement, with murder, depravity, corruption of the beautifully innocent, those things that seemed only obsessions in him once. But there they come true.

The other range of language available to contemporary authors also serves Styron well, and again doubly impresses upon us that people who lived in 1831 were human beings like us, and that we are human beings like them. How instantly and shockingly the scene leaps into focus when we overhear a Negro slave of 1831, in Virginia, saying, "*Shee-it,* man."

"*After this I saw in the night visions, and behold a beast, dreadful and terrible, and strong exceedingly; and it had great iron teeth: it devoured and brake in pieces. I beheld then because of the voice of the great words: I beheld even until the beast was slain, and his body destroyed, and given to the burning flame.*"

"Dey was a free nigger woman name Laurie, wife to old John Bright live up Cloud School way, you know? Well, dey took dat woman an' leant her up 'longside a fence and druv a three-foot spike right up her ole pussy like dey was layin' out a barbecue. Oh me, Nat, de tales I heerd tell dese months and days! Dey was two white mens I heerd about, come up from Carolina, has actual got dem a real bunch of black nigger heads all nailed to a pole and was out to git dem some mo' till de troops grabbed holt 'em an' run 'em back to Carolina—" "Hush."

"Nigger life ain't worth pig shit." "White fuckah." So far as I know, nobody else has ever seriously made this simple and frightening exchange of the smallest debased currency of talk to establish a sure transaction between our times and those other days.

Earlier, I remarked how the author, through Nat's voice, causes us to see, taste, and smell the events of the story. This amounts to more than "description." To Nat Turner, as to Huckleberry Finn (and to Macbeth) in justified precedent, the world of nature, the weather, the call of beast and bird, are more than background. They are signs charged with anima, they are portents, warnings, omens. "The light paled, the stark shadows of the barren wintry trees grew hazy and dull, lost definition; far off in the woods a flock of ragamuffin sparrows, late winter visitors, ceased their cheeping, became still in the false dusk." Or, "I sat still on the board, watching the dawn light grow and fill the cell like a cup, stealthily, blossoming with the color of pearl. Far off in the distance now I heard a rooster crow, a faint call like a remote hurrah, echoing, fading into silence. Then another rooster crowed, nearer now. For a long while I sat there, listening and waiting. Save for Hark's breathing there was no sound at all for many minutes, until at last I heard a distant horn blow, mournful and familiar-sounding, a hollow soft diminishing cry in the fields beyond Jerusalem, rousing up the Negroes on some farm or other."

Although with this pervading sense of atmosphere, and the ever-present power of the language itself, the events as drama are prepared and delivered with all the old art of storytelling and with the instruction of modern psychology. Nat's revelations come to him in pairs, reinforcing one another, thickening and deepening the significance of the movements of his mind and of the persons in the action. His first drive to raise himself comes when as a child he instinctively steals a book he cannot read, and almost simultaneously witnesses the rape of his helplessly compliant mother by a drunken white overseer. He becomes aware, then, for the first time, of what he is. "I feel a sense of my weakness, my smallness, my defenselessness, my *niggerness,* invading me like a wind to the marrow of my bones."

When Nat first becomes inflamed almost to the point of madness by the girl Margaret Whitehead, he had just bloodied his own thumb, building shelves in her mother's library, whereupon she enters on a girlish prattling errand—in her pantalettes. His first self-baptism follows a boyish incident of homosexuality; his first vision proceeds from a masturbation fantasy. On the whole, this texture of combined incidents seems to be one more of the necessities of the book. At the end, in the last pages—and the suspense of the foregone conclusion keeps up until those very last pages—maybe it becomes at last schematic, but only finally, only, as I have suggested earlier, in a way that no novel could avoid.

Another kind of schematicism appears here and there, minor and rather embarrassing to notice, like some tiny blemishes of the skin that indicate no serious disorder but rather an overindulgence in something too rich for the digestion. These are the phrases that echo unnecessarily the note of historical irony: Negro slavery will last a thousand years, like the Third Reich; mention is made of people ill-fed, ill-clothed, ill-housed, like Roosevelt's one-third of a nation. These could well be spared, as perhaps for the sake of the whole book as a novel the "love story" could not.

The deep connivance of the sexual instincts in all race relations has of course been remarked a million times. The white man's easy exploitation of Negro women, his paranoid fascination with the Negro penis, his projection of all his own forbidden sexual urges onto the Negro, particularly in the classic Southern preoccupation with sibling incest—these are all familiar matters today. (There is a tale of how William Faulkner once, at a Hollywood story conference, was asked to solve a crux the old Hays office had imposed. The movie needed to indicate clearly to the audience, without showing anything openly censorable, that a young man and a young woman had been having sexual relations. Faulkner: "Make them brother and sister.")

But sex today has become only another disappointment, rather like Emancipation or Desegregation or Free Dirty Speech. A Negro today can indeed, should he wish to obtain her consent, legally marry any white man's sister. This is less than the millennium. The general relaxation of sexual inhibitions in our society does not seem to have brought about, as once it was innocently supposed to do, any general relaxation of tyranny and murder, of violence. Human aggression is the problem of our time, not sex, and if the two are inextricably bound together in the roots of human biology and culture, if unkinking one of them will help straighten the other, then all we can say is that we have not yet begun. Dramatically, sex plays a central part in *The Confessions of Nat Turner,* and it does this in the traditional form of Western art, as love. Nat lusts for, loves most tenderly, and finally murders the beautiful Margaret Whitehead. Their scenes together provide some of the most astonishing evocations I have ever seen of how unspeakably desirable the young human female can be when our hearts have fixed upon some particular incarnation.

That Margaret all but openly, all but knowingly, loves Nat too is one of the things that most maddens him. Her love for him could never imagine crossing the hopeless gulf between them, except in death. "O Nat I hurt so. Please kill me Nat I hurt so." Well, today she could cross that gulf; if the gulf exists now it is as a recognized attraction. And at the climax of the novel, at its romantic, novelistic, *romance* climax, Nat crosses the gulf. Margaret, God, and his own sex are all, just before he is hanged, reconciled: "and the twain—black and white—are one. I faint slowly." God, who has been absent from Nat since the rebellion, leaving him in an emptiness beyond despair, speaks out at last. *Come, My son!* "Even so, come, Lord Jesus."

In plain words, Nat Turner has just masturbated and this is his masturbation fantasy. What irony the author intends by this I do not know, nor how much he wants us to dwell on it. Nat, at least, is left with the fantasy as it is to him, as revelation, as the final moment of truth and reconciliation before death. So what can this be except the author's final kindness to Nat, a benevolent deception to ease the truly unbearable thoughts that had been his as he lay in his cell in chains, defeated and alone? It is those thoughts, though, that the reader must be left with, and not the *Liebestod.*

In his cell, as the book begins, Nat has been meditating on the flies that buzz there "in haphazard elastic loopings from wall to wall. . . . In many ways, I thought, a fly must be one of the most fortunate of God's creatures. Brainless born, brainlessly seeking its sustenance from anything wet and warm, it found its brainless mate, reproduced, and died brainless, unacquainted with misery or grief. But then I asked myself: How could I be sure? Who could say that flies were not instead God's supreme outcasts, buzzing eternally between heaven and oblivion in a pure agony of mindless twitching, forced by instinct to dine off sweat and slime and offal, their very brainlessness an everlasting torment? So that even if someone, well-meaning but mistaken, wished himself out of human misery and into a fly's estate, he would only find himself in a more monstrous hell than he had ever imagined—an existence in which there was no act of will, no choice, but a blind and automatic obedience to instinct which caused him to feast endlessly and gluttonously and revolting-ly upon the guts of a rotting fox or a bucket of prisoner's slops. Surely, then, this would be the ultimate damnation: to exist in the world of a fly, eating thus, without will or choice and against all desire."

Nat reflects how he had once thought that the Negro's Christian faith, "his understanding of a kind of righteousness at the heart of suffer-ing," could save him. *"And the afflicted people thou wilt save, for thou art my lamp, O Lord; and the Lord will lighten my darkness.* But now as I sat there amid the sunlight and the flickering shadows of falling leaves and the incessant murmur and buzz of the flies, I could no longer say that I felt this to be true. It seemed rather that my black shit-eating people were surely like flies, God's mindless outcasts, lacking even that will to destroy by their own hand their unending anguish. . . ."

Nigger life ain't worth pig shit, Nat Turner's friend Nelson once said: *mought make a nigger worth somethin' to hisself, tryin' to get free, even if he don't.*

It will take some utmost devotee of suffering to deny that proposi-tion, as he reads this book, or to claim that there was any other choice for a Negro slave, to whom it had occurred that he might become a man, ex-cept slaughter. By the time Nat Turner's project begins to form, we can-not wait for the heads to roll. Then what of Newark and Detroit? What of burning stores and stealing television sets, or shooting a fireman in the back, supposing it was not the police or the National Guardsmen who did the shooting? Is this really required to make Negroes worth something? Easy for us to say it is not, but if what this book tells us is true, we are wrong. And wrong on other testimony too, if we are going to take art as testimony. William Faulkner was never able to imagine a Negro as more than a great sufferer—"they endured"—until he created his first real Negro man, Lucas Beauchamp, to whom precisely it first occurred, of all Faulkner's Negroes, that he might kill a white man.

Why is this so shocking? Why are we terrified by the notion that a Negro may kill a white person, when we are only saddened perhaps or in-dignant when whites kill Negroes with absolute impunity, assassinating Negro leaders in the most cowardly fashion possible, lying about it, and walking the streets afterward in secure self-congratulation; even, with ab-solute impunity, doing what no fanatic enemy of America could have imagined in his most inimical dreams, bombing a Sunday School full of children and killing them like dynamited fish?

The plain fact is that subject peoples are not supposed to retaliate against their subjection. Retaliation is shocking not for the real harm it does, but because it breaks a taboo. If we admit this right to retaliate, we have admitted our subjection of these people, and this our consciousness cannot afford. Americans have an absolute right to kill Vietnamese. If a Vietnamese kills an American, it is "terror"; the illegal, immoral violation of a taboo, as dreadful as patricide. But like so many of the other taboos, like those sexual ones, this taboo seems to have lost its *mana*, at least for those upon whom we used to enforce it so freely. Even, there is an element of this primitive magic in the thrilled reaction to the great Israeli war. Jews are supposed to suffer, not to fight back, and above all they are not supposed to win. Or they *were* not; the thrill is that now they have won the outrageous right to win. Negroes seem still at some early stage of freedom, believing still that they are not supposed to win; while the whites remain at an earlier age, in which Negroes may dare to sing hymns on white territory if they get permission.

It is a complicated and probably, as usual, a tragic day in history. We made a community here, agreeing to practice violence only minimally against one another, while reserving the right to practice it totally against others. Negroes, Puerto Ricans, they were not members of the community. Their nonviolence was imposed, not agreed upon. Now, uninstructed in the unconscious taboos that guard the rest of us from one another, they are free to commit random acts of aggression, pure aggression quite without other aim—or with the simple aim only, as in the instant switchblade reaction of the *macho* to some affront, of claiming a pitiful and disgusting runt's "manhood" by the murder of a stranger in the subway. To all this we are as blind as Nat Turner's confessor, the Court Commissioner who was honestly trying to understand the insurrection:

" 'For see here, Reverend, that's another item the people can't understand. If this was out-and-out tyranny, yes. If you was maltreated, beaten, ill-fed, ill-clothed, ill-housed—yes. If any of these things prevailed, yes. Even if you existed under the conditions presently extant in the British Isles or Ireland, where the average agricultural peasantry is on an economic level with a dog, or less—even if you existed under these conditions, the people could understand. Yes. But this ain't even Mississippi or Arkansas. This is *Virginia* in the year Anno Domini 1831 and you have labored under civilized and virtuous masters. And Joseph Travis, among others, you butcher in cold blood! That—' He passed his hand across his brow, a gesture of real lament. '*That* the people can't understand.' "

Nor can we understand. The final words are probably those of the tormented slave-owner who has sold Nat's friends and betrayed Nat, whom he loved.

"Surely mankind has yet to be born. *Surely* this is true! For only something blind and uncomprehending could exist in such a mean conjunction with its own flesh, its own kind. How else account for such faltering, clumsy, hateful cruelty? Even the possums and the skunks know better! Even the weasels and the meadow mice have a natural regard for their own blood and kin. . . ."

As for us, we seem doomed to remain oppressor and oppressed. Men of good will, we shall hope and pray that we can somehow alleviate all this through due process, through the natural decency of those of us who are enjoying our deserved prosperity in 1967, through the inspiration and leadership of the various millionaires we choose to guide our political destinies, and again, through the natural decency of those who may find themselves at some momentary if slightly fatal disadvantage in our company. This we may devoutly hope. But all we know for certain, considering now the truths of art rather than the blessings of politics or religion, is that from time to time men will rise and slay, if not the oppressor, then whosoever lies at hand in the oppressor's likeness.

Unslavish Fidelity

Anonymous*

Some writers regard a first-person narrative the way a film director would consider making a movie with only one camera. Yet the technical restrictions of the narrative "I" vary a good deal, depending on whether the confining ego is the author's autobiographical self or an imaginary character created by him. When he is writing as himself, he is presumably limited to the facts and fictions of his own experience; when he is writing as an imaginary character, he is limited only by what he can persuade the reader to accept. Even the autobiographical ego, however, seems wonderfully free when compared to a first person which belongs to someone who actually lived and whom the author is attempting to revive with his imagination: his sense of confinement as a writer must then be almost unbearably intense. We cannot check the detail of the author's own life nor that of an imaginary character, but we *can* track down his lies and evasions in the case of a literary Lazarus, and we can also be more sure about his achievement in drawing character. We knew of the real Lazarus; has he been brought back to life? Or is he perhaps another person using the same name, the same ego?

Although it is justifiable to base a novel on a real character, it is not as easy to justify writing such a novel in the first person. At one extreme in this biographical kind of novel is *The Moon and Sixpence*, in which Somerset Maugham built so much on his Gauguin base that he even used another name for the character and thus didn't have to worry about respecting the facts of Gauguin's life—or respecting Gauguin. Then, more in the middle of this group, come the floods of novels about artists with romantic, dramatic lives so popular in the last generation. Typical of these was *Lust for Life* about Van Gogh, which was written in the third person and usually had good documentary evidence for ascribing certain "thoughts" to its hero, "Vincent". We were in fact let in for a minimum of that kind of embarrassment we feel on reading trashy, patronizing interior monologues ostensibly put in the head of some hero we admire by a scribe lacking the hero's genius and eloquence. We can most easily under-

*Reprinted from *Times Literary Supplement* (London), 9 May 1968, p. 480, by permission of Times Newspapers Ltd.

stand the whole problem when we remember how little we know about even the way our own parents think and behave. Would the reader like Irving Stone, or a contemporary Somerset Maugham to write a novel about his father or mother describing their allegedly intimate thoughts and actions?

It is reasonable to pose this question in considering William Styron's new novel, *The Confessions of Nat Turner*, for which he has just been awarded the 1968 Pulitzer Prize for fiction, because Mr. Styron has not only chosen as his chief character a man who actually lived but he has written in the first person as if from Nat Turner's viewpoint. Most American critics when the novel first appeared applauded this as an extraordinary feat of the imagination, but unfortunately it appeared that they were greatly influenced by the fact that Nat Turner was a Southern Negro and Mr. Styron is a Southern White; and the twain never usually meet; they were really seeing it not in literary or even in human terms, but in a purely racial context. Nobody seemed to care what Nat Turner the man would have thought about having another man's thoughts—particularly some repressed puritanical ones—ascribed to him. Trying to repeat Mr. Styron's feat of imagining Mr. Turner's reactions, one suspects that he would not have liked it at all.

The essential drama of Nat Turner—the slave revolt he led in Virginia in 1831—is a great story, even in the bits and pieces left us after most of the evidence was suppressed. It naturally would attract an American novelist of our time because he might find in it so many reflections of today's racial tragedy. For those who read only newspaper headlines, Stokely Carmichael will seem to follow in the footsteps of Nat Turner; ten years ago Malcolm X might have seemed a successor. It would be impossible to convince such a reader that the real Nat Turner, in fact, would have had more in common with the late Dr. Martin Luther King, because they shared a great religious sense, although in action Nat Turner was more an Old Testament man and Dr. King was strictly a son of the New Testament. It is a story, in short, that has the raw material of all the great historical novels; it is a marvellous tale and also is very relevant to our own time.

But why tell it from Nat Turner's viewpoint in the first person? Firstly, it shows scant respect for Nat Turner, who was obviously an extraordinary man; secondly, hardly any documents remain, except his own brief confession, to justify guessing his thoughts or feelings; thirdly, he lived over 100 years ago as a slave, and we know very little about the day-to-day domestic lives of slaves, so that the author not only had to throw his imagination back over a century but also into an almost unknown society; also he is a white Southerner and therefore had all kinds of personal, social blocks to overcome in tackling this particular subject from the inside. Technically, too, there seem to be enormous advantages in giving us a third-person narrative without any of the restrictions of the first person, for surely there are restrictions enough without any purely technical ones: in this case, one would have thought the novelist needed all the help he could give himself.

Having raised the question of why this form was chosen—the first novel, in fact, Mr. Styron has written in the first person—we need now to consider how it works out in practice over 429 pages. Well, let us say this at once. Lazarus (that is, Nat Turner) hasn't been raised from the dead. This combination of Old Testament prophet and Southern white puritan isn't the Nat Turner who has so sturdily resisted the White South's attempts to erase him from history. And one wonders in the end, as he clearly isn't Nat Turner, whether he is anyone, or whether perhaps the author hasn't rolled back the gravestone and found the body arising in his novel to be no more or less than William Styron himself. Almost at times one can imagine the book as *The Confessions of William Styron* by Nat Turner, for the style is biblical (in a contemporary translation), though more rhetorical than Nat Turner's own confession (which anyway was taken down by a lawyer and may have been only a curt summary by an amateur stenographer); the style *could* be Nat Turner's on a garrulous day, but the person reflected there seems so often to be an outsider posing as an insider, i.e., Styron himself. The details of slave life, what a Negro slave thought (or thinks) of a white person, the racial smells, and so on down through the documentary details, are often expressed too badly in the way a white outsider often tells one some things about Negro life which he imagines are some great original discovery. Mr. Styron, who has come late to an appreciation of Negro life, might well write that way, but Nat Turner, who was born knowing all of it, would have written or talked much more naturally about it all and so fitted it more closely into the body of his narrative. It is the difference between knowing something at first hand and merely learning it at second hand. One might add, of course, that Mr. Styron presumably had to bear in mind that he was writing essentially for a white book-buying public even more ignorant of Negro life in America, then or now, than Mr. Styron, and therefore these bald explanations were necessary in his mind, however much they strike the wrong notes in a narrative pretending to be Nat Turner's.

Mr. Styron perhaps sought to defend himself from such a charge in his prefatory note, in which he calls his book "less an 'historical novel' in conventional terms than a meditation on history." Call it a novel, and perhaps Mr. Styron will reply: "Now, now, didn't I tell you it was a 'meditation on history'?" But unfortunately *The Confessions of Nat Turner* is a novel or it is nothing, although one leading American weekly did choose to have it reviewed by an historian. Its history, however, is at a freshman level and its meditating is no more profound that that of most talented novelists, even great ones. And this is no criticism of it as a novel, for history and literature serve different gods. History must at its most basic level be accurate as regards facts even if it is incapable of recapturing atmosphere. But a novel at the same basic level has to involve us in its atmosphere; it can dispense with facts altogether. If Mr. Styron's Nat Turner were a giant who involved us in his tragedy as if it were our own, we might have reservations about writing of someone who has lived in the first person (surely it is always condescending), but we would excuse it as the price for the writer's art. But Mr. Styron's Nat Turner does not so involve us. There are long stretches of fine descriptive writing—and when "Nat Turner" is involved simply in action, it is often moving—but the sum total is not a man, not a slave in nineteenth-century Virginia, but, as Mr. Styron suggests himself, the author meditating on slavery in his own home state, and perhaps his sense of the white Southerner's guilt in himself, though surely *The Confessions of William Styron* would have been more to the point there (how seldom white Southerners are willing to give us the kind of soul-stirring personal confessions we have come to expect from American Negro writers).

Some American Negro critics have questioned its historical accuracy (some think, for example, that rather than being the repressed puritan of Mr. Styron, Nat Turner was, in fact, married and deep in family life) but we must insist on considering it as a novel and therefore much more relevant to us is the liveliness of the chief character—call him "Nat Turner" or "Charles Strickland," it doesn't really matter, so long as you reject Mr. Styron's description of it as a "meditation." We know enough about contemporary slum life, ghetto life, Southern rural and plantation life, to guess what some aspects of slave life must have been like. Certainly in that kind of environment you must graduate sexually much earlier and take most sexual forms of expression much more for granted. Mr. Styron has his "Nat" and one of the other slaves trying to communicate with each other through a feeble little touch of homosexuality. The scene, though prettily written, was more like certain scenes that used to appear in novels about English public schools—or perhaps white Southern private schools. Nor is "Nat's" hungering for white womanhood and apparent rejection of Negro girls very convincing even in contemporary terms. Slave life by its very nature could not support such artificial, genteel, puritanical repressions. It is an essentially dry, reserved attitude and what one senses above all in the very little we know about slave life is the flood of soul feeling waiting to find an outlet, almost any outlet. Mr. Styron's "Nat", in the matter of sex, is more like a suburban white boy.

A big point of his characterization is that "Nat" could not bring himself to kill. Fifty-five white men, women and children were killed by "Nat's" army of slaves, but "Nat" himself kept finding his weapons too inefficient and succeeded at last in killing only one person—a young white girl he had yearned after. And after that one killing, the fanaticism that had kept him going seeped out of him. As Mr. Styron has him say: "My mouth was sour with the yellow recollection of death and blood-smeared fields and walls." He watches a white girl escape without trying to stop her. "Did I really wish to vouchsafe a life for the one that I had taken?"

It is a convenient way of looking at all the bloodshed. The ill-treated slaves, led by a biblical fanatic, rebelled and murdered, but their leader, finding action harder than words, is revolted by the bloodshed and gives up. It is the same hope of those white Americans today who fear some great violent act of Negro revenge: a hope that guilt will stop the Negroes. That is why the late Dr. King was admired by so many white people—he condemned the violence even before it began. His religious message, however, was lost. So, too, this way of looking at Nat Turner's revolt is much too convenient. Why accept it any more than the opposite interpretation—that Nat Turner was not a fanatic of the Old Testament who turned into a lover of the New Testament when he tried to carry out his revenge, but that he was really as much of an avenger as Abraham or David and that the slave-owners by their very way of life were human devils good only for fire and sword? Just as Mr. Styron does not delve deeply enough into the slaves' way of life but often seems to be transplanting the way of life he has known in *his* Virginia, so, too, he seems to be taking too easy, too convenient, too complacent a view of Nat Turner's outbreak and those fifty-five deaths, not to mention the execution of Nat Turner and his army and the destruction of most of the signs that they had ever existed. It is a view that obviously will appeal to most established readers—that is, most established whites—but that perhaps, too, is an illustration of how far short Mr. Styron has stopped before the full anguish he contemplated in the tragic life of Nat Turner.

Blacklash

Robert Coles*

"I don't know what to tell my son when he goes off to school. It may be different for the colored man up North, or even over in New Orleans and the big cities like that, but out here it's Mississippi, with only the fields here and the store and the sheriff here, and you know when they don't like what a colored man does, they just goes and takes matters into their own hands.

"My boy, he's doing something real different. I don't know how it come about. Not with my help, anyway. He's marching, that one is. They signed him up to march. Some one did, out of Jackson, I think. A civil rights man. He got my boy's ear. He told him that we're still slaves—and I can't deny it—and we shouldn't be. Well, of course, I agree there, too. We're not supposed to be slaves no more; and that was to be gone a long time ago, my daddy told me. His daddy, he was the son of one, but he was supposed to be the last one, though I can't really see what difference it makes, to call us a slave or not. We live the same way, and it doesn't make any difference what the name of us is.

"But my boy, he's all fired up. They got him to be like that. They kept on telling him things, about how bad it is, and how we've got to go get things for ourselves, the colored man, and stand up to the white people, stand up real strong. Well, that was a lot of wild talking, that's what I thought. But they came and said we could have our kids go to the white school, and things like that, if we wanted, and all we had to do was *petition* them, *petition* the white people and they'd go along.

"That's the biggest piece of foolishness I'd ever heard, when I heard it. First I thought my boy was pulling a big joke on me, but then I decided it was himself he was fooling—because he kept on saying, 'I'm going, Daddy,' and 'I'm going, Daddy,' until I thought he was in bad trouble, yes sir, real bad trouble, in his head.

"But his mother, she sided with him, and she said yes, he should go. And I thought the end of the world was coming, because sure as anything they'll come in the night and kill us, be it with dynamite or bullets or a

*Reprinted from *Partisan Review*, 35 (Winter 1968), 128–33, by permission of the author and journal. Copyright © 1968, Partisan Review, Inc.

fire that burns us down so fast we couldn't figure which fire it was, the one here or the one in Hell. And if we tried to escape, they'd be waiting for us up the road, guns pointing, like always, you know.

"Well, the next thing that happened was It. My boy—he's four-teen—he just walked off one day, right from this house here, with everyone watching us real close, not only him but us, too. They were lawyers and the news people, and they told me there was government people, the F.B.I. from up in Washington come, and they were to stand by, in case of trouble. And the next thing I knew, there was our James walking out of here, and he marched his way right into the school and sat there, with all those white kids, and God knows how he come out of it alive, and the fact that he's still alive today—well, I can't explain it, I'll have to admit. Because I thought they'd kill him, right on the spot, as soon as his black feet stepped inside of that white school, and no matter how many people were there to watch him and protect him. And to this minute, I hold my breath in talking of it all. Because the white man, he'll kill a nigger when he can, even for no reason, you see—just that he *wants* to; and my boy, he gave them a real good reason. But so far, they're holding their guns, and maybe waiting until the moment is quiet, and they'll strike. I fear they will. I believe they will. I do. And when they do, you know, they'll kill more than one—maybe the whole family, for all you can know. They don't stop until they figure they've drawn all the blood they need, and then we know that it's no use provoking them, not on this earth."

Those words were spoken in the autumn of 1965, well over a century since Nat Turner led his short-lived revolt and died by hanging; and presumably at a time when William Styron was writing *The Confessions of Nat Turner*, an unforgettable book, a feverish, convincing, redemptive book, a book by a contemporary American novelist that will be read and valued for generations. As I read Styron's novel I kept on thinking of that youth and his family. For years I spent time in Little Rock, in New Orleans, in Clinton, Tennessee, in Atlanta—but I have never seen anything to match what the man quoted above had to face: his son was not marching down a city's streets, in the company of others; nor could the youth fall back on the support of a Negro community, poor but massed together and somewhat able to defend itself. They were way out in the country, the father, the mother and their children; they were "sitting ducks," as they put it, sharecroppers who lived in Mississippi, virtual slaves, barely alive in isolated territory that may well be as dangerous for the "uppity" Negro even now as Nat Turner's Virginia ever was. When I watched that man say goodbye to his son I wondered what he could possibly be thinking. I saw the mixed pride and terror in his eyes and I heard him resort to history, just as "we" do in the most desperate of moments, just as Styron does in his novel; but I never quite dared imagine all that went through his mind—in contrast, that is, to what he was willing to say, and say to the likes of me. (Perhaps one day psychiatrists will realize that a lot more goes on in the mind than even willing and talkative patients can convey, *or* their doctors can comprehend and formulate, even by resort to such catch-all terms as the "unconscious," that large, rambling and convenient house which presumably shelters everything not spoken or remembered.)

And the son, what could I "make" of the son? What was "going on" in his mind as he took himself and his race into that white, rural, Mississippi school, in that hard-core segregationist county, with its active, powerful Klan? One of the first things the son did tell me had to do with members of the Klan. They were all about, he was told by a white boy in the locker room, and they meant business. They had their executions, and their next target was obvious. They would one day appear out of nowhere, a "healthy number" of them. So, the Negro boy told me what the white boy told him: "There are a healthy number of Klan people hereabouts." He spoke in a quiet, matter-of-fact voice.

He was too old for me to rely on drawings—paintings—as I do with young children when I want to get an idea of at least some of the things that pass through their minds. He was too shy, too reserved, too dignified for me to ask him direct questions. (Not all reluctance, even on the part of a self-declared patient, need be called "resistance"—by hungry listeners, psychiatrists who all too often want merely to hear confirmed what they already claim to know.)

So, at that time, I tried to *imagine* what was alive in the mind of that rather old child, that young man who one moment made me feel childish—not to mention excluded, ashamed and useless—and another moment seemed as open and direct and captivating as Wordsworth thought a "boy" of his age should still be. By that time I knew all the *conflicts* he had—psychological, social, the lot—and I knew the *defenses* he had or would soon be required to build, and I had some idea of what he was *thinking*, because I had asked many other Negro children what they had in mind when, say, they walked past a fierce mob on their way to an American school. I have never really known how to pull it all together, though—the conflicts, the defenses, the thoughts, the social and economic "background," the particular family's "goals." There is something more going on in the father and the son I have described here than a mind like mine, looking for what it is looking for, can really fathom. Psychiatrists are always on their way down, plumbing this or that depth; they don't quite know what to do with someone who is kicking *his* way *up*, fighting his way to the surface for air and rescue, for freedom, a word used possessively and cheaply in America to describe what white men obtained for themselves and denied to all others—Indians, Negroes, Mexicans.

I suppose it is true that William Styron has also tried to understand and give expression to the "innermost" feelings of a slave, and by extension the "real" Negro the rest of us simply fail to acknowledge or comprehend. In fact, it is a little sad to read some of the good and bad things said of his new novel, particularly the comments that dwell upon its psychological accuracy or deplore its historical failures. We hear that Styron has done the miraculous, transcended race, time and class to reach Nat Turner's "mind" and put its worst preoccupations and most noble moments to print. We hear that Styron has shown himself just another bourgeois writer: he makes something special and different out of Nat and out of one revolt among many; and he refuses Negroes their *general* anger and discontent, in the face of which the South inevitably had to be harsh and repressive (and was, *before* Nat Turner's rebellion).

And finally, we are told that Nat is simply not believable: the language is obviously Styron's, Styron straining hard rather than Nat talking naturally. Approved or disapproved as if it were a piece of research written by a social scientist—its *psychology* is good, its sense of *history* and its *sociology* or *anthropology* excellent or questionable—this is in fact a novel written by one of our best contemporary novelists. Styron either comes off knowing the virtually unknowable—for a white man; or he is told that he needs to know nineteenth-century society much better, needs a few "field trips," needs to pick up more of the Negro's dialect (which he actually uses to great effect) and then draw on *it*, rather than his own voice and style of expression. Styron himself makes it very clear that he is trying to write a "meditation on history." There is nothing evasive or sly about the expression; it tells as much or as little as the word "novel" does. Perhaps the author could not simply assume the integrity and validity of his own novel because he lives in our time, when old-fashioned literary critics are less menacing than their more "objective" successors, who have all those new "methodological tools" to fall back upon.

On New Year's Day, 1967, in Roxbury, Connecticut, Styron must have known "deep down" as he wrote his "Author's Note" that he would be called before Freud, or Marx, or Stanley Elkins, or Frederick Law Olmsted, or Malinowski or C. Wright Mills—even as Oscar Lewis is asked to read more B. F. Skinner, more Lukács, and become more "quantitative," less "qualitative" and more "historical"; and Freud is called a poor sociologist who never knew what Durkheim or Weber did. Again and again we choose to ignore exactly what a given man is doing, and when and where, and in the face of what professional resistance or prejudice. As critics we also refuse to invoke the most obvious and pertinent standards; and for Styron's *Confessions of Nat Turner* those standards have to do with the novel's success or failure as a work of the writer's imagination.

I think Styron has written an enduring book. He captures a whole region, the speech, the beautiful land, the moody weather and everywhere the open black fear and the white fear that masquerades as edgy pride. Whatever its historical merits, I think the book will *make* history, be a part of our history. Like Faulkner, Styron will not let up on the reader. He has some of Faulkner's passionate, withering power, and like him he is a Southerner, brought up on talk, on stories and on the region's calculated and desperate ambiguity. I do not see how anyone—regardless of race—can ever be the same again after reading his novel, after reading what the facts known about Nat Turner did to and brought out from the mind of William Styron. For me the book made the sharecropper quoted above become more "real," more of a "person." That is the point—and the irony—of what a writer can do. The sharecropper *is* real, *is* a person to me. God knows I have seen him often enough. Yet, when I recently went to see him again, with Styron's Nat in mind, something seemed different. The sharecropper's "life," his words and eyes and gestures became Nat's, and in a flash I felt myself "seeing" and "feeling" more than I could before. I suppose I could say that Styron's writing made me newly and gratefully impressionable, and as a result more broadly observant.

The obvious simplicity of the novel's plot binds together all sorts of complicated and tortuous "inner" events. Nat Turner has been caught after an abortive but striking, persistent and fearful rebellion. In Styron's book Nat sits in jail awaiting execution and speaks and speaks and speaks; and dreams and remembers and meditates and wonders and listens. In a few days he will be dead and the novel about his life and spirit over. Nat's listening is particularly important. Styron wants to bring Nat alive, make him seethe and cower, but as a writer Styron knows that the most private and withdrawn person lives with others, even if they populate an imaginary world of dreams and fantasies. And as a Southerner Styron knows that slavery or no slavery the region's twin distinctions have been its willingness to exploit the Negro ruthlessly and live beside him in fitful and peculiar closeness. *The Confessions of Nat Turner* conveys more than a believable, distinguished Negro, a would-be leader who never had a chance once he started himself and others marching; the book captures beautifully the "thing" that goes on between black and white—particularly the more educated of both races—in Virginia or Alabama or Louisiana. Perhaps a tentative generalization might be in order: Southern writers of whatever color are particularly sensitive to the terrible and humorous and impossible "goings-on" between men and women and children of both races; Northern writers who are Negro or white go deep into themselves, and even into the skins of "others," but somehow fail to capture much that happens *between* people whose racial differences mean so much to one another. Perhaps it is simply that not much *does* go on between whites and blacks in New York or Chicago. Or rather, they hate and fear one another, pure and simple, but as Baldwin has said, they don't "know" one another. Ellison's "invisible man" nevertheless had all sorts of palpable, sad, comic and ironic dealings with white men in the South; and Ellison knows that social customs and habits, no matter how formal, constrained or abusive, are not without their "deeper" or "inner" (read "psychological" today) significance. Like Ellison, Styron manages to catch the twisted intimacy that Southerners of both races live out—and Southern writers portray.

So Styron has wedded his voice, his personal experience, his generous heart to Nat's yearning, suffering, gifted life. In so doing he succeeds in making Nat a particular human being and a particular Negro, and thereby affirms himself a novelist who wants to enter the world with whatever sensibility he can summon. Yes, I find it all "valid": Nat's experiences with Negroes and whites, his memories of growing up, his various moods and "attitudes," his biblical rage and biblical resignation, his uncanny restraint as a commander-in-chief and his murderous vengeance—singly delivered upon Margaret, the white woman who came nearest him and drew him furthest from himself and his awful circumstances. But I do not believe it is the "validity" or the historical "accuracy" of *The Confessions of Nat Turner* that count all that much. William Styron has written words that will push hard at thousands and thousands of minds. He has awakened us, made us feel more and in that way given us a rather special glimmer of that elusive thing called "history" and that terribly concrete thing called "race." Following the tradition of writers like Faulkner and Tolstoy, he has made a bold and successful attempt to follow them quite directly—not by writing "responsibly" about a social issue, or writing "profoundly" about a psychological one, but by writing a haunting and luminous novel that incidentally breathes history and psychology and whatever on every page.

Mr. William Styron and
The Reverend Turner

Mike Thelwell*

We know within certain general and stable (though they appear to be constantly expanding) boundaries what a novel is. We know also what a historical novel is, and the terms by which such works can be judged. But when a work of fiction is cast in the form of a novel, utilizes those techniques of narrative, situation and structure that we associate with the novel, and which concerns an important historical event, but is declared to be "less an historical novel in conventional terms than a meditation on history," then what are we to make of it? Is its historicity more or less important than its meditativeness?

William Styron's *The Confessions of Nat Turner* straddles two genres, claims to be not quite either, and manages to combine the problems of both while to an extent reaping dual dividends as a novel which is in some way also "history." If the book were simply a novel, then there are things that could be said about its structure, characterizations and language. But how is one to judge the proper and appropriate language of meditation? If it were simply history, then we could point to certain violations of the rules for reconstructing history, and point out that, on the face of any objective reconstruction of the evidence, it could not have been how the book says it was.

The fanfare with which the book has been greeted is largely based on the duality of its claims. It is hailed as a major novel with a significant theme. As a work which recreates and significantly illumines a morally traumatic portion of the American past, it is held, *ipso facto*, to contribute to our awareness of ourselves and our subconscious postures toward present realities. In this context the work becomes a page in that sacred journal that marks the peculiarly American quest to master the truth of our past in a quest for historical and spiritual authenticity. This is doubtlessly an honorable and valid undertaking, but one which borders on absurdity on many sides. It is perhaps a function of this absurdity that I find myself writing in defense of a black rebel, dead since 1831, related

*Reprinted from *Massachusetts Review*, 9 (Winter 1968), 7–29, by permission of the author and journal. An abridged version appeared in *William Styron's Nat Turner—Ten Black Writers Respond*, ed. John Henrik Clarke (Boston: Beacon Press, 1968).

to me neither by blood or obligation, and whose shades, I suspect, have little concern with judgments of posterity as expressed through the person of Mr. Styron.

But my concern is less with the Rev. Turner's memory than it is with the future of his grandchildren—to whom he used to be a hero. And it is reasonably clear—if the notices with which the book was greeted mean anything at all—that Mr. Styron's book is being read as a kind of super historical novel by a public seeking what it seeks in all of its reading, the shock of mildly pleasurable outrage and, incidentally, information and insight.

Because the book is both "historical" and a "novel," a section of the public will invest it with qualities it does not necessarily possess. The facts and situations will be assumed to be accurate because by being "historical" it must of necessity be "true." And just as the facts of history are "true," so are, in a somewhat different sense, the insights of the novel. This is the great advantage of the form. By simulating a cosmos, its terms appear sufficient unto itself, its boundaries definitive and discrete, so that no further possibilities, no moral or philosophical dimensions, other than those existing within those boundaries, seem relevant to that cosmos. It is true, as Negroes are increasingly discovering, that what is excluded by historians is frequently as important as what they choose to record. This must be doubly true of the novel because of the cloak of self-containment which it wears, so that what is an extremely selective process takes on the illusory dimensions of being "the experience." So a book which according to its publishers "reveals in unforgettable human terms the agonizing *essence* of Negro slavery" can certainly be held accountable for what it selects and what it chooses to ignore. It is a solemn and rather prosaic truth that one cannot approach the essence by ignoring the *substance*, either in literature or in the laboratory. For an example, if it were true, or even suggested by the evidence—and this is not the case—that Nat Turner's first nineteen years were spent as a privileged and pampered house slave, favored (beyond all belief) by an ineffectually well-intentioned (beyond all belief) old Master of vaguely liberal bent, this would be neither the essence nor substance of the experience of slavery. The substance of that experience, as we well know, was the deadening accumulation of event, the experience of the slave ship, the auction block, the torture of body and spirit, undernourishment, overwork, the violation of spirit and body, the deprivation of a culture, of language, and the overwhelming presence of the apparatus of white power, that is to say the power to coerce, to mutilate and ultimately arbitrarily to kill. That, it seems to me, is the substance of reality out of which any "essence of Negro slavery" must be distilled. Those are realities that have conditioned our present situation for both whites and blacks.

Despite the necessary secondary tasks which Styron undertakes in this book, i.e., the fleshing out of various contemporary positions on "the question," the evocation of a historical period, the reconstruction of a culture inherently morally schizophrenic, and so on, the theme of the novel, the central mystery that engages us and clamors for insight is the personality and motivation of Nat Turner and the determined and desperate band of men who fought and died with him.

It is in this context that the questions which so plague our time become relevant. The question of the moral imperatives and consequence of violent rebellion, of its spiritual and political implications, the existential confrontation with the act of murder, and particularly the exquisitely painful responsibility of the instigator, who not only for himself must choose to resist—that is, to take the irrevocable step—but to be responsible for his followers taking it also. This is the ultimate revolutionary responsibility, and requires a certainty that approaches either love turned to desperation or madness. Styron's Nat Turner, in marked contrast to the historical Nat, has neither; lacking ideology or even the fervor of a prophetic fanaticism, he has only a pallid and unconvincing neurosis. It is perhaps, as one critic has proclaimed, that "only a white southerner could have written this book," this particular book. It is equally true that only a writer who is imaginatively familiar with the agonies of oppression and the morally convoluted dimensions of rebellion and who is in some measure liberated from that experience can do justice to this theme. Mr. Styron is not such a writer.

In selecting the subject and the strategy for this novel, Styron took certain calculated risks. In doing so—and one must assume a full awareness of the purely technical and creative problems they represented—he displays a *chutspah* which borders on arrogance. First, by selecting Turner, Styron chose a personality with a reality in history, caught up in actual events, within a specific historical situation, about which and whom some facts are known. By so doing Styron placed on his creative imagination the responsibility of working within the facts and events as we know them. This he has not done, and his failure is at once significant and revealing.

Then, by deciding to render the novel through the mind, voice and consciousness of Nat Turner, he undertook the challenge that finally ruined the book. Assume for a moment that a White Southern gentleman could, by some alchemy of the consciousness, tune in on the mind-set, thought-pattern, impulses, feelings and beliefs of a black slave in 1831. Having accomplished this miracle of empathy, since they lack common language or experience, he would still have the problem of creating a *literary* idiom in which to report his insights to his contemporaries. And as the linguists are discovering, and novelists have always known, language is not only a medium of communication, but also helps shape and express consciousness. It not only functions to formulate attitudes but to create them, it not only describes experience but colors the perception of it, so that dialects and idioms are evolved by people to serve the necessities of their experience. This is one reason why people in Harlem do not speak like people in Bucks County.

When black people were brought here they were deprived of their language, and of the underpinnings in cultural experience out of which that language comes. It is clear that they replaced it with two languages, one for themselves and another for the white masters. It is this latter that has been preserved, parodied is a better word, as the "Sambo" dialect in the works of southern dialect humorists (even Samuel Clemens at times)—to whom it was often simply quaint and humorous. The only vestiges we have of the real language of the slaves is in those spirituals which have survived. Mere vestiges though they are, most spirituals give a clue to the true tenor of that language. It is a language of conspiracy and disguised meaning, of pointed irony and sharp metaphor. It is a language produced by oppression, but whose central impulse is survival and resistance. It is undoubtedly the language in which Turner's rebellion and the countless other plots for insurrection were formulated. Anyone who has been privileged to catch the performance of a good black preacher in the rural south (or Martin Luther King talking to a black audience) understands something of the range and flexibility of this language. Lacking complicated syntactical structure and vast vocabulary, it depends on what linguists call para-language, that is gesture, physical expression, and modulation of cadences and intonation which serve to change the meaning—in incredibly subtle ways—of the same collection of words. It is intensely poetic and expressive since vivid simile and a creative juxtaposition of images and metaphor must serve (instead of a large vocabulary) to cause the audience to see and feel. It is undoubtedly a language of action rather than a language of reflection, and is as such more easily available to the dramatist than the novelist. Nevertheless it is some literary approximation of this language that the characterization of Nat Turner requires. And Mr. Styron's Nat speaks or rather meditates in (as Spenser is said to have written in) no language at all. His creator places in his mouth a sterile and leaden prose that not even sizeable transfusions of Old Testament rhetoric can vitalize. It is a strange fusion of Latinate classicism, a kind of Episcopalian prissiness, and Faulkner at his least inspired. At times it would seem that Mr. Styron was trying, for whatever reason, to imitate the stodgy "official" prose of the 19th century lawyer who recorded the original confessions. At other times Nat sounds like nothing so much as a conscious parody of the prose voice of James Baldwin, the Negro Mr. Styron knows best. This is not to say that the prose is not lucid, even elegant in a baroque Victorian way, especially in the functionally inexplicable passages of nature writing that continuously interrupt the narrative. But finally it is the language of the essay, heavy and declarative. It does not live.

This language combines with the structure of the novel to disastrous effect. Since the story begins after the fact, with Nat already in prison reflecting on his life, much of the book is in the form of long unbroken monologues, insulated in an inert prose. Even the most violent action or intensely felt experience seems distanced and without immediacy, strangely lumpen. Lacking the allusiveness of thought or the vitality of speech, and the quality of dynamic tension necessary to the illusion of the immediacy of the experience, the language reduces us to spectators rather than participants in the action.

Because the problem of language is inextricably caught up in the problem of consciousness, Styron's inability to solve this problem (and it may well be insoluble) is symbolic of, and operative in, his failure to bridge the gap of consciousness.

Nat Turner operates in this novel with a "white" language and a white consciousness. His descriptions of his fellow-slaves, for example, are not in the language of a man talking about his friends and family; they reveal, rather, the detailed racial emphasis best exemplified by slave-auction advertisements, or the pseudo-anthropological reports sent back from Africa by white missionaries in the 19th century. Lacking the idiom in which Nat might communicate intimately with his peers, and apparently any meaningful insight into what they might say to each other, Styron simply avoids this problem by having him spend most of his time in that paradoxically southern situation, close to but isolated from whites. This isolation in proximity becomes his obsession. And as his language is theirs, so are his values and desires. Styron's Nat Turner, the house nigger, is certainly not the emotional or psychological prototype of the rebellious slave, he is the spiritual ancestor of the contemporary middle-class Negro, that is to say the Negro type with whom whites and obviously Mr. Styron feel most comfortable.

Conspicuously intelligent—in their terms—he aspires hopelessly to the culture and stature of his white masters, to break his isolation by being recognized on their terms. Witness his ecstatic joy when he is able to spell a word, thereby demonstrating his intelligence to his master's guests. Naturally, to Mr. Styron, and his white audience, he must despise and hold in contempt the society of his own people whom he considers dumb, mindless, unsalvageable brutes unfitted either for freedom or salvation. Hating the blackness which limits the possibilities which he feels should be his by right of intelligence and accomplishment he becomes a schizoid nigger-baiter. That the speaker is supposed to be black merely obscures the issue. In the historical context it is impossible to imagine Nat Turner, a minister to his people, teacher, and above all, a venerated leader, displaying the kind of total alienation and contempt inherent in the following:

> A mob of Negroes from the cabins were trooping towards the house. Muffled against the cold in the coarse and shapeless, yet decent, winter garments Marse Samuel provided for them. . . . I could hear the babble

of their voices filled with Christmas anticipation and loutish nigger cheer. The sight of them suddenly touched me with a loathing so intense that I was filled with disgust, belly sickness, and I turned my eyes away.

What this Nat Turner really wants is to become white, and failing that, to integrate. This is the Negro whom whites, in the smug near-sighted chauvinism of their cultural and ethnic superiority, can understand. As a type it certainly exists *today*; 1831 is a different question. What is wrong with this characterization as applied to Nat Turner is simply that it has sprung full-blown out of Mr. Styron's fantasies. It does not logically derive from those facts of Turner's life that have come down to us. Indeed, to develop this characterization, not only did Mr. Styron have to ignore portions of this meager record, but he had to distort, in significant ways, many of the portions he did use.

In an author's note at the beginning of the novel, Mr. Styron says that he has "rarely departed from the *known* facts about Nat Turner and the revolt of which he was the leader." "However," he continues, "in those areas where there is little knowledge in regard to Nat . . . I have allowed myself the utmost freedom of imagination in reconstructing events—yet I trust remaining within the bounds of what meager enlightenment history has left us about the institution of slavery."

One can only assume from this note that the author intends us to regard this novel in a certain way. We must assume that it is an unbiased reconstruction of the events and probable motivations for the Nat Turner rebellion, true to the available facts. Where facts and events are missing, they are imaginatively supplied, carefully based on the logical extension of what is known. By virtue of this claim, and the book's being titled *The Confessions of Nat Turner*, thereby tying it to the event, we are led to expect the greatest possible dispassionate, unprejudicial objectivity and accuracy. It is with these minimum expectations that we approach the book, and they must affect how we react to it, and ultimately our attitudes to the subject it illumines. While we cannot realistically expect the novel to escape the influence of the author's private vision, his unique and subjective sensibilities and attitudes, we do expect it to be free of any kind of special pleading, fact-juggling, unsupported theorizing, and interpretations which answer not to the facts or logic of the events, but to an intellectual commitment to a version of history which is not only debatable but under serious question. We do not expect these specious qualities, because they are patently not the terms on which this work is presented to us. Yet Mr. Styron falls victim to all. If Mr. Styron presents his terms in good faith, we must conclude that he was betrayed by his own unconscious attitudes towards slavery, black people, and his ancestors whose myths, prejudices, and self-delusions are faithfully preserved in what must be one of the most touching examples of ancestral reverence outside oriental literature.

The primary source of information, of "known facts," is extremely brief, about 4,000 words. Why was it necessary, in this objective reconstruction, to depart from this source? In Nat's confession his formative years are deeply rooted in his family and within the slave society. His mother and father placed his first book in his hands and encouraged him in his efforts to read. His grandmother, to whom he claims to have been very attached, gave him religious instruction and predicted that he was too intellectually curious and intelligent to make a tractable slave. He taught himself reading and writing, and successfully deduced ways to make gunpowder and paper, being limited in these enterprises only by "the lack of means." The white lawyer who took his confession interrogated him about these processes and reports that he was "well-informed on the subject." From an early age, says Nat, he enjoyed the confidence of the "Negroes of the neighborhood," who would take him on their stealing expeditions to plan for them. What emerges from this is that Nat's character and attitudes in his formative years were molded by his family and peers. He becomes a leader and a plotter very early, and is involved with his black brothers in the clandestine resistance to slavery symbolized by stealing. Later he becomes a Preacher, that is, a leader and a minister among the slaves. When he stops fraternizing with his peers, it is not out of any disdain or contempt, but for the very good political reason that "having soon discovered to be great, I must appear so, and therefore studiously avoided mixing in *society*, and wrapped myself in mystery."

It is Mr. Styron's inability or unwillingness to deal with the notion of a slave "society"—the presence of a black culture, that is, a system of social organization and modes of collective response—with its own values, leaders, and rules, that more than anything else robs the novel of credibility. Because he cannot deal in convincing terms with the "culture" of slavery which produced and shaped Nat Turner, Styron, in contempt for the "known facts," simply isolates Turner from the blacks, places him among the whites, and attempts to create from that situation convincing motives and stimuli for his actions. If the case, historically, had been as Styron reconstructs it, it is difficult to imagine that a single slave would have followed Turner.

In Mr. Styron's "free ranging imagination," Nat's formative years are somewhat different. He has no knowledge of his father. His grandmother, a mute, catatonic, culturally shocked Corromantee wench, barely survives to give birth to his mother after disembarking from the slave ship. Nat's master, who is only mentioned once in his original confession, and then to say only that he was "religious," is elevated by Styron to be the major influence on Nat's life. Discovering Nat with a book stolen from his library (an occasion of great surprise since no nigger ever expressed interest in literacy), he has Nat tutored by his own daughter. Nat becomes a favorite, does light work around the great house, and observes the elegance, enlightenment and moral superiority of his owners and strives to emulate and impress them. He feels superior to all other "niggers." Of his kindly and benevolent master Nat reports,

> . . . I hold him in such awe, that I am forced to regard him physically as well as spiritually, in terms of such patriarchal and spiritual grandeur that glows forth from Moses on the mount. . . .

Such awe, indeed, that in his version rather than Styron's he is leading his fellow slaves in raiding his property.

This venerable patriarch is, as Styron is careful to report, educating Nat as an experiment to prove that Negroes are educable. After which presumably he will personally build schools and free them all since he feels that "it is evil to keep these people in slavery, yet they cannot be freed. They must be educated. To free these people without education with the prejudice that exists would be a ghastly crime."

Indeed, Marse Samuel does in due course reveal to Nat that, having educated him, he intends to free him. This contingency terrifies Nat, literate paragon among slaves though he is, since he simply is unable to conceive of assuming responsibility for himself. The wise and kindly master had however anticipated this insecurity and reassures Nat that he has devised a method to give him his freedom gradually, under his kindly and paternalistic guidance. Nat is satisfied. (No explanation—except that time passes—is given in the novel of the process by which Nat moves from this abject dependence to the self-confidence that will allow him to accept responsibility for a colony of free rebels that it was his intention to start in the Dismal Swamps.)

This response (Please good Massa, dis yer Darkie ain't studyin' no freedom) is, of course, one of the favorite clichés coming to us from a certain school of plantation melodrama. Its inclusion here violates the evidence of history. This is not to say that it had no basis in reality, but there were other realities which are not shown. In order to make this response credible in Nat (remember he is the most intelligent and enlightened of any slave shown), Styron includes an image of "The Freed Slave" who is starving, confused, and totally incapable of surviving, and presumably this wretch who is clearly worse off than the slaves, represents Nat's only experience or knowledge of freedom. This is misleading, since the fact is that every southern community and many northern ones had free Negroes, and at times whole colonies of them. These freemen worked as skilled artisans in many instances; some, to their discredit, even owned slaves. What is important here is that both slave masters and slaves knew this, and for the slaves these free Negroes represented a constant inspiration. What then is the purpose of this fanciful episode concerning Marse Samuel's plantation, Nat's fear of freedom, and the desperate straits of "The Freed Slave"?

The first figure is familiar: the gracious, courtly, humane, landed

Virginia gentleman, wracked by conscience, solicitous of his chattel, and obligated by conscience to take care of his slaves who could not survive on their own. For him slavery is not a financial operation, it is the exercise of a moral obligation. (The example of the freed slave proves this.) His home, in which the First Families of Virginia "with names like Byrd, and Clarke" gather in elaborate carriages, rivals Tara in its gentility, charm, and benevolence. This is the Golden Age of Southern Chivalry, and what is being reconstructed for us is the enlightened benevolence of the "Old Dominion" version of slavery, surely the least oppressive serfdom in mankind's history. This only applies, as Mr. Styron is careful to indicate, to slaves fortunate enough to be owned by the enlightened gentry; it is the poor white overseers, and small landholders who made the lot of slaves unendurable. Surely we have some right to expect serious novelists in 1967 to eschew this kind of fanciful nonsense? Especially if we know that it is precisely on these large Virginia plantations that the most degrading and debasing form of slavery was developed. Even as early as the 1830's, the Virginia land being increasingly exhausted by tobacco, these enlightened aristocrats had begun converting their plantations to breeding farms— that is to say, the business of breeding black men and women like animals for the purpose of supplying the labor markets of the Deep South. That's one reality which is only fleetingly mentioned in this novel.[1]

In Marse Samuel's great house, Nat becomes "a pet, the little black jewel of Turner's Mill. Pampered, fondled, nudged, pinched, I was the household's spoiled child." Enjoying great leisure he is enabled to lurk around for "a rare glimpse, face to face, of the pure, proud, astonishing, smooth-skinned beauty," of Miss Emmaline, one of the daughters of the household. It is clear that we are to be rewarded with some psychological insight into the emotional development of the young slave, and we are not disappointed. Nat, in his words, grows to "worship" Miss Emmaline, she who "moves with the proud serenity . . . which was good and pure in itself, like the disembodied, transparent beauty of an imagined angel," with a "virginal passion." For angels, what else?

Imagine then, the trauma of the poor youth who is raised in "surroundings where white ladies seemed to float like bubbles in an immaculate effulgence of purity and perfection" when he finds Miss Emmaline rutting with her cousin on the lawn and in her passion blaspheming God's name. When, having apparently enjoyed the act, she rushes with the inevitable "rustle of taffeta" into the house, she carries with her Nat's innocence and faith.

But for Nat, the experience, shattering as we are asked to believe it is, constitutes a form of emancipation. He had long rejected as too common the idea of sex with black wenches and substituted for it onanistic fantasies with faceless white women.[2] After his "Angel's" fall from grace, he says ". . . in my fantasies she began to replace the innocent imaginary girl with the golden curls as the object of my craving, and on those Saturdays when I stole into my private place in the carpenter shop to relieve my pent-up desires, it was Miss Emmaline whose bare, white full round hips and belly responded wildly to my lust and who . . . allowed me to partake of all the wicked and Godless yet unutterable joys of defilement." Well, after all, that is what comes of all that "fondling, petting and pinching." Nat becomes an inverted, frustrated, onanistic, emotionally short-circuited lecher after white women. Presumably, if he had given way to this secret lust and raped the white girl he is later to murder, the rebellion would never have occurred. The horror of this experience would probably have driven the young girl insane (almost a moral obligation for her in this tradition of southern literature) but some fifty-five white and two hundred black lives would have been saved. This moonlight, magnolia and Freud view of history is presented as the basic motivation for the rebellion, a sexual desire (or love if you will) turned malignant in frustration.[3] Even if it did not come dangerously close to reiterating the infuriating sexual slander of the Negro male that is the stock-in-trade of the American racist, it would still be unacceptable as a theory of Turner's motives because this kind of frustration-neurosis expresses itself in solitary, suicidal acts of violence, not in planned, public, political acts of rebellion.

The spare facts of Turner's life constitute grounds for a truly fascinating and illuminating meditation. Certainly more useful insight into Nat Turner's character and motives are to be achieved in the effort to reconstruct what it must have been like for the youth growing up in the influence of his family—two parents and a grandmother, his reacting to them and their attitudes towards slavery, his response to his father's running off, his early leadership in the stealing expeditions, his call to the ministry (while ploughing, not serving mint juleps) and his position among his fellows. Surely it is from these experiences that his personality and mission evolved.

Turner tells us, through Gray's, not Styron's, "Confessions," that as he grew to young manhood, the memory of what had been said about him as a child by "white and black"—that he would never be of use to anyone as a slave—began to obsess him, "finding I had arrived to man's estate and was a slave." But he says he is consoled by the spirit of prophecy which indicates to him that there is a preordained role for him in that position. He begins his ministry and continually exhorts his people who "believed and said my wisdom came from God." He obviously occupies a place of some importance among them on his own merit, not from being the favorite of a paternalistic Master. That he is a man of charisma and magnetism is evident. He seems totally preoccupied with his God and his people and the only mention of any white person at this time is of an overseer from whom he runs away and is at large for thirty days. He returns voluntarily because the Spirit orders him to return to his "mission," the exact nature of which he does not yet know. Upon his return the "negroes were astonished and murmured against me, saying that if they had my sense they would not serve any master in the world." This incident either did not impress Mr. Styron enough to be included, or else was at odds with his "interpretation." For one thing their unequivocal condemnation of Turner for returning establishes his peers' attitudes towards slavery, and it is different from the one generally found in the book. This is, significantly, one of the few cases on record of any slave returning voluntarily to slavery. What did it mean? Did Turner return out of a sense of solidarity with his black brothers, out of a sense of divine mission? Was it simply another case of nostalgia for the irresponsible security of slavery, did he get hungry? Subsequent events, and his own explanation, suggest some glimmering of a deliberate motive.

His given reason (at the time) for returning must stand as a masterpiece of irony. He simply quotes one of the Biblical texts best loved by slave owners: "he that knoweth his master's will and does not do it, shall be beaten with many stripes and flogged with a rod." To the slave master this must have been gratifying indeed, evidence further of the faithful darky well-steeped in the acceptable slave morality. To Nat, knowing that his master is God, a terrible vengeful God, who has selected him for a "mission," it meant quite something else. He may even have undertaken the episode simply to establish his trustworthiness, thereby getting the necessary mobility to organize.

Let us examine how this omission serves the "interpretation" presented in the novel. While the historical Turner is trying to regain the confidence of his fellows, who are angry, incredulous and suspicious at the idea of a man returning voluntarily to slavery, Styron's Nat Turner is fuming and fulminating endlessly at the spiritless subservience and servility of his fellow slaves who are presented as totally lacking in the will or imagination to change their condition. There can be no question that "Uncle Toms" existed, but it is also equally clear that these types and the attitudes they represented were seized upon by apologists for the institution and publicized and exaggerated, out of all proportion, while militance and rebelliousness were played down. Who can doubt this after hearing any contemporary Southern sheriff mouthing his eternal platitude, "our niggers are happy?" History testifies that the desire for freedom among the slaves was a constant problem to their owners.[4]

The reality of slavery was that the slaves were constantly resisting and rebelling, whether by sabotage, malingering, escape to the north, physical retaliation to attack, plotting insurrection (with a frequency that caused the masters to live in a state of constant apprehension and under conditions of continual vigilance and security), running off to join Indian tribes, or else to form small bands of armed guerillas operating out of swamps and remote areas. It is difficult to imagine why, if the majority of slaves were inner "sambos," broken in mind and spirit as Styron's Nat suggests, Southern Governors filled the official record with so many requests for federal troops to guard against insurrection. Why were meetings of slaves forbidden or so severely proscribed? Why were they required to have passes permitting them to use the roads? Why were curfews so rigidly maintained? Why were armed patrols abroad in every slave community at night? Why were firearms considered a necessary part of the overseer's equipment? Is it perhaps because the "Sambo" type was the product of "enlightened" Virginian slavery that no suggestion of this massive machinery of coercion and control is found in the novel? What does its absence do to the "essence of the experience of slavery" that the publishers boast about? It is rather like trying to capture the experience of the Nazi concentration camps without mentioning the barbed wire or armed guards.

Two examples of incidents reported in the original "confessions" and transformed by Mr. Styron's imagination are worthy of mention, as they are indicative of the pattern of interpretation that runs through the book. Turner tells of converting and baptizing a white man, an event unprecedented in Tidewater Virginia of the time, and which would probably cause an equally great furor were it to happen today. The two men are refused access to the church and repair to the river for the ceremony where they are mocked and threatened by a white crowd.

In Styron's version the white convert is a drunken, degenerate, child-molesting pederast who is about to be run out of the county anyway, and is shown as the typical sub-human, white trash "cracker" that one might find in Erskine Caldwell. Again the logic dictating such an interpretation is not clear, but this is what happens in this novel to the only white who is shown associating with slaves on anything that looks like simple human terms, outside of the paternalism and implied superiority of the social categories of the time.

The second instance of arbitrary and derogatory "interpretation" concerns a slave called Will, who invited himself to join the insurrection. He is different from the other conspirators by virtue of this fact: Will was not recruited, he volunteered. In the original confession Turner reports finding Will among his men when he joins them on the day of the insurrection.

> I asked Will how he came to be there, and he answered his life was worth no more than others, and his liberty as dear. I asked him if he thought to obtain it? He said he would or lose his life. This was enough to put him in full confidence.

In the subsequent violence Will is identified specifically as "dispatching" a number of people, while most of the other murders are not attributed to members of the band. The most that can be said of Turner's references to Will is that they show him operating with a singleminded efficiency in carrying out the work at hand, which is, after all the extermination of whites. In the context of Turner's narrative there is no suggestion of dementia or frenzy in Will's actions; like Joshua he is simply engaged in the destruction of the Lord's enemies. There is one probable explanation for Turner's specific references to Will other than his being particularly impressed by his murderous efficiency. This is simply that Will, being the last of the original band recruited, may have felt it necessary to stay close to the leader so as to demonstrate his sincerity, thus causing Turner to remember his actions more vividly than others in the group.

In the novel, Nat sees "the demented, hate-ravished, mashed-in face . . ." whose "wooly head was filled with cockleburrs. A scar glistens on his black cheek, shiny as an eel cast up on a mud-bank. I felt that if I could reach out I could almost touch with my finger-tips the madness stirring within him, a shaggy brute heaving beneath the carapace of a black skin." Will is "streaked with mud, stinking, fangs bared beneath a nose stepped upon and bent like a flattened spoon." His eyes shine "with a malign fire" and he bears a hatred "to all mankind, all creation." We learn that Will has been reduced to this condition of bestiality by the unendurable cruelties of a sadistic master so that his is not the "natural depravity" that another generation of Southern writers would have evoked. But even so, this characterization, this portrait of an evolutionary marvel, half-nigger, half-beast, is surely familiar to anyone who knows such classics of southern literature as Dixon's *The Klansman*. His has been a long history. He has been constantly and conveniently evoked for any number of purposes, to frighten children with or to justify lynchings. And as he sidles into the scene, stinking and licking his fangs, we recognize his function: like the others of his type who have preceded him, he will rape a white woman. And thirty pages later, despite Nat's injunctions against rape (no sexual incidents are mentioned in the record of the trial), an injunction all the nobler in light of his own perennial, frustrated cravings, we find this scene:

> There deserted of all save those two acting out their final tableau—the tar black man and the woman, bone-white, bone rigid with fear beyond telling, pressed urgently together against the door in a simulacrum of shattered oneness and heartsick farewell. . . .

and it looks as if Nigger-beast has struck again. One had hoped that this particular stereotype had served his time in the pages of southern fiction and could now be laid to rest. It is, to say the least, disappointing to see him resurrected by a writer of Mr. Styron's unquestioned sophistication—and to what purpose?[5]

In addition to these (and other) examples of pejorative "interpretation" there is finally the major invention that gives color to the entire novel. Mr. Styron, on no historical evidence, has Turner's final defeat coming as a result of the actions of loyal slaves who fought in defense of their beloved masters. That these slaves are identified as "owned by the gentry" further underlines the book's emphasis on the benignity of "aristocratic slavery" which was able to command the loyalty of these slaves who were in one white character's words "living too well." Asked about this in the *Per Se* interview, Mr. Styron, who really talks too much, said: "The slaves in many of these houses—and not at gun point either, but quite voluntarily—were rallying to their master's defense . . . I'm sure the cliché liberal of our time would ask for proof that this is true. But there are a lot of motives, quite real ones, that would cause a Negro to defend his white master against other Negroes. One was to preserve his own skin. He was shrewd [at all other times in the novel, with the exception of Nat, he is loutish and stupid] and he figured that if he played his cards right he'd get off better. And also I think that there was quite frankly often a very profound loyalty in those days. The fashionable historians can't convince me otherwise, because there's too much evidence."

He never, however, cites any of this evidence. Mr. Styron simply *knows*, like a Mississippi planter of my acquaintance, that "them old time darkies were loyal and true." This is an item of faith. Apart from the fact that there is no evidence of this having happened, is it logical? Can one really believe that a group of outnumbered and frightened slave-holders discovering themselves in the midst of a slave revolt would have armed other slaves, who might themselves [have] been part of the conspiracy?

This thing which did not happen is made into one of the central motifs of the book. Turner broods on the memory of "Negroes in great numbers . . . firing back at us with as much passion and fury and even skill as their white masters." When his lieutenant Hark falls, Turner recalls "three bare-chested Negroes in the pantaloons of *coachmen* . . . kick him back to earth with booted feet. Hark flopped around in desperation, but they kicked him again, kicked him with an exuberance not caused by any white man's urgings or threat or exhortation but with rackety glee. . . ."

This invention makes it possible for a white lawyer at the trial to "revise certain traditional notions about Negro cowardice," because "whatever the deficiencies of the Negro character—and they are many varied and grave—this uprising has proved . . . that the average Negro slave faced with the choice of joining up with a fanatical insurgent leader such as Nat Turner or defending his fond and devoted master, will leap to his master's defense and fight as devotedly as any man and by so doing give proud evidence of the benevolence of a system so ignorantly decried by Quakers and other such morally dishonest detractors." The "bravery of those black men who fought bravely and well" at their master's side is to be recorded "to the everlasting honor of this genial institution."

It is true that those lines are meant to be read as special pleading and polemical defense of the institution *by a single character*. But it was not that character who invented those black loyalists, it was Mr. Styron, and much in the novel—the picture of life at Turner's Mill and Turner's own reflections on the event—support this general position. It is built into the architecture of the novel.

When Gray, the lawyer who is taking Turner's confession, says to Nat,

> . . . you not only had a fantastic amount of Niggers who did not *join* up with you but there was a whole countless number more who were your active *enemies* . . . they were as determined to protect and save their masters as you were to murder them. . . . All the time that you were carrying around in that fanatical head of your'n the notion that the niggers were going to latch onto your great mission . . . the actual reality was that nine out of ten of your fellow burrheads just wasn't buying any such ideas. Reverend, I have no doubt it was your own race that contributed more to your fiasco than anything else. It just ain't a race made for revolution, thats all. Thats another reason why nigger slavery is going to last for a thousand years.

we are clearly meant to read it as one taunting rationale of an apologist for slavery. Because of the emphasis in the whole book, it is none too clear that this *is* a qualifiable position. Quite literally *nothing* that we are shown in the novel denies the fictional Gray's conclusions. Quite to the contrary, as I have indicated, characters and events which in fact support them are invented in a systematic way.

Turner himself acquiesces in this interpretation. Dispirited and broken, he sits in his cell feeling himself betrayed by his people and his God. He thinks "it seemed . . . that my black shit-eating people were surely like flies, God's mindless outcasts, lacking even that will to destroy by their own hand their unending anguish. . . ."[6]

A pathetic and almost obscene figure, Nat broods and sulks in jail awaiting his death. The night before his execution he is comforted by fantasies of a sexual encounter with the white girl he murdered. In the original confessions Turner shows no such uncertainty or ambiguity. When asked if he could not see that the entire undertaking was a mistake, he answers simply, "was not Christ crucified?" Gray's final description of him is significant ". . . clothed with rags and covered with chains: yet daring to raise his manacled hands to heaven, with a spirit soaring above the attributes of man: I looked on him and my blood curdled in my veins." This is the Nat Turner of historical record: the rebel whose "calm deliberate composure" and unshakeable defiance in defeat so troubled and puzzled his white captors. Unfortunately Mr. Styron has not escaped their fate; that is why his Nat Turner is such a grotesque reduction. If this novel is important, it is so not because it contributes anything to our awareness of the Negro experience and response to slavery, but because of the demonstration it presents of the truly astonishing persistence of white southern myths, racial stereotypes and derogatory literary clichés even in the best intentioned and most enlightened minds. Its largely uncritical acceptance in literary circles shows us how far we still have to go, and what a painfully little way we have come.

Its almost wholly favorable reception, up to now, is in some respects more significant and revealing than the book itself. Why, for example, in a book that alleges to deal with important themes and events in Negro history, was no black writer asked to comment on it in any major journal? Is it not a form of cultural condescension and indirect racism, that only one white critic bothered to check its historical accuracy? Would a book similarly interpreting the history of any other cultural minority be so uncritically accepted? Would the fate of this novel have been the same had it appeared in 1964, before the liberal literary intelligentsia had begun to feel estranged from the movement for black independence? These are, admittedly, sociological rather than literary questions. But forcing these questions upon us may ultimately prove to be this novel's real contribution to our awareness of contemporary realities.

Notes

1. In 1837 the Old Dominion exported to the death camps of the Deep South 40,000 black bodies for a net income of 24 million dollars.

2. There is some indication that the historical Nat, rather than being contemptuous of black women, was either married to one, or was the father of several children. Mr. Styron chose to discount this for several reasons. In the magazine *Per Se* (Summer 1966) he explains one of these reasons. "He was enormously unusual. He was an educated slave, and a man even of some refinement in a curious way. A man of that sort, I think, in a deep part of his heart would scorn the average, pathetic, illiterate colored woman, slave woman." It is unfortunate for the black woman of this country that Mr. Styron's ancestors, who were beating paths to the slave quarters after dark, were not of Turner's "refinement." This insult to black womanhood (wittingly or unwittingly) is an example of the kind of assumptions which underlie the novel.

3. To have this thesis seriously put forward is astonishing, and would be laughable if it were not for the easy acceptance that white reviewers have accorded it. It was, Mr. Styron tells us, suggested to him by the fact that the only murder that Turner admits to in his confession is that of a white girl. This is Styron's sole "evidence" for such a view. Along with millions of other Americans, we get another insight into Nat's character, here from the supremely authoritative and anonymous critic of *Time* magazine:

> Nat must have been what the book makes of him . . . spoiled by the sweet taste of humanity some of his masters allowed. "I will say this, without which you cannot understand the central madness of nigger existence," he [Turner] explains, "beat a nigger, starve him, leave him wallowing and he will be yours for life. Leave him with some unforseen hint of philanthropy, tickle him with the idea of hope and he will want to slice your throat."

This hodge-podge of cliché, stereotype and True Confessions psychology would be disappointing from a novelist of Mr. Styron's accomplishment, whatever the context. To have it accepted and disseminated as wisdom and insight is simply too much.

4. For the testimony of slaves, see B. A. Bodkin, ed., *A Folk History of Slavery* (New York, 1962).

5. James Wells Brown, a Negro whose book on the Negro in the American Revolution appeared in 1867, mentions the Nat Turner rebellion. His version does not in any way contradict the meagre record that is the original "Confessions," but it adds information not included. One may speculate as to the source of this information—possibly newspaper accounts of the time, or the testimony of black survivors of the incident—but the account is of interest, representing as it does an early account of the insurrection by a black man. About Will, Brown has this to say:

> Among those who joined the conspirators was Will, a slave who scorned the idea of taking his master's name. Though his soul longed to be free, he evidently became one of the party as much to satisfy revenge as for the liberty he saw in the dim future. . . . His own back was covered with scars from his shoulders to his feet. A large scar running from his right eye down to his chin showed that he had lived with a cruel master. Nearly six feet in height and one of the strongest and most athletic of his race, he proved to be one of the most unfeeling of the insurrectionists. His only weapon was a broad axe, sharp and heavy.

Brown then quotes from the "Confessions" of Will's path of carnage and describes his death in the final skirmish.

> In this battle there were many slain on both sides. Will, the blood-thirsty and revengeful slave, fell with his broad axe uplifted, after having laid three of the whites dead at his feet with his own strong arm and terrible weapon. His last words were, 'Bury my axe with me.' For he religiously believed, that, in the next world, the blacks would have a contest with the whites, and he would need his axe.

No sociological comment is necessary. But from a purely literary standpoint, it should be clear that Will, lifelong rebel and archetypal destroyer, presents possibilities which Mr. Styron simply ignored in favor of the "ravening, incoherent black beast" stereotype.

6. Brown's version makes it clear, as does the court record, that Turner's defeat came at the hands of whites. No black loyalist mercenaries are mentioned, but he does give an instance of a Master's life being saved by a slave. That, too, is instructive.

> On the fatal night, when Nat and his companions were dealing death to all they found, Capt. Harris, a wealthy planter, had his life saved by the devotion and timely warning of his slave Jim, said to have been half brother to his master. After the revolt had been put down, and parties of whites were out hunting the suspected blacks, Capt. Harris with his faithful slave went into the woods in search of the negroes. In saving his master's life Jim felt he had done his duty, and could not consent to become a betrayer of his race; and, on reaching the woods, he handed his pistol to his master, and said, 'I cannot help you hunt down these men: they, like myself, want to be free. Sir, I am tired of the life of a slave: please give me my freedom or shoot me on the spot.' Capt. Harris took the weapon, and pointed at the slave . . . The Capt. fired and the slave fell dead at his feet."

I do not claim that this incident necessarily took place in exactly the way that Brown relates it. But it also seems too specific to be pure invention by Brown, who was, after all, writing history and not fiction. It seems most probable that this was one of those minor incidents which become part of the "folk-lore" surrounding any major event; it is discussed, passed on, almost certainly distorted in the telling, but for some reason not included in "official" records. In this case, moreover, the nature of the incident suggests a reason for its exclusion.

William Styron before the People's Court

Eugene D. Genovese*

The praise given to William Styron's current prize-winning, best-selling novel, *The Confessions of Nat Turner*, has been followed by strong dissent and hostility from many members of the black intelligentsia. Black writers have denounced the novel in essays and public statements; black actors have threatened to boycott the film version. *William Styron's Nat Turner: Ten Black Writers Respond*[1] presents the essential points of the attack. It is a book that demands attention not so much because of the questions it raises about Styron's novel as for what it reveals about the thinking of intellectuals in the Black Power movement.

That the novel lends itself to historical or other criticism is true but irrelevant to this collection. What is at issue here is the ferocity and hysteria of the attack, which claims Styron to be a racist, a liar, an apologist for slavery, and a man who displays "moral cowardice" and "moral senility." A few of the writers dissociate themselves from these slanders and argue that his book is "objectively" racist and ahistorical—an argument that at least makes discussion possible—but the editor, John Henrik Clarke, editor of *Freedomways* magazine and a member of the staff of HARYOU, is right in claiming that the authors as a group insist on the "deliberate" quality of Styron's alleged crimes. The writers insist on most points as a group, and the essays themselves repeat one another; thus most of the criticism may properly be discussed as a collective effort.

Except for occasional entertainment, we need deal only with the essays of two writers, Mike Thelwell, who teaches English at the University of Massachusetts, and Vincent Harding, who directs the Institute of the Black World in Atlanta, Georgia. Virtually all the serious points made in the book may be found, skillfully presented, in Thelwell's essay, but for some suggestive material on slave religion we must turn to Harding's. Of the rest, the less said the better.

Clarke's introduction begins with a quote from Herbert Aptheker: "History's potency is mighty. The oppressed need it for identity and in-

*Reprinted from *Red and Black: Marxian Explorations in Southern and Afro-American History* (New York: Pantheon, 1968), pp. 200–17, by permission of the author.

spiration: oppressors for justification, rationalization, and legitimacy." This nonsense sets the tone for the book. I should respectfully suggest that although the oppressed may need history for identity and inspiration, they need it above all for the truth of what the world has made of them and of what they have helped make of the world. This knowledge alone can produce that sense of identity which ought to be sufficient for inspiration; and those who look to history to provide glorious moments and heroes invariably are betrayed into making catastrophic errors in political judgment. Specifically, revolutionaries do not need Nat Turner as a saint; they do need the historical truth of the Nat Turner revolt—its strength and its weakness.

One might have thought that black and white Americans who are committed to racial equality would be pleased that William Styron, a white Southerner, has rescued the great rebel slave leader, Nat Turner, from obscurity. Instead, the claim is made throughout these essays that black America has always known of and admired the historical Nat Turner. This is pretense. When Vincent Harding, for example, writes of a Nat Turner who exists "in the living traditions of black America," he is deceiving himself and, inadvertently, the rest of us. Certain great slave revolts in Brazil and the Caribbean have been celebrated in tales and in songs and have contributed to subsequent uprisings; but we have yet to be shown evidence that slaves and postslavery blacks kept alive a politically relevant legend of Nat Turner or of any other Southern slave leader. If Nat Turner is now a name widely known to black and white America, and if the existence of armed resistance to slavery is now generally appreciated, William Styron deserves as much credit as any other writer.

The burden of the attack on Styron's book is the charge of historical falsification. These writers claim that he transforms Turner, the revolutionary general, into a man of indecision and even cowardice; presents slavery as a benign system and reduces the causes of the revolt to trivial personal complaints; denies the influence on Turner of the slave quarters, and makes his virtues the result of his having been a pampered "house nigger"; fails to understand the hold that Turner had on his people as a preacher; and—greatest offense of all—ignores evidence that Turner had a black wife and assigns a central role to his relationship with a lily-white Southern belle. For the most part the criticisms are historical and ideological, and only rarely aesthetic. Some critics praise Styron's writing and see it as enhancing the ideological threat; others deride it, more or less in passing. Thelwell's sarcastic discussion of Styron's handling of Turner's preaching style is a brilliant set piece on black language and deserves to be read quite apart from either Styron or Nat Turner. The social content, not the artistic performance, is, however, the issue and therefore will be my concern here.

The novel is historically sound. Styron takes liberties with fact, as every novelist does, but he does not do violence to the historical record.

The same cannot be said for his critics. Thelwell criticizes Styron for denying that Virginia masters deliberately bred slaves, and refers to the incontrovertible evidence of huge slave sales to the lower South. Certainly every historian knows of those sales, and so does Styron. But had Thelwell read the historical literature carefully, he would have found there a distinction between a system of deliberate breeding and the process of transferring surplus populations. Styron understands the distinction, which is of great importance to the moral question of slavery, but Thelwell misses it completely. There is no disagreement on this matter among historians, black and white, radical, liberal, or conservative.

William Styron's Nat Turner: Ten Black Writers Respond contains a useful appendix with the original confessions of Nat Turner as told to T. R. Gray. For clarity, since Styron's novel has the same title as that Gray gave to the original, I shall refer to the latter as Turner's *Testimony*. Lerone Bennett, the editor of *Ebony* Magazine, tells us that the historical data reveal the real Nat Turner as commanding, virile, and courageous whereas Styron makes him impotent and cowardly. The historical data reveal no such thing; in fact, they do not reveal much at all about Nat Turner's qualities. In his *Testimony*, Turner naturally makes himself appear as if he always knew what he was doing, but his words merely suggest a human being who had respect for himself and no wish to bare his innermost thoughts to the enemy. The historical Turner had resourcefulness and courage, as his conduct shows, but surely nothing in the novel suggests anything else. Styron gives him a human complexity, attributing to Turner doubts and self-doubts, and thereby makes his action the outcome of intelligent and sensitive consideration.

To this extent Styron may well exaggerate Turner's virtues, for it is possible to read the *Testimony* as the reflections of one of those religious fanatics whose single-minded madness carried him to the leadership of a popular cause. Instead, Styron sees enough in the *Testimony* and in the events of the time to suggest that Turner may well have had a more impressive character, including a humanity and sensitivity that could sharpen his resolve to liberate his people and, at the same time, fill him with doubt and foreboding about the means. When Styron sees Turner as racked by self-doubts and unable to kill anyone except Margaret Whitehead, he does not convict him of cowardice. When it could no longer be avoided, he killed. The inner conflict and pain can be interpreted as cowardice and irresolution by those who wish to do so, but this interpretation seems to me more revealing of its authors than of either Styron or the historical Turner.

The historical record is clear enough: Turner hit a defenseless man on the head with a hatchet and could not kill him; he hit a woman on the head with a sword and could not kill her. He explains: it was dark, the hatchet glanced, the sword was dull and light. But neither darkness nor inferior weapons kept his associates from doing better. Surely a serious novelist might be moved to meditate on the reasons. That Turner did kill only Margaret Whitehead—and then only with considerable difficulty—raises questions about human character that are appropriate to a serious novel. Yet the description of the ambivalent relationship between Turner and Margaret, which is of course fictional, has infuriated Styron's critics perhaps more than anything else in his novel.

What of "General Nat," about whom we hear so much? According to the *Testimony,* Turner met with his associates the night before the insurrection to devise a plan. Although he had brooded over his revolutionary calling for a long time, he had as yet no plan at all. Nat Turner led a slave revolt under extremely difficult conditions and deserves an honored place in our history, but there is a limit to what may be claimed for a general who on the day he marches does not know where he is marching to. In fact, Turner had no place to go. These facts do not make Turner a fool or a madman or less than a hero; they do suggest the desperate circumstances in which he and other Southern slave rebels had to operate. If Styron's presentation of a white-influenced, doubt-ridden Turner insults the hero, what shall we do with the historical figure of the greatest of black revolutionaries, Toussaint L'Ouverture, who enjoyed a privileged position in slavery; who played it safe while his fellow slaves sent the fertile North Plain of Saint-Domingue up in flames; who, when in command, offered to deliver masses of blacks back into slavery in return for amnesty and freedom for his own officers; and who took care to lead his master's family to safety before doing anything at all? Toussaint stands as one of the greatest revolutionary leaders in world history, but not being a statue, he had all the frailties and contradictions common even to the greatest of men.

Styron draws especially heavy fire for showing loyal slaves helping to shoot down the insurgent blacks. Relying on the authority of Aptheker, the black writers tell us that it did not happen and could never have happened. This is nonsense. Many planters claimed that it did happen, but we may dismiss their testimony for a moment. During the War for Southern Independence some loyal slaves defended their masters' families with guns in hands, but we may put that fact aside also. When we turn from the United States, which had only small and scattered slave revolts, to Brazil and the Caribbean, where large black slave revolts were frequent, we find all the evidence we need. Armed, loyal slaves often fought against insurgents, as every historian of those regions knows. It is pardonable for Styron to take liberties with the particular history of the Nat Turner revolt, so long as he does no violence to the history of the slave revolts generally. Here, as in his handling of the rape episode, he has proved himself a better student of history than his critics.

Styron apparently knows, as his critics do not, that a ruling class incapable of applying the rule of divide and conquer could not last a year. Turner's *Testimony* itself tells of loyal slaves who protected their masters.

Of special relevance is Turner's own account of his last days in hiding, wherein he tells us of being discovered by two Negroes to whom he revealed his identity; he adds that they immediately fled and that he knew they would betray him.

Styron's critics miss his irony. In the novel, Gray reveals to Turner the slaveholder's conventional wisdom on slave loyalty when he announces, with all the sensitivity and genius for miscalculation characteristic of ruling classes, that this is why "nigger slavery will last a thousand years." Styron invokes here the image of the Thousand-Year Reich, which lasted twelve years; by linking the two systems he is ironically demonstrating the stupidity of those who think that divisions among the lower classes may forever be counted upon to maintain systems of oppression. For this he is accused of being a "white Southern racist." It is not surprising that the White Citizens Councils cannot recognize Styron as one of their own, and have denounced him as a traitor to his race and class; but it is surprising that Styron's black critics have insisted on reading the incident with eyes of a T. R. Gray.

In the novel, Turner winces when Gray tells him that his revolt has been crushed with black help; and throughout Styron's book, Turner expresses contempt, even hatred, for his fellow blacks. The critics of Styron's book insist that love, not hatred, must have driven Turner forward. Such love for his people is also in the novel. Had he not loved them, he would not have protested so much against their weakness in the face of oppression; he could not even have perceived them as victims of oppression. No revolutionary could be free of such feelings of hatred, which is essentially a hatred for the oppression rather than for the oppressed.

John Oliver Killens cites David Walker's magnificent call for slave insurrection (1829), *The Appeal to the Colored Citizens of the World*. But Walker never feared to mix his professions of love for his people with the harshest condemnation:

> Why is it that those few, weak, good for nothing whites are able to keep so many able men, one of whom can put to flight a dozen whites, in wretchedness and misery? It shows at once what the blacks are, we are ignorant, abject, servile and mean—and the whites know it, they know that we are too servile to assert our rights as men—or they would not fool with us as they do. . . . Why do they not bring the inhabitants of Asia to be body servants to them? They know they would get their bodies rent and torn asunder from head to foot.[2]

This, the language of a genuine revolutionary, is what Styron gives Nat Turner; both display the humanity of men capable of doubt and anguish.

The critics claim that Styron's Turner and his followers revolted for trivial personal reasons, and that Styron pictures slavery as a benign and reasonably humane system. None of this is true. By giving Turner a kind master, Styron shows, as Mrs. Stowe did long ago, that the kindest masters could not offset the inhumanity and injustice of the system. Styron's Turner chooses insurrection because a series of betrayals, which his old master could not help, awakens him to the injustice of his general, not specific, condition. Will, the slave, makes the same choice because the exceptional brutality to which he is subjected produces the same effect. Hark, one of the most attractive and interesting of the rebels, has to be urged by Turner to transform his own personal misery into political consciousness.

All this is simple and sound both as history and as psychology. One of the essential qualities of a great revolutionary leader (or, for that matter, of a great counterrevolutionary demagogue like Hitler) is the ability to raise the consciousness of his people from the personal to the social. People, especially simple people, normally experience an oppressive social system in a thousand seemingly meaningless and disconnected ways: It is the leader's task to make them see their oppression as flowing from a common social source and to help them to identify the oppressor. The "personal" suffering Styron describes flows from the slave condition; he is correct to dwell on this as the basis for revolutionary consciousness and to make Turner's religious preaching the vehicle for the transformation. Styron does not, as some charge, make Turner's feeling for Margaret Whitehead the spring of his action. Nothing in the novel suggests anything so absurd.

The critics accuse Styron of presenting Turner as a pampered house nigger and denying the influence on him of the slave quarters. Styron's Turner allegedly does not adequately reflect the influence of his own mother and father and the friendship of his fellow slaves; the positive influences on his life seem to have been white. Historians, black and white, have done little work on house slaves, drivers, preachers, and especially field slaves, so that if Styron underestimates the influence of the slave quarters on the personality and character of its inhabitants, so does virtually everyone else who has written on the subject. Nat Turner, in his *Testimony*, does say a few words about a grandmother, about his parents who taught him to read, and about some relations with other slaves. Because Turner is taught to read by the white family in the novel, Styron is accused of falsifying history, of denying a vital culture among the blacks, and of seeing slave life from the view of the Big House.

How much can we make of Turner's having been taught to read by his parents? Who, after all, probably taught them? Turner himself says that he used white children's books. Styron did not invent white paternalism. That attitude was part of the history of slavery and, as Styron shows in many ways, in no way could compensate for the injustice of the system.

Thelwell condemns Styron because Turner aspires to white culture, speaks a white language, and thinks and dreams like a white man, although Frantz Fanon, whose work Thelwell must know, provides ade-

quate theoretical justification for this side of the experiences of the oppressed. Thelwell cites sections of the *Testimony* which suggest Turner's
early alienation from the system and a distinctly religious and political
opposition to it. It is hard to believe that so sophisticated a man as
Thelwell should take Turner's claim to lifelong dedication at face value.
Every revolutionary can give the social reasons for his conduct, but we
must still explain how the same circumstances make one man a revolutionary and his brother the opposite. It is impossible to expect the
Testimony to yield more than unconscious hints. Out of these, Styron
created a believable Nat Turner although by no means the only possible
one. But then, nothing prevents (or has ever prevented) black intellectuals, who claim to have the living traditions of black America at their
disposal, from creating their own version.

Turner's aspiration to white culture is not the same as hatred for
things black. Slaves of any race normally reach out for the culture of the
class above them, even as they create a viable world of their own. So do
colonials, as Fanon shows. So do industrial workers, for all their freedom
and leisure, unless they are organized in a struggle to develop a larger
view. Again, consider the example of Toussaint and the other black
leaders who were, at one bad moment, prepared to betray their army
back into slavery. Their excuse was that the newly imported African
Coast Niggers "cannot even speak two words of French"!

Styron's black critics, especially Harding and Thelwell, insist that
there was a special kind of subterranean life in the slave quarters which
might have proven far more powerful than we now appreciate. Since we
know so little and can say so little, the anger and hostility toward Styron,
who has created something out of what we do know, is hard to justify.
One is tempted to say, if you say that black folk life can be unearthed and
made relevant, then do it; if white historians—for whatever reasons—
have been blind to whole areas of black sensibility, culture, and tradition,
then show us. We can learn much from your work, but nothing from your
fury.

The most important and damaging criticism by Thelwell and Harding concerns religion. They argue that Styron pays insufficient attention
to Turner's role as a preacher and misses the central role of black religion.
It is true that all black slave revolts in the Americas had a religious side,
which provided ideological and often organizational cohesion. But
Styron's critics claim more than an artistic failure to convey the full power
of Turner's preaching. According to Harding, Styron shows Turner as a
man abandoned by God until he repents, not for the dead white children
but for the young white woman who opened him to love. Such a God
ostensibly belongs neither to the black man nor to the white, but only to
the private world of William Styron. Harding is entitled to his reading,
but I fail to see much in it. The young woman in question was the one person Turner did kill—in the novel and in fact—and guilt tends to be an in-

tensely personal matter. In saying that he would have spared her, Styron's Turner acknowledges the love that accompanied his hatred; he repents not for having led his slaves in revolt—he affirms his cause decisively—but for having allowed the justice of his cause to generate personal hatred. He thereby reaffirms his Christianity and his humanity: he sees his own tragedy in his inability to wage uncompromising class war without personalizing the hatred it engenders.

Of all the criticisms, the most violent are directed at Turner's relationship with Margaret Whitehead. The objections are primarily these: that the historical Nat Turner had a black wife whom Styron ignores; that Styron-Turner's romance with Margaret goes hand in hand with Styron's portrayal of Will as a lunatic hell-bent on raping white women; that Styron gives Turner homosexual and asexual tendencies and thereby denies his manhood; and that the interracial love affair arises from a white man's fantasy life, has racist overtones, and has nothing to do with Nat Turner and the slave experience.

The evidence for Turner's alleged black wife is slim and not beyond challenge. The black critics make much of Turner's references to his grandmother and his parents in the *Testimony*. How incredible, then, that he failed to mention his wife. Perhaps she existed, perhaps not; perhaps she had some importance in his life, perhaps not. We do not know. Given the slim thread of evidence—or gossip—Styron has not falsified history by ignoring her. The discussion, therefore, must focus on whom and what he put in her place.

A similar attack is aimed at the characterization of Will as a man obsessed with the idea of rape. We know little or nothing of the historical Will. One historical account, without evidence to support it, presents a different man from that in the *Testimony*. Styron had nothing to work from, and was free to invent him as bloodthirsty, nihilistic, consumed by hate—a type who has appeared in the noblest of uprisings and revolutions throughout history. It is ridiculous to infer an insult to black people from this characterization. We are told that, in fact, there was not a single episode of rape during the revolt and that the issue is, therefore, viciously injected. No rape did occur, but so far as I can recall, no one except Herbert Aptheker bothered to note the absence until Styron himself commented on it in an essay published several years ago. In any case, there are no instances of rape in Styron's book. If Styron's Will is hungry for white women, his Nat Turner is a man who will stand for none of it and who is strong enough to prevail.

What, then, is the complaint? The rape question is supposed to be Styron's invention and the creation of his racist mind. But Styron knows, as his black critics ought to know, that evidence of rape appears frequently in the histories of the slave revolts. It would be astounding if it did not. Evidence from the United States is cloudy, but we can also turn to Saint-Domingue's great revolution. The radical and black (by United

States classification) historian of the revolution, C. L. R. James, in his superb book, *Black Jacobins*, refers without fuss to the raping of white women and says all that needs to be said: those whose women had for so long been objects of white violence settled old scores. To deny these common occurrences during social struggle is to betray a curiously rosy view of the effects of oppression.

Styron's Turner has a homosexual experience and afterwards remains continent; accordingly, we are told that Styron has deprived him of his manhood. Twenty years ago the *Kinsey Report* reported that the majority of white males had homosexual experiences during pre- and early adolescence. By assuming that black men follow similar lines of development, Styron merely gives Nat Turner something of a normal early life. Perhaps black men do not share with decadent whites these delightful early encounters. *Che peccato!*

The second matter is more serious. Why does Turner abstain from sexual relations? The answer seems to me clear throughout the novel. Styron has, in this way, dramatized Turner's single-mindedness, his devotion, even to the point of monomania, to his revolutionary calling. This characteristic, in its general if not necessarily specific form, may be found in many great revolutionaries. As a literary device it may or may not be successful; it is clearly meant not to denigrate, but to link Turner with a great historical tradition of revolutionary heroes. And those who think that sexual abstinence deprives a man of his manhood have a few questions to answer themselves.

Finally, we come to Margaret Whitehead, whose place in the novel has drawn the heaviest fire. The charges are by now familiar: Styron insults black men by suggesting that they hanker after white chicks; he insults black women by denying them the charms to lure their men away from these white chicks; and he is immersed in a white-racist sexual fantasy. To begin with, we may recall what his detractors never mention: Margaret Whitehead displays a feeling for Turner parallel to his feeling for her. She unconsciously tries to seduce him several times; Turner is, after all, the only sympathetic, different, and unobtainable man in her life. Perhaps the complaint should be reversed: Styron insults white women and attributes to them an irresistible fascination for that celebrated black penis. This is, in fact, exactly what white racists, especially in the South, are saying.

The attack on Styron's handling of the sexual aspect of race relations comes at a strange time, for in recent years various black writers have been exploring the issue in a similar way—e.g., Fanon's *Black Skin, White Masks*, Earl E. Thorpe's *Eros and Freedom in Southern Life and Thought*, and especially Calvin C. Hernton's indispensable *Sex and Racism in America*. With creditable research, professional integrity, and considerable good humor, Hernton argues that the racial problem in America does have a sexual aspect and that the sooner we face its implications, the better. American life throws whites and blacks together under circumstances in which they constantly affect one another and yet they remain apart. As one result, the sexual fantasies common to both sexes and races tend to be translated into racial terms. For example, whites often regard blacks as sexually uninhibited and more desirable, and blacks regard whites in exactly the same way. If the racial translation of sexual fantasy proves so strong in modern America, what must it have been like in the slave South?

By focusing on this side of the black-white confrontation, Styron does expose one of the most tragic features of the slave regime. On the one hand, slavery threw whites and blacks together intimately in relations often harsh and brutal, sometimes affectionate and loving, sometimes all at once. On the other hand, it forbade fruition to those feelings of love which its intimacy engendered. The tension was at once a matter of race and class. In Styron's novel, Margaret and Turner are drawn together because they glimpse a special sensitivity in each other. Each is drawn to the other by the attraction of the forbidden; but each is so remote from the other that neither can even know what he or she is feeling. The novel describes a social system that brought people together in intimate relationships, negated that intimacy, relentlessly suppressed any awareness of the feelings created, and necessarily turned love into hatred and fear. Here Styron sees how slavery crushed the feelings of those who faced each other from different sides of the line.

Styron's Turner is impressed by the fine white ladies, with their polish and elegance, and it would have been perfectly natural for Turner to focus his feelings on a lovely girl who seemed to embody everything in life that was desirable and unattainable. One wonders if Styron was thinking of the great Toussaint L'Ouverture, who, as our black critics surely know, steadily plowed his way through those aristocratic French ladies of Le Cap who sought his favors. If Styron's critics find some racial insult here, then they fail to see that the issue transcends race and is a question of class and status as well. The Margaret Whiteheads of the WASP bourgeoisie have long fluttered before working-class boys of other ethnic groups quite as much as they must have fluttered before black slaves.

The power of Styron's performance lies in his having carried his confrontation further. In establishing genuine love he also establishes genuine understanding, for to some extent Turner does come to see Margaret as a particular human being, rather than as a social type. That, I should suggest to Harding, is the reason he must repent of her murder before he can reestablish a relationship with his God. In repenting, he does not repudiate his revolt; he repudiates the hatred which led him to deny the love he felt for a human being who was as trapped as he. This may or may not be convincing artistically, but the charge that this part of the novel stamps Styron as a racist is outrageous. If anything, it may stamp him as an integrationist—which for some may well be his ultimate crime. Certainly, it stamps him as a man who has the courage to confront the depths of America's racial tragedy.

Of other complaints, great and small, little need be said, for they are, at best, more of the same and generally a good deal worse. I will only mention the complaint of Dr. Alvin F. Poussaint, a psychiatrist. After telling us that Styron, as a white Southerner, must be the victim of racist ideology, Poussaint notes that Styron calls Turner "Nat" and then asks if this is an attempt by a white Southerner to keep Turner in his place. Perhaps. But what shall we say of Vincent Harding, the title of whose essay is "You've Taken My Nat and Gone"? Or of Aptheker, who also calls Turner "Nat" and who is cited throughout this book as a solid authority? And what of Genovese—I hold my breath!—who calls Turner "Turner," for surely Poussaint knows that Turner was the name of the master's family.

William Styron's Nat Turner: Ten Black Writers Respond shows the extent to which the American intelligentsia is splitting along racial, rather than ideological, lines. As such, the book needs to be taken with alarmed seriousness, no matter how absurd most of the contributions are. It is enough that Vincent Harding and Mike Thelwell appear here with no less passion than the others, although with considerably more grace and intellectual power. Certainly, we need not probe the motives of these ten writers as they try to probe Styron's. But it is clear that the black intelligentsia faces a serious crisis. Its political affinities lie with the Black Power movement, which increasingly demands conformity, myth-making, and historical fabrication. No one need believe that any of these writers would resort to deliberate falsification—which they so readily accuse Styron of—but the intellectual history of popular and revolutionary movements has overflowed with just such crises, in which dedicated, politically committed intellectuals have talked themselves into believing many things they have later had to gag on. The black intellectuals seem to be going through what Marxist intellectuals went through in the 1930s and 1940s. Let us hope that they come out a good deal better.

One thing remains certain: If they follow the line laid down by Aptheker with which they open the book, and if they proceed in a hysterical way, to demand new myths in order to serve current ends, they will find the same moral, political, and intellectual debacle at the end as did most of the Marxists of those days. Their political movement, being a genuine popular force, can only be served by the truth. The history of every people exhibits glory and shame, heroism and cowardice, wisdom and foolishness, certainty and doubt, and more often than not these antagonistic qualities appear at the same moment and in the same men. The revolutionary task of intellectuals is, accordingly, not to invent myths, but to teach each people its own particular contradictory truth. This historian has never been sure which lessons can be drawn from the past to serve the future. Except perhaps one: Until a people can and will face its own past, it has no future.

Postscript

The reaction to Styron's fictional treatment of the relationship between Turner and Margaret Whitehead has easily been the most obscene part of the discussion. For what it is worth, I think it appropriate to glance at one or two black treatments of the sexual dimension of the racial confrontation. Vincent Harding's essay, "Black Radicalism: The Road from Montgomery," Alfred F. Young, ed., *Dissent: Explorations in the History of American Radicalism* (DeKalb, Illinois, 1968), contains some thoughts and a quotation surprisingly missing from the polemics against Styron:

> How significant was the constant discussion of black revolution? One of its foremost exponents, Ron Karenga, said: "We are the last revolutionaries in America. If we fail to leave a legacy of revolution for our children we have failed our mission and should be dismissed as unimportant." Although Karenga, like others, believes the cultural revolution of black consciousness is most important at the present time, he has vividly pictured the next stage:
>> When word is given we'll see how tough you are. When it's "burn," let's see how much you burn. When it's "kill," let's see how much you kill. When it's "blow up," let's see how much you blow up. And when it's "take that white girl's head too," we'll really see how tough you are.

June, 1970

Notes

1. John Henrik Clarke, Lerone Bennett, Jr., Alvin F. Poussaint, Vincent Harding, John Oliver Killens, John A. Williams, Ernest Kaiser, Loyle Hairston, Charles V. Hamilton, and Mike Thelwell (Boston, 1968).

2. Herbert Aptheker, ed., *"One Continual Cry": David Walker's Appeal to the Colored Citizens of the World (1829–1830)* (New York, 1965), p. 129.

William Styron and
The Southampton Insurrection

Arthur D. Casciato and James L. W. West III*

Much of the controversy over *The Confessions of Nat Turner* in 1967 and 1968 concerned William Styron's alleged distortion of historical fact in the novel. Many important critics, black and white, added fuel to the racial fires that surrounded Styron's book. Most of them took up the tired debate over historical "fact" versus imaginative "fiction," and in some of their writings they engaged in guessing games about Styron's motives for distorting the historical record. *Nat Turner* became an extraliterary event—a moral and political issue on which critics and reviewers could take sides. As Richard Gilman points out, "The book was immediately swept up into areas of power and influence wholly outside its existence as literature, and, even more crucially, before such existence could even be brought into question."[1]

Given this background, it is surprising to discover that Styron's known historical sources for the novel have not been investigated in any systematic way. In interviews and public appearances Styron has made no secret of the fact that he relied heavily, for information and detail, on specific books about slavery and the antebellum South. To date, however, no one has followed Styron's leads.[2] This article utilizes an important document—Styron's annotated copy of *The Southampton Insurrection* —to uncover specific details that he borrowed for his novel. The article also demonstrates that Styron was by no means careless about his use of historical fact, as many of his detractors have maintained.

Styron has often noted that the only *contemporary* source on which he drew for his novel was a five-thousand-word document called "The Confessions of Nat Turner." This pamphlet, supposedly dictated by Nat to a Southampton County lawyer named T. R. Gray, was Styron's main source for information about the 1831 rebellion and its leader.[3] A later source which Styron has frequently mentioned is William S. Drewry's *The Southampton Insurrection*. Published in Washington by The Neal Co. in 1900, the book was originally Drewry's doctoral dissertation at Johns Hopkins. About his use of Drewry's work Styron has said, " 'The

*Reprinted from *American Literature*, 52 (Jan. 1981), 564–77, by permission of the journal.

Southampton Insurrection,' while obviously biased, served me quite well. It helped give me a sense of the feeling and smell of the revolt, after, of course, I sieved out what I instinctively sensed was irrelevant, false or biased."[4]

Fortunately Styron's personal copy of Drewry's volume has survived. Housed today in the Manuscript Department of the William R. Perkins Library at Duke University, the book has been annotated by Styron throughout.[5] His marginalia contain many speculations about Margaret Whitehead, the only person murdered by Nat in the rebellion, and about Nat's failure to kill except in that one instance. Styron also notes Drewry's frequent borrowings from the Gray pamphlet and comments repeatedly in the margins on Drewry's bias. The most interesting markings, however, are found on the front preliminary blanks (see Figures 1 and 2). Styron's notes here are significant for two reasons: first, they indicate specific passages in Drewry that he has used for his fictional purposes; second, they direct us to previously undiscovered source material for *Nat Turner* in Frederick Law Olmsted's *A Journey in the Seaboard Slave States.*

The history of Styron's copy of Drewry's book is in itself interesting. A Tidewater Virginia native, Styron had always wanted to write about the 1831 Nat Turner Rebellion which occurred near his birthplace in Newport News. As a youngster he first learned of the slave insurrection while studying a benighted grammer school text of Virginia history. Here Nat was briefly mentioned as a fanatical Negro preacher who led a blood-thirsty reign of terror against the whites of Cross Keys. In 1947, while enrolled in a creative writing class at the New School for Social Research in New York City, Styron spoke to his teacher Hiram Haydn about the possibility of writing a novel about Nat Turner. Haydn, who was later Styron's editor at Bobbs-Merrill and Random House, told the novice author to write about a subject he understood better.[6] Styron followed Haydn's advice and wrote *Lie Down in Darkness,* a novel set in contemporary eastern Virginia. That novel won the Prix de Rome for Styron, and the award paid his passage to Europe in the early spring of 1952.

By the time he reached Paris, Styron was again thinking about Nat Turner. In a letter dated 1 May 1952, he told his father back in Newport News that Nat would be the subject of his next book:

> I've finally pretty much decided what to write next—a novel based on Nat Turner's rebellion. The subject fascinates me, and I think I could make a real character out of old Nat. It'll probably take a bit of research, though, and I've written to people in the U. S.—among them Prof. Saunders Redding (whom I saw Christmas, you remember) of Hampton Institute—asking them to pass on any reference material they might have. Perhaps you know of a book or something on Nat Turner and would be willing to get it sent to me somehow. Actually, I'd be extremely interested in anything on life around the Southside-Caroline Border country of Virginia in the 1820–1850 period. If you can get your hands on something

on that order without too much trouble I'd appreciate your letting me know. I don't know but whether I'm plunging into something over my depth, but I'm fascinated anyway.[7]

Styron's father did some research for his son and put together a list of published source materials on Nat's rebellion. Professor Redding was also willing to help, and on 20 May Styron wrote his father to contact Redding so that no duplication of effort would result. A short time later Redding sent Styron a package of materials, including a copy of *The Southampton Insurrection*.[8] It was this copy that Styron read and kept with him over the next ten years as the idea for *The Confessions of Nat Turner* grew in his imagination. In 1962, when he finally began writing the novel, he turned to this copy as one of his principal sources for information.

It is well to remember that Drewry's study is a highly colored account written by a Southerner who believed in white supremacy. Early in the book, for example, Drewry writes that "slavery in Virginia was not such as to arouse rebellion, but was an institution which nourished the strongest affection and piety in slave and owner, as well as moral qualities worthy of any age of civilization" (p. 44). Styron was aware of the slanted nature of Drewry's writing; frequently his marginalia point out Drewry's obtuseness and prejudice.[9] But for all his bias, Drewry was an energetic researcher who gathered many valuable data on the Turner insurrection. Styron found these data invaluable in writing his own novel, and he would later characterize Drewry's study as "a book of considerable information and detail, and valuable to that degree."[10]

Styron's first specifically paginated annotation in the front of the book, for instance, reads, "Drunkenness (apple brandy ever-prevalent) p. 104." Drewry's description, bracketed by Styron on p. 104 of his copy, does indeed provide valuable detail about the problem of slave intoxication during the insurrection:

> Apple brandy was the principal source of revenue. Cotton, corn, and tobacco grew in the orchard, and while they were maturing the apples were gathered and manufactured into brandy and cider. Thus the apple crop was clear profit. The following are the words of a native of Southampton at the time of our narrative: "Apple brandy was a factor, and an important one, in those bloody scenes. But for that many more would have been murdered. Nearly everybody at that time had an orchard, and it was probably the largest source of revenue in a county where revenues were small. I know my father's income was derived chiefly from the brandy he made and sold. Whenever they (the negroes) stopped in their raids they drank abundantly of it."

Styron accordingly emphasizes the importance of liquor in the defeat of the rebellion, mentioning apple brandy and cider several times in *Nat Turner*. The first reference is significant: Nelson, a powerful member of Nat's inner circle of revolutionaries, agonizes over the problem of drunkenness in the ranks: *"Us jes' gots to keep de niggers out'n dem cider*

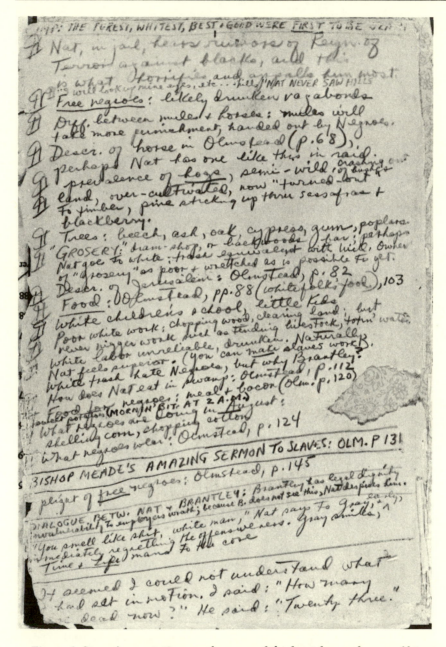

Figure 1: Styron's annotations on the verso of the front free endpaper of his copy of *The Southampton Insurrection*. This illustration and the one opposite are reproduced with the permission of the Manuscript Dept., Duke University Library, and of William Styron.

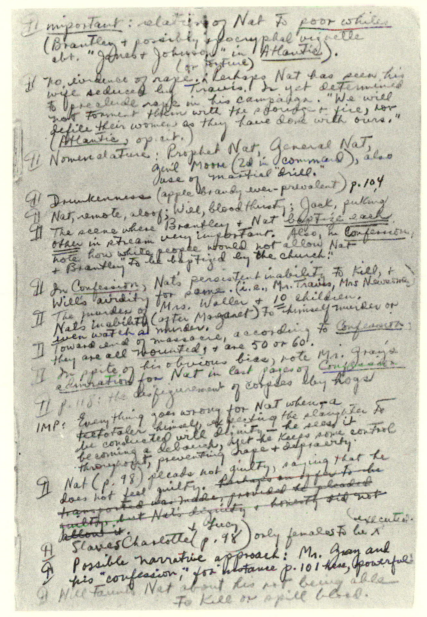

Figure 2: Styron's annotations on the initial blank page of his copy. The reference to " 'Jones + Johnson' in *Atlantic*" is found in Thomas Wentworth Higginson's article "Nat Turner's Insurrection," *Atlantic Monthly*, 8 (Aug. 1861), 173–87. These men were poor whites whose property was threatened by Nat and his followers.

presses. Let dem black bastids get at dat cider an' brandy and us done lost de war."[11] Later Nat himself speaks of the wealth of apples in the countryside:

> This was the estimable brandy distilled from apples growing so plentifully throughout the county. For if the soil of Southampton was utterly wrecked for tobacco and could produce cotton in quantities adequate only for subsistence, a cornucopia of apples ripened on every hand—wild and in cultivated orchards, in bramble-choked groves on dead plantations, by the wayside of each land and road. They grew in all sizes and colors and varieties, and what had once lain in wormy, decaying heaps on the ground were now dumped by the wagonload into the stills which had become each farmer's most valued asset. (p. 320)

Styron's second paginated annotation ("p. 118: the disfigurement of corpses by hogs") refers to Drewry's observation that "all along the route lay the murdered victims, so mangled by the murderers and disfigured by hogs as to be unrecognizable even to their friends." Drewry's sentence is only a gruesome detail, but Styron transforms it into a brief and powerful set-piece that captures the dehumanizing effect of the rebellion on Nat:

> As I crept past the chicken shed and into the barnyard I heard a grunting and a snuffling noise, and saw two razorback wild hogs devouring the body of a man. It must have been the overseer. The corpse was parted from its head and I knew that the last face the man had ever seen had been that of Will. I watched the hogs rooting at the man's intestines for a moment and I was without feeling; the iniquitous mud-smeared beasts may as well have been feeding upon slops or offal. (p. 401)

The next paginated annotation reads, "Nat (p. 98) pleads not guilty, saying that he does not feel guilty." This note refers to Drewry's statement that "Nat, upon his arraignment, pleaded not guilty, declaring to his counsel that he did not feel so." Styron employs this bit of information twice in the published novel. On p. 392 Nat tells Gray, "That's right, Mr. Gray. I fear I would have to plead not guilty to everything, because I don't feel guilty. And try as I might I simply can't feel—as you put it, sir— a pang of remorse." Later, shortly before Nat's execution, Gray presses him again about his guilt:

> "Well, I got to go, Reverend. I'll see you tomorrow. Meanwhile, I'll put down in my deposition to the court which precedes your confession that the defendant shows no remorse for his acts, and since he *feels* no guilt his plea will be that of 'not guilty.' Now, one last time, are you *sure* you feel no remorse at all? I mean, would you do it again if you had the chance? There's still time to change your mind. It ain't goin' to save your neck but it'll surer'n hell look better for you in court. Speak up, Reverend."
> When I made no reply to him he left without further word. (pp. 397–98)

Styron's speculation about Nat's plea is even more interesting: following his note on the end paper is the cancelled statement, "Perhaps an offer to be transported was made, provided he pleaded guilty, but Nat's dignity + honesty did not allow it." Styron rejected this idea, though, and did not use it in his novel, probably because the historical record did not support the speculation.

Styron's fourth paginated annotation concerns his own search for a narrative voice: "Possible narrative approach: Mr. Gray and his 'confession,' for instance p. 101 here, powerful!" In this note we see Styron considering, perhaps for the first time, the narrative strategy he would eventually adopt for the published novel. In *Nat Turner* he begins with an excerpt from Gray's "Confessions" and then depicts Gray's arrival in Nat's cell to interview him, a visit which triggers Nat's retrospective narration of the story.

These paginated annotations only begin to suggest the influence of Drewry's book on Styron's novel. *The Southampton Insurrection* is in fact a storehouse of detail which Styron appropriated in order to give *Nat Turner* a realistic flavor. For example, Drewry describes Nat's escape and subsequent capture at some length and relates that Nat kept accurate time during this period "by means of a notched stick, which was found in the cave at the time of his capture" (p. 90, n. 1). In *Nat Turner* Styron uses the device of the notched stick in his description of Hark's ill-fated attempt at escape:

> His difficulties about finding the way began that night and plagued him all the long hours of his flight into freedom. By notches cut with his knife on a small stick each morning, he calculated (or it was calculated for him by someone who could count) the trip as having lasted six weeks. (p. 279)

Drewry's book is also the source for a horrifying bit of information about Nat's treatment by his captors. In his copy of *The Southampton Insurrection* Styron underlined the phrases "Persecuted with pinpricks" on p. 93 and "ladies actually being accused of sticking pins in him" on p. 94, noting in the margin of the latter page that Nat "obviously *had* pins stuck in him." In the published novel, Styron describes Nat's torment in more detail:

> The day before, when they had brought me up by foot from Cross Keys, there had been two women—banshees in sunbonnets, egged on by the men—who had pricked my back deep with hatpins a dozen times, perhaps more; the tiny wounds along my shoulders had begun fiercely to itch and I yearned to scratch them, with a hopeless craving which brought tears to my eyes, but I was prevented from doing so by the manacles. (p. 13)

Styron garners an even more gruesome detail from Drewry's description of the murder of the Travis infant. Drewry's version reads this way:

> Then, remembering his resolve to spare neither age nor sex, and reflecting, as he said, that "nits make lice," Nat sent Henry and Will back to take it by its heels and dash its brains out against the bricks of the fireplace. (p. 36)

In *Nat Turner*, Gray attributes an almost identical statement to Nat:

> "So you say out loud, 'Nits breed lice!'—there's a delicate sentiment, I'll vow, Reverend, for a man of the cloth—and you send Henry and Will back to the house an' they take that pore pitiful little babe and dash its brains out agin the wall." (p. 392)

These annotations and borrowings show much about the uses to which Styron put Drewry's study. Certainly Styron took nothing of his imaginative reconstruction of Nat's personality from Drewry, but he did mine Drewry's book for historical detail.

The annotations also reveal a second volume used by Styron— Frederick Law Olmsted's *A Journey in the Seaboard Slave States*. This book rivals Drewry's as a source of realistic detail for Styron's novel. Perhaps best known for his collaboration with Calvert Vaux in designing New York City's Central Park, Olmsted published his influential study of the South in 1856.[12] The book was based on a series of letters written by Olmsted to *The New York Times* from December 1852 to April 1853 during a journey which extended as far west as New Orleans. Olmsted, a Northerner born in Hartford, Connecticut, painted a dismal picture of Southern society and especially of the institution of slavery. But contemporary critics applauded him for the objectivity of his reporting—a quality lacking in most anti-slavery tracts of the time. In his introduction to a later edition of Olmsted's book, W. P. Trent writes:

> *A Journey in the Seaboard Slave States* must probably rank along with *Uncle Tom's Cabin* and *The Impending Crisis* as one of the three books that did most to open the eyes of the North to the true nature of the plague of slavery and to the inflamed condition of public opinion at the South during the decade preceding the Civil War. . . . [Olmsted's book] is by far the most valuable to the historian and to the reader interested in reconstructing the past.[13]

Styron's major burden in *The Confessions of Nat Turner* was to reconstruct the past, and it is therefore not surprising that he relied heavily on Olmsted. But Styron has only mentioned Olmsted once in his published interviews and then only in an oblique reference in defense of his use of Negro dialect in the novel.[14] Styron's annotations in the Drewry book, however, reveal that he gleaned many important details from Olmsted's *Journey*. Styron refers to Olmsted in eighteen different annotations—half of them paginated. Of these eighteen only nine point to material that eventually appears in the published novel, but even those references which do not directly contribute to the finished work are significant because they show Styron doing his homework, bolstering his knowledge of life in antebellum Southampton County, and gathering material for possible use in his novel. For example, Styron notes a "Descr. of horse in Olmstead (p. 68)" that may prove valuable:

> The filly was just so pleasantly playful, and full of well-bred life, as to create a joyful, healthy, sympathetic, frolicsome heedlessness in her rider—walking rapidly, and with a sometimes irresistible inclination to dance and bound.

In the annotations Styron speculates that "perhaps Nat has one like this in raid." Styron may have been attracted to Olmsted's filly because of the dramatic possibility of having Nat, the grim avenging angel, seated on so lively and friendly a mount. Apparently Styron abandoned this idea, though, since the horse does not appear in *Nat Turner*.

These annotations also reveal Styron's healthy skepticism concerning the surviving historical record. He questions, for example, the feasibility of the rebel slave's survival in the Great Dismal Swamp ("How does Nat eat in swamp"). Styron finds his answer on p. 112 of Olmsted:

> "But, meanwhile, how does the [runaway] negro support life in the swamp?" I asked.
> "Oh, he gets sheep and pigs and calves, and fowls and turkeys; sometimes they will kill a small cow. . . . If it is cold, he will crawl under a fodder-stack, or go into the cabins with some of the other negroes, and in the same way, you see, he can get all the corn, or almost anything else he wants."

Satisfied that Turner and his band could indeed have survived, Styron retains the Dismal Swamp as the destination of Nat and his rebels in the published novel.

Many of the annotations to Olmsted refer to minor specifics. One note, for instance, reads, "Diff. between mules + horses: mules will take more punishment, handed out by Negroes." On p. 51 of his study, Olmsted writes:

> So, too, when I ask why mules are so universally substituted for horses on the farm, the first reason given, and confessedly the most conclusive one, is, that horses cannot bear the treatment that they always *must* get from negroes; horses are always soon foundered or crippled by them, while mules will bear cudgelling, and lose a meal or two now and then, and not be materially injured, and they do not take cold or get sick if neglected or overworked.

Styron changes this passage slightly, including oxen along with horses as animals which are mistreated by slaves:

> I could hear Hark in the barn with the mules. The oxen that Moore once owned he had replaced with mules, partially because mules—unlike oxen and certainly horses—would sustain almost any punishment handed out

by Negroes, a people not notably sweet-natured around domestic animals.
(p. 293)

Styron also demonstrates his eye for realistic detail in two other annotations. These notes read, "Food for negroes: meal + bacon (Olm. p.
120)" and "*Food:* Olmstead, pp. 88 (white folk's food), 103." Of Negro
food Olmsted writes, "I was assured, however . . . that, generally, the
slaves were well provided for—always allowed a sufficient quantity of
meal, and, generally, of pork" (p. 120). According to Olmsted, white
Southerners ate substantially better: "There was fried fowl, and fried
bacon and eggs, and cold ham; there were preserved peaches, and
preserved quinces and grapes; there was hot wheaten biscuit, and hot
short-cake, and hot corn-cake, and hot griddle cakes, soaked in butter"
(p. 88). In the novel Styron juxtaposes these diets in order to underscore
the humane treament Nat receives from Joseph Travis: "Instead of the
nigger food I was accustomed to at Moore's, fat pork and corn pone, I got
house food like the white people—a lot of lean bacon and red meat, occasionally even the leavings from a roast of beef, and often white bread
made of wheat" (p. 48).

Styron also draws on Olmsted in his portrayal of two other interesting sub-classes of the pre-war South—the free Negroes and the poor
whites. Two of Styron's annotations read, "*Free negroes:* likely drunken
vagabonds" and "White labor unreliable, drunken. Naturally, Nat feels
superior." Of the former class Olmsted writes, "Our free negroes . . . are
a miserable set of vagabonds, drunken, vicious, worse off, it is my honest
opinion, than those who are retained in slavery" (p. 48). Styron's picture
of Arnold, the drunken free Negro in the novel, is similar:

> Now having been set free through the grace and piety of his late mistress
> (who had left him a hundred dollars—which he had squandered in bran-
> dy during his first free year—but who had not thought to teach him a
> trade), the oafish old fellow dwelt upon life's furthest rim, more insignifi-
> cant and wretched than he had even been in slavery. (p. 261)

Olmsted's portrait of the poor white Southerner is equally distressing:

> I have been once or twice told that the poor white people . . . are worse
> off in almost all respects than the slaves. They are said to be extremely ig-
> norant and immoral, as well as indolent and unambitious. (pp. 93–94)

Styron's description of the poor white trash of Jerusalem is even more
damning:

> These white idlers were the rogues and dregs of the community: penniless
> drunks and cripples, scroungers, handymen, ex-overseers, vagabonds
> from North Carolina, harelipped roustabouts, squatters on pineland bar-
> rens, incorrigible loafers, cretins, rapscallions, and dimwits of every de-
> scription . . . allowing the slaves from their market promontory a brac-

ing glimpse of white men worse off—in certain important respects at least—than themselves. (pp. 304–05)

The most interesting item of source material—"BISHOP MEADE'S AMAZING SERMON TO SLAVES"—is taken by Styron directly from pp. 131–33 of Olmsted's text. This sermon, which Olmsted calls "a specimen of the most careful kind of preaching, ordinarily addressed by the white clergy to the black sheep of their flocks" (p. 131), was originally delivered by Bishop Meade, of the Church of England in Virginia. After changing some of the wording and deleting about a third of Meade's sermon, Styron put the bishop's words into the mouth of Richard Whitehead, a young Methodist minister and brother of Margaret Whitehead. Richard's sermon places him in opposition to both Margaret and Nat: his obvious pro-slavery sentiments are the antithesis of his sister's humanistic attitudes, and his advocacy of subservience is directly opposed to Nat's religion of revolt. More importantly, Styron ironically counterpoints Nat's description of his fanatical co-conspirators with Whitehead's message of forbearance. Nat's description of half-mad Will is preceded by Whitehead's advocacy of earthly obedience:

> *And though you could manage so cleverly as to escape the eyes and hands of man, yet think what a dreadful thing it is to fall into the hands of the living God, who is able to cast both soul and body into hell. . . .*
>
> And now through the soft moaning of the black crowd . . . I hear another voice behind me and very near, almost at my shoulder, a harsh rapid low muttering, almost incoherent, like that of a man in the clutch of fever: . . . *me some of dat white stuff, yas, get me some of dat white stuff, yas* . . . (pp. 101–02).

Styron's annotations and marginalia in his copy of *The Southampton Insurrection* point to some of the details he took from Drewry and Olmsted. A careful reading of both books reveals additional passages and information appropriated by Styron for his novel. And these two books represent only one corner of Styron's research: future investigators should explore his extensive reading on the history of slavery for other important materials. According to one's persuasion, of course, Styron may still be guilty of distorting "history" in the larger sense, simply by having been bold enough to enter imaginatively into the mind of a nineteenth-century black rebel. But in the more narrow and exacting sense, Styron was quite faithful to the historical record. His annotations show him to have been an attentive and accurate researcher in recreating an historical event, and not, as some of his critics have contended, a careless distorter of historical facts.

Notes

1. Gilman, "Nat Turner Revisited," *The New Republic*, 158 (27 April 1968), 23.

2. The only attempt at a scholarly investigation is Henry Irving Tragle's "Styron and His Sources," *Massachusetts Review*, 11 (Winter 1970), 134–53. Tragle, an historian, was one of Styron's most severe critics; his article concentrates on the sources Styron chose not to use rather than on those he did employ.

3. "The Confessions of Nat Turner" (Baltimore: Lucas and Deaver, 1831).

4. Frederic Kelly, "William Styron tells the story of the Nat Turner Rebellion," *The New Haven Register*, Sunday Pict. Sec., 14 August 1966, p. 7.

5. Styron's copy is part of an extensive collection of his scrapbooks, clippings, correspondence, and manuscripts at Duke. We are most grateful to Dr. Mattie Russell, Curator of Manuscripts at the Perkins Library, for permission to examine Styron's copy and for having its pages microfilmed for our use.

6. George Plimpton, "William Styron: A Shared Ordeal," *The New York Times Book Review*, 8 Oct. 1967, p. 2.

7. Styron's letters to his father are among the holdings at Duke. Permission to publish this passage, the quotations in this article from Styron's annotations, and the facsimiles of those annotations, has been granted by the Manuscript Department, Perkins Library, Duke University, and by William Styron; these materials may not be reproduced without Mr. Styron's permission. Jay Saunders Redding, a distinguished black educator and scholar, taught at Hampton Institute from 1943 to 1966, finishing his tenure there as Johnson Professor of Creative Literature. From 1966 to 1970 he served as Director of the Division of Research and Publication, National Endowment for the Humanities. Styron likely met Redding through their mutual publisher Bobbs-Merrill, which had issued both Styron's *Lie Down in Darkness* and Redding's *On Being Negro in America* in 1951.

8. A label on the front paste-down endpaper of the book reveals that it was apparently a discarded copy from the library of The Hampton Normal and Agricultural Institute. Redding also sent Styron several other items; these too are preserved with Styron's papers at Duke. The items are photostats of Gray's original "Confession"; Samuel Warner, *Authentic and Impartial Narrative of the Tragical Scene Which Was Witnessed in Southampton County . . .* (New York: Warner & West, 1831); "Nat Turner's Insurrection," *Atlantic Monthly*, Aug. 1861; and "The Light Dragoons," *Southern Historical Society Papers*, August 1899.

9. Also of interest are Styron's comments, in the margins and front blanks, on Nat's wife. In the front he writes, "No evidence of rape. Perhaps Nat has seen his wife seduced by Travis." And in the margin of p. 33 he queries:

Nat's wife: Fannie?
  "   son: Gilbert?

But in the published novel, Nat never marries and in fact never experiences heterosexual intercourse. Styron's detractors have criticized him severely for being ignorant of historical evidence which suggests that Nat was married. Styron has always insisted, however, that he knew of this evidence (which is scant and inconclusive) and simply chose to make Nat unmarried and virginal for fictional purposes. These speculations in the front blanks and margins show that Styron was aware early on of the possibility that Nat had had a wife and son.

10. Robert Canzoneri and Page Stegner, "An Interview with William Styron," *Per/Se*, 1 (Summer 1966), 39.

11. William Styron, *The Confessions of Nat Turner* (New York: Random House, 1967), p. 100. Subsequent references are cited parenthetically.

12. Olmsted, *A Journey in the Seaboard Slave States* (New York: Dix & Edwards; London: Sampson Low, Son & Co., 1856).

13. Olmsted, *Journey*, 2 vols. (New York: Putnam's, 1904), I, xxxi–xxxii. This is the edition used by Styron in his researches; subsequent references to its text are cited parenthetically.

14. Plimpton, "Ordeal," p. 2.

Acceptance Speech for the Howells Medal

William Styron*

Just as I started to set down these few words my attention was caught by an advertisement for a book of essays which claimed to challenge, among other things, *The Confessions of Nat Turner*, and its "condescending and degrading opinions about Negroes." It was not the modifiers—*condescending and degrading*—that bothered me so much as the key word: *opinions.* I had an old hurtful twinge of resentment and my first impulse was to say here something mean-spirited and elaborately defensive about this familiar response to my work. I am sure there is some wisdom in my not doing so, for this award is one which by its very essence tends to make any bitterness I might still harbor quite unimportant.

It seems to me that in honoring my work this award underscores some certainties about the nature of literature. One of these is that a novel worthy of the name is not, nor ever has been, valuable because of its opinions; a novel is speculative, composed of paradoxes and riddles; at its best it is magnificently unopinionated. As Chekhov said, fiction does not provide answers but asks questions—even, I might add, as it struggles to make sense out of the fearful ambiguities of time and history. This award therefore implies an understanding that a novel can possess a significance apart from its subject matter and that the story of a nineteenth-century black slave may try to say at least as much about longing, loneliness, personal betrayal, madness, and the quest for God as it does about Negroes or the institution of slavery. It implies the understanding that fiction, which almost by definition is a kind of dream, often tells truths that are very difficult to bear, yet—again as in dreams—is able to liberate the mind through the catharsis of fantasy, enigma, and terror.

By recognizing *Nat Turner* this award really honors all of those of my contemporaries who have steadfastly refused to write propaganda or indulge in myth-making but have been impelled to search instead for those

*Reprinted from the *Proceedings of the American Academy of Arts and Letters and the National Institute of Arts and Letters,* 2d series, no. 21 (1971), publ. #269, pp. 30–32. This is Styron's acceptance speech for the Howells Medal for Fiction, awarded every five years for the most distinguished work of fiction published during those five years. Styron received the medal at the Joint Ceremonial, 26 May 1970, for *The Confessions of Nat Turner.* Reprinted by permission of the author and journal.

insights which, however raggedly and imperfectly, attempt to demonstrate the variety, the quirkiness, the fragility, the courage, the good
humor, desperation, corruption, and mortality of all men. And finally it
ratifies my own conviction that a writer jeopardizes his very freedom by
insisting that he be bound or defined by his race, or by almost anything
else. For one of the enduring marvels of art is its ability to soar through
any barrier, to explore any territory of experience, and I say that only by
venturing from time to time into strange territory shall artists, of
whatever commitment, risk discovering and illuminating the human
spirit that we all share.

IN THE CLAP SHACK

Playwriting Debut for Styron

Clive Barnes*

NEW HAVEN, Dec. 16—A first play by a new playwright is always a tense event—tense for the playwright, tense for the audience and, to be honest, tense for the critic. And this tension is felt all the more strongly if the playwright is not in fact a young unknown, but a distinguished author who is making his playwriting debut.

Certainly, Mr. Styron is distinguished. He is a Pulitzer Prize-winning novelist and well known as a writer and essayist. His play was produced last night at the Yale Repertory Theater. Called "In the Clap Shack," it is set in the venereal-disease ward of a naval hospital during World War II.

Perhaps the subject matter makes it sound more original than it in fact is. Nowadays, and rightly so, venereal disease is widely discussed in public, and indeed is even the subject of a rather well-made little television commercial. But Mr. Styron's purpose is not to discuss V.D., but rather to describe life in a V.D. ward and, despite the plight of most of the men, long discussions on the effect of syphilis and its diagnosis and the treatment of gonorrhea, the play is rather conventional.

An 18-year-old Marine is admitted into the hospital ward with what appears to be syphilis; certainly his Wassermann test is alarmingly positive. Once there, he finds himself with a mixed group of men. One is dying from hypertension (he doesn't make it through the first act). There is a friendly Jew, suffering from an incurably tubercular kidney rather than V.D. He is full of rabbinical wisdom and compassion and vainly hopes to start a pet shop after the war. And there is also an ironically embittered black sailor, who is dying of some quite terrible venereal infection, which is causing him much pain.

The inmates are looked after by a very sympathetic homosexual ward attendant, by a paranoid physician with unusual sexual proclivities and by a mildly mad captain, who quotes Kipling and feels that sex is an un-American activity.

Unfortunately, and as I admire Mr. Styron this is not easy to say, the play comes out resembling a pilot for a TV series. Of course, on TV the

*Reprinted from *New York Times*, 17 Dec. 1972, p. 67, by permission. © 1972/79 by The New York Times Company.

ward would be a casualty ward, but that is the level of the writing, plotting and characterization. At times the tone is satiric, at times a little more cozy. And Mr. Styron exaggerates everything.

The homosexual ward attendant, for example—and this may be partly the director's fault—flits across the stage like the queen of the May. The Jewish philosopher is all too Jewish and too philosophical. The crazy officers, taking down sexual confessions on a recorder, are too much to be believed, but too little to be satirical. And the dialogue never has that effortless flight of truth.

Men do not talk like this except on television series of the sixties, movies of the fifties and plays of the forties. I welcome Mr. Styron to the ranks of playwrights—it is good that he should have a go—but, if he wants to hear what real men sound like on stage in an all-male environment, he should perhaps either read David Rabe's "The Basic Training of Pavlo Hummel" or take a trip to New Haven's other resident theater, the Long Wharf, to see David Storey's "The Changing Room." Mr. Styron's play lacks any dimension of received reality, yet it is realistically intended.

At its own level, it is adequate enough. Alvin Epstein's staging is bright, it underpins the play's structure and underlines its tendency toward the obvious.

It must be difficult to make the V.D. ward of a hospital visually interesting, and I cannot pretend that the designer, Tony Negron, has succeeded in what was probably an impossible task. The acting, on the other hand, was frequently good.

As the hero, Miles Chapin looked more disgruntled than dismayed, and he never came to grips with a role the author himself had not fully delineated. Eugene Troobnick, his voice resonant with accepted agony, was fine as the long-suffering Jew, and Hannibal Penney Jr. impressed as the smilingly bitter black. Jeremy Geidt proved splendidly disturbed, not to say crazy, as Dr. Glanz. And, although he had to swish incredibly, Nicholas Hormann did very well as the homosexual orderly.

Mr. Styron had a serious idea. He wanted to show how V.D. can place a man outside of majority valuation—so that a syphilitic is a minority group, like a Jew or a black. The idea is more interesting than the play. But it is, after all, only a first play.

Styron's Play

Irvin Malin*

In the Clap Shack is Styron's first play. It was performed in December, 1972, at the Yale Repertory Theatre. Although it was not reviewed widely, it deserves close attention because it deals with many of his characteristic themes—the nature of freedom, the quality of official language—in a "relaxed," open way.

Of course, the play is inferior to Styron's best fictions. It lacks, for example, the stunning images, the "romantic" views of nature, and the tense development of character. But like the plays of McCullers and Bellow, it helps us to understand more clearly the impulses behind the fiction; it thrusts Styron's obsessions at us.

In the following essay I explicate the written version, hoping to show that it is a finished, substantial—if not complex—work which must be read by anyone interested in the career of one of our best writers.

In the Clap Shack begins with these stage directions:

> The time is the summer of 1943. The place is the Urological Ward of the United States Naval Hospital at a large Marine Corps base in the South. The entire action of the play takes place on the ward, which differs little in appearance from hospital wards throughout the world. . . . The beds are staggered, so that the audience obtains a view of each bed and its patient. At extreme stage left is the office of the Chief Urologist, Dr. Glanz, who rules the ward from the cluttered room filled with urological instruments and medical books.

The directions introduce the tensions which dominate the entire play. There is a contrast between the "ward" (a closed space) and the outside world, but this contrast is somewhat misleading—*the ward is really as violent as the distant battlegrounds*. Furthermore, the patients and Dr. Glanz are directly opposed. War and illness reign; there is little resting in "the summer of 1943."

Styron is so interested in the warfare between men—one of his favorite themes—that he does not develop "character." He gives us stereotypes—the mad scientist, the innocent hero, and the philosophical

*Reprinted from *Southern Literary Journal,* 6 (Spring 1974), 151–57, by permission of the author.

Jew—because he believes that only when men battle authoritarian forces do they break out of their roles and achieve some "unique" identity. Thus his play is drawn in black and white—in vivid, polemical contrasts.

Act One begins with Lineweaver, the "chief male nurse," ordering the men to "rise and shine." He is a caricature; he never seems to be more than the cynical underling who uses his authority (gained from Dr. Glanz and Captain Budwinkle) for self-pleasure. He "masturbates"—in terms of the sexual imagery underlying the play. He is less natural—and more "effeminate," Styron tells us—than his sick patients. Once we realize that he is cruel, ironic, and compulsive, we sympathize with the patients he "helps."

The various patients are even more crudely characterized than Lineweaver. They are "fenced in"—the radio plays "Don't Fence Me In"—by their illnesses; they merely laugh or rage at their condition. But in the opening scene, we recognize that some of them are capable of "rising and shining," of transcending their unwilling imprisonment. Schwartz, the "solemn, bespectacled Jew," demonstrates concern for a dying patient (instead of just feeling "creepy"). Magruder, who has arrived the night before, has also not learned the proper responses. He does not know the daily routine. He has syphilis—or, at least, the official tests proclaim so—and, therefore, he stands out. He is, as Lineweaver ironically claims, "a prince among commoners."

The various conflicts become more apparent when Dr. Glanz and Captain Budwinkle arrive to inspect the patients. Both men are in charge, but they have surrendered to their roles. They, like Lineweaver, have lost *personality*. Dr. Glanz, for example, always speaks in the plural; he views the patients (and himself) as "specimens" to be labelled and treated. He resembles, therefore, many of Styron's authority figures who use official language. (He is less strong than Templeton in *The Long March*, who forces his men to use such words as "courage" and "heroism"—words *he* never defines.) He "knows all." He calls the ward "corrupt and discouraging"; he cites "moral breakdown." Dr. Glanz is a theologian (or, at least, a moralist), asserting meanings without correct, full information.

Captain Budwinkle goes along with him. But he lacks the skill of Dr. Glanz. He is, in fact, more comic than either the doctor or the nurse. He speaks in Hollywood clichés—"we'd better batten down all ports and man the fire stations."

Dr. Glanz and Captain Budwinkle consider Magruder a perfect reflection of their symbolic fantasies. Surely he is a case of "moral breakdown"—not only does he have the "soft full mouth of a voluptuary" and the deceptiveness of a potential "artist"—he cannot even understand military routine. Magruder is *marked* for unusual inspection. (Styron usually employs the marked man as his rebel. Think of Nat Turner marked by color or Cass Kinsolving marked by art.) He must come to terms with his special case before he gains manhood. As the first scene ends he wears a robe marked with a "yellow 'S'." He likens the symbolic letter to Hawthorne's letter and to Nazi stars worn by Jews. He recognizes that by adopting *other people's symbols*, he is less free. He screams: "I'll never get used to my new status. Never!"

In the second scene we remain in the ward—"*the routine now is similar to that of the early morning*"—and we begin to feel as claustrophobic as the patients. Before the tensions build forcefully, Styron introduces a comic chaplain who, upon being told that he is in the "urological and venereal" ward, shudders and says "Heavens!" He leaves quickly. The implications are clear—the usual comforting words of orthodoxy, like the military clichés of Captain Budwinkle, do not help the patients very much.

Schwartz and Magruder continue to communicate. Their conversation about poetry, love, ethics, is rather simpleminded—the Jew, for example, quotes easy passages from a popular book called *Tolerance for Others*, but it is more appealing than the hostile, dark words of the dying patient, Clark. Styron applauds the warmth of Schwartz and Magruder, but he recognizes the wisdom of Clark, who mutters angrily: "I'll get sleep. And you too, Jew-boy. Because you and me—us gwine *die!*" The scene is powerful because of the clashing philosophies of the three outsiders. It is little wonder that Magruder—who is more innocent and "alive" than the others—finally screams: "Jesus Christ, I feel like I've died and waked up in hell!"

There is little rest for Magruder. Now he faces the inquiry of Dr. Glanz, a tyrannical "father" (unlike Schwartz, his other "father"). The doctor claims the authority of experience: "You do not see a callow, gullible young intern eager to swallow any harebrained invention that might pass a patient's lips." He insists upon direct answers. He calls Magruder a liar, coward, and pervert. We are shocked because knowing the young patient, we realize that Dr. Glanz is less interested in "health" than in "disease." He delights, indeed, in the pains of life, those pains which render men helpless and force them to surrender to his authority. He uses Magruder for his own sick purposes.

The scene concludes with sudden laughter. (Such laughter continually undercuts the scientific jargon.) Clark says, "Food for de worms. Equal." The equality extends apparently not only to him and the outsiders but to the doctor (and chaplain) as well. The ward is the body; the ward is the cage. What can help us to transcend the "stink"?

Act Two begins with the sense of elapsed time, of sleepy, half-shaped meanings. (Even Lineweaver dozes.) Sleep tends to acquire symbolic meaning—it suggests that the patients, especially Magruder, are not fully aware of their human condition.

There is little action in the first scene. Styron concentrates upon the syphilis textbook which is stolen from Dr. Glanz's office by Magruder (upon Schwartz's urging). By reading it, Magruder hopes to gain knowledge: "*Knowledge* might make me able to get through this." Later he says: "I try to worm a little knowledge out of Dr. Glanz, but I can't even get a word of consolation from him, much less any facts." The book is symbolic. (It reminds us of the Bunyan read by Nat Turner.) It seems to contain the information which will help Magruder to transform himself, to become an "*authority*." But there is irony. The book merely forces him to lose whatever hope he possesses. He soon yields to written "symptoms" of paresis.

Styron's insistence upon words should not surprise us. He recognizes that a man can control others by forcing them to use *his* language. Only an artist can battle official clichés (propaganda) and create "pure," free patterns of meaning. Magruder is trapped now by military *and* scientific language; he has not shown the strength of Wallace Stevens—a poet he mentioned earlier—that strength which can liberate him from the routine symbols which imprison us. He cannot create "poetry."

The contrasts between poetry and science are underlined in the next scene. Dr. Glanz interviews Magruder, trying to establish a "sexual profile" of his patient. As they talk about sex, we see the differences in their philosophies of life. Dr. Glanz says: "First, it is our recollection that you told us that you had sexual congress with only quote two women unquote in quote my entire life unquote, these females being quote an older woman unquote and quote my girl unquote." He uses such words as "carnal connection" and "relations." Sex—or nature itself—is cold, impersonal, and curiously abstract. Magruder equates sex with poetry and religious experience: "It was the first time for me, the first time I had made love to anyone, and somehow it was all mixed up with this poetry we'd discovered together. I imagine you could say it was like a religious experience. . . ." The clashing descriptions force Magruder to cry (especially when Dr. Glanz hints at the infection of his girl friend). And these cries hover in the darkness as the scene (and act) ends.

Act Three ironically resolves the established tensions. It contains three scenes.

The first begins with the clichés of blackjack play: " '*Hit me, I'll stick.*' " (These words acquire new meaning in the context.) Soon Dr. Glanz and Lineweaver inform one patient that "he'll be free." But, unlike Stancik, Magruder is less free than ever. He believes that his illness has won; he lacks the strength to write his girl or even to argue with Clark's nasty remarks about Schwartz as "thief." *He does not know the correct words to use for anyone.* Finally he and Schwartz fight. Suddenly he realizes that he may be out of control: "Like Dr. Glanz said, it's gone to my brain! I'm mad! Stark raving mad! Stark raving mad! Stark raving mad!" The repetitions with which the scene abruptly ends are particularly strong; they imply that not only does Magruder lack the ability to create "poetry" (or admire it!)—he can do little more than *babble hysterically*. Words fail him!

The pains, losses, and deaths continue in the second scene. Clark dies; Schwartz approaches his end. Although the Jew dreams of a pet shop in which the animals run free—an ironic contrast to this "clap shack"—he realizes as he watches Clark die, that freedom may be a dream. He preaches love, "tolerance for others," but these words are destroyed by social realities. Thus Clark's last words suggest that only miracles can cure the hostility of the patients.

Styron won't have us stay in the pit. He "interferes" with this downward swing of events (and persons), implying that nature itself is arbitrary, possibly "unplotted." Suddenly a "miracle" occurs—at least for Magruder, who discovers that his "syphilis" is a false diagnosis (due to trench mouth). He is saved.

The wheel turns again. Now that he is "healthy," he can, according to Lineweaver, "die a hero on a wonderful Pacific beach somewhere. That's a lot better, isn't it, than ending up with the blind staggers, or in the booby hatch? And if you really die with enough dash and style, they might even give you the Navy Cross." What a choice! Magruder does not still comprehend the absurdity of things—is death as a war "hero" more meaningful than death as a patient?—but he soon asserts himself more strongly than we have yet seen.

He rushes into Dr. Glanz's office and fights his authority. He says: "You're a loathsome little functionary with a dirty mind and a stethoscope. . . ." He continues: "You're a ghoul. You feed off the very dregs of death." He is extreme; he uses words for his own violent ends, trying to vent the rebellious feelings he had previously contained. Of course, it is easy to object to this sudden change of personality. It is pat, didactic, unreal. Styron is so involved with the underlying principles of private expression and individual liberty, that he tends to sermonize. Nevertheless, he cleanses us, especially when we hear Dr. Glanz *adopt Magruder's words*, and we feel a strange kind of relief.

The relief is short-lived. In the third scene (the shortest in the play), we meet a stranger, a Marine Corporal, who guards Magruder. The innocent hero needs police protection; he is going to the brig, having assaulted a "superior officer." The official words "superior officer," "terrible crimes in the naval service" assert themselves. Magruder, however, seems at ease. He knows that prison is better than the ward (and a death like that of Schwartz). He gets as close to Schwartz as possible before his departure: "Whatever else, I think I've gotten rid of my hypochondria. Breathe on me, Schwartz! . . . Fantastic. The breath of a babe! It was like a zephyr!" These are his last words. They are "poetic," suggesting that he is at the point of creating new patterns of meaning. Although they are *half-formed*, they cheer us.

The play ends with Lineweaver (who, we remember, began the play). He is less cynical; he has also learned some compassion. He reads about the pet shop to Schwartz: " 'As a veterinarian with over thirty years of experience in handling all the canine varieties, I can testify that the notion of smaller dogs being more neurotic is strictly a myth. . . .' "

Styron ends the play with the word "myth." It is a useful word. It suggests "bigness," extreme behavior, poetic theory. It captures the feelings generated by the play.

In the Clap Shack deals, as we have seen, with universal patterns of meaning—with the nature of freedom (rebellion against authority) and the quality of language. (It fuses these two themes.) It is primarily a didactic work, sublimating character and plot to theme, but it still works powerfully at times—especially in the ironic, "accidental" turn of final events. Then it goes "beyond" sermon, meditation, or polemic—it moves us. Although this play is not a major achievement—like that of *The Confessions of Nat Turner*—it convinces us again that Styron is an important, *necessary* writer who continues to experiment, grow, and express his freedom.

SOPHIE'S CHOICE

Breaking Sacred Silences

Larzer Ziff*

In the summer of 1947, the narrator of *Sophie's Choice*, whom William Styron asks us to accept as his twenty-two-year-old self, rents a room in the Brooklyn house of Mrs. Yetta Zimmerman. The lodgers in the house and the tone of the surrounding neighborhood are so intensely Jewish as to be positively exotic for the ex-Marine, ex-Duke University, ex-Tidewater author bent on writing a novel in which he must imagine himself into the causes of the suicide of his heroine, Maria Hunt, a young woman he had known in high school. She had died in despair, but the young Styron is all too aware that he has led a life much like the life of other Americans of his age, troubled only by minor guilts and major yearnings and remote from the psychic condition at the center of his intended work, for all his familiarity with its milieu. Although he does not then realize it, he is in Jewish Brooklyn to borrow the trouble his art needs.

Rather than accepting the exoticism of his environment as a desirable hedge around the privacy of his creative consciousness, then, he casts forth furtive Southern filaments with which to attach his new surroundings to the needs of his inner self. Southerners, he reasons, have always responded more warmly to Jews than Northerners: in part because of a shared affinity for the obdurate patriarchs and prophets of the Old Testament, and in part—baleful fact that becomes a tie that must be made to bind—because Southerners already have their sacrificial lamb in the Negro race. Indeed, Styron would not have been in those Brooklyn lodgings, freed for a season from the need to earn his bread, were it not for a legacy of $500, his share of his father's freaky discovery that year of a cache of money in the family house in Virginia. Successfully hidden for almost a century, the money had been received by his great-grandfather for the sale of a slave, a particularly nasty transaction in that it broke up a family and sent a sixteen-year-old boy (notably named Artiste) from the relative comfort of a Tidewater farm to the hell of the Georgia turpentine mills.

At Mrs. Zimmerman's the young author is immediately and intensely

*Reprinted from *Commonweal*, 11 May 1979, pp. 277–78, by permission of the author.

attracted to Sophie, the survivor of another hell, Auschwitz, and although the pull is strongly erotic—she is beautiful and her couplings with her lover, Nathan, occur audibly over his head—it also gains strength from the promise it has of shriving him of his guilty acceptance of Artiste's head-price. In the long run, Sophie, whom he learns is Polish, not Jewish, so that for all her otherness, her being victimized in parallel with Artiste, she is also akin to him, another white Christian island in a sea of Jews, this Sophie will become the center of another novel, *Sophie's Choice*, completed more than thirty years after that summer. But in 1947 her anguish initially serves to sensitize him to the despair of his heroine, Maria, of whom she reminds him.

During the historical present of *Sophie's Choice*, the young author sees the relationship of Sophie and Nathan through to its fatal end and listens at great length to her conflicting, evasive, calculating, yet eventually full and passionate account of her life. She has been the generalized victim of an incomprehensible historical atrocity and the personal victim of a deliberately satanic moral atrocity, yet she feels the guilt of a perpetrator. He comes to experience what it will take him another thirty years to articulate, the structure of feeling summarized thus by Simone Weil: "Affliction stamps the soul to its very depths with the scorn, the disgust and even the self-hatred and sense of guilt that crime logically should produce but actually does not."

The historical present of the novel, then, comes to us within the controlling voice of the contemporary present of a celebrated, mature author who shares his musings about his subject with the reader. He speaks of the research he conducted into the holocaust and he sees what he experienced in the late '40s through the meaning it acquired from events in the '50s and '60s. Sophie's story must be the vehicle for his understanding the nightmare of contemporary history.

In one of the novel's early scenes the narrator is at a beach with Sophie in company with a group of young, clever, bookish, attractive Jews whose conversation is sharp with the pain of their self-awareness, at which, it seems, they have all arrived through psychoanalysis. The young author, a glutton for words, is sated, made positively dizzy by the novelty and daring of their terms—penis envy, oral sex, orgasmic function. But for Sophie, the survivor, there is only disgust. In what the author calls "a lovely gem of a phrase," she denounces the mood of the group as "unearned unhappiness."

Indeed, in context, it is a gemlike phrase (one also, it must be noted, that Styron slyly invites us to apply to the fiction of his Jewish contemporaries who were also beginning their assault upon American literature in 1947). But it is a phrase that can be brought home to Styron's door. Here still remains, we might say, this sprawling, slovenly America, a rural bumpkin converted in a twinkling into an urban terrorist, a society electric with implicit patricide of a scope to match the explicit fratricide of a century ago. With so much earned unhappiness in his America, why must the possessor of the intelligence that realized *Nat Turner* in its symbolic fullness and of a mastery of naturalistic narrative technique unmatched by his American peers (so that he is almost single-handedly sustaining the tradition of the novel as the tradition of great storytellling), why must he seek a vehicle for our condition outside the circumstances of this continent? Why import unhappiness?

It is a question of which Styron is acutely aware throughout *Sophie's Choice*. At the close of the summer of '47 Sophie comes to his bed, although she is on the eve of returning to her lover and to certain death, and gives him as an unconditional gift the fulfillment of every erotic fantasy that haunted him since his puberty. She matches the capacity of his imagination. But she is unaffected by the encounter, and Styron thus reveals, consciously or not, that the creative task he undertook in writing about Sophie is one in which he can only hope to unburden himself; the horror remains intact and unaffected for all his profound and passionate concern.

Still, he has to make Sophie's story yield its larger meaning, spurred, among other things, by his reading of George Steiner on the holocaust. For all he learned from Steiner, he resents the suggestion that silence is the only fit answer to what occurred, that what was unspeakable is best left unspoken. To acquiesce, he affirms, is to conspire to permit evil to retain a privileged status. Rather, through telling Sophie's story he will have his stab at understanding massive evil.

Sophie's Choice, then, continues on from *Nat Turner;* it is a further study of the intrusion into human history of an evil so enormous that historical determination alone is inadequate to account for it. But whereas Nat, unable to pray in the opening scene in jail, does in the morning scene at the close have a Bible given him and with it once again bridges social evil and divine benevolence—foreshadows, that is, the actual end of the institution of Negro slavery—the narrator of *Sophie's Choice* has since the holocaust experienced no correlative to emancipation but is ridden by the renewed horrors of the '50, '60s, and early '70s. In the final scene, the young author having recently masqueraded as a Presbyterian minister awakes on the beach in the morning to find that it is morning—excellent and fair but not a judgment day—only morning.

The Nazi perpetrator of the central, personal crime against Sophie's moral identity assaults her because as a deathcamp official he has become so accustomed to gross atrocities that, he realizes, they are acceptable and sinless because there is no God to enforce such a judgment of them. Once a religious man, he longs for the return of God and so devises an act so sinful that it must be recognized as sin and therefore must restore a judging God. His action and reasoning are at the core of Styron's attempt to understand Auschwitz, and before the reader assesses his success Styron himself measures it in the line quoted on these pages.

There is a certain weakness inherent in Styron's dependence upon Sophie's voice for so much of the narrative because she talks of a moral and physical landscape alien to the listening young man. Although her listener, he is, of course, also her creator and the convention of his listening and reflecting at times appears not so much to enrich what she says as to compensate for deficiencies in the power of the telling. But his narrative mastery continues to be astounding and since Sophie's story is always part of the particular story of what happened in Brooklyn in 1947 as well as part of the monumental story of what happened in Poland during the war his sheer virtuosity keeps the frail acount of Sophie from snapping under the weight it must bear.

When Styron himself bypasses Sophie and directly imagines the Polish scenes, calling them up almost as incantations, he is superb. The greatest of these scenes occurs toward the close of the novel, and as in *Nat Turner* he evokes pity, fear, terror, and theological anguish without recourse to extended descriptions of the sensationally brutal episodes that lie ready to hand in the record. The description of the journey of the trainload of prisoners from Warsaw to Auschwitz cuts through every callus that has grown upon our consciousnesses after our many exposures to holocaust literature, and in such writing, far more than in the story of Sophie herself, Styron does, indeed, assert art's power and thus art's right to break in upon even sacred silence.

A Novel of Evil

John Gardner*

[*Editorial Note:* Mr. Gardner has asked that the following statement be printed as a headnote to his review of *Sophie's Choice.*]

Book reviews are necessarily written under pressure; at most one has a matter of days to figure out what one thinks and feels about a book that may have, like *Sophie's Choice*, taken years to write. After this review, I received a good deal of angry mail from Polish Americans, which makes me sorry I was not more careful to show my sympathy with the Polish and my large dependence on Mr. Styron's carefully documented and immensely sympathetic account. But what I regret most of all was my review's disservice to Styron himself.

Though I recognized the power and beauty of *Sophie's Choice*, I did not guess, at the time I wrote, the novel's staying power. Scene after scene comes back now, long after I last read the book, with astonishing vividness—perhaps the most obvious mark of a masterpiece. I think the reason is not solely that one of the novel's important subjects is the holocaust. Very few writers have been able to deal with the red hot subject without in the end being burnt up by it. In retrospect I would say that Styron succeeded where many failed, and, more than that, that among the few who succeed he stands alone—if one does not count personal diaries or memoirs—as a writer who could fully dramatize the horror, the complexity, and something at least approaching the full historical and emotional meaning of the thing. He found the connections between the vast historical horror and the psychological equivalents in ordinary life, not to mention the eerie connection between what happened in Germany and what happens in these divided United States. But as I was saying, it is not just this subject matter that makes *Sophie's Choice* memorable. His descriptions of Brooklyn life and scenery have a vividness just as

*This review is reprinted from *The New York Times Book Review*, 27 May 1979, pp. 1, 16–17. The headnote appears for the first time in this volume. Review reprinted by permission of the author.

uncanny, and his analysis of the young writer's anxieties (any young writer's, not just Stingo's), to say nothing of his psychologically original and convincing analysis of Nathan and Sophie, make one look at people—and oneself—in a new way.

I regret, too, that I did not mention the novel's humor. I suppose I was overawed by the horror; but the fact is that one of the reasons Styron succeeded so well in *Sophie's Choice* is that, like Shakespeare (I think the comparison is not too grand), Styron knows how to cut away from the darkness of his material, so that when he turns to it again it strikes with increasing force.

Another of my regrets is that I read the book with a somewhat bigoted Yankee eye. I will say the inevitable: Some of my best friends are Southerners. Nevertheless, I reacted with disbelief and distaste to some extremely Southern material—for instance Stingo reading the Bible with an old black woman. If Styron had been faking the scene, I would have been right. But I am now convinced he was not; he was simply reporting real experience of a kind foreign to me, and, given my own Yankee reserve, embarrassing. Though none of my best friends are ancient Greeks, I am much fairer to Homer (who had some *very* odd opinions) than I was to my fellow American and contemporary. What makes the matter worse is that the scene is in fact not only authentic but symbolically crucial. Rightly understood, it negates my criticism that the "moral" of the novel is inadequate, the idea that all those people died so that Stingo might become a novelist. (I should mention that I write this without the review in front of me, and I'm not sure I voiced this objection. I remember thinking, at the time I wrote, that *Sophie's Choice* was faulty in the way Wallace Stegner's masterpiece, *Big Rock Candy Mountain*, was faulty, explaining away tragedy as a thing of value to the writer. I hope I decided not to say this, in the end, since in Styron's case at least, it's wrong. But whether or not I said it, other reviewers did. I hope they will join me apologizing for the mistake.)

I'm not sorry to have pointed out that *Sophie's Choice* transmutes the old "Southern Gothic" to a new, universal gothic, and I'm not sorry to have claimed that the Southern Gothic is an inherently inferior form. But I would like to take this opportunity to say that the general implication of my remarks was ill-considered. What I suggested, I'm sure, was that, in following the gothic formula, *Sophie's Choice* was a castle built on sand. What I now think is this: Most great American art is an elevation of trash. New Orleans tailgate funeral jazz was (or so I think on this particular Friday) aesthetically mediocre stuff, but out of it came the high art of Ellington, Gershwin, and the rest. Out of trash films, including Disney at his worst, came writers ranging from William Gass and Ishamel Reed to (forgive the self-congratulation) myself. Styron did not simply use the gothic formulae, he transmuted them. What is wrong with the gothics is not wrong with *Sophie's Choice*. When Dostoievsky published *Crime and Punishment* (I think it was), somebody important—I forget who—made a long trip to him (I think) to tell him, "You are the savior of all Russia!" After *Sophie's Choice*, I wish I had said, instead of what I did say, or at least in addition to what I did say, "You are the savior of all America!"

JOHN GARDNER
July 3, 1981

Early in William Styron's new novel a character named Nathan Landau tells the narrator, an aspiring young Southern writer, "I admire your courage, kid . . . setting out to write something else about the South." And Landau adds a moment later, "you're at the end of a tradition." The aspiring writer is a virtually undisguised William Styron at 22 (we get allusions, from the now mature narrator, to his earlier fiction, easily recognizable as *Lie Down in Darkness, The Long March, Set This House on Fire* and *The Confessions of Nat Turner*); and what Landau says to the young Styron is clearly very much on the mature Styron's mind as he works out the immense Gothic labyrinth that is the weighty, passionate novel we are reading now.

Sophie's Choice is a courageous, in some ways masterly book, a book very hard to review for the simple reason that the plot—even the double entendre in the title—cannot be given away. Certain things can be said without too much harming the novel's considerable effect: The story treats two doomed lovers, Nathan Landau, a brilliant, tragically mad New York Jew, and Sophie Zawistowska, a beautiful Polish survivor of Auschwitz, and their intellectual and emotional entrapment, for better or worse, of the novelist-narrator.

Thematically, the novel treats the familiar (which is not to say trivial) Styron subject, the nature of evil in the individual and in all of humanity. Brooding guilt is everywhere: in the narrator's story of how, when his mother was dying of cancer and could not take care of herself, he once went on a joy ride with a friend, failed to stoke up the fire in his mother's room and, when he returned, found her half-frozen, teeth chattering, shortly after which catastrophe—whether or not as a result of it—she died; in the narrator's awareness that the money he lives on as he writes his first novel comes directly from the sale of a 16-year-old slave, a boy who, having been falsely accused of accosting a Southern young lady, was sent into a kind of slavery few survive; in the memories of the novel's wonderful complex heroine, Sophie, a Catholic turned atheist and a woman who, for love of her son, made inept attempts at collaborating with the German SS; in the drug addiction and occasional fiendish violence of the gentle, humorous, intelligent and humane—but also mad—Nathan Landau. In the stories of Sophie's Resistance friends; in the stories of the narrator's father and his friends; and so on.

The novel's courage lies partly in this: After all the attacks on Styron, especially after *The Confessions of Nat Turner*, which some blacks and liberals (including myself) found offensive here and there, we get in *Sophie's Choice* the same old Styron, boldly and unmercifully setting down his occasional lapses (or his narrator's) into anti-Semitism, anti-feminism and so forth, baring his chest to whatever knives it may possibly deserve, even begging for it. Those who wish to can easily prove him anti-black, anti-white, anti-Southern, anti-Yankee, anti-Polish, anti-Semitic, anti-Christian, anti-German, anti-American, anti-Irish—the list could go on and on. No bigotry escapes him; the worst that can be said of humanity Styron claims for himself, wringing his hands, tearing his hair, wailing to all the congregation, *Mea culpa!* (Only in their taste in music are he and his favored characters faultless.)

Such all-inclusive, self-confessed sinfulness should absolve a man, and in a way, of course, it does; no reader of *Sophie's Choice* can doubt that Styron has put immense energy into trying to understand and deal justly with the evils in American history and the European holocaust, to say nothing of the evil (as well as the good) in his characters. Yet for all the civilized and, in the best sense, Christian decency of Styron's emotions when he's watching himself, the rabid streak is always ready to leap out and take command.

One example must suffice: After the double suicide of Nathan and Sophie at the end of the novel, the narrator, trying to get to their bodies, finds himself blocked by a police cordon. Styron's observation is that "everywhere stood clots of thuggish policemen chewing gum and negligently swatting their thick behinds." He adds: "I argued with one of these cops—a choleric ugly Irishman—asserting my right to enter." The scene is crowded with these piggish policemen, also "a cluster of wormy-looking police reporters"; not one of them is portrayed as timidly decent; none of them can be seen as, merely, confused children in grown-up bodies. Styron is far more just in his treatment of the Southern racial bigot Senator Bilbo, or Sophie's viciously anti-Semitic, woman-enslaving father, Prof. Zbigniew Bieganski, or even the master of Auschwitz, Rudolph Höss.

My point—and I labor it because it seems to me important—is this: Styron's justice and compassion, the desperate struggle to get to the bottom of even the most terrible, most baffling evils—the holocaust, above all—and to come back a just and loving man are impressive, almost awesome, precisely because we know by his slips that they are not natural to him but earned. When he forgets the ideal he sets for himself, as he does with the cops, with a Unitarian minister we meet later, with the

McGraw-Hill organization men we meet in the first chapter, and as he does in numerous other places, he shows us how serious this novel is as not merely a story of other people's troubles, but a piece of anguished Protestant soul-searching, an attempt to seize all the evil in the world—in his own heart first—crush it, and create a planet fit for God and man.

In a moving passage near the end of the novel, Styron admits that he has not succeeded, quite, in doing what he set out to do. He writes (recalling his earlier dream):

> *Someday I will understand Auschwitz.* This was a brave statement, but innocently absurd. No one will ever understand Auschwitz. What I might have set down with more accuracy would have been: *Someday I will write about Sophie's life and death, and thereby help demonstrate how absolute evil is never extinguished from the world.*

Though no one will deny that writing about the holocaust and its aftermath in personal terms—"Sophie's life and death"—may be the best thing one can do to wring at least some fragmentary sense out of those numbing times, I wonder if Styron's scaled-down goal is not as innocently absurd as the earlier goal. "Absolute evil." What a chaos of medieval phantoms nestles in those words! Like absolute good, a concept abandoned in Styron's vision as in much of modern Christianity, absolute evil is the stuff of which witch cults, country sermons and Gothic tales are made.

As I said at the outset, Styron is very conscious of being one of the last to work a dying literary tradition—in effect, the Southern Gothic, the vein mined by, among many others, Walker Percy, Robert Penn Warren and, possibly, William Faulkner. (In my opinion, Faulkner has too much humor, even joy, to belong.) Styron makes a point, in *Sophie's Choice*, of naming his influences—Thomas Wolfe, Faulkner, Robert Penn Warren, etc.—and claims, in Nathan Laudau's voice, that he has surmounted them. In *Sophie's Choice* he does far more than that: He transfers, down to the last detail, the conventions and implicit metaphysic of the Southern Gothic—especially as it was handled by Robert Penn Warren—to the world at large. It is no longer just the South that is grandly decayed, morally tortured, ridden with madmen, idiots and weaklings, socially enfeebled by incest and other perversions: it is the world.

The requisite madman is Nathan Landau; the requisite webs of guilt reach out toward the present from Auschwitz and the American North and South. For slavery and the necessary racial-taint theme, Styron chooses (besides America) Poland, occupied for centuries first by one cruel master, then another, pitifully devoted to both German culture and Nazi-style anti-Semitism, and genetically so mixed that blond Polish children can be saved from the death camps by being slipped into the Aryan Lebensborn, or New Youth Program. The Southern Gothic must have vaguely symbolic weather—if possible, murderously hot and muggy

(Brooklyn in the summer will do fine)—and some crazy old house—Styron chooses Yetta Zimmerman's huge old apartment house, entirely painted, from end to end, in Army-surplus pink. Doom must hang over everything, ominously, mysteriously forewarned throughout the novel; and of course there are special requirements of style and plot.

Styron is, of course, a master stylist; but notice the precisely Gothic quality of the following passage, which I've chosen by opening at random. Note the intricacy of the sentences, the ironic use of jarring images, sly biblical hints (the Professor's hiss), the inclination to choose objects that are old, "authentic" and likely to spell doom; note the fondness for suspense and rhythms that seem to pant. Sophie's father, the Professor, I ought to explain, having long ago written a Polish tract arguing that Jews should be exterminated, is now trying to get an audience with some—any—bureaucrat among the occupying German forces, hoping to curry favor. Styron writes:

> Loathing her father now, loathing his lackey—her husband—almost as much, Sophie would slip by their murmuring shapes in the house hallway as the Professor, suavely tailored in his frock coat, his glamorous graying locks beautifully barbered and fragrant of *Kölnischwasser,* prepared to sally forth on his morning supplicatory rounds. But he must not have washed his scalp. She recalled the dandruff on his splendid shoulders. His murmurings combined fretfulness and hope. His voice had an odd hiss. Surely today, even though the Governor General had refused to see him the day before—surely today (especially with his exquisite command of German) he would be greeted cordially by the head of the *Einsatzgruppe der Sicherheitzpolizei,* with whom he had an entree in the form of a letter from a mutual friend in Erfurt (a sociologist, a leading Nazi theoretician on the Jewish problem), and who could not fail to be further impressed by these credentials, these honorary degrees (on authentic parchment) from Heidelberg and Leipzig, this bound volume of collected essays published in Mainz, *Die Polnische Judenfrage,* etc. and so on. Surely today . . . [The ellipsis is Styron's.]

The hothouse quality of the style—the scent of overripe black orchids—seems to be thoroughly appropriate, as suited to rotting Europe as to the decaying Old South. The only question I would raise is Heisenberg's: Does the instrument of vision—in this case, the transferred Southern Gothic form—seriously alter the thing seen?

But even more than style and setting, the glory of the Southern Gothic is plot. We must get surprise after surprise, revelation after revelation, each more shocking and astonishing than the last. (Unavoidably, but nonetheless to my great annoyance, I have already given away one surprise: We do not know till near the end of the novel that our beloved Nathan Landau is a maniac.) Insofar as plot is concerned, *Sophie's Choice* is a thriller of the highest order, all the more thrilling for the fact that the dark, gloomy secrets we are unearthing one by one—sorting through lies and terrible misunderstandings like a hand groping for a golden nugget in a rattlesnake's nest—are not just the secrets of some crazy Southern family but may be authentic secrets of history and our own human nature: why people did what they did at Auschwitz—people on every side—why often the Polish underground hated the Jewish underground, on which their lives sometimes depended; how the Catholic, Protestant and Jewish souls intertangle in love and hate, and can, under just the right conditions, kill.

Sophie's Choice, as I hope I have already made clear, is a splendidly written, thrilling book, a philosophical novel on the most important subject of the 20th century. If it is not, for me, a hands-down literary masterpiece, the reason is that, in transferring the form of the Southern Gothic to this vastly larger subject, Styron has been unable to get rid of or even noticeably tone down those qualities—some superficial, some deep—in the Southern Gothic that have always made Yankees squirm.

Judging at least by its literary tradition, the South has always been an intensely emotional and, in a queer way, idealistic place—emotional and idealistic in ways not very common in, say, Vermont or New York State, or, anyway, upstate. I would never claim that Yankees are more just and reasonable than Southerners; I would say we hide our evil in a different style. Though we may secretly cry our hearts out at a poem like, say, James Dickey's "Celebration," we wince at novels in which the characters are always groaning, always listening in painful joy to classical music, always talking poetry—much of it having to do with terminal disease. And we blush at passages like the following:

> I don't recall precisely when, during Sophie's description of those happenings [I] began to hear [myself] whisper, 'Oh God, oh my God.' But I did seem to be aware, during the time of the telling of her story . . . that those words which had commenced in pious Presbyterian entreaty became finally meaningless. By which I mean that the 'Oh God' or 'Oh my God' or even 'Jesus Christ' that were whispered again and again were as empty as any idiot's dream of God, or the idea that there could be such a Thing.

Which is not to deny that the story that follows this Gothic introduction is not terribly moving and shocking.

In short, though I am profoundly moved by *Sophie's Choice* and consider the novel an immensely important work, I am not persuaded by it. Styron's vision may have humor in it—he tells us about Nathan's hilarious jokes, none of which turn out to be funny on the page—but if so, not an ounce of that humor is in the novel. Perhaps it may be argued that, in a book about American guilt and the holocaust, humor would be out of place. But it seems to me that humor is central to our decency. It cannot be replaced, as it is in *Sophie's Choice,* by great classical music or (a major concern in the novel) sex. If anything, classical music leads in exactly the wrong direction: it points to that ideal Edenic world that those master musicians, the Poles and Germans, thought in their insanity they might create here on earth by getting rid of a few million "defectives." I'm not, God knows, against Bach and Beethoven; but they need to be taken with a grain of salt, expressing, as they do, a set of standards unobtainable (except in music) for poor silly, grotesque humanity; they point our hearts toward an inevitable failure that may lead us to murder, suicide or the helpless groaning and self-flagellation of the Southern Gothic novel.

Styron's Stingo

Robert Alter*

From the beginning of his career, William Styron, with the echoing fictional edifices of Joyce, Faulkner, and Wolfe as his models, has been a writer boldly committed to ambitious undertakings. *Sophie's Choice*, however, his first novel since *The Confessions of Nat Turner* (1967), is in several respects his most ambitious book. In it he tries to address himself simultaneously to some of the fundamental issues of his own life as a writer and to a central dilemma of the moral history of our century. The novel he has shaped to confront these urgent questions is remarkably compelling, eloquent at its best, but not altogether satisfying—perhaps chiefly because the intertwined stories of a writer's coming of age and the meditation on the horrors of the Nazi death camps generate more static than resonance between them.

The first-person narrator, identified only by the nickname Stingo, would appear to reflect the autobiographical facts of Styron's life with considerable literalness. Like Styron, he was born in the Virginia Tidewater country in 1925, served in the Marines during World War II, attended Duke University, and in 1947 (at the beginning of the novel) arrives in New York where he begins work on a large first novel that in plot, manner, and intention sounds very like *Lie Down in Darkness* (1951), though it is given another title here. In this retrospective narrative, told from his vantage point as a mature and successful writer, Stingo alludes in passing to a brief second novel based on his military experience—clearly *The Long March* (1953)—and repeatedly mentions his fascination with Nat Turner's slave-rebellion, which finally issued, so he informs us, in a 1967 novel that stirred vehement national debate. Of Styron's published works, only *Set This House on Fire* for some reason is not alluded to.

Styron rather consciously represents himself in his fictional surrogate Stingo as a Young Man from the Provinces: an inexperienced small-town Southerner among Northern urbanites; a youth with a traditional genteel literary education among psychoanalytically minded New York intellectuals; and, above all, a Christian among Jews. The basic structure of the novel, then, is an attempted movement from the periphery to the center.

*Reprinted from *Saturday Review*, 7 July 1979, pp. 42–43, by permission of the author.

Superficially, this involves geographical displacement—from Virginia to Manhattan, then to the heart of Jewish Brooklyn, where Stingo takes up residence in a rooming house maintained by one Yetta Zimmerman and becomes intimately involved with Nathan Landau, a brilliant, manic, hostile, paternally affectionate intellectual eight years his senior. More essentially, the movement from the circumference is a moral and an imaginative one. What Stingo finds at the center, during this long mid-century moment of his initiation to adulthood, is a reality too obscene to be conceived by the mental equipment his comfortable Southern boyhood has given him.

Nathan, as a Jew, is periodically obsessed with the Holocaust. His beautiful blonde mistress, Sophie Zawistowska, who also lives in the rooming house, and whom he alternately adores and abuses hideously, has herself lived through the Holocaust, interned at Auschwitz not for her race—she is a lapsed Polish Catholic of eminently "Nordic" appearance—but for trying to smuggle a ham into Warsaw for her sick mother. Sophie's identity as a Christian victim of the Nazis serves both a psychological and a thematic purpose in Stingo's story. He falls hopelessly in love with her and soon becomes her confidant in matters of her personal history about which she has been reticent even with Nathan. Through this lovely woman with the blue numbers of the bureaucracy of death tattooed on her arm, Stingo makes contact with the ultimate horror, all the more readily because he can identify with her as Southerner with Pole (both offspring of proud but conquered lands) and as one kind of ex-Christian with another. Thematically, Sophie's presence at the heart of this evocation of the Holocaust enables Styron to make the polemic point that the evil of Nazism was by no means directed against Jews alone and that they differed from the others, as one character is made to say, by being also "the victims of victims." Styron argues that the very rationale of Nazism was an unending, dehumanizing process of enslavement and mass murder: first the Jews, then, had there been time, the Slavs and still others. It is an argument worth attending to, even if it may give insufficient weight to the very special eschatalogical fury with which the Nazis singled out the whole Jewish people for destruction.

Styron's novelistic strategy for approaching the abysmal center of recent European history is a simplified version of the technique of oblique multiple narration Faulkner used to move gradually toward the core of racial blight of Southern history in *Absalom, Absalom!* Sophie's tale is told in overlapping fragments, occasionally in her own words but by and large through Stingo's reconstruction, which bring us gradually closer to the final revelation of the unspeakable choice that the Nazis forced her to make. There are a good many moments when this procedure of narrative mediation works brilliantly: The American writer cannot presume to see the horror directly, but he can intimate its awful magnitude by imagining how it looked through the eyes of a figure who was there, desperately wishing she did not see what was around her. Thus Sophie, glancing out from a window in the house of Auschwitz Commandant Rudolf Höss, where she is briefly employed as a secretary, tries to "blot out of her sight the fragmentary and flickering apparitions which from this vantage point registered only imperfectly, like the grainy shadow-shapes in an antique silent newsreel: a rifle butt raised skyward, dead bodies being yanked from boxcar doors, a papier-mâché human being bullied to the earth."

Unfortunately, the execution of this plan of embedded narration is flawed in a number of ways. To begin with, Styron, conscious of the moral extremity of his subject, strains too hard to produce intensities. In the European scenes, this is sometimes reflected in a melodramatic contrivance of details. I realize that I am touching here on a sensitive question of moral and aesthetic tact, but to me, at least, it seems like a sentimental contrivance for a novelist to describe to us, with all our nightmarish knowledge of those mountains of slaughtered children, a little girl being marched off to the gas clutching her flute in one hand and her one-eyed teddy in the other. Stylistically, the striving for intensity results in an overwrought quality that mars a good deal of the prose, whether Styron is writing about Sophie among the Nazis or Stingo coming of age intellectually and sexually. There are abundant Faulkneresque epithets of ultimacy like "immemorial" and "perdurable," an occasional touch of D. H. Lawrence ("now the fire . . . blazed to the core of herself, somewhere near the womb"), but, most pervasively, a tendency to hopped-up language that is either cliché, or grotesque overstatement, or even plain redundancy. Survivors writing about the Holocaust "have tried to limn the totally infernal in their heart's blood," just as Stingo produces his first novel "by spilling quarts of [his] heart's blood"; he dreads loneliness like "the onset of some terminal disease," finds his emotions in "a dark tangle," notes Sophie's compulsion "to scrape out the rest of her appalling and inconceivable past to its bottommost dregs."

Beyond such effusions of style and detail, there are two aspects of the framing narrative that tend to interfere with the central vision of history gone awry. One is Nathan's evident psychopathology and, perhaps, Sophie's as well. This magnetic intellectual turns out to be a paranoid schizophrenic, and one wonders whether his response to the Holocaust, his treatment of the dismayingly compliant Sophie do not constitute a rather special case from which it is impermissible to generalize as Styron would have Stingo generalize. More blatantly, the painful, dubiously comic efforts of the 22-year old Stingo to disembarrass himself of his virginity—efforts to which an inordinate number of pages is devoted—progressively detract from the seriousness of the moral issues pursued in Sophie's story. I cannot think of a recent novel that is so compromised artistically by exercising the full prerogatives of the new sexual candor. All these post-adolescent erotic imaginings at the foreground of the novel may faithfully reflect aspects of the novelist's recollected experience, but autobiography has to work for the novel, not for itself, and it is hard to see how such concentration on a writhing priapic Stingo helps us grasp the novel's subject of absolute evil. The penultimate moment of the book, Stingo's long-postponed sexual initiation by Sophie, is more a beautiful masturbatory fantasy than a credible novelistic scene. With a little ingenuity, of course, one might find a "symbolic" justification, but the tenor of the scene, and of others like it, seems all wrong.

Styron has obviously devoted much careful reading and much serious reflection to the implications of the Hitler years, and he has made a daring effort to focus his vision of that awful time through the lens of autobiographical fiction. There are flashes of probing perception, and the narrative itself is constantly absorbing, but finally the ties between personal frame and historical subject do not quite hold.

Styron's Survivor:
An Honest Witness

Benjamin DeMott*

Sophie's Choice, William Styron's fifth book, is chiefly about Europe, Jewry, and the Holocaust, and the choice of subjects is likely to puzzle readers who know the author's earlier work. His career began with *Lie Down in Darkness*, a family chronicle set in the South and composed in a Gothic-Faulknerian mode; fame and the Pulitzer prize arrived with the appearance of the controversial *Confessions of Nat Turner*, a historical novel about a slave rebellion; neither these nor Styron's other books connect, in substance or manner, with *Sophie's Choice*.

Everyone familiar with the shameful media treatments of Nazidom over the years has to have felt an obligation to protest. (To cite just one example, there's a long-rerunning TV sitcom featuring laff-riot SS men—*Hogan's Heroes*—that qualifies as a minor national disgrace.) But I wouldn't have predicted that, among American fictionists of established reputation, the author of *Set This House on Fire* would have been the figure who met that obligation. And certain signs in *Sophie's Choice* suggest that Styron isn't entirely at ease in his role.

We notice these signs because in this book we often notice William Styron himself. When first glimpsed, the narrator is a provincial youngster in Greenwich Village dreaming of writing the great American novel. The time is 1947. The character's name is Stingo and the reader is encouraged in a dozen ways to identify him with the author. (Like the young Styron, Stingo hails from Virginia, is a graduate of Duke, served in the Marines, and did a term as a junior editor at McGraw-Hill; like Styron the novelist, Stingo begins his career with a family chronicle set in the South and composed in the Gothic-Faulknerian mode, and wins fame later with a controversial novel about Nat Turner.) The reader is also encouraged—strongly at the start, intermittently throughout—to regard Stingo the autobiographee as a pivotal person in the tale. In the course of *Sophie's Choice*, several members of Stingo's family are introduced, most notably his father, a southern gentleman of liberal cultivation and some humor. Stingo's old girlfriends, former bosses, and treasured ancestors (Civil War heroes)—not to mention his hypochondria and drinking

*Reprinted from *Atlantic Monthly*, July 1979, pp. 77–79, by permission of the author.

habits—are reviewed at length. Chapters are devoted to his bizarre and comic passage through the straits of virginity. And there are many reminders of his effort to write—discussions of obstacles, progress reports, hints of future success. (A trusted friend remarks, after reading the first third of the manuscript of Stingo's Gothic novel: "That's the most exciting hundred pages by an unknown writer anyone's ever read.")

Yet while the narrator's perfectly conventional frustration and aspiration are always in the picture, his life furnishes much less of the material of the story than do the lives of people distant from Virginia. In an early chapter of the work, Stingo, fired by McGraw-Hill and lent breathing space by a tiny legacy, moves from Manhattan to a rooming house overlooking Prospect Park in Flatbush, ready to commence writing in earnest. Above him, as he discovers, lives a young, extraordinarily beautiful, polylingual Polish widow named Sophie—Zofia Maria Bieganska Zawistowska—a survivor of Auschwitz whose American sanctuary is a job as secretary to a Queens chiropractor. Stingo meets her and quickly becomes her friend; her life, revealed sometimes through her monologues, sometimes through his historical reconstructions, gradually emerges as central in the book.

A fearful and ponderable life it is, almost from the beginning. Born in Cracow, where both her parents—practicing Catholics—are members of the Jagiellonian University faculty, Sophie is afflicted with an anti-Semitic father, a Germanophile sexist and pedant who dominates her marriage as well as her childhood (her husband is also a university professor and the couple has two children), simultaneously mocking her as an inferior intelligence and indoctrinating her in the language and culture of the super-race. And her entire life is dogged with ironies in which anti-Semitism is mysteriously pervasive. Her father, author of a pamphlet advocating the extermination of the Jews, is himself murdered by the Nazi invaders (Sophie's husband perishes in the same execution). Sent to Auschwitz with her two children as punishment for smuggling meat to her consumptive mother, Sophie tries in desperation to use her father's wretched writings as part of a mercy plea addressed to the camp commander; the effort crazily backfires. In America, having survived (as her children did not) the abominations of the concentration camp, Sophie comes under the protectorship of one Nathan Landau, self-identified as a scientist—only to learn, in a final crisis, that she still isn't free of the coils of *Antisemitismus*. Landau, it appears, is both more and less than a savior; he's a drug addict, an obsessive, a sadomasochist—and, in his own concept, an avenger of the slain Jews. He perceives Sophie as a soulless hypocrite, one whose survival is proof of her participation in the unspeakable atrocities committed by her captors. (Landau is a second link to Stingo; all three principals of *Sophie's Choice* live in the same Flatbush rooming house and are, briefly, an inseparable trio—music enthusiasts, Coney Island fans, confidants.)

A long narrative (more than 500 oversized, tightly printed pages), circumstantially detailed, *Sophie's Choice* has defects as a work of fiction. About many events in the heroine's life the narrator has no direct knowledge, which means that Sophie must tell all, slipping into a volubility awkward in someone first presented as a human being of style and dignity. (Stingo asks us to believe that a taste for American bourbon, rather than a spell of the novelistic clumsies, lies behind Sophie's garrulousness, but he's unconvincing.) The events are both hideous and unsurprising. At Auschwitz, with the smoke of burning Jews in her lungs, Sophie is raped by a female guard, obliged to choose which of her children will be murdered first, and endures unimaginable degradation—yet scarcely a word of what happens to her is new to print. And the narrator is hyperconscious of this, alluding often to the literature of the Holocaust—works by Hannah Arendt, Bruno Bettelheim, George Steiner, and others—for parallels to, and commentaries on, Sophie's case.

Subtler problems grow from these roots, erupting from page to page and frequently disengaging the reader's feelings. The author's honorable sense of responsibility to sources leads to incongruous, reductive juxtapositions. At one of the most intensely imagined moments in the book, Sophie, at work in the camp headquarters, suddenly hears sacred music issuing from a phonograph that usually plays nothing but *dreck*:

> The Elysian chorus, thrusting itself up through the muttering chatter of [the camp commandant] and his aide below, stabbed her with such astonished exaltation that she rose spontaneously from her seat at the typewriter, as if in homage, faintly trembling. What on earth had happened? . . . The ecstatic hosanna moved across her skin like divine hands, touching her with ecstatic ice; chill after chill coursed through her flesh; for long seconds the fog and night of her existence, through which she had stumbled like a sleepwalker, evaporated as if melted by the burning sun.

She goes to the window and finds the seasonably drab natural world outside—bare meadow, grazing livestock, autumnal woods beyond— "transmuted by the music's incandescence into a towering frieze of withering but majestic foliage, implausibly beautiful, aglow with immanent grace." She begins to pray, but the music is abruptly cut off, stopping the words of the paternoster in her throat, and, as she remembers later, "it was at that moment that I [began] to lose my faith. . . . I felt this emptiness. It was like finding something precious in a dream where it is all so real—something or *someone*, I mean, unbelievably precious—only to wake up and realize the precious person is gone."

After a second or so the phonograph resumes, this time with "The Beer Barrel Polka,"—a touch of the banality of evil that fascinated Dr. Arendt—but it's not the musical banality that dissipates the force of the scene. It is instead an academic banality. One moment after seizing the imagination with a vision of Sophie at the borders of unbelief, the narrator launches a discourse on treatises concerning the technology of depots of mass murder. (" . . . Richard L. Rubenstein has written in his masterful little book *The Cunning of History*," etc.) Ears tuned to the Elysian chorus and the powerful purities of Psalms, caught and held by the sound of an inner shattering of faith, adjust only with difficulty to the judgmental tinkle of "surveys of existing scholarship."

Uneasy disengagement is one result, as I say. Another is a tic of skepticism—fear that the novelist, when he undertakes to probe the foundations of individual behavior, is settling too quickly for the received wisdom of those who have preceded him in the "field." Why does Sophie hang on so doggedly with Nathan Landau, her accuser and tormentor? How can love nourish itself on insult and mauling? Obvious: she's victimized by a survivor's sense of guilt; feels vulnerable because, where millions were slain, she escaped; knows that, had she dared to risk herself fearlessly, she might have helped someone else to live. This is the "answer" ratified in Holocaust literature—nothing sounder, nothing more psychologically right, than the theory of survivor guilt. Yet the answer feels, in this context, pat and unparticularized—too much like a solution to a problem, too little like an entrance into the full mystery of a unique self.

Other problems surface, large and small, none more significant than that presented by the narrator himself—or rather by the immense gap between the youthful Stingo's level of comprehension and the inexpressible horror through which his friend has passed. William Styron is by no means unaware of this gap. His Stingo quotes an apposite passage in George Steiner which asserts that "it is not clear 'that those who were not themselves fully involved should touch upon these agonies unscathed.' " Stingo hungers to recall what toys held his attention as a southern boy in America on the day Sophie arrived at Auschwitz:

> And what, I have asked myself . . . were the activities of old Stingo, buck private in the United States Marine Corps, at the moment when the terrible last dust—in a translucent curtain of powdery siftings so thick that, in Sophie's words, "you could taste it on the lips like sand"—of some 2,100 Jews from Athens and the Greek islands billowed across the vista? . . .

A letter of his that his father saved discloses that, on the day in question, his entire eighteen-year-old being was focused upon an upcoming Duke versus Tennessee football game. But while Stingo is shaken by this discovery, he isn't transformed by it; he's incapable of becoming the fit audience for Sophie's story because the measure of her tragedy is beyond him. And his weakness inevitably diminishes the emotional impact of the work.

From none of this does it follow, though, that *Sophie's Choice* is a failure—merely another of the relentlessly overreaching blockbusters that litter the landscape of late twentieth-century American letters. Looked at in terms of craft, even with defects weighed, it's a far from negligible enterprise. Three complex stories—the friendship of Sophie, Nathan, and Stingo, Sophie's youth and her fifteen months at Auschwitz, the chaos and ruin of her love affair with Nathan Landau—are artfully woven into Stingo's youthful self-absorption. Changes of key and pace are unobtrusively managed. The principals speak with recognizably personal accents, becoming characters by virtue of possessing individual voices.

And, enormously more important, the book is animated throughout by a courageously judged sense of mission. At times, to be sure, the grip loosens—as when Stingo beamishly concludes that *his* mission is laboriously to construct his thoughts and actions in the days and years of the Holocaust. But in the main William Styron holds fast to two most urgent and relevant truths. The first is that the task of searching for a language not wholly incommensurate to the slaughter of the six million can never be finished. The second is that, in Western culture, in quarters more influential than those in which sitcoms such as *Hogan's Heroes* are manufactured, that search has in recent times taken a turn that is potentially dangerous to the future of our kind.

A widely acclaimed Italian film—Lina Wertmüller's *Seven Beauties*—presents the gas chambers as an interlude in an entertainment: absurdist *chic* in which GIs and Nazi Jew-burners are indistinguishable. A widely acclaimed contemporary historical analysis—Terrence Des Pres's *The Survivor*—presents the gas chambers as a setting for the triumph of existential heroes (the survivors) over cowardly dwarfs (the slain): a beyond-culture epic in which the arrival of Allied troops is immaterial to those still alive in the concentration camps. A widely acclaimed television program—NBC's *Holocaust*—presents the gas chambers as a fadeout of a contest between white hats and black hats: an Old World western that "personalizes" cataclysm. Everywhere, as Bruno Bettelheim points out in a recent essay surveying these and related contemporary intellectual responses to the Holocaust, "the survivors are . . . being used to bear witness to the opposite of the truth."

No such witnessing occurs in this book. Like several works in the Styron canon, it is smutched in places by morbidity and exhibitionism, and, to repeat, it never takes full command of the heart in the manner of classic fictional achievement. But its reading of mass murder is serious to the core. The portrait of Sophie in terror of the gas chambers reaches toward the full truth of human panic at the edge of oblivion. The portrait of Nathan Landau grasps the maddening force of the "outsider's" impotent rage at the slaughter of his people. The portrait of Stingo, despite its embarrassments, shows us the lameness of our own incomprehension. And the overall scale and tone, the willingness to ask some height of the reader, the quality of the book's ambition to be adequate to a major moral challenge, stand forth, well before the end, as thoroughly admirable.

There are successes in letters whose measurement requires alertness first to pressing cultural need rather than to formal excellence and aesthetic accomplishment. *Sophie's Choice* is one of them.

A Vast Dehumanization

Philip W. Leon*

When William Styron's *The Confessions of Nat Turner* (1967) appeared, most of the critical reception was highly favorable, the publication of that book assuming the proportions of an *event*. But, in the feverish climate of the late sixties, some black writers, professors, and college students mounted a strident protest against Styron and his work, claiming that his fictional treatment of Nat Turner robbed them of one of their folk heroes. A book, *William Styron's The Confessions of Nat Turner: Ten Black Writers Respond*, was issued, charging Styron with the deepest racism, likening Nat to Uncle Tom. Styron came under fire from many quarters, and though the controversy engendered several books and dozens of articles dealing with Styron's historical inaccuracies, he also sold many copies of the novel as a result of the debates.

Sadly, the black critics who disparaged *The Confessions of Nat Turner* denied the writer his creative act of selecting or ignoring facts about his characters. That Styron chose to create a Nat Turner who engages in homosexual activity and who lusts after the beautiful Margaret Whitehead indicates the creative process. Whitehead's name, incidentally, provides Styron with what Mary McCarthy calls a "natural symbol." To argue, as many did, that, in actual fact, Nat Turner was married, says little about the worth of Styron's fiction. To resent a white writer's attempt to enter the consciousness of a Negro slave severely restricts the creative impulse. Who, for example, would argue that James Baldwin can write only about blacks since it would be impossible for him to understand the white consciousness? Despite the controversy, most critics agree that *The Confessions of Nat Turner* is a major work of fiction and that it fully deserved the Pulitzer Prize it received in 1968.

Now that a decade has passed, Styron brings forth *Sophie's Choice*, his long-awaited novel about a survivor of a Nazi death camp; this book could possibly bring from the Jewish community a similarly indignant outcry, charging that Styron has trespassed on Jewish suffering and death at the hands of Hitler's executioners. Styron seems to have anticipated

*Reprinted from *The Virginia Quarterly Review*, 55 (Autumn 1979), 740–47, by permission of the author and journal.

charges of historical inaccuracy, having conducted extensive background research before committing himself to paper. He said in the *New York Times Book Review* in January 1979, "I've been scrupulous about the facts and used the historical record. It [the novel] has a lot about the workings of the camp. But it is a novel, a novelist is not a scholar, and the book is not buried in footnotes." In the novel itself Styron refers to Richard L. Rubenstein's *The Cunning of History* (1975) and its thesis that the death camps were "a new form of human society." Styron's creative mix of fact and fiction becomes clear when one discovers that Styron also published a review of Rubenstein's book in *The New York Review of Books*, June 29, 1978. He has also read the opinions of George Steiner and Bruno Bettelheim on life in the camps.

If the historicity of *Sophie's Choice* proves acceptable, Styron could still receive criticism on two other points. First, Styron never experienced the agony of a Nazi death camp. Second, Sophie is not Jewish. Both arguments diminish after consideration. Styron's narrator says in his novel, "I have been haunted, I must confess, by an element of presumption in the sense of being an intruder upon the terrain of an experience so bestial, so inexplicable, so undetachably and rightfully the possession alone of those who suffered and died, or survived it. A survivor, Elie Wiesel, has written: 'Novelists made free use of [the Holocaust] in their work. . . . In so doing they cheapened [it], drained it of its substance. The Holocaust was now a hot topic, fashionable, guaranteed to gain attention and to achieve instant success. . . . ' I do not know how ultimately valid any of this is, but I am aware of the risk." Clearly, Styron did not set out simply to write any novel, settling on the Holocaust as a "hot topic" for convenience and to sell books. I saw parts of *Sophie's Choice* in manuscript when I interviewed Styron at his home in 1973, and he outlined the entire novel in another interview in 1975 at Duke University. Styron's slow, meticulous pace of writing precludes any motive such as mere topicality. *Sophie's Choice* fits into the established pattern of Styron's other novels, which show the struggle of individuals as representative of our collective struggle to survive.

The second objection, the fact that Sophie is not Jewish, could cause the louder protest because it seems to intrude on the proprietorship Jews feel for the deaths at Treblinka, Auschwitz-Birkenau, Belsen, Dachau, and the other infamous camps. Little research is required to establish that millions of non-Jews also died in the camps. Poles, Russians, Gypsies, and Serbs perished by gas and were cremated along with their Jewish cellmates. The first victims of Cyclon B gas at Auschwitz were almost one thousand Russian prisoners of war, not Jews. Sophie is not a German Jew—the stereotypical victim of the camps—but a Polish Catholic, sent to Auschwitz for the crime of smuggling meat. The Nazis appropriated all such luxuries for German soldiers, just as they indiscriminately appropriated human beings to work at the I. G. Farben plants manufacturing goods for the war effort. When these conscripted human beings had exhausted themselves in a short time as slave laborers, they were then efficiently gassed and cremated or buried in mass graves. Most of the victims, of course, were Jews, but not all. To protest that Styron has no right as a novelist to create a non-Jewish character who suffers in a death camp is as hollow as saying only blacks can feel degradation and suffering from being owned.

I am certain that in Styron's mind there is a correspondence between coffles of Negro slaves being "sold down the river" as we see in *The Confessions of Nat Turner* and boxcars of prisoners being shipped like cattle to the death camps such as Auschwitz in *Sophie's Choice*. At one point in the novel the narrator compares the American South with Poland. After describing several similarities, he says, "In Poland and the South the abiding presence of race has created at the same instant cruelty and compassion, bigotry and understanding, enmity and fellowship, exploitation and sacrifice, searing hatred and hopeless love. While it may be said that the darker and uglier of these opposing conditions has usually carried the day, there must also be recorded in the name of truth a long chronicle in which decency and honor were at moments able to controvert the absolute dominion of the reigning evil, more often than not against rather large odds, whether in Poznan or Yazoo City." Because the sincerity of Styron's portrait of Nat Turner was misunderstood, perhaps his artistic creation of Sophie will similarly be viewed as an encroachment by an outsider, but let us hope that thinking readers will grant to Styron his use of a terrible period in history to express his faith in the ultimate goodness in man.

We read of Sophie's Auschwitz experience through the narration of Stingo, a Styron-like 22-year-old Virginian who lives in the same rooming house in Brooklyn as Sophie and her Jewish lover, Nathan. The picaresque Stingo falls in love with Sophie, a beautiful and compassionate girl whose attachment to Nathan arises from the fact that he single-handedly undertakes to feed and clothe her, provides her with medical care, and gives her love shortly after her arrival in America. Their energetic and vocal lovemaking in the room above Stingo fills him with envy and later bewilderment when Nathan becomes unpredictably vicious and treats Sophie with abuse. Later we learn that Nathan has had a lifelong history of mental imbalance, his instability now compounded by his use of drugs. Stingo's naïveté that a seemingly respectable, well-dressed person could indulge in marijuana, cocaine, and amphetamines rings true when we remember that the time of the novel is 1947.

Stingo's sexual inexperience provides a contrapuntal humor to the very serious business of Sophie's Auschwitz imprisonment. One of Stingo's attempts at sexual discovery was excerpted from the novel in progress and published in *Esquire*, September 1976, as "The Seduction of Leslie." Styron's only play, *In the Clap Shack* (1973), shows his talent for writing humor, mixing laughter with suffering in a venereal disease ward of a

Navy Hospital during World War II. There are no humorous scenes when Sophie relates her life at Auschwitz; there is no intrusion or ridicule on that subject. As Sophie's life flows out to the reader, Stingo's insouciance ebbs. Styron's technique of affixing humor to Stingo but not to Sophie and Nathan shows how Stingo's life has been uncomplicatedly pleasant and predictable in relation to Sophie's unspeakable misery. Stingo's only problem is in finding the money, dependably supplied by his father, to write his first novel. Thus Stingo's most challenging episode in his life, having the financial freedom to perform a creative act, pales compared to Sophie's efforts merely to survive.

Stingo becomes Sophie's confidant, hearing not only her problems with Nathan but eventually hearing her life story. Whether or not the novel succeeds could well rest on how readers view Styron's use of Stingo as narrator to tell us Sophie's story. Styron's narrative technique has long endeared him to the French whose *nouveau roman*, as espoused by such writers as Michel Butor and Roger Asselineau, thrives on episodic, backward and forward shifts in time to achieve some final stasis. Styron's novels all reflect his interest in the narrative structure. *Lie Down in Darkness* (which is mentioned from time to time as Stingo's first novel in *Sophie's Choice*) uses the points of view of several characters to reveal to us the causes of Peyton Loftis's suicide, a plunge to her death from a tenement building in New York City after a luckless marriage and love affair. In *The Long March* (1953) Lieutenant Culver appears to be the central figure, but Captain Mannix emerges as the hero who rebels against the Marine Corps. In his third novel, *Set This House on Fire* (1960), Styron uses Peter Leverett to tell us the story of Cass Kinsolving. As the novel progresses, Cass dominates to the extent that we lose all awareness that we should be hearing of Peter's search for meaning and existence. Nat Turner's confessions, as represented by Styron, are set down by a white lawyer serving as amanuensis "with little or no variation, from [Nat's] own words."

A similar but much smoother narration is at work in *Sophie's Choice*. We learn of Sophie's most agonizing choice through Stingo, who functions as a sort of priest for Sophie's confessions. In order to make clear her relationship with Nathan in time present, Sophie must make Stingo understand her life in Poland during the war and especially in Auschwitz, where she nearly dies. Stingo says, "I began to see seeping out of Nathan, almost like some visible poisonous exudate, his latent capacity for rage and disorder. And I also began gradually to understand how the turmoil that was grinding them to pieces had double origins, deriving perhaps equally from the black and tormented underside of Nathan's nature and from the unrelinquished reality of Sophie's immediate past, trailing its horrible smoke—as if from the very chimneys of Auschwitz—of anguish, confusion, self-deception and, above all, guilt. . . ."

What, then, is Sophie's "choice"? Of course, there are several, just as we all make moral or ethical decisions several times each day. But Sophie must choose which one of her two children will survive and which one will be gassed and cremated at Birkenau. When she arrives at Auschwitz, having been erroneously incarcerated with a group of captured resistance fighters, she faces a Nazi doctor who must select only the fit prisoners for temporary survival as slave laborers. He scourges himself of his guilt by making himself suffer all the more, like a religious ascetic who does physical penance to cleanse himself of former physical indulgences. The doctor allows Sophie to pass on to the Auschwitz camp but tells her she must choose one of her children to go to nearby Birkenau for certain death. Both or one will die; the choice is hers.

Styron is not using a cheap emotional trick in structuring this choice for Sophie. His intent is to show the labyrinthine, inexplicable nightmare that engulfed both captive and captor. The Nazi doctor will doubtless survive the war while victims will not; but the doctor must continue to live with the knowledge of the perverse horror and suffering he helped inflict on innocent people. The full impact of Sophie's choice is withheld until near the end of the novel, and in this regard Styron shows his mastery of his craft. By carefully plotted degrees we learn that Sophie was married, that her father and her husband were both executed by the Germans, that she had a son and later a daughter, until finally we learn of her agonizingly irreversible choice. Living with her decision imposes a burden of guilt that neither Nathan nor Stingo nor the vast opportunities of America can relieve.

To escape Nathan's homicidal intentions, Stingo and Sophie set out for Southampton County, Virginia, the site of Nat Turner's rebellion, where Stingo's father owns property. Along the way Stingo learns of the ineluctable memories which drive Sophie to Nathan who, though deranged, still offers her love in her otherwise loveless existence. When it becomes clear that she cannot live without Nathan, she leaves Stingo and returns to Brooklyn. Of course, she cannot live *with* Nathan either, and they commit suicide. Stingo, crushed by their deaths—he had loved them both—wants to weep for "the beaten and butchered and betrayed and martyred children of the earth. I did not weep for the six million Jews or the two million Poles or the one million Serbs or the five million Russians—I was unprepared to weep for all humanity—but I did weep for these others who in one way or another had become dear to me." Stingo confronts his grief when he can no longer avoid it, and, having expended it, wakes the next day to a new morning, "excellent and fair."

Styron seems to be urging a universal confrontation of the reality of the unutterable dehumanization which took place in our very recent history, because only through such confrontation and examination can the truth be made clear. Styron wanted to say essentially the same thing about slavery, but that vision became clouded with extrinsic criticism. *Sophie's Choice* reveals the truth of Auschwitz indirectly. There are no detailed descriptions of beatings, tortures, medical experiments, and the like. There are no cinematographic ploys in the battle of wits between Sophie and Rudolf Höss, the commandant of Auschwitz for whom she works. The truth which Stingo confronts frees him of grief when he realizes that Sophie could never, except in death, be free from her guilt. While eschewing exploitative descriptions of death camp horror, Styron stuns the reader in a convincing revelation that mere physical survival does not preclude emotional destruction.

Styron's Case and *Sophie's Choice*

G. A. M. Janssens*

The novels of William Styron have proved both compelling and embarrassing. All literary markers seem to point in the opposite direction from his approach to the novel, but we read him avidly, only to turn upon him afterwards for having enthralled us by illegitimate means. He is, as everyone knows, the author of the grand theme, the large subject carefully "researched," whereas the more representative interest of the modern American novel has focussed on the individual's tenuous, often abrasive relation with a limiting, imprisoning environment. And while everyone else seems to be neurotically self-conscious about the possibilities of form and language for the novel in our time, Styron uses the well-tried, timeworn conventions of the Southern romance. He simply continues where his literary forebears, William Faulkner, Robert Penn Warren, Thomas Wolfe and F. Scott Fitzgerald left off. It is not that he is impervious to the literary situation; on the contrary, he has been sensitive to criticism and ambitious for literary success. As a matter of fact, his erstwhile friend and lifelong rival Norman Mailer early accused him of literary logrolling.[1] It is rather that nothing has convinced him to abandon his conception of the novel, and he puts the burden on us to prove him wrong.

In reading Styron's new novel, *Sophie's Choice* (1979), we are made to ponder his literary career, for one thing because his narrator, nicknamed Stingo (earlier prep-school Stinky), whose surname follows on the heels, alphabetically, of "Strohmyer" and "Stutz,"[2] is the author fictionalized. The degree of fictionalization increases with the distance in time. When the narrator returns to "those faraway afternoons of First Novelhood" (p. 112) in 1947, he is a fictional re-creation invoked, ironically and at times affectionately, by William Styron in his early fifties; in 1947 Stingo was passionately engaged in the writing of *Inheritance of Night* (read *Lie Down in Darkness*), a twenty-two-year-old innocent from Virginia come to Manhattan and soon after to Brooklyn to confront

*Reprinted from *From Cooper to Roth: Essays on American Literature*, ed. J. Bakker and Dr. D. R. M. Wilkinson (Amsterdam: Rodopi, 1980), pp. 79–92, by permission of the author and publisher.

the European experience of Sophie Zawistowska, a Polish Roman Catholic survivor of Auschwitz. The closer the narrator approaches the present time of the writing of *Sophie's Choice*, which itself is part of the subject-matter of the novel, the more straightforwardly informative, and didactic, his voice becomes. To be alive to the tone of the narrative is to be aware of the fallibility, the "staggeringly puerile inexperience" (p. 203) of twenty-two-year-old Stingo, "a gullible and simple-minded waif" (p. 432) from the South among the Jews of Brooklyn. During the summer of 1947 he is initiated into the mysteries and perplexities of sex and of death, the two subjects, incidentally, upon which his own "most memorable dreams" turn (p. 45). Again and again he proves inadequate to the experience; and Stingo/Styron in middle age comes to write Sophie's story, as Sophie herself had wanted to write a novel about Auschwitz, partly to lay the ghost of his own past guilt.

In 1947 Stingo's youth is "at its lowest ebb" (p. 3). He had left the Marine Corps two years earlier, too young to have seen actual combat, this in contrast to his experienced friend Jack Brown who lost a leg on Iwo Jima; the ghastliness of recent history has passed Stingo by. He reads lousy manuscripts at McGraw-Hill leveling at them the scorn that could only have been mustered by "one who had just finished reading *Seven Types of Ambiguity*" (p. 5). Indeed, in the evening hours, Stingo reads all the right literary texts, and hoards the prologue to a novel readied to preface the experience he still lacks. It is heavily indebted in tone to the opening passages of *All The King's Men*, but his own words bowl him over at every rereading. The experience soon reaches him in a letter from his father announcing the suicide by leaping from the window of a Manhattan building, of his hometown flame, Maria Hunt, but it is only days later, when the shock has worn off, that he recognizes its potential for his novel:

> Again and again I pored over the newspaper clipping my father had sent, becoming warm with excitement as the awareness grew that Maria and her family might serve as the exemplary figures for the novel's cast of characters. The rather desperate wreck of a father, a chronic lush and also something of a womanizer; the mother, slightly unbalanced and a grim pietist, known throughout the upper-middle-class, country-club and high-Episcopal echelons of the city for her long-suffering tolerance of her husband's mistress, herself a social-climbing dimwit from the sticks; and the daughter finally, poor dead Maria, doomed and a victim from the outset through all the tangled misunderstandings, petty hatreds and vindictive hurts that are capable of making bourgeois family life the closest thing to hell on earth—my God, I thought, it was perfectly marvelous, a gift from the sky! (p. 111)

This description, of course, closely approximates the characters in *Lie Down in Darkness* (1951), the novel that made Styron famous at twenty-six. But characters alone do not make a novel, and Stingo himself must first be driven to suicidal despair by living through the degradation and death of Sophie, who so resembles Maria, before he can fully dramatize the plight of his heroine.

Already now, too, Nat Turner casts a shadow. "I'm going to make a *book* out of that slave," Stingo tells his friend, Sophie's Jewish lover, Nathan Landau. Styron is by turns outrageous, sly and defensive about *The Confessions of Nat Turner*. It is of course the novel that is freshest in everybody's mind, including the author's, as are the attacks on it by militant blacks and some whites. Its theme of slavery in the American South increasingly insinuates itself into the texture of *Sophie's Choice* as a muted parallel to the total enslavement in the Nazi deathcamps. So Nat Turner also will have to be exorcised, but first Stingo has to deal with his "beloved and bedeviled bourgeois New South family whose every move and gesture, I had begun to realize were played out in the presence of a vast, brooding company of black witnesses, all sprung from the loins of bondage" (pp. 420–1). Stingo cannot elude the "fearsome and ungodly history" (p. 72) of his native ground; indeed the events of 1947 throw that history into high perspective.

As with most Styron characters, dreams play an important part in Stingo's life. They are never as mysterious and imaginatively satisfying as Nat Turner's recurring dream of "the strange building standing so lonely and remote upon its ocean promontory,"[3] but they do help to bring out more clearly certain submerged significances. As Maria tends to merge with Sophie in Stingo's imagination, so does Nat Turner fuse into a dream about another Negro slave, Artiste, and thereby passes into Stingo's family history, even as Stingo in the end is admitted to the dead bodies of Sophie and Nathan as "a member of the family" (p. 507). For by a curious and intriguing twist that is the very stuff of fiction, the money that Stingo's great-grandfather made from the sale of his slave Artiste into the hell of the turpentine forests of Georgia pays for Stingo's keep in the "Pink Palace," Yetta Zimmerman's "Liberty Hall," the rambling roominghouse in the Flatbush part of Brooklyn where, after leaving McGraw-Hill, he spends the summer in close companionship with Sophie and Nathan. In later years that money will haunt him, but by then he has made a packet on another slave. "What the hell, once a racist exploiter always a racist exploiter" (pp. 32–3)—Styron tries to needle his detractors still. Also, the peanut farm in Southampton County, scene of Nat Turner's insurrection, that Stingo's father offers to his son as a haven away from the "barbarity" (p. 188) of New York City, the father inherited from a bachelor friend, who was also a rabid racist, "10 miles to the right of Mussolini" (p. 107).

That farm is the scene of the following daydream:

> In my mind's prism the years like blue hills rolled peacefully away toward the horizon of the far future. *Inheritance of Night* a remarkable success, gaining laurels rarely shed upon the work of a writer so young. A short novel then, also acclaimed, having to do with my wartime experiences—a

taut, searing book eviscerating the military in a tragicomedy of the absurd. Meanwhile, Sophie and I living on the modest plantation in dignified seclusion, my reputation growing, the author himself being increasingly importuned by the media but steadfastly refusing all interviews. "I just farm peanuts," says he, going about his work. At age thirty or thereabouts another masterpiece, *These Blazing Leaves*, the chronicle of that tragic Negro firebrand Nat Turner. (p. 450)

Conspicuously lacking here is mention of Styron's longest novel—as long, that is, as *Sophie's Choice*—*Set This House on Fire* (1960), a Gothic tale of sexual perversion, rape and murder, set mostly in Italy, that was remaindered in hardbound within a year of publication. Styron himself has expressed affection for parts of it, but it is also the only novel where very significant cuts were made in the proofs;[4] this is remarkable for a writer who works slowly, but usually has done with a novel once he has put it into the hands of his publisher. Several reviewers noticed the omission of Styron's Italian novel, and one of them expressed surprise that the author of *Set This House on Fire* should have written *Sophie's Choice*.[5] In reply it might be argued that *Sophie's Choice* is Styron's rewriting of the earlier novel.

Set This House on Fire has been criticised for two defects especially: its deficient structure and its fortuitous ending. Whether or not one wants to argue for a special relation between the two novels, one can proffer a comparative judgment to the effect that both structure and ending are better managed in *Sophie's Choice*. For one thing, Stingo is a more personable narrator, who must indeed soon share the limelight with Sophie as her story moves to the centre, but who is not relegated to near insigificance, as is Peter Leverett in *Set This House on Fire*. Stingo is given the advantage of the long perspective, whereas Peter is still rather naive when, at a remove of only two years, he tries to reconstruct the macabre events in Sambuco. So Cass Kinsolving comes to dominate the story—to such an extent that one critic has seen him as a continuation of Peter Leverett and a more mature autobiographical projection of the author.[6] Peter is a colourless Nick Carraway; "you look so *ordinary*," Cass's ingenuous wife tells him at first meeting, and his friend from prep-school, Mason Flagg, addresses him as: "Squarest of the Square."[7] So it does not surprise us that Cass finally speaks the words that ought by rights to have been Peter's:

> And I kept thinking of the new sun coming up over the coast of Virginia and the Carolinas, and how it must have looked from those galleons, centuries ago, when after black night, dawn broke like a trumpet blast, and there it was, immense and green and glistening against the crashing seas. And suddenly I wanted more than anything in my life to go back there. And I knew I would go . . . (*Set This House on Fire*, p. 500)

Shades of "the matchless *Gatsby*."[8]

At the close of *Sophie's Choice*, Sophie and Nathan, decked out in theatrical garb, are stretched out on Sophie's bed, their love couch, a double suicide. If for a moment, for the sake of argument and much too schematically, we identify Sophie with Cass and Nathan with Mason in the triangles formed with Stingo and Peter, the pat parallelism is disfigured by Cass's ultimate affirmation. And then we remember that, not only had Cass, like Sophie, been frequently suicidal, there had been moments when he had felt an urge to blot out his family as well; but, for all the rhetoric of doom, Sophie might have described Cass's plight, unkindly, as "undeserved unhappiness" (p. 130). Indeed, today's reader may well conclude that in *Set This House on Fire* Styron's rhetoric is in excess of the suffering of his characters. This is equally true for the novella *The Long March* (1953), which some readers, in disparagement of the novels, have tried to promote too generously to Styron's *Seize the Day*. It does not hold for *Sophie's Choice*, be it that one wants to challenge the viability of Styron's rhetoric altogether. This is a question we shall let rest till later.

It may be instructive to juxtapose a few passages:

> . . . as we zoomed toward the far green reaches of the island he talked his head off, and with a sorcerer's charm. Jokes tumbled from his lips, and witty wicked allusions, and airy ballooning puns; his spoofery was a marvel, so wild and preposterous that Celia, rosy with laughter, had to implore him to stop, put her head down in his lap and cried, "Stop! *Stop it!*" while I collapsed in merriment among the wrenches. (*Set This House on Fire*, p. 159)

> We walked in the gayest of spirits toward the subway station—Sophie between us now, her arms linked in ours—and he returned to that grits-and-molasses accent he rendered with such fantastic precision; there was no sarcasm this time, no intent to needle me, and his intonation, accurate enough to fool a native of Memphis or Mobile, caused me to nearly choke with laughter. But his gift was not mimicry alone; what emanated from him so drolly was the product of dazzling invention. (p. 75)

It is indeed the resemblance between Mason Flagg and Nathan Landau, both brilliant and self-educated, and both masters of make-believe, that is most striking.[9] Peter finds Mason "immensely attractive" (*Set This House on Fire*, p. 63), and Stingo is beguiled by Nathan's "devastating attractiveness" (p. 416). Both Stingo and Peter long try to stave off the awareness of the darker side of their delightful friends. It is the minor characters who bring it out into the open: Maggie, who calls Mason "a *monster*" (p. 231), a name also, and with similar emphasis, applied to Nathan by Morris Fink, part-time janitor at the Pink Palace (p. 60). Or consider the following passage:

> Once more she was silent, but now I felt a tremor run through her body. "He scares me when he hits me like that." Her lips were trembling and I held her very close against my side, as I would a little girl. "But that's all

right," she blurted out suddenly. "I'm mad for him, just positively *mad* for him!"

This could have been Sophie to Stingo about Nathan, but it is actually Celia to Peter about Mason (*Set This House on Fire*, p. 165). In the end Celia can take charge of her own fate and go to Reno, but Sophie's doom was sealed even before she knew Nathan.

The two novels have the same literary progenitor, Thomas Wolfe. In *Set This House on Fire* his influence was particularly felt in Cass Kinsolving's hyperbolic monologues. As *Sophie's Choice* is a writer's book with frequent references to the literary world, Wolfe can be introduced by name. He is first mentioned in the opening pages when Stingo relates how his fortunes at McGraw-Hill began to decline with the arrival of a new editor in chief, "whom I secretly called the Weasel—a near-anagram of his actual surname" (p. 15). The Weasel, he tells us, was Wolfe's second editor. (An anagram, then, of Edward Aswell;[10] no doubt we are encouraged to remember Wolfe's own portrait of "the Fox" in *You Can't Go Home Again*, a take-off on his first editor, Maxwell Perkins.) Stingo utterly fails to make contact with the Weasel, "a cold company man" (p. 16), and that is unfortunate because "I would have given all I had to spend a chummy, relaxed evening with a man like the Weasel, pumping him for fresh new anecdotes about the master" (p. 30).[11] Wolfe has other admirers. Stingo's mother had been "a devoted fan long before I had read a word of Wolfe," and we come upon her, racked by cancer, seeking oblivion from her pain in *You Can't Go Home Again*. And Sophie, after her arrival in the United States making up for lost time, read Dos Passos, Hemingway and Dreiser, but it was *Of Time and the River* that "excited her the most of all the books she read that winter and spring," before she met Stingo. But the name of Wolfe also occurs in connection with Auschwitz. Its commandant, Rudolf Höss, is born in the same year and under the same sign as Wolfe (p. 149), and, irony of the time relation, Sophie meets Höss for the first time, Stingo tells us, on "the birthday of three of my heroes: of my father, of the autumn-haunted Thomas Wolfe, and of wild Nat Turner, that fanatical black demon whose ghost had seared my imagination throughout my boyhood and youth" (p. 220).

Both tales are told as detective stories. In *Set This House on Fire*, the question at stake is actually the resolution of a murder, but when we finally learn who did it, we feel keen disappointment because the village half-wit Saverio does not meet the measure of our imagination; he is simply sprung upon us by the author. The choice offered Sophie is as vile as any murder, "in the realm of the unspeakable" (p. 365), and she can work herself up to the revelation of it, the speaking of it, only towards the end of her tale. Peter was actually in Sambuco when the murder took place which is described at the end of the first part of the novel. In the second part he recollects those wild Italian days in tranquillity, from a distance, and, with the help of Cass Kinsolving, a much more perceptive participant more deeply involved in the outlandish events, establishes the truth of the latter's guilt. Stingo was not present at the scene of Sophie's choice; what indeed appalls him is the time relation: "on that afternoon, as Sophie first set foot on the railroad platform in Auschwitz, it was a lovely spring morning in Raleigh, North Carolina, where I was gorging myself on bananas" (p. 217); Stingo was trying to satisfy the minimum weight requirement for entrance into the Marine Corps, like other young innocents—remember Studs Lonigan and his friends?—before him.

Whereas Cass's voice takes over much of the second half of *Set This House on Fire*, Stingo tells most of Sophie's story himself. Judging from the moments he hands the tale over to Sophie, this was a wise decision. Sophie was raised bilingual in Polish and German and has a good knowledge of French; her English is not bad at all, but the shape of her sentences is monotonous and her idiom distracting. Of course Stingo/Styron is aware of the problem; he had faced a similar one when he decided to tell Nat Turner's story in the first person. His solution then drew much criticism—undeservedly on the face of it, if one considers that the author gave the best language he could muster to his slave protagonist. This time he has decided to try to duplicate only sparingly "the delicious inaccuracies of Sophie's English" (p. 51).

Styron is very skillful at structuring his narrative: interweaving the stories of Stingo and Sophie, managing the frequent timeshifts and changes of scene, and highlighting the cruel ironies of the time relation. "What's Owswitch?" (p. 213), asks Stingo's impervious, Jewish fellow lodger, Morris Fink. The question remains unanswerable—"no one will ever understand Auschwitz" (p. 513)—but blatant ignorance is criminal. So Stingo will help demonstrate how *"absolute evil is never extinguished from the world"* (p. 513) by writing about Sophie's life and death. But the language he has chosen for the story is different shades of Southern purple and that creates a measure of embarrassment. It is a language that never lets go of the reader, that will not trust to understatement, and, in its metaphors, will plump for clichés rather than for the original image that might slow the reader down. It delights in sound effects and in dictionary words like "mucilaginous" (p. 168), "paludal" (p. 188), "matutinal" (pp. 257, 498), "luminiferous" (p. 302) and "unguentary" (p. 457); "parturition" (p. 215), "tintinnabulation" (p. 226), "famishment" (p. 319) and "depredation" (p. 349); and, of course, the Faulknerian "immemorial," "perdurable," etc. Emotions are described as physical sensations, most characteristically the sensation of choking—"despair over her loss encircled my throat like hands" (p. 318)— but other expressions of physical outrage as well: "anguish similar to that of being buried alive under a ton of cinders" (p. 291); "a pain of nostalgia so intense that it was like being impaled upon a spear" (p. 421). And we might as well face the worst (Stingo has just made some rash remarks): "I now saw that I could not have caused her worse pain had she possessed a hot inflamed cicatrix from which I had savagely yanked the stitches in a horrible ball of fresh sutures and outraged flesh" (p. 308).

These instances are not cited to dismiss Styron. Although they are not always seamlessly embedded in their context, the reader stumbles less frequently than listing them in isolation would suggest. Styron is, of course, aware of the pitfalls of the literary tradition he follows. When Nathan really wants to get at Stingo he says: "You have a pretty snappy talent in the traditional Southern mode. But you also have all the old clichés" (p. 208). This is meant to hurt—it is indeed a far cry from Nathan's earlier extravagant praise—but especially because it applies to Stingo/Styron's first novel, it is not entirely unjust. For some readers *Lie Down in Darkness* is still the first novel that never dies, and that has never been equalled. Rereading it today one is still impressed by the skillful structure and the created sense of place, but the pervasive impression is of precocity rather than of lived experience; the emotional and intellectual life does not quite fill out the potentialities of the mastered form. One way of illustrating the point is to consider Faulkner's influence. It has been remarked upon from the very beginning, could indeed hardly have been missed, and starting with Malcolm Cowley,[12] readers have maintained that Styron borrowed Faulknerian techniques and situations but transformed them for his own ends. This is not the effect on the reader today; when he comes to Peyton's interior monologue he forgets about Styron and is overcome by his *memory* of Faulkner, because Peyton's plight, in contrast to Sophie's, has not been made sufficiently challenging to appropriate the means of its portrayal.

At this point one may tentatively propose a rough distinction between *Lie Down in Darkness* and *Set This House on Fire* as novels that deal with literary situations, and *The Confessions of Nat Turner* and *Sophie's Choice* that tackle historical, or public themes. Now, it is arguable that clichés of language are more easily absorbed by the texture of "public" novels than of "literary" novels, possibly because the printed texts closest to the "public" novel deal with history and society and are non-literary. This differentiation may also apply to clichés of situation. If readers of *The Confessions of Nat Turner*, for instance, complain that Nat's passion for white Margaret is a cliché, they mean something different from the objection that Milton Loftis in *Lie Down In Darkness* is a cliché of a Southern gentleman. The first objection refers primarily to a social stereotype—it does not immediately suggest comparison with the fiction of, say, Richard Wright or Ralph Ellison—whereas the second refers us to the Southern literary tradition. Again, it may be easier to bring the social stereotype to literary life because the writer dramatizes a notion rather than reflects a literary practice.

Stingo's experiences fit more snugly in the mould of the "literary" novel, Sophie's of the "public" novel, and the distance between the two is bridged by the voice of the narrator. Stingo's main preoccupation during the summer of 1947 is his obdurate virginity, and his inspiration as the teller of that tale is Philip Roth. In his twenty-second year, "the most anxiety-filled of all" (p. 438), he is "the prey of an ever-unfulfilled randiness" (p. 348). Sophie, meanwhile, is tortured by a survivor's guilt, and in order to delve down to the sources of that guilt Styron read widely about the concentration camps, and was most particularly struck by Richard L. Rubenstein's *The Cunning of History* (1975). Indeed, Rubenstein's book stands in the same relation to *Sophie's Choice* as Stanley Elkins' *Slavery* does to *The Confessions of Nat Turner*. Styron elaborates on this in a passionate endorsement of Rubenstein's argument in an article, "Hell Reconsidered," published a year before the appearance of the novel.[13] The article augured ill for the novel because Styron had written it with the proselytizing zeal of the converted; one was not looking forward to another rumpus about a Styron novel, this time under attack by outraged Jews.

As a matter of fact, Rubenstein's book has proved particularly useful for the novel. It is central to Rubenstein's argument that Auschwitz was both a slave camp and an extermination camp, and constituted a "society of total domination" of both Jews and Gentiles based on the simple but "absolute *expendability* of human life" (p. 235). Stingo, who has noticed the tattooed number on her wrist, is surprised to learn that Sophie is not Jewish. This is of the essence of the tale that she unfolds, because her guilt turns out to be that not only of the survivor but, to some extent, of the accomplice. Sophie and Stingo are fellow Gentiles self-exiled among the Jews in Brooklyn. He becomes her confidant, which her Jewish lover, obsessed with the Holocaust, can never be, because they hail from similar backgrounds. Poland conjures up images of the American South—"or at least the South of other, not-so-distant times;" like the Old South it was tormented into its shape "out of adversity, penury and defeat," and the "sinister zone of likeness" between the two has to do with the matter of race (p. 247). While Sophie has to live with memories of "a nation which practically invented anti-Semitism" (p. 472), Stingo is heir to a region that breeds racist politicians like Senator Theodore Gilmore Bilbo and that mutilates and lynches Bobby Weed.

"Like numerous Southerners of a certain background, learning and sensibility, I have from the beginning responded warmly to Jews," Stingo tells us; indeed he has to conclude that "an unconscious urge to be among Jews" had been at least part of his reason for coming to Brooklyn (p. 39). In his hometown in Virginia the Jews had been an integral part of the social world; only their religious and domestic lives had seemed mysterious to him.

> It was out of the glare of daylight and the bustle of business, when Jews disappeared into their domestic quarantine and the seclusion of their

> sinister and Asiatic worship—with its cloudy suspicion of incense and
> rams' horns and sacrificial offerings, tambourines and veiled women,
> lugubrious anthems and keening banshee wails in a dead language—that
> the trouble began for the eleven-year-old Presbyterian. (p. 162)

But, then, the mind of eleven-year-old Stingo had been full of extraordinarily charged images—of sexual intercourse, for instance, which he
had visualized as "a brutish act committed in secrecy upon dyed blondes
by huge drunken unshaven ex-convicts with their shoes on" (p. 311). It is
the gorgeous Leslie Lapidus who will, he hopes, enlighten him on both
counts. She turns out to live in thoroughly American opulence, a Cadillac
at the front door and a Pissarro (genuine) on the wall, and she puts sex
where her mouth is rather than where she ought to. Stingo will only begin
to understand her type when he comes to read books like *Goodbye,
Columbus*.

Sophie's relation to Jews is of course infinitely more complex and
tragic. Her father was a virulently anti-Semitic professor of law at
Cracow, "a superconservative in a faculty of right-wingers" (p. 238). Initially Sophie must hide the truth about him, tell lies because the truth
that he preached the extermination of the Jews even before the Nazis in-
stitutionalized it, is too horrible to endure; and it is only towards the end
of her tale, when other horrors have been revealed, that she remarks: "I
sometimes got to think that everything bad on earth, every evil that was
ever invented had to do with my father" (p. 466). Styron takes time out
for a formal sketch of Professor Zbigniew Bieganski:

> He was a tall robust-looking man, usually garbed in a frock coat and a
> shirt with wing collar and a broad foulard tie. Old-fashioned dress, but
> not at all grotesque in Poland for that time. His face was classically Polish:
> high wide cheek-bones, blue eyes, rather full lips, the broad nose tilting
> up, large elfin ears. He wore sideburns and his light fine hair was swept
> back evenly, always nicely coiffed. A couple of artificial teeth made of
> silver slightly marred his good looks, but only when he opened his mouth
> wide. Among his colleagues he was considered something of a dandy,
> though not absurdly so; his considerable academic reputation was a
> safeguard against ridicule. (p. 238)

The professor is a domestic tyrant who exploits his daughter and despises
her. He creates an ambience of "rapturous Germanism" (p. 369), but
grafted on a time long past and gone, so that this romantic zealot is cut
out to be one of the first victims of "the stainless-steel, jackbooted, mam-
moth modern power, the first technological state" (p. 250). With him dies
his colleague and disciple, Sophie's cold husband Kazik.

The professor is one of Styron's finest characterizations. He was the
overwhelming reality of Sophie's formative years, and indeed beyond,
and he is brought to full life in the novel. Stingo's father is equally present, a loving portrait that reminds one of Updike's homage to his father

in *The Centaur*.[14] For all the guilt of its history, the South has an honourable legacy also—as indeed has Poland as represented in the resistance fighter Wanda—and this legacy is dramatized by Stingo's father with his concern for the past and family, his basic liberalism and his running fight with "the monstrous leviathan known as American business" (p. 108), in particular its lieutenants, "those piratical devils, Washington Duke and his son, 'Buck' Duke" (p. 30). But, above all else, he represents the rurally rooted values of the South vs. the treacherous North, especially that "octopus of a city," New York; "I've never been there, but really, is it *possibly* true that, as you wrote me, there are parts of Brooklyn that remind one of *Richmond*?" (p. 291)

South meets North when Stingo's father confronts a Manhattan taxi-driver. But the Northerners never get down South, although Stingo, Nathan and Sophie are all excited about a prospective trip to Dixie, with a special excursion to Nat Turner country. In flight from Nathan, Stingo and Sophie do not get beyond Washington, and when Stingo continues flight on his own, he discovers that the "sprawling concrete blight" of the North has spread south of the "broad Potomac viscid with sewage" and has contaminated his home state. "Was all this not merely Yankee carcinoma, spreading its growth into my beloved Old Dominion?" (p. 504). The South will not shelter him now; he must return to Brooklyn to face the disaster at the end of that summer of 1947.

Doom has hovered over the novel from the very first meeting of Stingo with Sophie and Nathan whose violent lovemaking is followed by Nathan's vociferous attack on Sophie and, when he gets in the way, on Stingo. It is a pattern that will be repeated time and again, and it is Stingo's guilt through inexperience and thoughtlessness that he fails to help forestall the disaster. He has a knack of being distracted when he ought to act decisively. Nathan, in his dark moments, sits in vituperative judgment on his friends' racist heritage, but at other times he can be "utterly, fatally glamorous" (p. 187). He is "the ranting ogre become Prince Charming" (p. 74); there are fleeting moments in which "the attractive and compelling in him seemed in absolute equipoise with the subtly and indefinable sinister" (p. 116). His brother Larry, a physician, is in a position to put it more tersely: "The truth is that my brother's quite mad" (p. 424). For all that, he is a fascinating character, the most interesting Jew in Styron's fiction. Stingo is "quite simply devoted to Nathan" (p. 416) who is something of an older brother to him; Sophie is totally, masochistically in love with Nathan; and the reader can go along with that.

Still the question remains: is Nathan's significance to be limited, ultimately, to that of prompter of Sophie's and Stingo's guilt feelings? Could not Styron have imagined a more meaningful explanation for Nathan's behavior? He lamely reads into him a prophecy for aftertimes—"his image has always seemed to foreshadow these wretched unending years of madness, illusion, error, dream and strife" (p.

445)—but after Auschwitz, what is so bad about the post-World War II era? Styron never gets beyond the occasional rhetorical reference to "several barbaric American wars" (p. 23). If the resolution of Nathan's case, which is moving as it is, had been sought in the moral rather than in the pathological sphere, it might have been better attuned to the weighty questions the novel poses.

In any novel the author takes a number of calculated risks hoping they will pay off, and in a novel like *Sophie's Choice*, which lives as much by its structure as by its texture, mistakes are especially noticed. The novel's worst mistake occurs in the wake of its most excruciating scene when, on the railroad platform at Auschwitz, a drunken camp doctor offers Sophie a truly satanic choice. The scene is well paced and forcefully narrated, but is immediately followed by a deflating explanation of the doctor's psychology. If there were any doubt that Styron was conscious of taking a risk at such a crucial point in the narrative, we only have to read the first sentence of the chapter that follows his disquisition on the doctor's psyche: "All my life I have retained a streak of uncontrolled didacticism" (p. 489). Indeed, as the protagonist is also the novelist we come across frequent statements of authorial quirks and intentions. On the whole the structure of the novel is very artful, but inevitably the reader will challenge certain decisions. For instance, Stingo's tug of war with Leslie Lapidus is well told and functional, but when much later he has a similar exhausting bout with a girl named Mary Alice Grimball (yes), he might have let it go at his first notebook entry that Mary Alice was "something *worse* than a Cock Tease, a Whack-off artist" (p. 432), for the reader can very well imagine the mores of "that sexually bedeviled era" (p. 120), the nineteen-forties, for himself. Or the theft of Stingo's money: the reader expects it to be meaningful but it turns out to be a mere matter of plot, a means of the author to get his character to move.

Some of the Polish underground scenes are distracting and overly didactic, but the train transport from Warsaw to Auschwitz and the scenes in the commandant's house, which Styron, not trusting to Sophie's English, relates mostly in his own voice, are starkly told, with outrage contained but close to the surface of the prose. The train reaches Cracow at night, "the familiar station, moonlit railroad yard where they lay stranded hour after hour. In the greenish moonglow an extraordinary sight: a German soldier standing in *feldgrau* uniform and with slung rifle, masturbating with steady beat in the half-light of the deserted yard, grinningly exhibiting himself to such curious or indifferent or bemused prisoners as might be looking through the peepholes" (p. 479). A foul act and a grim sight indeed. Or the music in Haus Höss:

> Sophie scarcely ever heard the music, indeed blanked most of it out, for it
> was never anything but noisy German backyard schmalz, Tyrolean joke
> songs, yodelers, choirs of glockenspiels and accordions, all infused with

recurring strains of treacly *Trauer* and lachrymal outpourings from Berlin cafés and music halls, notably such cries from the heart as "Nur nicht aus Liebe weinen," warbled by Hitler's favorite songbird Zarah Leander and played over and over again with merciless and monotonous obsession by the chatelaine of the manor—Höss's garishly bejeweled and strident wife, Hedwig. (p. 230)

Music plays an even more important thematic part in *Sophie's Choice* than it did in *Set This House on Fire*. One remembers *Don Giovanni* booming forth from Cass Kinsolving's apartment; Nathan actually knows the libretto by heart. It is the shared passion for music that cements the bond between Sophie, Nathan and Stingo. Their taste is thoroughly mainline, "music in the grand tradition, nothing remotely popular and very little composed after Franz Schubert, with Brahms being a notable exception" (p. 117). So it is fitting if saddening that at the half-baked funeral service led by the unspeakable Reverend DeWitt, "a whiny Hammond organ" plays Gounod's "Ave Maria" (p. 509). And, most outrageous of all, the welcoming prisoners' band at Auschwitz plays the Argentine tango "La Cumparsita"—"Ba-dum-*ba*-dum!"—while Sophie with her two children faces the S.S. doctor whose task it is to look over the prisoners and send them in two different directions, either straight to the gas at Birkenau or to slave labor at Auschwitz (p. 482). " 'Ich möchte mit dir schlafen'," (p. 481) are his very first words to Sophie, and soon he offers her her choice:

> "You may keep one of your children."
> "*Bitte?*" said Sophie. (p. 483)

At this writing *Sophie's Choice* has been on the bestseller list for almost forty weeks, but of course the relation between commercial success and critical acclaim is never predictable. Already in the early sixties, John Aldridge accused Styron of using the clichés of the highbrows to impress the middlebrows, and, at about the same time, Marvin Mudrick clobbered Styron for having "coldly chosen the garden path to the drawing-rooms of the Establishment."[15] Initially *The Confessions of Nat Turner* was a remarkable critical—as well as commercial—success, but soon Herbert Aptheker and the black critics moved to the attack; Richard Gilman, revisiting the novel, assured them they were right on target and sought to teach them how they could have made their case in literary critical terms.[16] During the time of creative exhaustion that followed, Styron worked on a novel about the Marine Corps, but with the continuation of "the filthy war," he abandoned *The Way of the Warrior* and started on *Sophie's Choice*.[17] Meanwhile, with the passage of time, *The Confessions of Nat Turner* regained some of its initial critical esteem.[18] Now with the publication of *Sophie's Choice* Styron's case is wide open again.

Notes

1. Norman Mailer, *Advertisements for Myself* (New York: Signet, 1960 [1959]), p. 415; Styron has answered in kind: "For his own peace of mind I fervently hope that he wins the Nobel Prize" ("The Editor Interviews William Styron," *Modern Occasions*, 1 [Fall 1971], 503); and "the concept of 'the white Negro' is . . . preposterous" ("Overcome," *The New York Review of Books*, 26 September 1963, 18).

2. William Styron, *Sophie's Choice* (New York: Random House, 1979), p. 221; all further references are to this edition.

3. William Styron, *The Confessions of Nat Turner* (New York: Random House, 1967), p. 4.

4. *Set This House on Fire* "has some of my most passionate and best stuff, and I'm proud to have written it" (Robert K. Morris, "An Interview with William Styron," in *The Achievement of William Styron*, eds. Robert K. Morris and Irving Malin, Athens: Univ. of Georgia Press, 1975, p. 30). "There was a great amount, an enormous amount, that was cut out of *Set This House on Fire*" (James L.W. West III, "A Bibliographer's Interview with William Styron," *Costerus*, N.S., 4, 1975, p. 22).

5. Benjamin DeMott, "Styron's Survivor: An Honest Witness," *Atlantic*, July 1979, 77. Cf. also Robert Alter, "Styron's Stingo," *Saturday Review*, 7 July 1979, 42: "Of Styron's published works, only *Set This House on Fire* for some reason is not alluded to." Elsewhere in *Sophie's Choice*, however, Styron mentions "other works of fiction" (p. 215), which may be taken to include *Set This House on Fire*.

6. Louis D. Rubin, Jr., "Notes on a Southern Writer in Our Time," in *The Achievement of William Styron*, pp. 79–87; Rubin makes the same point more succinctly in "William Styron and Human Bondage," in *The Sounder Few: Essays from the 'Hollins Critic'* (Athens: Univ. of Georgia Press, 1971), p. 307.

7. William Styron, *Set This House on Fire* (New York: Random House, 1960), pp. 39, 152.

8. William Styron, "An Elegy for F. Scott Fitzgerald," *The New York Review of Books*, 28 November 1963, 2.

9. It is surely fortuitous that a Washington hotel clerk who has not quite caught Nathan's name ventures "Mason?" (p. 499).

10. See Andrew Turnbull's biography of *Thomas Wolfe* (New York: Scribner's, 1967) which Styron reviewed for *Harper's Magazine*, April 1968, 96–104.

11. "There was a moment when I think I would have ransomed my soul to meet Wolfe" (Styron's review of Malcolm Cowley, *A Second Flowering*, *The New York Times Book Review*, 6 May 1973, 8). See also Styron, "The Shade of Thomas Wolfe," *Harper's*, April 1968.

12. Malcolm Cowley, "The Faulkner Pattern," *The New Republic*, 8 October 1951, 19–20, reprinted on pp. 16–17 of this collection.

13. *The New York Review of Books*, 29 June 1978, 10–14.

14. *Sophie's Choice* is dedicated to the memory of Styron's father (1889–1978).

15. Aldridge, "William Styron and the Derivative Imagination," in *Time to Murder and Create: The Contemporary Novel in Crisis* (New York, 1966), p. 49; Mudrick, "Mailer and Styron: Guests of the Establishment," *Hudson Review*, 17 (Autumn 1964), 366.

16. "Nat Turner Revisited," *The New Republic*, 27 April 1968, 23–32.

17. Styron, "In the Jungle," *The New York Review of Books*, 26 September 1968, 11. See James Atlas, "A Talk with William Styron," *The New York Times Book Review*, 27 May 1979; Tony Schwartz, "The Choosing of 'Sophie'," *Newsweek*, 28 May 1979; West, "A Bibliographer's Interview;" and especially Ray Ownbey, "Discussions with William Styron,"

Mississippi Quarterly, 30 (1977), 283–295, and Ben Forkner and Gilbert Schricke, "An Interview with William Styron," *The Southern Review*, 10 (1974) 923–934.

18. See especially Richard Gray, *The Literature of Memory: Modern Writers of the American South* (London, 1977), pp. 291–305.

The Message of Auschwitz

William Styron*

Springtime at Auschwitz. The phrase itself has the echo of a bad and tasteless joke, but spring still arrives in the depths of southern Poland, even at Auschwitz. Just beyond the once-electrified fences, still standing, the forsythia puts forth its yellow buds in gently rolling pastures where sheep now graze. The early songbirds chatter even here, on the nearly unending grounds of this Godforsaken place in the remote hinterland of the country. At Birkenau, that sector of the Auschwitz complex that was the extermination camp for millions, one is staggered by the sheer vastness of the enterprise stretching out acre upon acre in all directions.

The wooden barracks were long ago destroyed, but dozens of the hideous brick stable-like buildings that accommodated the numberless damned are still there, sturdily impervious, made to endure a thousand years.

Last April, as this visitor stood near "Crematorium II," now flattened yet preserved in broken-backed rubble, his gaze turned and lingered upon the huge pits where the overflow of the bodies from the ovens was burned; the pits were choked with weeds but among the muck and the brambles there were wildflowers beginning to bloom. He reflected that "forsythia" was one of two loan-words from Western languages that he recognized amid his meager command of Polish. The other word, from the French, was *cauchemar*—"nightmare." At the beginning of spring, the two images mingle almost unbearably in this place.

At Auschwitz itself, in the original camp nearby, there is still the infamous slogan over the main gate—*Arbeit Macht Frei*—and only yards away, unbelievably, a small hotel. (What does the guest really order for breakfast? A room with *which* view does one request?) It is hardly a major world tourist attraction but Auschwitz is not unfrequented. Many of the visitors are Germans, festooned with Leicas and Hasselblads, whose presence does not seem inappropriate amid the *echt*-German architecture.

These grim warrens, too, were built to last the Hitler millennium. Hulking and Teutonic in their dun-colored brick, the rows of barracks

*Reprinted from *New York Times*, 25 June 1974, p. 37 (Op-Ed Page), by permission of the author.

where hundreds of thousands perished of disease and starvation, or were tortured and hanged or shot to death, now shelter the principal museum exhibits: the mountains of human hair, the piles of clothes, the wretched suitcases with crudely or neatly painted names like Stein and Mendelson, the braces and crutches, the heaps of toys and dolls and teddy bears—all of the heart-destroying detritus of the Holocaust from which one stumbles out into the blinding afternoon as if from the clutch of death itself. Even thus in repose—arrested in time, rendered a frozen memorial, purified of its seething mass murder—Auschwitz must remain the one place on earth most unyielding to meaning or definition.

I was unable to attend the recent symposium on Auschwitz at the Cathedral Church of St. John the Divine in New York City, but many of the aspects of the proceedings there, at least as reported, troubled and puzzled me, especially because of the overwhelming emphasis on anti-Semitism and Christian guilt.

My interest in the meeting was deep, since although I am nominally a Christian my four children are half-Jewish and I claim perhaps a more personal concern with the idea of genocide than do most gentiles.

There can be no doubt that Jewish genocide became the main business of Auschwitz; the wrecked crematoriums at Birkenau are graphic testimony to the horrible and efficient way in which the Nazis exterminated two and a half million Jews—mass homicide on such a stupefying scale that one understands how the event might justify speculation among theologians that it signaled the death of God.

The Holocaust is so incomprehensible and so awesomely central to our present-day consciousness—Jewish and gentile—that one almost physically shrinks with reticence from attempting to point out again what was barely touched on in certain reports on the symposium: that at Auschwitz not only the Jews perished but at least one million souls who were not Jews.

Of many origins but mainly Slavs—Poles, Russians, Slovaks, other— they came from a despised people who almost certainly were fated to be butchered with the same genocidal ruthlessness as were the Jews, had Hitler won the war, and they contained among them hundreds of thousands of Christians who went to their despairing deaths in the belief that *their* God, the Prince of Peace, was as dead as the God of Abraham and Moses.

Or there were the few ravaged survivors, like the once devoutly Catholic Polish girl I knew many years ago, the memory of whom impelled my visit to Auschwitz. It was she who, having lost father, husband and two children to the gas chambers, paid no longer any attention to religion since she was certain, she told me, that Christ had turned His face away from her, as He had from all mankind.

Because of this I cannot accept anti-Semitism as the sole touchstone by which we examine the monstrous paradigm that Auschwitz has become. Nor can I regard with anything but puzzled mistrust the chorus of *mea culpas* from the Christian theologians at the symposium, rising along with the oddly self-lacerating assertion of some of them that the Holocaust came about as the result of the anti-Semitism embedded in Christian doctrine.

I am speaking as a writer whose work has often been harshly critical of Christian pretensions, hypocrisies and delusions. Certainly one would not quarrel with the premise that Christian thought has often contained much that was anti-Semitic, but to place all the blame on Christian theology is to ignore the complex secular roots of anti-Semitism as well.

The outrages presently being perpetrated against the Jews by the secular, "enlightened," and anti-Christian Soviet Union should be evidence of the dark and mysterious discord that still hinders our full understanding of the reasons for this ancient animosity.

To take such a narrow view of the evil of Nazi totalitarianism is also to ignore the ecumenical nature of that evil. For although the unparalleled tragedy of the Jews may have been its most terrible single handiwork, its threat to humanity transcended even this. If it was anti-Semitic it was also anti-Christian. And it attempted to be more final than that, for its ultimate depravity lay in the fact that it was anti-human. Anti-life.

This message was plainly written in the spring dusk at Auschwitz only short weeks ago for one observer, who fled before the setting of the sun. To linger in Auschwitz after nightfall would be unthinkable.

STYRON *EN FRANCE*

William Styron and
the *Nouveau Roman*

Melvin J. Friedman*

A novel by a gifted young Frenchman Yves Berger, *The Garden*, captures a unique sense of place which seems to elude a great number of American Southern writers. Although Berger's novel has its real setting in France it is symbolically haunted by a utopian dream of nineteenth-century, antebellum Virginia. Susan Sontag, reviewing *The Garden* for the September 15, 1963 *Book Week*, had this to say about it:

> But M. Berger goes the American Southern writers one better. For him, America, the American South, becomes literally an item of the imagination. Virginia is not a place, but an idea, upon which a mad provincial French family immolates itself. The public myth of America as the land of revivifying contraries (of youth and materialism, of innocence and brutality, of virgin forests and the asphalt jungle) has been refined . . . into the study of a cancerous private myth of America. (p. 28)

This "private myth of America" has been a peculiarity of the French temperament, from the Symbolists on. When Baudelaire and Mallarmé, and more recently Valéry, decided to give the Virginian Edgar Poe a "French face," they started a series of literary efforts—which have continued to our own time—to revaluate American writers in French terms. The preference has clearly been in the direction of Southern novelists or those transplanted to the South. G. A. Astre in his *L'Oeuvre de John Dos Passos* (Lettres Modernes, 1956) wrote the first book-length study in any language of the novelist who once lived in Westmoreland, Virginia. Sherwood Anderson, who spent long periods of his life in New Orleans and Marion, Virginia, was the subject of a long essay, *Réalisme, Rêve et Expressionnisme dans "Winesburg, Ohio" de Sherwood Anderson* (1957), written by Roger Asselineau, and of a *Configuration critique de Sherwood Anderson* (1963), edited by Roger Asselineau (both published by Lettres Modernes).

Another member of the literary generation to which Anderson and Dos Passos belonged far outdistanced their reputations—and even Poe's—

*Reprinted from *William Styron* (Bowling Green, Ohio: Bowling Green Univ. Popular Press, 1974), pp. 19–36, by permission of the author and publisher.

in France. I am thinking of William Faulkner. He was known and appreciated in France before he was in his native America. An introductory essay by Maurice-Edgar Coindreau (Faulkner's most accomplished translator) in the *Nouvelle Revue Française* in June 1931 had started the landslide of Faulkner criticism in France.[1] André Malraux and Valery Larbaud followed with suggestive prefaces to the French translations of *Sanctuary* and *As I Lay Dying* in 1933 and 1934 respectively. The French took their "Faulkneromanie" seriously from the start. They insisted on a "pure" Faulkner, subject to all the critical demands of their own "roman pur." Thus, for example, French critics have insisted from the start that *The Wild Palms* and *Old Man* be read in alternating chapters, as a single work, in the way Faulkner originally published it; they have found intolerable and disrespectful our fragmentation of the book into virtually unrelated novellas. Faulkner seems to be the inspiration behind the impressive number of French books on twentieth-century American fiction; the best of these are built around a central chapter on the creator of the mythical Yoknapatawpha County: Maurice-Edgar Coindreau's *Aperçus de littérature américaine* (1946), Claude-Edmonde Magny's *L'Âge du roman américain* (1948), and Michel Mohrt's *Le Nouveau roman américain* (1955).

Only Mohrt's book deals with the most recent generation of American writers, those who came to prominence after the Second World War. Mohrt's title might suggest to some of us that he is extending the French name for the new avant-garde fiction (*nouveau roman*) to American soil. One of the young novelists introduced to the French reader in *Le Nouveau roman américain* is William Styron. His presence at this crucial moment in Franco-American literary history is especially intriguing because he, more than any other American writer, seems the rightful heir of Faulkner's techniques, themes, and literary settings; and he more than any other of his generation in America seems daringly close to the practices of his French contemporaries, like Michel Butor and Claude Simon. The Faulkner side of Styron, as we have already seen, was evident to most reviewers of his first novel. Malcolm Cowley, for example, writing in *The New Republic* for October 8, 1951 said:

> It is a general rule that novels which stay close to their literary models have no great value of their own, but *Lie Down in Darkness* is an exception; in this case the example of Faulkner seems to have had a liberating effect on Styron's imagination. One might even say that his book is best and most personal when it is most Faulknerian. (p. 20)

The *nouveau roman* connection is reenforced by a sympathetic preface to the French translation of Styron's 1960 novel, *Set This House on Fire*, by Michel Butor. The demon of historical coincidence is apparent again in the haunting presence of Maurice-Edgar Coindreau who turned from splendid translations of *As I Lay Dying, The Sound and the Fury, Light in*

August, and *The Wild Palms* to a very sensitive rendering of *Set This House on Fire* (*La Proie des flammes*, Gallimard, 1962).

Thus the stage has been neatly set for Styron's entrance into the history of Franco-American literary relations. A Virginian was turned into a Symbolist theoretician and poet by the generation of 1870; a Mississippian, who divided his last years between Charlottesville, Virginia, and Oxford, Mississippi, was turned into a Bergsonian novelist by the generation of 1930; and now another Virginian (who currently lives in Roxbury, Connecticut) threatens to become the first American addition to the ranks of the *nouveau roman*.

We can measure the French response to Styron by the number of reviews in the major journals and weeklies of *La Proie des flammes*. On March 22, 1962 *Les Nouvelles Littéraires* carried an interview with Styron, Butor, and Coindreau; on the following week it carried a review of Styron's novel by R. Las Vergnas. The *Figaro Littéraire* reciprocated with two pieces on Styron, one by Robert Kanters who is among the more gifted of the younger French critics. Most of the significant journals were also represented: the list includes *La Nouvelle Revue Française, La Revue des Langues Vivantes*, Sartre's *Temps Modernes*.[2] This was a very different reception from that accorded the French translation of *Lie Down in Darkness* (*Un Lit de ténèbres*) when it was published by the Éditions Mondiales in 1953: Styron's first novel passed practically unnoticed. Another detail of literary history might be useful here. In 1953 the notion of a *nouveau roman* as a defined type of novel was still several years away and the only genuine example of the species available was Alain Robbe-Grillet's *The Erasers* (which was published that year). The next decade witnessed a deluge of *nouveaux romans* by Robbe-Grillet, Nathalie Sarraute, Michel Butor, Marguerite Duras, Claude Simon, Maurice Blanchot. Thus 1962 was a better year for Styron in France than was 1953.

So much for literary reception and historical coincidence. The one symptomatic document we possess is Michel Butor's preface to *La Proie des flammes*. Like so many novelists-turned-critic Butor seems to be holding the mirror up to his own work as much as he is studying Styron's novel. Thus the title of the preface, "OEdipus Americanus," reveals an important preoccupation of Butor with the Oedipus myth and, indeed, with myth in general. In his novel *Passing Time* (*L'Emploi du temps*), published in 1956, we have this revealing passage:

> The detective is a true son of the murderer Oedipus, not only because he solves a riddle, but also because he kills the man to whom he owes his title, without whom he would not exist in that capacity (without crimes, without mysterious crimes, what would he be?) because this murder was foretold for him from the day of his birth or, if you prefer, because it is inherent in his nature, through it alone he fulfills himself and attains the highest power.[3]

At another point in the novel, a tapestry is described in detail, one scene of which depicts Theseus greeting the aged Oedipus at Colonus.

Butor, in his Styron preface, is the first critic to point out the Oedipus parallel, especially the analogy between Cass Kinsolving and the old Oedipus at Colonus. Cass does, after all, refer several times to Sophocles' late play:

> "Tell me this, Signor Regista," he [Cass] said, still grinning. "What said the chorus when old Oedipus was at Colonus"—he seemed fearfully close to pitching backward over the rail—"and old Theseus dragged his poor old bones off . . ." (p. 117)

(The Theseus-Oedipus confrontation here doubtless delighted the Michel Butor of *Passing Time*.) In a later passage, Cass revealingly identifies himself with the blind Oedipus:

> "Anyway, when you mentioned how I started quoting at length from Sophocles that night, it all came back to me. The sweat and the horror and this bleeding awful view into the abyss. Long before I ended up in Sambuco I'd memorized great hunks and sections out of those two volumes. And when you saw me that night I was really in a bad way—as blind-drunk off of *Oedipus* as I was off of booze. . . . I was so completely blind . . . All I know now is that I had some sort of drunken truth that I'd dredged up out of that play, and that it sure as hell had to do with evil, and that Mason . . ." (p. 130)

There are at least three other sustained references to the *Oedipus at Colonus* (see pages 281, 362 and 388) as well as several mentions of either the play or Sophocles' name. Yet Styron's many references to works of literature and music (especially to Mozart's *Don Giovanni* and *The Magic Flute*) and his special fondness for myth[4] might distract most commentators from the Oedipus parallel. Not Butor, however, who has attempted to redefine Oedipus for readers of his neo-detective, mythically centered novels.

The Oedipus-detective metaphor—"The detective is a true son of the murderer Oedipus"—which Butor suggests in *Passing Time* seems also to have found its way into *Set This House on Fire*. Cass Kinsolving only becomes Oedipus after he kills Mason Flagg ("the man to whom he owes his title, without whom he would not exist in that capacity"). The murder offers Cass the astonishing release to return to his native America and to become "himself." The formula for the Oedipus changes here, offering the positive note of salvation denied the Sophoclean original; thus the "Americanus" part of the title of Butor's preface.

The reading I have just offered is based on the passage I quoted above from *Passing Time* applied to *Set This House on Fire*. Butor does not suggest the Oedipus-detective rapprochement in his "OEdipus Americanus." He dwells more on the purging of Cass's guilt, the paradoxical result of his murder of Mason— who for Butor is both Cass's father and his "jumeau" (which means both twin and "double"—in the Dostoev-skian sense). Butor gets too caught up in the Freudian possibilities of his subject: he speaks of Cass's "other self" and classifies the "new Cass" as "the son of Mason's violation of Francesca." He goes on, "One sees that the Oedipian incest is achieved here in a very unexpected way, in reverse. As for the 'twin' who has disappeared, Cass has obviously killed him when he killed Mason . . ."[5] This would seem to be a more fitting solution for the Henry James of "The Jolly Corner" than for the William Styron of *Set This House on Fire*.

Butor curiously missed his cue by not reviving his Oedipus discussion of *Passing Time*. Not only does it explain the successive relationships in Styron's novel in convincing mythical terms, but it also accounts for the burlesque detective ingredients of *Set This House on Fire*. The amateur sleuthing of Peter Leverett (the ineffectual narrator of the novel) leads in improbably indecisive directions. Leverett is present at Sambuco (the mythically etched southern Italian town) during the atrocities yet remains blissfully ignorant of the murderer's identity and other contributing de-tails. Leverett is in the finest mock-detective tradition; he has been com-pletely de-heroicized and manages artlessly to fade into the woodwork:

> My name is Peter Leverett. I am white, Protestant, Anglo-Saxon, Virginia-bred, just past thirty, in good health, tolerable enough looking though possessing no romantic glint or cast, given to orderly habits, more than commonly inquisitive, and strongly sexed—though this is a conceit peculiar to all normal young men. (pp. 4–5)

This is perhaps what Dostoevsky asked for in the famous passage in *The Idiot* when he expressed the need for "ordinary" people in fiction, but he did not cast them in crucial positions in his novels. Styron calculatingly goes to every length to preserve the anonymity of his narrator—in much the same fashion as Beckett and Nathalie Sarraute—even to the point of having two of the other characters confuse his name on first meeting (Poppy calls him "Levenson" and Mr. Garfinkel "Levitt").

The second of the curious "detectives" in *Set This House on Fire* is the Fascist-Humanist, Luigi: Cass, unbelievingly, classifies him on first meet-ing, "(An intellectual policeman! I could hardly believe my ears)." (p. 194) Luigi is responsible for the sympathetic miscarriage of justice which sends Cass, the real murderer of Mason Flagg, home to America, to (in Butor's words) "regain his roots, to review the complete account." (p. xx)

The job of reviewing the complete account falls squarely on Cass's shoulders, the third and most legitimate in the series of detectives. We should now recall Butor's *Passing Time* definition once again. Cass is both the solver of the crime ("because he solves a riddle") and the murderer ("because he kills the man to whom he owes his title"—in this case, Mason).

This elaborate and systematic mockery of detective fiction, through the devious byways of the Oedipus myth, links Styron emphatically with the *nouveau roman*. Sartre, in a famous preface to Nathalie Sarraute's *Portrait of a Man Unknown*, set the record straight for Nathalie Sarraute and, by implication, for the new type of novel by speaking of it as "an anti-novel" which moves ahead like a detective story and, more revealingly, as "a parody on the novel of 'quest'." We might also recall Malraux's suggestion of the infiltration of the elements of Greek tragedy in detective fiction in his preface to the French translation of Faulkner's *Sanctuary*.

Indeed many of the novels of Butor, Sarraute, Robbe-Grillet, and Beckett seem to be linked to detective writing in the same way that *The Rape of the Lock* is linked to the Homeric and Virgilian epic: they offer a caricatured recipe of the original form. Butor's *Passing Time*, for example, has as its "detective" a young Frenchman, Jacques Revel, who spends a year in an English city, Bleston. Jacques senses from the beginning an ambiance of murder. Bleston offers Jacques a "symbolic landscape" to practice his newly-acquired art of detection. He studies the principal *object d'art* of the city, a stained glass window depicting Cain's murder of Abel. He frequents the Bleston museum which features a series of tapestries tracing the career of the legendary Theseus, another man of violence. Jacques has a curious way of linking the real inhabitants of Bleston with mythical figures. The city becomes for this self-appointed detective the labyrinth which he must solve Theseus-style.

Butor further complicates Revel's task by having him pick up a volume in the Penguin "Crime and Detection Series" which bears the ominous title, *The Bleston Murder*. The murder described and the identity of the author intrigue Revel to the point of obsession. Thus we have all the ingredients of the classic detective novel: symbolical foreshadowing, murder, systematic detection. Revel is not, however, a successful sleuth; he is no more fitted for the role than Peter Leverett or Cass. He pieces together an elaborate crime story, complete with symbolical and mythical overtones, based ingeniously but often inaccurately on details from *The Bleston Murder*. The theory and practice are expected to coincide in serious detective fiction. They do not in *Passing Time*. This novel is, as Malraux said about Faulkner's *Sanctuary*, "a novel with a detective-story atmosphere but without detectives."

Jacques Revel shares another trait with Cass Kinsolving. He also has the diary habit. Revel has made a serious matter of his *journal intime*. It seems to work on the principle of the palimpsest in which one period of time appears to be written over another, with the intention of expanding the texture of time.[6] Revel's imagination, which wanders freely and associatively through myth and history, enlarges the framework of the crime out of realistic proportion.

Thus Butor has compressed the ineffectuality of Styron's three "detectives" into a single one. The "symbolic landscape" of southern Italy has been moved northwards to England; still Sambuco and Bleston function in the same way. Cass and Jacques Revel, both types of Butor's "Oedipus Americanus," return to their native countries after the cathartic experience of temporary "exile."

There is probably no question of influence here. *Set This House on Fire* and *Passing Time* are merely symptomatic of their time. Alain Robbe-Grillet has also tampered with most of the serious conventions of detective fiction in his novels. In his first book, *The Erasers*, the detective ends by committing the murder, Oedipus fashion.[7] In *The Voyeur* the narrator himself commits the murder and is, in fact, as implausible a murderer as he is a detective. There are clueless paths leading nowhere in Nathalie Sarraute's novels; her "detectives" go through all the expected motions but usually discover that the money has not been stolen or that the crime has not been committed. Beckett's characters have long dress-rehearsals in which they itemize their possessions and enumerate their physical incapacities before they start on their quests: Moran, the narrator of the second part of *Molloy*, for example, dons his salt-and-pepper shooting suit, readies his bicycle, and begins his search for Molloy in good Sherlock Holmes fashion; he not only does not bring back Molloy but returns home, himself, physically disrupted. The *crime de passion* which launches Marguerite Duras' *Moderato Cantabile* serves only as a distracting leitmotiv through the novel; it merely acts as a vehicle for bringing together two obviously mismatched people for conversation and wine. Claude Simon's novels, the most Faulknerian of the group, have what Laurent Le Sage calls "a cosmic atmosphere of doom and bewilderment."[8] The setting acts in the same paradoxical and confusing way as it does in Butor and Nathalie Sarraute.[9]

Although the figure of Oedipus is not literally conjured up in all of these novels the ingredients of the legend are very often present: suggestions of incest and parricide, for example. The mock-detective fiction, with its mythical core, is one of the staples of the *nouveau roman* as it is of Styron's *Set This House on Fire*.

II

The reassuring reception which the French translation of *Set This House on Fire* received in France combines convincingly with Styron's application of the *nouveau roman* "detective" formula to suggest a kinship between the Virginia-born novelist and France's recent generation of fiction writers. There is more in common, however, than a thematic preoccupation. There are some genuine similarities in technique.

Styron offers one of the last strongholds for stream-of-consciousness writing, Faulkner-style. He is especially fond of interior monologues—built around recurring metaphors—which practice Bergsonian displacements in time. Both *Lie Down in Darkness* and *Set This House on Fire* are concerned, in the manner of Greek tragedy, with events which occur in a single day: the burial of Peyton Loftis and the murder of Mason Flagg. In each case the rectilinear movement of the occurrence is disturbed by what we might call interruptions of consciousness (not far removed from Proust's "intermittences du coeur"). Thus the burial procession in *Lie Down in Darkness*, which does not arrive at its destination until the end of the novel, is broken in upon by a restless series of recapitulative monologues by all the principal characters. Most of them are third-person. When Styron reverts to the first-person he usually resorts to italics:

> *How can I talk about, tell anyone of this tender rapture? Loving a man so for all these years. Now untied from the tie that binds, poor Pookie gone to Knoxville, Tennessee, and Melvin at college, my tie is to him alone. Together we can never die. A farm girl from Emporia: what would Papa say now? I sophisticated and fancypants, vice-chairman of the Red Cross and member in good standing of the Tidewater Garden Club too. Sweet and ruinous, Milton says, with a soft sweet corruption about the mouth. I love him so.*
>
> *Wanting him for so long, holding off, having to, sitting back on these hips he says drive him frantic, like a saint yearning for perfect communion. Holding off. Having to because he says we're both upcaught in the tragedy of a middle-class morality.* (pp. 70–71)

This passage is symptomatic of the use of interior monologue in Faulkner, Joyce, Larbaud, Dujardin, and Dorothy Richardson. It does all the expected things. Its principal concern is sexual, like Bloom's monologues of sexual longing and Molly's monologue of sexual repletion in *Ulysses*, like Daniel Prince's elaborate monologue of sexual preparation in Dujardin's *We'll to the Woods No More (Les Lauriers sont coupés)*. The logical connectives are left out so the monologue has all the qualities of free-flowing impressionism. The sentences in certain cases have been deprived of necessary syntactical ingredients, thus reducing them to clipped phrases. Although there is little imagery in the passage, there is enough alliteration (of "t" and "s" especially) to give it a kind of poetic foundation.

The cliché-ridden thoughts of the monologuist Dolly Bonner are not untypical either. Hers is clearly the type of mind which practitioners of interior monologue enjoy investigating. What is most surprising is how *un*distinctive the passage is. It could have been written by any novelist of the Twenties without arousing curiosity. It should, however, arouse curiosity in a novel published in 1951, especially by a novelist of Styron's unquestioned ability.

We should withhold judgment until we examine another passage from *Lie Down in Darkness*; this one is taken from Peyton's fifty-page monologue—entirely in the first-person—placed toward the end of the novel and acting as a kind of coda to it. Except for the opening lines and an occasional phrase, the monologue is in roman type. The following is representative:

> I thought of feathers, birds, and when he went in it hurt, but no more than the other pain quiescent in me now like the claw of some bird waiting: I put my arms around him, feeling the hair. I could hear the clock whir so near me it brushed against my ear: *tick-tick-tick*, that minute hand making its perfect orbit in space, bearing us like freight through the sky, Harry and I sprawled along the springs and drowsing there to yawn and stretch and turn and watch the revolving diamonds, rubies red as blood from the cut throat of a pigeon, set perfect and complete among the precisely ordered, divinely ticking wheels. Sheltered from the sky like drowning, only better: the sun within submarine, aqueous, touching the polished steel with glints and flickers of eternal noonday light; so we'd have our sun among the springs and our love forever. (p. 323)

The subject of this passage curiously resembles that of the other, except that this concerns sexual fulfillment while the other sexual anticipation. Yet the language here is richer, more metaphorical. The symbols are the same which recur through the entire fifty-page monologue: birds and the clock. Both have sexual associations—the bird suggests the male reproductive organ and the clock the womb (elsewhere in the monologue we find "and the Benrus clock, my womb all jeweled and safe"). The clock is not only the central metaphor of this passage but of the entire monologue and refers not only to the womb but also to the problem of time which obsesses Peyton.

This is vintage interior monologue. Unlike the selection from Dolly Bonner's mind, this excerpt demands the combined gifts of the poet and novelist. But it is really no more distinctive than the other passage. So many of the stream-of-consciousness writers were nurtured on Symbolist poetry and felt keenly the need of bringing poetry into the novel: Dujardin, Larbaud, and Joyce, for example, had all published volumes of poetry before they turned to fiction. Thus we are once again confronted with techniques that were already stale by 1951.

This all convinces me that Styron turned to interior monologue to engage in elaborate literary pastiche.[10] In the same way that he mocked detective fiction—and indirectly myth—in *Set This House on Fire*, he caricatured another literary "sacred cow" in *Lie Down in Darkness*. The pastiche of interior monologue is somewhat more subtle than William Carlos Williams' parody of it in *The Great American Novel* (1923) or Giraudoux' in *Juliette au pays des hommes* (1924). Styron has learned the stream-of-consciousness lesson of Joyce and Faulkner so convincingly that he can reproduce their techniques almost as if he had indeed discovered them.

Peyton's long monologue acts as a kind of *ave atque vale* for the whole stream-of-consciousness movement. It is filled with the favorite symbols and poetic devices of the Bergsonian novel. Thus we can explain the obsessive appearance of the clock which is the favorite symbol of so many of the novelists of the Twenties who were intent on destroying chronological time in favor of "human" or "psychological" time. Peyton's clock is a near-relative of Quentin Compson's watch which Faulkner describes as "the mausoleum of all hope and desire." It offers the same insistent reminder of Peyton's failure to escape from time which Big Ben offers Clarissa Dalloway. In most stream-of-consciousness fiction the time is sounded periodically: Dujardin's *We'll to the Woods No More* begins on a Paris street corner as the chimes announce 6 P.M.; Leopold Bloom receives periodic reminders of the time of day; the Marcel of Proust's "Overture" keeps trying to determine the intervals of time.

Thus it seems likely that Styron uses Peyton's monologue and especially the unifying symbol of the clock as a sympathetic pastiche of interior monologue. At this point his work seems to beg comparison again with the *nouveau roman*. Styron is closest to Robbe-Grillet's first two novels on this occasion. The Oedipus-detective of *The Erasers*, Wallas, has difficulty with a wrist watch which has stopped during the significant twenty-four hour period which led to the murder:

> Wallas looks at his watch; it shows seven thirty-five. Then he remembers that it had stopped at seven-thirty. He raises it to his ear and hears the faint ticking. It must be the detonation that has started it going again—or else the shock, if he bumped it when he threw himself to the floor.[11]

There is a clear connection between Wallas' *neglect* of his watch, in other words of mechanical time, and the Oedipal murder he commits. There is a clue to this in the passage from Sophocles which Robbe-Grillet borrows as the epigraph for his novel: "Time that sees all has found you out against your will." Wallas' attempt to triumph over clock time fails him as disastrously as Peyton's. Wallas cannot avoid the destructive effects of time by allowing his watch to stop just as Peyton cannot avoid them by imagining herself protected, hidden within the springs of her Benrus clock.

Mathias, the principal character of Robbe-Grillet's second novel, *The Voyeur*, is similarly a victim of time pieces. He is a watch salesman who mismanages the time he has allotted himself to sell his wares. He fails to account for the human factor of delay which slows up his sales considerably. He ends up the same ambiguous murderer as Wallas. His selling watches no more exempts him from the compelling presence of "human" or "psychological" time than does the neglect of Wallas or the stratagem of Peyton. The quotation from Sophocles, "Time that sees all has found you out against your will," applies as well, it would seem, to Mathias as it does to Wallas.

None of Butor's characters is symbolically linked with a time piece. Yet Jacques Revel skillfully tries to avoid the uncertainty of the present by taking refuge in his diary jottings which fuse several periods of time. He gains a certain montage effect by superposing the time of the diary notation on the time in which the action related occurred. Thus he seems able to move through several periods at once, with relative freedom and fluidity. Yet he leaves Bleston untriumphant at the end of the year, with no more mastery of time than Peyton or Robbe-Grillet's characters achieved.

In a long, almost Proustian meditation about time in *The Grass* (*L'Herbe*), Claude Simon describes the same kind of frustration:

> . . . but to have the consciousness of time passing constantly present to the mind, and, in hotels that like this one were near a station, this passing of time assuming a solemn character from the fact of no longer being doled out, pecked at by tiny gears, but marked by the slow displacement of monumental and luminous hands suspended in the night on the pediment or the belfry of the station, filling the window's entire rectangle, conferring, with the night's help, a monumental quality on time passing, black and thick in an incessant and catastrophic racket of clashing couplings, rumblings, whistles, as if it consisted of a material as hard as metal, capable of pulverizing and destroying; hearing, then, time groan, collide, gasp, and remorselessly advance in the darkness. . . .[12]

The deliberate, slow, heavy cadence of the prose reveals a kind of exhaustion induced by time. The passage ends with the inevitable reference to the broken clock: ". . . while the lugubrious and frivolous Louis XV clock, broken for good, its hands immobilized forever. . . ." (p. 78)

These examples from Robbe-Grillet, Butor, and Simon offer a further similarity between Styron and the *nouveau roman*. While Styron seems to be consciously offering a pastiche of the earlier generation's obsession with time and its symbols, the "new novelists" are suggesting a negative aspect of the problem. Proust's narrator escapes chronological time by seeking refuge in his "involuntary memory" which induces privileged moments of recollection. Joyce's characters fall back on their "epiphanies" while Virginia Woolf's characters enjoy their "moments of being." There is no such salvation for the characters of Robbe-Grillet, Butor, and Simon who find no way out of their temporal dilemma; they are as much victimized by "human" time as Proust's, Joyce's, and Virginia Woolf's characters are redeemed by it.

The clocks and watches which prove to be the undoing of Robbe-Grillet's characters assume a special importance in the *nouveau roman*. They enter a world of "things" which have a crucial existence apart from fictional characters.[13] (It is no accident that one of the names given to the "new novelists" was *chosiste*.) The turning to objects and giving them almost talismanic importance may be partly a compensation for the "betrayal" of psychological time. Thus while the Bergsonian novelists seemed to temporalize all experience (think of Proust's notion that time has a "form" and of his metaphor of a three-dimensional "solid" psychology) the "new novelists" tend to spatialize it. Robbe-Grillet explains this in his preface to *In the Labyrinth* (*Dans le labyrinthe*, 1959):

> Yet the reality in question is a strictly material one; that is, it is subject to no allegorical interpretation. The reader is therefore requested to see in it only the objects, actions, words, and events which are described, without attempting to give them either more or less meaning than in his own life, or his own death.[14]

The object, then, does not represent something; it is meant to be taken in its own terms. Nathalie Sarraute, in a collection of short pieces interestingly called *Tropisms* (*Tropismes*), has this to say:

> Things! Things! They were her strength. The source of her power. The implement she used, in her instinctive, infallible, sure way, for triumph, for crushing defeat.

> When you lived with her, you were a prisoner of things, a cringing slave burdened with them, dull and dreary, continually being spied upon, tracked down by them.

> Things. Objects. Bells that rang. Things that should not be neglected.[15]

The theory has been turned into practice in most *nouveau roman* fiction. Robbe-Grillet not only gives special importance to watches, but also metaphorically enlarges an eraser (*The Erasers*), a centipede (*Jealousy; La Jalousie*), the figure eight (*The Voyeur*). Samuel Beckett has the destinies of most of his characters attached to umbrellas, bicycles, hats, "sucking stones," pencil stubs, rocking chairs, wheel chairs. Even in an early Beckett book like *More Pricks Than Kicks* we find the symptoms: "Belacqua, who could on no account resist a bicycle. . . ." or "Turning aside from this and other no less futile emblems, his attention was arrested by a wheelchair. . . ."[16] Nathalie Sarraute seems almost capable of writing an entire novel around a physical object (*The Planetarium* comes very close to this); as Anne Minor has said, ". . . in Nathalie Sarraute the object comes into direct conflict with the characters."[17] Butor is less "objectal," perhaps more Balzacian, in his descriptions. Yet the railroad car in *A Change of Heart* (*La Modification*); the diary, tapestry, stained glass window, and murder novel in *Passing Time*; and the classroom in *Degrees* (*Degrés*) are very close to what we have been talking about.

It would be an exaggeration to say that William Styron pays the same attention to physical objects and responds to them with similar fanatical devotion. There is none of Robbe-Grillet's geometrical fascination or Beckett's anguished attachment anywhere in his fiction. Yet Styron has his own reverence for "things." In *Lie Down in Darkness* the mimosa—which fondly recalls Proust's hawthorn—recurs with the insistence and frequency of a leitmotiv. One characteristic description is: "Outside the mimosa seemed to come alive; the pink, mossy blooms groped at the air. . . ." (p. 23) The clock and the birds in Peyton's monologue fulfill the demands made by Nathalie Sarraute's *Tropisms*: "Things! Things! They were her strength. The source of her power. The implement she used. . . ."

The vase which Cass Kinsolving breaks when he first arrives in Sambuco seems perpetually to be connected with his person, almost in the manner of an "objective correlative."[18] There is perhaps more symbolism here than Robbe-Grillet is willing to allow for in his preface to *In the Labyrinth* but most of the other conditions of *chosisme* are satisfied by the vase. It is as much a talisman for Cass as the watch is for Robbe-Grillet's "detectives."

Styron has given more than ordinary attention, then, to certain physical objects; this is not perhaps as essential a part of his aesthetics as it is of that of the "new novelists" but it must still be taken seriously. Another direction in which Styron has extended his experimentation is closely linked to his *chosiste* tendencies. His fiction, thus far, has been a strenuous and unceasing effort to make his peace with the various "points of view" available to the novelist. While Peter Leverett is the narrator of the entire *Set This House on Fire*, his point of view gradually gives way to Cass Kinsolving's in the second half of the novel. More and more, Cass's disjointed diary jottings and his hallucinative monologues replace Leverett's sure but unspectacular view of the events. (Beckett has done something very like this in the second half of *Molloy* where Moran's controlled narration is gradually replaced by a frantic and illogical transcription of thoughts very close to Molloy's monologue of the first part.) The texture of the prose thickens as the novel gives way to the neo-existentialist reverie of Cass Kinsolving.[19]

The experimentation in *Lie Down in Darkness* not only involves frequent changes in point of view—involving each of the relatively articulate characters in the novel—but the use of first, second, and third person discourse. The alternation between the first and third offers no surprises. But second-person discourse is rare enough to attract attention.[20] In the second paragraph of *Lie Down in Darkness* we have a sampling of this:

> Suddenly the train is burrowing through the pinewoods, and the conductor, who looks middle-aged and respectable like someone's favorite uncle, lurches through the car asking for tickets. If you are particularly alert at that unconscionable hour you notice his voice, which is somewhat guttural and negroid—oddly fatuous-sounding after the accents of Columbus or Detroit or wherever you came from—and when you ask him how far it is to Port Warwick and he says, "*Aboot* eighty miles," you know for sure that you're in the Tidewater. (p 7)

This continues through two uninterrupted pages and finally gives way to the third person. The second person sets the guide-book tone for the tour through Styron country. These early pages of *Lie Down in Darkness* are especially interesting for us because of their resemblance to a novel which appeared six years later, Michel Butor's *A Change of Heart*. This novel is written entirely in the second person and takes place on a train. Butor's narrator seems mainly to be addressing his other self as "you" (very much like Eliot's Prufrock). Yet there is some of Styron's guide-book discourse apparent in this scenically plotted Paris-to-Rome train ride:

> If you want further information about the train on which you're traveling (as for the other, the Rome express, you know its times almost by heart, and when you take it you don't need this square booklet in which, for all your experience, you find your way with some difficulty) you will have to consult Table 500, in which the itinerary is far more detailed, mentioning all the stations, even those at which the train doesn't stop, then, after Mâcon, where it leaves the main Paris-Marseilles line, Table 530, but after Modane you'll need an Italian time-table, for in this one there's only this page with the principal stops—Turin, Genoa, Pisa—whereas there are bound to be some other stops, at Leghorn probably, possibly at Civitavecchia.[21]

We have now come full circle back to the original "matter" of the Oedipus Americanus. What may have drawn Butor originally to *Set This House on Fire* were the opening pages of *Lie Down in Darkness*.

III

William Styron published his third full-length novel, *The Confessions of Nat Turner*, in 1967. Like *Set This House on Fire* before it, it was translated into French by Maurice-Edgar Coindreau.[22] Styron has continued, in the meantime, to indulge his penchant for essay-writing; he has become in the past several years a contributor of reviews and articles to such periodicals as *Esquire, Harper's, The New York Review of Books,* and *The New York Times Book Review* on a fairly regular basis.[23] The "new novelists" have always been essayists as well as novelists. Butor, Robbe-Grillet, Maurice Blanchot, and Nathalie Sarraute, for example, have written studies of the novel which eloquently complemented their fiction. Nathalie Sarraute even occasionally lapses into judgments of other writers in her novels.

Styron's kind of "literariness" has kept him apart from such American contemporaries as Kerouac, Mailer, and James Jones, who plead a kind of cultural poverty. He is much closer in spirit to his French *nouveau roman* contemporaries who thrive on, what seems to be, the same Symbolist inheritance: the total commitment to literature. It is no accident that both Styron and the "new novelists" returned to Flaubert for his technique, his "style indirect libre"; *Madame Bovary* has offered them an irreproachable model.[24] Styron feels his responsibility to write about literature almost as keenly as his responsibility to write it. He may have acquired this habit during the years spent living and writing in Paris (when he helped found the *Paris Review*). Several of the "new novelists" have reciprocated Styron's gesture by making excursions to various parts of the United States. In the last several years, Nathalie Sarraute, Claude Mauriac, Robert Pinget, Alain Robbe-Grillet, and Claude Ollier have all lectured in America. Michel Butor has served a series of extended terms as a visiting professor; *Mobile* (1962), which he subtitled "Study for a Representation of the United States," is an intriguing expression of his views of America.

This cultural exchange has doubtless enriched both French and American letters. Whatever the literary rapprochements between Styron and the "new novelists," Franco-American relations are the richer for them.

Notes

1. The subject has been important enough to merit a full-length study, S. D. Woodworth's *William Faulkner en France (1931–1952)* (Paris: Lettres Modernes, 1959); a skillful bibliographical essay by Percy G. Adams, "The Franco-American Faulkner," *Tennessee Studies in Literature*, 5 (1960), pp. 1–13; a recent critical analysis by Percy G. Adams, "Faulkner, French Literature, and 'Eternal Verities'," *Proceedings of the Comparative Literature Symposium*, Vol. VI, eds. W. T. Zyla and W. M. Aycock (Lubbock, Texas: Texas Tech University, 1973), pp. 7–24; a chapter from Ward Miner's and Thelma Smith's *Transatlantic Migration: The Contemporary American Novel in France* (Durham, North Carolina: Duke University Press, 1955); and M. E. Coindreau's "William Faulkner in France," *Yale French Studies*, No. 10 (1952), pp. 85–91. Coindreau's essays have recently been gathered together in the splendid volume, *The Time of William Faulkner: A French View of Modern American Fiction*, edited and chiefly translated by George M. Reeves (Columbia, South Carolina: University of South Carolina Press, 1971). This last represents a milestone in scholarship.

2. More recently, the well-known French critic of American literature, Cyrille Arnavon, has published a useful study, "Les Romans de William Styron," *Europe* (Paris), 41 (September 1963), pp. 54–66. See also Simone Fraisse, "Une tragédie de notre temps: La Proie des flammes de William Styron," *Esprit*, No. 321 (October 1963), pp. 483–488.

3. Michel Butor, *Passing Time and A Change of Heart*, trans. Jean Stewart (New York: Simon and Schuster, 1969), p. 154. There are a series of worthwhile studies which touch on certain aspects of myth discussed here: see Leon S. Roudiez, "The Embattled Myths," in *Hereditas*, ed. Frederic Will (Austin, Texas: University of Texas Press, 1964), pp. 77–94; André Bonnichon, "William Styron et le second OEdipe," *Etudes*, 315 (October 1962), pp. 94–103; David D. Galloway, "The Absurd Man as Tragic Hero: The Novels of William Styron," *Texas Studies in Literature and Language*, 6 (Winter 1965), pp. 512–534; L. Hugh Moore, "Robert Penn Warren, William Styron, and the Use of Greek Myth," *Critique: Studies in Modern Fiction*, 8 (Winter 1965–66), pp. 75–87; and Kenneth A. Robb, "William Styron's Don Juan," *Critique: Studies in Modern Fiction*, 8 (Winter 1965–66), pp. 34–46.

4. Styron has the same sense of mythical urgency as Mann and Joyce, for example. He cannot resist dilating the most ordinary situations into myths and classical harmonies. Even in describing a forced march in the Marine Corps he is metaphorically tempted: "In the morbid, comfortless light they were like classical Greek masks. . . ." (p. 29) When reviewing Andrew Turnbull's edition of F. Scott Fitzgerald's letters (*The New York Review of Books*, November 28, 1963), when writing Faulkner's obituary (*Life*, July 20, 1962), or when describing plans for *The Confessions of Nat Turner* (*Esquire*, July 1963), he is invariably seduced by the mythical possibilities of his subject.

5. "Oedipus Americanus," in William Styron, *La Proie des flammes*, trans. M. E. Coindreau (Paris: Gallimard, 1962), p. xix. All references will be to this edition. The translations from Butor's French are my own. The essay is reprinted on pp. 135–45 of this collection.

6. See my discussion of this in "The Neglect of Time: France's Novel of the Fifties," *Books Abroad*, 36 (Spring 1962), p. 127. See also Bruce Morrissette's fine study, "The New Novel in France," *Chicago Review*, 15 (Winter-Spring 1962), pp. 1–19.

7. See Bruce Morrissette's brilliant discussion, "Oedipe ou le cercle fermé: *Les Gommes* (1953)," in his *Les Romans de Robbe-Grillet* (Paris: Les Éditions de Minuit, 1963), pp. 37–75. See also Ben F. Stoltzfus' discussion, "The Gum Erasers: Oedipus the Detective," in his *Alain Robbe-Grillet and the New French Novel* (Carbondale, Illinois: Southern Illinois University Press, 1964), pp. 67–81.

8. *The French New Novel: An Introduction and a Sampler* (University Park: Pennsylvania State University Press, 1962), p. 137.

9. One can look back to Heimito von Doderer's *Every Man a Murderer* (*Ein Mord, den jeder begeht*), which was originally published in 1938, for an early instance of the mock-detective motif. Here, as in several of the novels we have been discussing, the detective turns out to be the murderer.

10. See J. D. Scott's "New Novels," *New Statesman and Nation*, 43 (April 19, 1952), p. 473.

11. *The Erasers*, trans. Richard Howard (New York: Grove Press, 1964), p. 245.

12. *The Grass*, trans. Richard Howard (New York: George Braziller, 1960), pp. 77–78. All references will be to this edition.

13. See J. Robert Loy, " 'Things' in Recent French Literature," *PMLA*, 71 (1956), pp. 27–41.

14. *In the Labyrinth*, trans. Richard Howard (New York: Grove Press, 1960).

15. *Tropisms and The Age of Suspicion*, trans. Maria Jolas (London: John Calder, 1963), pp. 24–25.

16. *More Pricks Than Kicks* (London: Chatto and Windus, 1934), pp. 28, 48.

17. Anne Minor, "Nathalie Sarraute: *Le Planétarium*," *Yale French Studies*, No. 24 (1959), p. 99.

18. Cass's broken vase should probably be connected with Myshkin's in *The Idiot* and with Julien Sorel's in *The Red and the Black*. In each case, the breaking of the vase precedes an event of "epiphanic" importance. Cass's stay in Sambuco which ends in his murder of Mason is as much expressed metaphorically by the vase as Myshkin's epileptic seizure which prepares for his return to the asylum in Switzerland or Julien's actions which lead to the shots he fires at Mme. de Rênal.

19. Cass's words offer a convincing echo of Sartre, especially the Sartre of *Being and Nothingness*: ". . . that as for being and nothingness, the one thing I did know was that to choose between them was simply to choose being, not for the sake of being, or even the love of being, much less the desire to be forever—but in the hope of being what I could be for a time." (pp. 500–501).

20. Bruce Morrissette, in his "The New Novel in France," points to Valery Larbaud's "Mon plus secret conseil" (1923) as an early use of the "narrative 'you'." Morrissette has also published a virtually definitive discussion of the use of the second person; see his "Narrative 'You' in Contemporary Literature," *Comparative Literature Studies*, 2 (1965), pp. 1–24. W. M. Frohock, in his "Faulkner and the 'Roman Nouveau': An Interim Report," *Bucknell Review*, 10 (March 1962), points to an early use of the second person in several pages of *Absalom, Absalom!* (Modern Library edition, beginning p. 214). The contagion has apparently spread to the weeklies: the March 14, 1964 *New Yorker* carried a vignette, "Jimmy Bennett Doesn't Work Here Any More," written entirely in the second person.

21. *Passing Time and A Change of Heart*, trans. Jean Stewart (New York: Simon and Schuster, 1969), p. 334.

22. The moral climate and sense of place in *The Confessions of Nat Turner* are really not very far from the utopian dream of nineteenth-century, ante-bellum Virginia conceived of in *The Garden* (although I doubt strongly that Styron had Yves Berger's book in mind). We seem to be quite removed in *The Confessions of Nat Turner* from the narrative mode of the *nouveau roman*, even from the frantic monologues of Beckett. It would seem then, as I indicated earlier, that in his most recent novel Styron has found a narrative solution favored by an earlier generation of French fiction writers—the generation which uncomfortably accommodates both Proust and Camus—so the *nouveau roman* does not pertain here as it did with *Lie Down in Darkness* and *Set This House on Fire*.

23. See especially Styron's incisive and blistering attack on Lt. Calley (he comments, in passing, about him, "One thinks of Eichmann.") in the lead review in *The New York Times Book Review* for September 12, 1971.

24. Styron had this to say to Thérèse de Saint Phalle in *Le Figaro Littéraire* (October 28 to November 3, 1968): "France is my spiritual home. Of all the countries which have translated my books, I believe that it is here [in France] where one understands them best. Flaubert, whom I have read in college and a hundred times since then, has been one of my guides. *Madame Bovary* should be read by everyone. What mastery of composition!"

William Styron in France

Valarie M. Arms*

William Styron has drawn with unremitting honesty a picture of the American "la dolce vita." Styron's portraits of the ugliness in our society have occasioned much critical disagreement on this side of the Atlantic. But, on the other side, they have been widely acclaimed. While his position at home is still being debated, in Europe Styron has received serious critical attention and been warmly received by students and writers from France to the Soviet Union. His novels have sold well abroad and in his frequent travels he has often been interviewed about them. Especially in France, where Styron feels "at home," his interviews and the articles on his works reveal a great deal that has not been expressed in the United States. As J. Hillis Miller has said recently, "literary criticism at this moment is an international enterprise. Even if one is working on an entirely English or American topic, to ignore criticism in other countries is to risk being provincial."[1] Particularly with Styron, whose harsh picture of American society may cloud the eyes of American critics, it is important to consider his foreign reputation.

William Styron is well aware that he is more highly regarded abroad than he is at home. He has made almost yearly trips to Europe since he won the Prix de Rome in 1951 and each time has granted several interviews. He finds the European critics perceptive and he is, in turn, responsive to their queries. Consequently his statements in foreign interviews are often more revealing and detailed than in American interviews. In fact, the only place that Styron discusses his trip to Russia is in a French interview. Besides Styron's own perception of his work, which he elucidates in fluent French, there are numerous foreign reviews and critical essays that illuminate the novels.

Styron has frequently named foreign writers such as Flaubert, Camus, Joyce, and Dostoevsky as influences; in France, he has not only been compared to them but also ranked with them on the prestigious Agrégation list, a compulsory reading list for graduate students in all French universities. In 1974, Styron was invited to lecture in France at several universities of his choice, and he selected four. Among them was

*This essay was prepared especially for this collection; it has not previously been published.

the Sorbonne, where his appearance on stage occasioned a standing ova-
tion.[2] The French recognize that they accord Styron more distinction than
he has received in his own country, and they note proudly that they also
preceded Americans in recognizing the merits of two other Southerners,
Edgar Allan Poe and William Faulkner. As Styron has said: "France is my
spiritual home. Of all the countries in the world which have translated
my books I think that they understand them best here."[3]

One of the reasons for Styron's popularity in France is the excellent
quality of the translations. His first novel, published in French in 1953,
was quietly noted. However, when Maurice-Edgar Coindreau asked to
translate *Set This House on Fire* in 1960, Styron gained widespread
retrospective recognition. Coindreau, a highly esteemed critic, had
taught at Princeton and had translated some of Faulkner's and Hemingway's novels. His personal interest in Styron and his connection with
Gallimard, an important French publishing house, assured Styron of a
thoughtful reception. French critics were quick to detect the European influences in *Set This House on Fire* and to applaud its honesty in depicting
the evil in American society. Its success occasioned renewed interest in the
earlier novels. Gallimard acquired the rights to *Lie Down in Darkness*
from Del Duca Publishers, who had published a translation by Michel Ar-
naud in 1953. After the success of *Set This House on Fire*, published as *La
proie des flammes* in 1962, Gallimard published both *Lie Down in
Darkness (Un lit de ténèbres)* and *The Long March (La marche de nuit)* in
1963. The excellent translations attracted public attention and quickly
established Styron as a major writer. As James West has noted in consideration of the sales record abroad, "The French translations of Styron's
writings and the history of Styron's reception and reputation in France,
will both be of great importance in any future assessment of Styron's
career."[4]

One Frenchman, Michel Mohrt, heralded Styron's novels even before
the Gallimard editions. In his 1955 study, *Le nouveau roman americain*,
Mohrt included *Lie Down in Darkness;* with the study's subsequent
translation into Spanish, Styron was introduced in both France and Spain
as a writer with promise. Mohrt saw that promise fulfilled in *Set This
House on Fire*, which he reviewed before it was translated. Calling the
novel "the American la dolce vita," Mohrt theorized that, like Faulkner
and Flaubert, Styron is unpopular at home because of the unpleasant
view he presents of his countrymen. Mohrt sympathized with the lack of
understanding Styron had received from American critics. "Like
Flaubert, he is scandalous in his own country. The official critics are
basically against him, but the approval of M. E. Coindreau, who
translated his book, seems much more important to him. It was in France
that Faulkner was first recognized and understood."[5] For Mohrt, the
comparison between Styron's and Flaubert's careers is dramatized by
their shared belief in a quiet lifestyle. Seeing Flaubert's motto in Styron's

study prompted Mohrt to ask Styron how he accounted for the fact that, like Flaubert, he is not highly valued at home. With particular reference to *Set This House on Fire*, Styron said that the hostility of the public response was owing to the "severity of my depiction of America and Americans," and that, in recompense, the novel's success in France was especially gratifying.[6]

Mohrt sees a similarity in Styron and Faulkner in their use of their Southern background and of existentialism. He finds a recurrent pattern in both writers in which man despairs of freeing himself from an inherited guilt. Mohrt's discussion of *La proie des flammes* is dominated by existential terms. Styron assents to Mohrt's interpretation that "one finds in this book that you are working on the obsessions which all the characters of your preceding works have been victimized by: sin, the despair born from an absolute lack of faith, the desire to escape from a world blocked by all possible means: alcohol, rape, murder."[7] Such willingness to see recurrent patterns is encouraging to Styron who suggests that Americans are unable to accept tragedy and are, consequently, unable to accept Cass' metaphysical crisis. Mohrt recognizes that Styron's interest in each of the first four novels has been in man's search for meaning, for a spiritual center. He answers his own question to Styron in discussing the continuity of themes in the novels: "What remains in this house where God is absent with its two beautiful refrigerators, its televisions, its comfortable sofas and all its gadgets? Nothing. When one has realized this emptiness, one comes to wish for some holocaust or some monstrous purification—that probably sought by your Nat Turner, that which the brutal translation of the title of your last novel expresses: *Set This House on Fire*."[8]

French critics such as Mohrt have the advantage of literary distance in viewing the American foibles that Styron depicts. Styron admits that writers often have an antipathy for critics, but he complains of the vehemence of many of the reviews of *Set This House on Fire*. "Writers do not easily accept the judgment of critics, they find always that they are unjust . . . that they do not understand them. . . . Just the same, I must say that I was surprised by the violence of the assault that *Set This House on Fire* received. They all said that it was an unbelievable story, stupid, a piece of filth." Another French critic, Madeleine Chapsal, who shares Mohrt's view, responds: "I have read *Set This House on Fire* and, indeed you do not mince words. It is a violent critique of certain aspects of American society. Now according to what I have heard, American society does not like very much to be criticized." Fortunately, though Styron is pained by the lack of critical understanding at home, he feels committed to his vision. He agrees with Chapsal's comment and adds that "the works of writers like Tennessee Williams, Henry Miller, and Nelson Algren, who paint a somber picture of America, receive almost the same treatment as mine. Nevertheless, I believe that these books are necessary, even indispensable."[9] America is no longer the land of innocence and Styron is one of those writers who acknowledges that his pen is an instrument to make us see ourselves as the rest of the world sees us. *Set This House on Fire* is not just his version of what Fellini immortalized as "la dolce vita," but a "dolce vita à l'Americaine." "This second book by Styron was rather poorly received by the American critics. They criticized his crudity and vulgarity. But if one judges by the way which he judges American politics, the way he describes Hollywood stars, their stupidity, their sexuality, one may think that there are deeper reasons for their bad mood."[10] Certainly Styron concurs with the French critics who saw his book in such a light; speaking on the theme of innocence recently he said: "Let's face it—we're no longer innocent. *Set This House on Fire,* for whatever value it had, was more or less an attempt (I see it retrospectively) as a description of the fact that Americans were evil in this particular case, not Europeans. . . . Also, we're not really innocent; by now we have Viet Nam and we're as dirty as the rest."[11]

Mohrt, for one, can appreciate "the ugly American" in *La proie des flammes,* but he also recognizes the universality of Styron's themes and draws attention to it in the note to the novel which he translated, *La marche de nuit.* Mohrt sees the Marines not as an American anomaly but as symbolic of any military establishment. "Any Frenchman who, in war or peace, has marched on the highways, knapsack on his back and blisters on his feet, will feel a friendship of complicity for the heroes of this story."[12] It is less important that the action takes place in the South than that it could happen to anyone anywhere. One of the anomalies of civilization is that every peace-keeping system has included an army. *The Long March* belongs to a worldwide tradition of literature that has struggled to reconcile the necessary evil of a military force with the purported purpose of keeping the peace. While American critics tended to dismiss *The Long March* because it failed to develop the theory that Styron was a new Southern writer, French critics praised it: "It is not a war novel but a novel of a garrison, a study of the military spirit more successful than anything since Stendhal."[13] Although *La marche de nuit* is less popular than the other novels in France, it is well regarded. Mohrt, noting that it shows little Faulknerian influence, still praises the translation. "It was a question of preserving in each sentence, charged with parenthetical clauses and dashes, its sinuous enveloping movement, its baroque richness, without damaging its clarity."[14]

The French freely admit to their "Faulkneromanie," so it is important to see that they admire Styron even when he is unlike Faulkner. Clearly their initial interest stresses his role as Faulkner's heir. For example: "Un énorme mélodrame à la Faulkner," is the way *L'Express* (27 December 1962) introduces its review of *Un lit de ténèbres.* "The characteristics the two share are a sense of tradition, suicides, adulteries, alcoholism, racism, incest, and metaphysiques." However, *L'Express* finds *La marche de nuit* the better novel: "brief and profound book, strong and discreet, [it] is probably among the great Southern tragedies."

In one of the best essays in any language on the novella, "En Suivant *La marche de nuit,*" Roger Asselineau explicates the symbols such as the young girls and the Haydn refrain in depth. He believes that the book has not received the attention it deserves and, like *L'Express,* he classifies it as a "tragedy." Asselineau suggests that the reason "*La marche de nuit* has not until now received all the attention that it deserves" has to do with the Americans' distaste for seeing themselves in an unfavorable light.[15] The novella illuminates a dichotomy in our society which makes us uncomfortable. As Asselineau says, *La marche de nuit* is thus, among other things, "the protest of an American civilian against the presence in a democratic society of a career army by nature essentially antidemocratic."[16] Asselineau, like Mohrt, recognizes that Styron's ties to Faulkner are less noticeable in *La marche de nuit,* but that fact does not dampen his praise.

As in America, *Un lit de ténèbres* provokes the most comparison with Faulkner. The comparison is invited by the comment on the French blurb (which echoes the American one): "They were in the presence of a more than promising writer, and as *Set This House on Fire* has recently proven, one of the chosen few worthy of succeeding the giants of the 'lost generation.' " The characteristics isolated in the review in *L'Express* are repeated in many other reviews. Several also stress the quality of the characterizations which the French find fully developed in *Un lit de ténèbres.* Several of the commentaries delineate what we recognize as endemic Southern qualities. Styron admits to being influenced by Faulkner, but stresses his attempt to grow beyond that influence. No writer can totally escape his environment or exist in a vacuum. Styron says: "You cannot become a writer without falling under influences and being affected by them, in order to create a universe in your image. The shadow of Faulkner glides over my first works, but no responsible critic can say that I am a disciple of Faulkner. I am my own master."[17]

In writing *Lie Down in Darkness,* Styron built on his love of place—Virginia, but he deliberately excised parts of the manuscript that were redolent of Faulkner's style. Many critics, American and French, failed to notice other influences in the novel—the epigraph from Joyce's *Finnegans Wake,* the echo of Thomas Wolfe's famous refrain "O lost, and by the wind grieved, ghost, come back again," and the opening framework in the second person which Styron had patterned on Robert Penn Warren's *All The King's Men.* Styron drew on a broad background in literature and music, and consciously expanded his theme beyond a regional limitation: "I wanted to write a novel whose implications would go beyond one region. I wanted to avoid the ancestral themes, the strangely perverse characters so frequent in the works of Faulkner, Caldwell, and other Southern writers. Moreover I didn't want to exploit the old theme of decay and destruction as a strictly Southern phenomenon. These elements are not absent from the novel but they describe characters rather than places. I like to think that my story would have taken place in Massachusetts as well as in Virginia."[18]

Lie Down in Darkness presents the evil in society but, asked if he thought his novel was completely pessimistic, Styron answered, "Not in any way. You have to be able to look at the horrible side of existence but believe in something better."[19] For Styron, Helen Loftis embodies the most horrible side of existence, the evil that corrupts and kills. She is best described in a French study of American writers, *Présences contemporaines: écrivains américains d'aujourd'hui* by Pierre Brodin. Brodin discusses *Un lit de ténèbres* at length, and he views Helen in the light that Styron intended for his portrait of evil: "This austere woman, a hypocrite, who regularly practices her religious duties has, rather than religion, a religiosity stripped of profound spirituality. She practices the ceremonies of a religion emptied of its supernatural content and deprived of its sense of forgiveness."[20] After praising both form and content in the novel, Brodin concludes that "of all the American writers of today, Styron is probably the most *flaubertien* and I say willingly, going further, one of the most apt to be appreciated in France."[21] What he is praising in Styron is most likely Styron's world view, which is indebted to the French existentialists, and his Flaubertian concern for the craft of fiction. Brodin sees Styron's world view not as limited by Southern regionalism, but as a metaphor for the individual groping for a religious and moral order in society.

Set This House on Fire has been examined by Melvin J. Friedman in its relation to French literature.[22] However, it is the French author and critic, Michel Butor, who gives some real insight into Styron's intent. Butor, in his lengthy preface to the French edition, "Oedipus Americanus," describes the novel in existential terms which elevates it to a universal meaning: "We see that what happens in the theatre of Sambuco is nothing less than an allegory of the American condition, an invitation to overcome it."[23] Butor gives a sensitive interpretation of the plot and, perhaps because of his own interest in myths, turns his attention to the relation of Cass to Oedipus at Colonus. Cass has quoted Sophocles' play at length, and Butor notes that "the unfortunate king of Thebes is thus a fundamental reference and Cass identifies with it more and more in the course of the night but we can already see that the interpretation which is given here differs profoundly from that to which classical psychoanalysis has accustomed us."[24]

Styron was quite pleased with Butor's sensitive interpretation of *Set This House on Fire*; in an interview in France conducted just after the book's publication, he mentioned that Butor was the first critic to note the importance of the Oedipus myth. Asked if he thought the preface which

Butor wrote was true to the author's intent, Styron replied: "Absolutely. And Butor was the only critic to discover the importance of the Oedipus myth which was used there."[25]

Although quite impressed by Butor, Styron only met the man and read his works after Butor had written the preface to *Set This House on Fire*. In an interview with Butor and M. E. Coindreau, the translator, Styron was asked about a possible indebtedness to the *nouveau roman*, the movement to which Butor belongs. Styron responded: "I believe myself independent. But perhaps I would find myself—in spite of myself— associated one day with some school. However, I do not think that the writers themselves create schools. But they can find themselves united by a sort of fraternity, by certain currents of thought or of forms of expression."[26]

Styron found himself united with European critics to a much greater degree when he wrote his historical novel *The Confessions of Nat Turner* (1967). Though his original note to the book called it "a meditation on history" because he feared the pejorative connotations of the real classification, he now freely admits it is an historical novel. A European understanding of the historical novel has allowed him to see its merits despite the derision the term often receives in American circles. A Marxist study, *The Historical Novel* by Hungarian critic Georg Lukács, changed Styron's thinking. The book relies heavily on Balzac and Flaubert to define and illustrate the value of historical novels. Lukács emphasizes one of Balzac's statements which best explains Styron's intent: "Talent flourishes where the causes which produce the facts are portrayed in the secrets of the human heart, whose motions are neglected by the historians."[27] The blurb to *Les confessions de Nat Turner*, which M. E. Coindreau translated in 1969, comments on the same distinction made in *The Historical Novel*. It reads in part, "William Styron, in *The Confessions of Nat Turner*, does the work of a sociologist, a painter of habits, and of a psychologist without ever forgetting that he is above all a novelist. That leads him to take certain liberties with the facts."[28] And Styron, when questioned in France, gave a response consistent with those he gave to his American detractors about his infusing Nat Turner with the soul of William Styron: "It is evident that book is like me. How is it possible to write a book that does not betray the sensibility of its author, his deportment, his world view? The essential thing is to avoid clichés and to stay faithful to the spirit of the time."[29] The French, more familiar with the goals of a good historical novel, were willing to take Styron at his word.

As a consequence of the understanding he is accorded in France, Styron has been very free, in his French interviews, in discussing *Sophie's Choice*, the historical novel which he has recently published. Like *The Confessions of Nat Turner*, the new novel deals with human bondage and has overt confessional overtones. For those willing to accept Nat Turner's bondage as a metaphor for the human condition, Styron has correlated Southern slavery and Nazi prison camps: "In a certain sense it is a repetition of slavery. . . . Beyond certain differences, I would like to emphasize the incredible dose of inhumanity of which man is capable with respect to his fellow being. We reach the deepest abysses when we ourselves enslave our brothers. Auschwitz is only an extreme case."[30]

Styron admits he is troubled by "the hysterical violence" of some American criticism. He believes that the French respect the writer more and understand his role in society better. As Styron has said many times to his French interviewers, the writer in America suffers from a lack of respect: "You cannot realize it in France where the writer is esteemed, respected for his profession and always feels necessary to the culture of his country. But in America, the writer is much less well accepted; it is not exactly that he is scorned but he inspires mistrust. . . . Considering his cousins, I think in America, a writer comes after a doctor and even after a politician."[31] Yet Styron believes that the writer is in part an educator and a moralist to his readers, and certainly in *Sophie's Choice* his goal is to caution against a recurrence of a Holocaust. By depicting the tragedy which befell a Polish Catholic girl at Auschwitz, Styron aims to expand the limited historical interpretation of the Holocaust as a Jewish genocide.

In France, Styron unashamedly states his goals, but it is difficult to imagine an American interviewer even asking the question, "What power does a writer have?" Especially with respect to *Sophie's Choice*, Styron says: "The young generation does not know about the concentration camps. Perhaps it is the role of the writer to revive the conscience and to remind us in a discreet way, that such things must not happen again. If you are moved after having read a book, or if your way of seeing things is modified, then you have participated in an act of illumination. Such is the function of literature, of music, and all forms of art."[32]

The French appreciation of Styron is documented by a book of essays evaluating his achievement, *Configuration critique de William Styron*, which appeared in 1967, nine years before the appearance of a comparable American volume, *The Achievement of William Styron*. His reputation is also growing elsewhere throughout Europe. The novels have been published in Mexico, Argentina, Brazil, and Japan; Styron was surprised to find that his novels are even read in the Soviet Union. Only the French press documents Styron's visit there: "In Moscow, at a meeting of Soviet writers, I was surprised to see a group of fourteen or fifteen novelists or critics ask to question me about my work which they knew well. The artists threw out questions which men in the United States would be incapable of even framing. Art is a universal language which binds more than it divides."[33] Styron's novels do indeed speak a universal language, a concern for understanding and accepting the brotherhood of man, not just of regional next-door neighbors.

Notes

1. "J. Hillis Miller on Literary Criticism," *The New Republic,* 29 Nov. 1975, p. 30.

2. Ben Forkner and Gilbert Schricke, "An Interview with William Styron," *The Southern Review,* 10 (Oct. 1974), 923.

3. Thérèse de Saint Phalle, "William Styron: 'En U.R.S.S.—et en France—je suiz chez moi'," *Le Figaro Littéraire,* 28 Oct.–3 Nov. 1968, p. 26.

4. James L. W. West III, *William Styron: A Descriptive Bibliography* (Boston: G. K. Hall and Co., 1977), p. xvii. This discussion of Styron's foreign reputation is indebted to West's bibliography, especially to Section B on French editions, which will be cited by his labels.

5. Michel Mohrt in "La Proie des Critiques," *Les Nouvelles des Littéraires,* 22 Mar. 1962, p. 8.

6. "Interview de William Styron," *Nouveau Candide,* 29 Aug. 1962, p. 13.

7. "Les Trois Obssessions de William Styron," *Arts,* 28 Feb.–Mar. 1962, p. 3.

8. "Les Trois Obsessions," p. 3.

9. [Madeleine Chapsal], "Entretien," *L'Express,* 8 Mar. 1962, pp. 26–27.

10. A.M., "William Styron: Nouveau Faulkner," *Nouveau Candide,* untraced clipping in the collection of the Manuscript Division, Perkins Library, Duke University.

11. Interview in Valarie M. Arms, "William Styron's Literary Career," Diss. Temple University 1977, pp. 57–58.

12. West, B 3.I.a.1†[b]

13. "Deux autres Styron," *L'Express,* 23 May 1963, clipping, Perkins Library, Duke University.

14. West, B 3.I.a.1†[b]

15. In *Configuration Critique de William Styron,* ed. Melvin J. Friedman et August J. Nigro (Paris: Lettres Modernes, 1967), p. 73.

16. *Configuration Critique,* p. 74.

17. Pierre Dommergues, "William Styron à Paris," *Le Monde,* 26 Apr. 1974, p. 19.

18. Dommergues, *Les U.S.A. à la recherche de leur identité: Rencontres avec 40 écrivains américains* (Paris: Éditions Bernard Grasset, 1967), p. 270.

19. Annie Brierre, "William Styron," *Les Nouvelles Littéraires,* 14 Aug. 1952, p. 4.

20. *Présences contemporaines: écrivains américains d'aujourd'hui* (Paris: Nouvelles Editions Debresse, 1964), p. 173. Incidentally, Styron describes Helen in similar terms in an interview which postdates Brodin. See Jack Griffin, Jerry Homsy, and Gene Stelzig, "A Conversation with William Styron," *The Handle* (undergraduate magazine of the University of Pennsylvania), 2 (Spring 1965), 16–29.

21. *Présences contemporaines,* p. 177.

22. Friedman, *William Styron* (Bowling Green, Ohio: Bowling Green Univ. Popular Press, 1974), chap. 2.

23. "Preface," *La proie des flammes* (Paris: Gallimard, 1962), p. xi. Reprinted on pp. 135–45 of this collection.

24. "Preface," p. xviii.

25. "La Proie des Critiques," p. 8.

26. "La Proie des Critiques," p. 8.

27. Lukács, *The Historical Novel,* trans. from the German by Hannah and Stanley Mitchell (Boston: Beacon Press, 1963), orig. Russia 1937, p. 42.

28. West, B 4.I.a.1†[b].

29. Dommergues, "William Styron à Paris," p. 26.

30. Dommergues, "William Styron à Paris," p. 26.

31. Chapsal, "Entretien," p. 27.

32. Dommergues, "William Styron à Paris," p. 26.

33. Thérèse de Saint Phalle, "William Styron: 'En U.R.S.S.—et en France—je suis chez moi,' " p. 26.

INDEX

316